S E V E N   N

THE CULTURAL DIMENSION OF GLOBAL BUSINESS

Gary P. Ferraro

The University of North Carolina at Charlotte

Elizabeth K. Briody

Cultural Keys LLC

PEARSON

Boston   Columbus   Indianapolis   New York   San Francisco   Upper Saddle River
Amsterdam   CapeTown   Dubai   London   Madrid   Milan   Munich   Paris   Montréal   Toronto
Delhi   Mexico City   São Paulo   Sydney   Hong Kong   Seoul   Singapore   Taipei   Tokyo

Editorial Director: Craig Campanella
Publisher: Nancy Roberts
Editorial Assistant: Molly White
Production Manager: Meghan DeMaio
Executive Marketing Manager: Kate Mitchell
Art Director, Cover: Jayne Conte
Cover Designer: Suzanne Duda
Cover Photo: Yuri Arcurs/Quantum/Glow Images and Getty Images, Inc.
Editorial Production and Composition Service: Anand Natarajan, Integra Software Services
Printer/Binder/Cover Printer: Courier Companies

Credits and acknowledgments borrowed from other sources and reproduced, with permission, in this textbook appear on page 281.

Library of Congress Cataloging-in-Publication Data
Ferraro, Gary P.
  The cultural dimension of global business / Gary P. Ferraro, Elizabeth K. Briody.—7th ed.
    p. cm.
  Includes bibliographical references and index.
  ISBN-13: 978-0-205-83559-1 (alk. paper)
  ISBN-10: 0-205-83559-7 (alk. paper)
  1. International business enterprises—Social aspects.   2. Intercultural communication.
  3. Technical assistance—Anthropological aspects.   I. Briody, Elizabeth Kathleen.   II. Title.
HD2755.5.F48 2013
302.3'5—dc23

2012013804

2 3 4 5 6 7 8 9 10—15 14

ISBN-10:   0-205-83559-7
ISBN-13: 978-0-205-83559-1

Contents

Preface

For more than two decades this book has demonstrated how the theories and insights of anthropology have positively influenced the conduct of global business and commerce. It has provided a foundation for understanding the impact of culture on global business, and global business on culture. From the beginning we have used our orientation to culture as a holistic and evolving process to explain the themes, patterns, and lessons that emerge from cross-cultural business situations. Yet, as the saying goes, "nothing is as constant as change," and this is particularly true of the world during the period of the life of this book. Beginning with this new (seventh) edition, we are introducing a number of significant changes.

WHAT'S NEW IN THIS EDITION

- The word *International* in the previous title of the book has been changed to *Global*, reflecting the fact that nondomestic business relationships are no longer confined to two companies headquartered in two different nation-states, but rather to all companies operating in a much more tightly integrated world, where the lines between organizations, nation-states, and NGOs have become increasingly blurred.
- A new chapter on Partnering Across Cultures has been added.
- Many of the new examples, vignettes, and scenarios found in this edition came from in-depth interviews with more than 30 business anthropologists and a number of other business professionals who shared with the authors the cross-cultural issues they encountered in the global business arena.
- While previous editions have focused primarily, but not exclusively, on the relationship between the individual and the world of business, our book now incorporates a focus on the complex organizational environments within the global arena.
- And this last bulleted point—the broadening of focus to include a more structural/organizational perspective—is the direct (and deliberate) result of our addition of a new coauthor, Elizabeth Briody. Whereas the original author, Gary Ferraro, has spent most of his career as primarily an academic anthropologist, Elizabeth Briody is a business anthropologist. She spent 24 years as an in-house applied anthropologist with General Motors R&D, and is now helping other businesses and non-profit organizations as a consultant. She is recognized as one of the world's leading anthropological experts on the culture of work and organizations, with numerous publications, a patent, innovative tools, and awards. Dr. Briody's experience as a researcher, a scholar, and a change agent within one of the largest corporations in the world makes her the ideal coauthor to provide this book with a comprehensive refocusing on the organizational/structural dimensions of global business.

While containing much that is new, this seventh edition maintains the essential organizational structure it established in its inaugural edition. Chapters 1 and 2 from the previous edition have been collapsed into Chapter 1. Several chapters are now in a slightly different order. There is one new chapter. In addition, all chapters have been revised and updated. Yet, like earlier versions, this new edition takes a fourfold approach to understanding the cultural dimension of global business.

Exploring the Relationship between the Discipline of Cultural Anthropology, Its Central Concept of Culture, and the Conduct of Global Business

Chapter 1 begins with a discussion of the enormous potential for business opportunities throughout the world, but cautions that business ventures are likely to fail without an adequate understanding of the concept of cultural differences. The chapter then provides an in-depth look at the concept of culture, what generalizations hold true for all cultures of the world, and the implications of those generalizations for global business in the 21st century. This chapter is predicated on the notion that it is impossible for anyone to master all of the specific cultural facts about the thousands of cultures found in the world today. Thus, a more conceptual approach is needed. The chapter includes various definitions of the culture concept, followed by some important generalizations that can be usefully applied to any cross-cultural situation. The importance of these cultural generalizations for the conduct of global business is then discussed.

Comparison and Cultural Self-Awareness in Global Business

Chapter 2 presents a number of different models or "lenses" for understanding cultural differences, including contrasting values and metaphors. The discussion of contrasting values—which examines such dimensions of values as individualism versus collectivism, equality versus hierarchy, and certain aspects of time—is designed with three purposes in mind. First, it aims to show that people from different cultures view the world from the perspective of their own cultural assumptions, not necessarily ours. Second, it encourages Western businesspeople to increase their cultural self-awareness—that is, their ability to recognize the influences of their culture on their thinking and behavior. And third, a better understanding of other cultures and our own should make it easier to diagnose difficulties when operating in a foreign business setting or in a situation involving global partnerships or global virtual teams. It should enable the global businessperson to discover how a cross-cultural misunderstanding may have arisen from his or her own cultural assumptions rather than from some shortcoming of the culturally different person.

Building and Maintaining Relationships through Communication: Nonverbal and Verbal

In Chapter 3 we discuss the importance of knowing the nonverbal communication patterns prevalent in the international business arena. As important as language is to sending and receiving messages, nonverbal communication is perhaps even more important. Not only do nonverbal cues help us interpret verbal messages, but they are also responsible in their own right for the majority of the messages that make up human communication. Seven major modes of communicating nonverbally— body posture, gaze, facial expressions, hand gestures, dress, proxemics, and visual media—are discussed in a cross-cultural perspective. The aim of this chapter is to demonstrate the possibility of miscommunication in a cross-cultural business setting unless one is familiar with the nonverbal patterns of communication in addition to the linguistic patterns.

Effective communication between people from the same cultural and linguistic group is often difficult enough, but when one is attempting to com- municate with people who speak little or no English—and have different ideas, attitudes, assumptions, perceptions, and ways of doing things—the chances for misunderstandings increase enormously. In Chapter 4 we examine the critical importance of language competence in an international business context, the scale of linguistic diversity, the interrelatedness between language and culture, linguistic style, the situational use of language, and some additional factors (such as slang and euphemisms) that can further complicate verbal communication in a global business context.

Understanding Global Business Processes in Cross-Cultural Perspective

The final approach taken in this book examines three functional processes critical to success in conducting global business: negotiating, partnering, and managing.

Chapter 5 deals with negotiating in a global business context. Although it is recognized that no two international negotiating situations are ever identical, some negotiating strategies are generally valid in most instances. Based on the experiences of successful and culturally sensitive international negotiators, this chapter provides such general guidelines as (1) concentrating on long-term rela- tionships, (2) focusing on the interests behind the positions, (3) being attuned to timing, (4) maintaining flexibility, (5) preparing carefully, (6) listening, and (7) acting ethically.

Chapter 6 includes a discussion of building and maintaining partnerships between corporations and other organizational entities headquartered in different parts of the world. Significant emphasis is given to cultivating relationships as the key to business success, with attention to the elements of cooperation, trust, and conflict. This chapter focuses on (a) business meetings as opportunities for col- laboration among global partners, (b) understanding different decision-making models to facilitate working efficiently and effectively among partners, and (c) developing relationships and problem-solving capacities among partners.

Chapter 7, devoted to the topic of managing culture shock when working and living abroad, is directly related to the successful mastery of those leadership competencies that can best be learned by operating in a global context. Chapter 8 examines developing global leaders, expatriate excellence, and a number of other important global human resource issues. This chapter argues that short-term and long-term expatriate assignments must be managed in a more systematic, holistic, and long-term way than they have been managed in the past. This requires global firms to be attentive to all phases of transferring personnel abroad, including selection, cross-cultural preparation, in-country support, repatriation, and the integration of those skills gained abroad into the firm's ongoing operations.

As a final note, attention should be given to the scenarios appearing at the end of Chapters 1 through 8. The reader is encouraged to analyze these mini-case studies in an attempt to determine why a cultural conflict has arisen and how the conflict or misunderstanding portrayed could have been avoided. Although it is impossible to include examples of *every* possible cross-cultural conflict in a business setting, these end-of-chapter scenarios are designed to help the reader gain a greater sensitivity to the wide range of *potential* conflicts that could arise. Moreover, they provide the active reader with opportunities to develop analytical, problem-solving, and decision-making skills. Explanations of these scenarios appear in Appendix A.

ACKNOWLEDGMENTS

Many people have played a role in the development of this edition. We interviewed many anthropologists and businesspeople to learn firsthand some of the issues they have encountered in the global business arena. Many of these interviews led to examples, vignettes, and scenarios created for this seventh edition. We would like to thank the following people for providing us with their experiences and insights: Wendy Bartlo, Mary Beauregard, Geneviève Bien, Clark Bien, Jeanette Blomberg, Ralph Bolton, Marjorie Briody, Dominique Charmillon, Jean-Louis Charmillon, Tomoko Hamada Connolly, Laura Corrunker, Cathleen Crain, Natasha Crundwell, Tara Eaton, Patricia Ensworth, Ken Erickson, Yasunobu Ito, Julia Gluesing, Wolf Gumerman, Ann Jordan, Sunil Khanna, Adam Koons, Datta Kulkarni, Nicole Laflamme, Jeff Lewis, Timothy Malefyt, Ejiro Onomake, Tracy Meerwarth Pester, Crysta Metcalf, Christine Miller, Bob Morais, Riall Nolan, Helena Ottoson, Richard Reeves-Ellington, Ken Riopelle, Andrew Robinson, Marc Robinson, Anulekha Roy, Ruth Sando, Joerg Schmitz, Susan Squires, Niel Tashima, Bob Trotter, François Vardon, and S.J. Yoon.

Several people provided photos and other visuals for inclusion in the book: Duncan Crundwell, Ken Erickson, Julia Gluesing, Wolf Gumerman, Ken Kim, Adam Koons, Timothy Malefyt, Phil MacKenzie, Tracy Meerwarth Pester, Bruno Moynié, EjiroOnomake, Richard J. Rybak, Bob Trotter, and Carole Vardon. Laura Corrunker deserves special mention due to the multiple roles she played. Whether she was compiling bibliographic sources, offering input on using this book in the classroom, or critiquing key sections of text, Laura served as a valuable colleague. Finally, Elizabeth Briody would like to thank her husband, Marc Robinson, for his ongoing support, ideas and perspectives, and good-natured cheerfulness during the research and writing process.

To one degree or another many people over the years have contributed to this text. Some have made very explicit suggestions for revisions, many of which have been incorporated into various editions over the past two decades. Others have contributed less directly, yet their fingerprints are found throughout the text. We are particularly grateful to our many colleagues over the years who have shared generously their thinking and insights. While there are far too many names to mention here, we are confident that they know who they are and will accept our most sincere gratitude. And finally, after more than four decades of teaching, Gary Ferraro wants to thank his many students who have helped him define and refine the anthropological concepts and interpretations found between the covers of this book.

Gary P. Ferraro
Elizabeth K. Briody

1

■ ■ ■

Cultural Anthropology and Global Business

INTRODUCTION: GLOBAL CONNECTIONS

In little more than two decades, the world has become increasingly more interrelated. To illustrate, computer parts manufactured in six different countries are assembled in Malaysia before being transported by a Dutch freighter and sold to a Russian entrepreneur. Since joining the World Trade Organization in 2001, China has become one of the largest (and certainly one of the most rapidly expanding) economies in the world. Clothing for children's dolls, sewn on Korean-made machines by Taiwanese workers, are assembled on dolls by Mexican workers according to U.S. specifications and then sold to parents in London and Chicago in time for Christmas. The American-based computer giant IBM has more than 430,000 employees working in some 40 different countries. Recently, a North Carolina man traveled to Bangkok, Thailand, to receive 22 dental crowns (and other dental work) by a Western-trained oral surgeon for less than one-third of what it would have cost back home. A German becomes the president of a Swedish kitchenware company, while an Indian university professor purchases (online) shares from a Swiss-based mutual fund for his retirement portfolio. The examples of the world becoming inextricably interconnected are simply too numerous to count.

To remain competitive in this rapidly globalizing world, most businesses, both here and abroad, have needed to enter into international/cross-cultural alliances. The overall consequences of this trend have been that more and more companies have engaged in activities such as joint ventures, licensing agreements, turnkey projects, and foreign capital investments. Since the end of the Cold War in the late 1980s, world economies have experienced dramatic changes; collectively these changes have been subsumed under the term *globalization*. This term has become one of the most overused and poorly understood words in the English language. To be certain, countries and cultures have been interdependent for centuries, but when the Berlin Wall came down in 1989, the world began to change in some dramatic ways. Forces were unleashed that have had, and will continue to have, profound effects on all cultures and nations of the world. These include a new integration of world markets, technology, and information that is oblivious to

1

both national and cultural borders. This post–Cold War globalization is driven by free-market capitalism and the questionable idea that the more a country opens up its markets to free trade, the healthier its economy will become. The economics of globalization involve lowering tariff barriers while privatizing and deregulating national economies. The North American Free Trade Agreement (NAFTA) and the European Union are two examples of the globalization of markets. The result of the globalization of markets is that goods, services, and ideas from all over the world are making their way into other cultures.

A FLATTER WORLD

What follows are just a few illustrations of how extensively the lives of all of the world's peoples are interconnected:

- The percentage of the U.S. population that is foreign-born has grown from six percent in 1980 to eight percent in 1990 and to 12 percent in 2010.
- Coca-Cola sells more of its product in Japan than it sells in the United States.
- Foreign-owned firms operating in the United States employ more than 5,000,000 workers, approximately one in ten manufacturing jobs.
- Internet users worldwide increased approximately 545 percent between 2000 and 2010.
- Direct foreign investments in the United States have increased from $66 billion in 1990 to $162 billion in 2006, an increase of 245 percent. And, in the opposite direction, U.S. direct investment abroad has grown from $430 billion in 1990 to $2.3 trillion in 2006, an increase of 540 percent.
- Many high-skilled jobs formerly performed in the United States are now being performed abroad, such as a CPA in Bangalore, India, filling out state and federal income tax forms for someone in San Francisco; a mathematician in Mumbai, India, tutoring a high school student in Cleveland via e-mail; or a Western-trained Thai surgeon in Bangkok performing a heart valve operation (which costs over $200,000 in the United States) on a New Yorker for $10,500.
- More than half of U.S. franchise operators (e.g., Dunkin' Donuts or KFC) are in markets outside the United States.
- Owing to a shortage of priests in North America, local Catholic parishes are sending mass intentions (requests for masses said for a sick or deceased relative) to India. Catholic priests in India (who have more time than North American priests and need the money) are now conducting the masses in Hindi on behalf of North American Catholics after receiving the requests via e-mail. Americans are outsourcing not only manufacturing jobs, but also their religious rituals to India.
- Artistic styles and traditions also are being globalized. In recent years we have witnessed recording artist Paul Simon collaborating musically with Ladysmith Black Mambazo, a singing group from South Africa; Sting recording fusion music with Cheb Mami from Algeria; and Jaz Coleman, lead singer with a British rock group, collaborating with Maori singer and poet Hinewehi Mohi.

At the same time that world trade barriers are falling, a concomitant revolution is going on in the world of information technology (IT). In the mid-1980s, only a handful of people in the world could operate a computer. Today, computers are as common in the home as the radio was in the 1940s. Moreover, the development of digitization, fiber optics, satellite communication, and the Internet now enables people to communicate with one another instantaneously. With the advent of e-commerce, anyone with a good product, a computer, a telephone, access to the Internet, a website, and a FedEx account can become a potential entrepreneur. Globalization has encouraged the participation of large numbers of new players in the world market. It is now possible to enter the global economy virtually overnight, with very little capital outlay, and become a global competitor by the next afternoon.

Indeed, the nation-state of the 21st century sometimes plays second fiddle to the powerful forces of the highly integrated global economy. During the early summer of 2002, India and Pakistan, both with nuclear capabilities, were on the brink of war over the issue of Kashmir. The two countries were rattling their sabers, as the leaders of the United States and Western Europe tried to bring the two parties back from the brink. In the end, the de-escalation of hostilities between India and Pakistan was brought about by pressure exerted by the IT industry—not the U.S. government (which has more military firepower than the next 15 most powerful nations). The global revolution in IT since the early 1990s has had an enormous impact on the Indian economy, accounting for 40 percent of India's gross domestic product. Drawing upon the large tech-savvy Indian population, many of the world's largest companies (including American Express, Motorola Solutions, Siemens, Shell, Nike, Sony, and General Electric) have their back rooms and research facilities in India. If you lose your luggage anywhere in the world, it will likely be tracked down by an Indian techie in Bangalore (India's Silicon Valley). Accounting, inventory control, payroll, billing, credit card approval, and customer service, among other functions, for many of the world's largest corporations are electronically managed by highly skilled engineers, computer scientists, and information technicians in India. With India so intimately involved in the IT lifeblood of so many large corporations, the possibility of India going to war could seriously disrupt the world's economy. In the final analysis, it was the powerful international corporations that convinced the Indian government to disengage with the Pakistanis under the threat of taking their IT business elsewhere. Thus, in the words of Thomas Friedman (2002: 13), "in the crunch, it was the influence of General Electric, not General (Colin) Powell, that did the trick."

THE PERSPECTIVE OF CULTURAL ANTHROPOLOGY

Cultural anthropology seeks to understand how and why contemporary peoples of the world differ in their customs and practices and how and why they share certain similarities. It is, in short, the *comparative* study of cultural differences and similarities found throughout the world. But learning about the wide range of cultural variations serves as a check on those who might generalize about "human nature" solely on observations from their own society. It is not at all unusual for people to assume that their own ways of thinking and acting are unquestionably rational, "natural," or "human." Consider, for example, the nonverbal gesture of negation (found in the United States and in some other parts of the world), shaking the head from side to side. In some parts of India, people use this very same gesture to communicate not negation but affirmation. In fact, there are any number of ways of nonverbally communicating the idea of negation, all of which are no more or no less rational than shaking the head from side to side. The study of cultural anthropology provides a look at the enormous variations in thinking and acting found in the world today and how many different solutions have been generated for solving the same set of human problems. Moreover, the cross-cultural study of the workplace and consumers by anthropologists can help global corporations craft solutions to problems of working together as efficiently as possible.

Anthropology does more than simply document the enormous variation in human cultures. As a social science, anthropology works to identify, describe, and explain the commonalities. For example, for any society to continue to exist over the long run, it must solve the basic problem of how to pass on its total cultural heritage—all the ideas, values, attitudes, behavior patterns, and so on—to succeeding generations. Should that complexity of cultural traditions not be passed on to future generations, that society will very likely not survive. Saudis have solved this problem by developing Koranic schools, which pass on the cultural traditions to the younger generations; in parts of West Africa, "bush schools" train young adolescents to become adults; in our own society, we rely on a formal system of compulsory education, complete with books, desks, and teachers. Although the details of these educational systems vary enormously, all societies in the world—today or in the past—have worked out a system for ensuring that new generations will learn their culture. Thus, the science of anthropology attempts to document the great variations in cultural forms while looking for both the common strands that are found in all cultures.

In addition to being comparative, the anthropological perspective has several other distinctive features. First, to a greater extent than other social sciences, anthropologists analyze cultural differences and similarities *firsthand.* Rather than relying on secondary information gleaned (often by other people) from questionnaires, interviews, and census reports, cultural anthropologists use *participant observation* as a major method for collecting culturally comparative information. When cultural anthropologists use participant observation, they share in the everyday activities of the local people while making systematic observations of people eating, working, playing, conversing, dancing, exchanging goods, fighting, or any other activity that might illuminate their cultural patterns. A second distinguishing feature of anthropology is that it is "holistic" to the extent that it studies (a) all peoples throughout the world and (b) many different aspects of human experience, including family structure, marital regulations, house construction, methods of conflict resolution, means of livelihood, religious beliefs, language, space usage, and art. And finally cultural anthropology, unlike other social science disciplines, emphasizes viewing another culture from the perspective of an insider. For decades, anthropologists have made the distinction between the *emic (insider) approach* (describing another culture in terms of the categories, concepts, and perceptions of the people being studied) and the *etic (outsider) approach* (in which anthropologists use their own categories and concepts to describe the culture under analysis). For the last half century, there has been an ongoing debate among anthropologists as to which approach is more valuable for the scientific study of comparative cultures.

Thus, cultural anthropologists are trained to analyze the cultural and social organizations of various types of societies. In the early 20th century, cultural anthropologists devoted their energies to the analysis of small-scale, technologically simple, and usually non-Western peoples. Over the last several decades, however, cultural anthropologists have become more involved in the study of complex

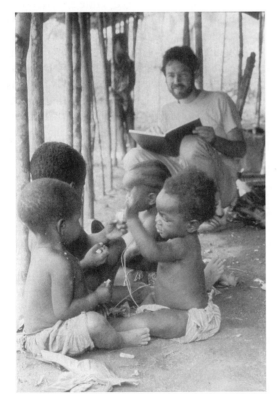

Cultural anthropologist Ed Tronick conducts participant observation fieldwork among the Efe people of Zaire.

societies. Yet whether dealing with simple or complex societies, the focus of cultural anthropologists has been the comparative study of sociocultural organizations wherever, or in whatever form, they may be found.

When hearing the phrase *cultural anthropologist*, the average American often imagines a drab, eccentric, elderly, bookish professor wearing sensible shoes and natural fiber clothing, and having little or nothing to do with anything outside the classroom. Anthropology, however, is neither dangerous (like the movie version of Indiana Jones) nor irrelevant. To counter this popular view that cultural anthropology is of little use in helping to understand the world around us, an increasing number of cultural anthropologists have applied their theories, findings, and methods to a wide range of professional areas, including economic development, business, health services, education, and urban administration. In fact, business and organizational anthropologists work inside some of the leading manufacturing and service companies in the world. These firms understand that anthropology brings a unique perspective on sociocultural issues to their organizations, both at home and abroad. Anthropologists not only help companies design products, but also develop culturally sensitive marketing strategies and organizational processes that incorporate an understanding of consumers, employees, and external communities.

This book rests on the fundamental assumption that to operate effectively in today's global business arena one must master the cultural environment by means of purposeful preparation as well as by becoming a lifelong student of culture. Now, as in the past, most globetrotting businesspeople acquire their cross-cultural expertise while on the job, and they consider hands-on factors such as business travel and overseas assignments to be the most important experiences. While not minimizing the value of experiential learning, this book argues that, *in addition to* on-the-job learning (and in most cases, before entering the global marketplace), successful international businesspeople must prepare themselves in a very deliberate manner to operate within a new, and frequently very different, cultural environment.

CULTURAL ANTHROPOLOGY AND BUSINESS

Anthropologists have been working in business and industry since the early 1930s; useful historical and contemporary overviews of the field are those by Marietta Baba (1986, 2006, 2009) and Ann Jordan (1994, 2003, 2010). The human relations school of organizational research emerged from the Hawthorne Project and produced a number of ethnographies (i.e., a descriptive and systematic account of a particular culture) showing how informal cultural patterns could influence managerial goals (Mayo 1933; Roethlisberger and Dickson 1939; Gardner 1945; Warner and Low 1947; Richardson and Walker 1948). Also during this early period, some anthropologists turned their attention to consumer behavior (Warner and Lunt 1941; Gardner and Levy 1955), and later, a focus on occupations (Van Maanen 1978; Gamst 1980; Applebaum 1981; Coy 1989).

Consumer anthropologist Timothy de Waal Malefyt conducts a videotaped interview with a female consumer in her home.

Since the last two decades of the 20th century, the field of business anthropology has evolved into two prominent streams of research and practice. One research stream has focused on organizational cultures, both domestic and global, along with global teams and partnerships (Gregory 1983; Serrie 1986; Suchman 1987; Dubinskas 1988; Sachs 1989; Hamada 1991; Hamada and Sibley 1994; Orr 1996; Jordan 2003; Gluesing and Gibson 2004; Briody and Trotter 2008; Cefkin 2009; Meerwarth, Gluesing, and Jordan 2008; Briody, Trotter, and Meerwarth 2010; Van Marrewijk 2010; Caulkins and Jordan 2012). For example, Frank Dubinskas' edited volume examines how time is understood in such places as high-energy physics laboratories, start-up biotechnology firms, hospital radiology departments, and an engineering company. Dubinskas writes, "Managers appear as short-term and biologists as long-term planners...What managers see as 'immaturity'—not coming to completion—the scientists see as necessary, ongoing development" (Dubinskas, 1988: 26–27). We discuss the dimension of time in Chapter 2.

A second stream consists of a critical mass of business anthropologists in consumer research, product design, and advertising (Miller 1994; Sherry 1995; Moeran 1996; Squires and Byrne 2002; Blomberg, Burrell, and Guest 2003;

Malefyt and Moeran 2003; Arnould and Thompson 2005; Metcalf and Harboe 2006; Sunderland and Denny 2007; Diamond et al. 2009; McCracken 2009; Wasson and Squires 2011). Nina Diamond and her colleagues, for example, conducted a large field study of the American Girl brand (Diamond et al., 2009). American Girl is an emotionally powerful brand because of the *Gestalt* created by its various elements—the dolls themselves (from many ethnic groups and historical periods), the young doll owners who play with them, the books and DVDs, the founder's philosophy, and the shopping experience with relatives at American Girl Place. A key insight for this research team was the importance of studying a brand in its totality so that it could be managed effectively. We feature numerous examples of product design and marketing throughout the book.

The anthropological perspective can be useful in the study of purely domestic business organizations, which are frequently composed of many social components that come from different backgrounds, hold contrasting values and attitudes, and have conflicting loyalties. For instance, the company vice president will not likely have much in common with the assembly-line worker, the union representative, the president of the local Sierra Club, the inspector from OSHA (the U.S. Occupational Safety and Health Administration), the janitor, or many members of that diverse group called the "buying public." And yet, if the organization is to function effectively, that corporate manager needs to know about the values, attitudes, expectations, concerns, and behavioral patterns of all these people, and others as well. In short, domestic business organizations can be viewed as minicultures (composed of different people with different roles, statuses, and value systems) that operate within the wider national cultural context.

The number of MA and PhD anthropologists working in the private sector for corporations and consulting firms has increased dramatically in the past three decades. Many high-tech multinational firms such as Microsoft, Google, and IBM have anthropologists on their staff working in the areas of research, marketing, management, human resources, and new product development. What is it that well-trained cultural anthropologists bring to the private sector? They are valuable because of their cross-cultural perspective, their capacity to study very specific behavior in its proper cultural context, and their primary research technique of participant observation, which reveals what people *actually do* in contrast to what *they say they do.*

Today, research and design firms, which develop new products, are actively recruiting anthropologists to help them gain deeper insights about their customers through participant observation research. One such anthropologist, Susan Squires, who has worked in new product development for many years, conducted participant observation research on U.S. families during breakfast time (Squires 2002: 108–14; http://practicinganthropology.org/?s=Squires). While hanging around the breakfast tables in middle-class homes, Squires found that, with both parents working, getting children ready for school was hectic at best, and often children ate "on the run" rather than having a traditional sit-down breakfast. She also observed that both parents and children frequently ate bananas on the way to office and school respectively, because they are nutritious, portable, disposable, and fun to eat. If a new breakfast product was to be developed, it would have to meet the needs of a number of family members. For example, it would need to be nutritious, banana-like, portable, disposable, versatile, and fun to eat. Based on her anthropological observations of actual behavior, Squires developed a new breakfast product designed for the children of a two-parent working family on-the-go called "Go-Gurt." The first yogurt served in a tube, Go-Gurt is a healthy, high-protein food that had sales of over $37 million during its first year on the market.

Failure to consider the cultural context in the domestic organization can lead, and has led, to misunderstandings, miscommunication, costly marketing blunders, lawsuits, and generally an undermining of organizational goals. When moving into the area of international business, the need to be aware of cultural environments becomes even more critical. Here the magnitude of the cultural differences is vastly greater; consequently, breakdown of communication usually increases geometrically. One of the most common factors contributing to failure in global business is the erroneous assumption that if a person is successful in the home environment, he or she will be equally successful in applying technical expertise in a different culture. Yet, research has shown that failures in the global business setting—including partnerships and joint ventures—most frequently result from an inability to understand and adapt to foreign ways of thinking and acting rather than from technical or professional incompetence (Black, Gregersen, and Mendenhall 1992; Adler 2002; Thomas, 2002; Maurer and Li 2006). At home, U.S. businesspeople equip themselves with vast amounts of knowledge of their employees, customers, and business partners. Market research provides detailed information on values, attitudes, and buying preferences of U.S. consumers. Middle- and upper-level managers are well versed in the intricacies of their organization's culture. Labor negotiators must be highly sensitive to what motivates those on the other side of the table. Yet when Americans turn to the global arena, they frequently deal with customers, employees, and fellow workers with a dearth of information that at home would be unimaginable.

The literature is filled with examples of business miscues when U.S. corporations attempted to operate in a global context. Some are mildly amusing; others are downright embarrassing. All of them, to one degree or another, have been costly in terms of money, reputation, or both. For example, when firms try to market their products abroad, they often assume that if a marketing strategy or slogan is effective in, say, Cleveland, it will be equally effective in other parts of the world. But problems can arise when changing cultural contexts. To illustrate, an airline offering service to Brazil advertised that it had comfortable "rendezvous lounges" in its business class section, without realizing that the word *rendezvous* in Portuguese refers to a room for illicit sexual encounters. Chicken entrepreneur Frank Perdue decided to translate one of his very successful advertising slogans into Spanish, but the translated slogan didn't produce the desired results. The slogan "It takes a tough man to make a tender chicken" was translated into Spanish as "It takes a virile man to make a chicken affectionate." And the American Dairy Association's wildly successful ad campaign "Got Milk?" had the unfortunate translation "Are you lactating?" when used in Mexico. Although all these cross-cultural advertising blunders cause us to chuckle, they can result in a loss of revenue and even product credibility.

These are only a few of the examples of the price paid for miscalculating—or simply ignoring—the cultural dimension of global business. The most cursory review of the global business literature will reveal many other similarly costly mistakes. If American businesspeople are to meet the challenges of an increasingly interdependent world, they will need to develop a better understanding of how cultural variables influence global business enterprises. A healthy dialogue between cultural anthropologists and members of the global business community—which this book seeks to foster—is an important step in achieving that needed understanding.

ANTHROPOLOGY'S MAJOR CONCEPT: CULTURE

Anthropologists do more than simply accumulate and catalog information on the world's exotic and not-so-exotic cultures. Like other scientists, they attempt to generate theories about culture that apply to all human populations. Because it is impossible for any individual to master every cultural fact about *every culture* of the world, anthropologists have developed a number of general concepts about culture that can be applied to a wide variety of cross-cultural situations, whether they involve differences in national culture, organizational culture, occupational culture, work group culture, consumer culture, regulatory culture, or other kinds of cultural groupings with an impact on global business.

In this section we explore what is meant—and what is not meant—by the term *culture*. In addition to defining this central anthropological concept, we also examine six important generalizations concerning the concept of culture and their significance for the U.S. businessperson operating in the world marketplace.

In everyday usage, the term *culture* refers to the finer things in life, such as the fine arts, literature, philosophy, and classical music. Under this very narrow definition of the term, the "cultured person" is one who prefers Bach to Lady Gaga, can distinguish between the artistic styles of Monet and Manet, prefers pheasant under glass to grits and red-eye gravy, and 12-year-old scotch to beer, and spends his/her leisure time reading Kierkegaard rather than watching wrestling on television. For the anthropologist, however, the term *culture* has a much broader meaning that goes far beyond mere personal refinements. The only requirement for being cultured is to be human. Thus, all people have culture. The scantily clad Dani of New Guinea is as much a cultural animal as is Yo-Yo Ma. For the anthropologist, cooking pots, spears, and mud huts are as legitimate items of culture as symphonies, oil paintings, and great works of literature.

While you will find many definitions of the concept of culture in the literature, we will define culture as: *Everything that people have, think, and do as members of their society.* The three verbs in this definition (*have*, *think*, and *do*) can help us identify the three major structural components of the concept of culture. For a person to *have* something, some material object must be present. When people *think*, ideas, values, attitudes, and beliefs are present. When people *do*, they behave in certain socially prescribed ways. Thus, culture is made up of (1) material objects; (2) ideas, values, and attitudes; and (3) normative, or expected, patterns of behavior. The final phrase of our working definition, "as members of their society," should serve as a reminder that culture is shared by at least two or more people. In other words, there is no such thing as the culture of a hermit.

In addition to this working definition, a number of features of the concept of culture should be made explicit. In the remainder of this chapter, we briefly examine these features that hold true for all cultures, and discuss why they are valuable insights into the cultural environment of global business.

Culture Is Learned

Culture is transmitted through the process of learning and interacting with one's environment, rather than through the genetic process. Culture can be thought of as a storehouse of all the knowledge of a society. The child who is born into any society finds that the problems that confront all people have already been solved by those who have lived before. For example, material objects, methods for acquiring food, language, rules of government, forms of marriage, systems of religion, and many other things have already been discovered and are functioning within the culture when a child is born. A child has only to learn the various solutions to these basic human problems established by his culture. Once these solutions are learned, behavior becomes almost automatic. Thus, culture is passed on from one generation to another within a society. It is not inborn or instinctive.

It is sometimes easy to fall into the trap of thinking that because the Australian Bushman and the Central African Pygmy do not know what we know, they must be childlike, ignorant, and generally incapable of learning. These primitives, the argument goes, have not learned about calculus, Shakespeare, or the Nobel Peace Prize because they are not as intelligent as we are. Yet no evidence whatsoever suggests even remotely that people in some cultures are less efficient learners than people in other cultures. What the comparative study of culture does tell us is that people in different cultures learn different cultural content—that is, different ideas, values, and behavior patterns—and they learn that content every bit as efficiently as anyone else. For example, despite the inability of a rural Kikuyu farmer from Kenya to solve a problem by using differential equations, she would be able to recite exactly how she is related (step by step) to a network of hundreds of kinsmen. Kikuyu farmers have mastered what to us is a bewildering amount of kinship information because their culture places great emphasis on such knowledge if the rather complex Kikuyu marriage and kinship system is to work. Hence, people from different cultures learn those things that contribute to adjusting to their particular environments.

Although these children growing up on the Solomon Islands learn different cultural content than do North American children, the process of acquiring culture through learning is common to all cultures.

This notion that culture is acquired through the process of learning has several important implications for the conduct of global business. First, such an understanding can lead to greater tolerance for cultural differences, a prerequisite for effective intercultural communication within a business setting. Second, the learned nature of culture serves as a reminder that because we have mastered our own culture through the process of learning, it is possible (albeit more difficult) to learn to function in other cultures as well. Thus, cross-cultural expertise for global businesspeople can be accomplished through a combination of direct experience and mentoring; effective training programs and readings may be helpful as well.

Culture Influences Biological Processes

If we stop to consider it, the great majority of our conscious behavior is acquired through learning and interacting with other members of our culture. Even those responses to our purely biological needs (e.g., eating, coughing, defecating) are frequently influenced by our cultures. For example, all people share a biological need for food. Unless a minimum number of calories is consumed, starvation will occur; therefore, all people eat. But *what* we eat, *how often* and *how much* we eat, *with whom* we eat, and *according to what set of rules* are all regulated, at least in part, by our culture.

This Masai girl and this middle-class North American woman put holes in their ears for exactly the same reason—because their cultures teach them that it enhances their feminine attractiveness.

Anthropologist Clyde Kluckhohn provides us with a telling example of how culture affects biological processes (Kluckhohn, 1968: 25–26). He once knew a woman in Arizona who took a somewhat perverse delight in producing a cultural reaction. At her luncheon parties she would serve delicious sandwiches filled with a pleasant tasting white meat similar to chicken. After her guests had eaten their fill, she would tell them that they had just eaten sandwiches filled with rattlesnake flesh. The results were always the same. Some of her guests would vomit, sometimes violently. Here, then, is a dramatic illustration of how culture can influence biological processes. In fact, in this instance, the natural biological process of digestion was not only influenced but was actually reversed. A learned part of our culture (the idea that rattlesnake meat is a repulsive thing to eat) actually triggered the sudden interruption of the normal digestive process. Clearly, there is nothing in rattlesnake meat that causes people to vomit, for those who have internalized the opposite idea—that rattlesnake meat is good to eat— have no such digestive tract reversals.

The basic anthropological notion that culture channels biological processes can provide some important insights when managing or marketing abroad. For example, in Chennai, India, such a concept can be a reminder not to serve beef noodle soup in the plant cafeteria, for to do so might cause a mass exodus to the infirmary. Or, even though foot binding is no longer widely practiced in China, the notion of equating small feet with feminine beauty should be taken into account by shoe manufacturers who hope to sell shoes to Chinese women in the 21st century. Or, an understanding of the fascination with plastic surgery in the United States should encourage cosmetic manufacturers around the world to do their homework on what constitutes attractiveness for both men and women in the United States.

Cultural Universals Do Exist

All cultures of the world, despite many differences, face a number of common problems and share a number of common features, which we call cultural universals. As we encounter the many different cultural patterns found throughout the world, there is a tendency to become overwhelmed by the magnitude of the differences and overlook the commonalities. But *all* societies, if they are to survive, are confronted with fundamental challenges that must be addressed. When cultures develop ways of addressing those challenges, general cultural patterns emerge. Differences in the details of cultural patterns exist because different societies have developed different approaches and solutions. Yet, a number of commonalities exist. Let's briefly examine the issues that all cultures face and the universal cultural patterns that emerge in response.

ECONOMIC SYSTEMS   One of the most obvious and immediate issues of a society is to meet the basic physiological requirements of its people. To stay alive, all humans need a certain minimal caloric intake, potable water, and, to varying degrees, protection from the elements in terms of clothing and shelter. No society in the world has access to an infinite supply of basic resources such as food, water, clothing, and housing materials. Because these commodities are always in finite supply, each society must develop systematic ways of producing, distributing, and consuming these essential resources. Thus, each society must develop an *economic system.*

To illustrate this principle of cultural universals, we can look at one component of economic systems—namely, forms of distribution. In the United States, most goods and services are distributed according to capitalism, based on the principle of "each according to his or her capacity to pay." In socialist countries, on the other hand, goods and services are distributed according to another quite different principle—that is, "each according to his or her need." The Pygmies of Central Africa distribute goods by a system known as "silent barter," in which the trading partners, in an attempt to attain true reciprocity, avoid face-to-face contact during the exchange. The Hadza of Tanzania distribute the meat of an animal killed in the hunt according to the principle of kinship—each share of meat is determined by how one is related to the hunter. But whatever particular form the system of distribution might take, there are no societies—at least not for long—that have failed to work out and adhere to a well-understood and systematic pattern of distribution.

MARRIAGE AND FAMILY SYSTEMS   For a society to continue over time, it is imperative that it work out systematic procedures for mating, marriage, child rearing, and family formation. If it fails to do so, it will die out in a very short time. No society permits random mating and all societies have worked out rules for determining who can marry whom, under what conditions, and according to what procedures. All societies, in other words, have patterned systems of *marriage.* And since human infants (as compared with the young of other species) have a particularly long period of dependency on adults, every society must work out systematic ways of caring for dependent children. Otherwise, children will not survive to adulthood and the very survival of the society will be in jeopardy. Thus, we can say that all societies have patterns of child rearing and family institutions.

And yet, it is absolutely essential that one knows something about the specific features of the marriage and family system that exists in those particular parts of the world in which one may have business interests. For example, where people have many obligations to attend family/kinship functions, labor contracts should include flexible working hours and perhaps slightly lower pay, instead of a rigid 40-hour workweek and somewhat higher pay. Workers, in other words, would be willing to give up higher pay rates if they knew they could attend family gatherings without being penalized.

EDUCATIONAL SYSTEMS   Along with ensuring that the basic physical needs of the child are met, a society must see to it that the children learn the way of life of the society. Rather than expecting each new child to rediscover for himself or herself all the accumulated knowledge of the past, a society must have an organized way

Although the marriage practices among the Ndebele of South Africa differ in many ways from this wedding under the Chuppah *in British Columbia, Canada, both sets of practices are responses to the universal interest in orderly systems of mating and child rearing.*

of passing on its cultural heritage from one generation to the next. The result is some form of *educational system* in every society.

Despite the universality of education systems, the specific features of any given system vary widely from culture to culture. For example, are the patterned forms of education formal (schools, books, professional teachers) or informal (information passed from parents to children or from older to younger siblings)? Is the emphasis on rote memorization or the development of analytical carryover skills? Are students exposed to a broad "liberal arts" education or a narrow, more occupationally oriented curriculum? Are various levels of education (kindergarten through graduate school) open to all members of the society or only to the privileged classes? The answers to these and other questions have important implications for any international businessperson engaged in the management of foreign workforces, the negotiation of international contracts, or the development of marketing strategies abroad.

SOCIAL CONTROL SYSTEMS　If groups of people are to survive, they must develop some established ways of preserving social order; that is, all societies must develop mechanisms that will ensure that most of the people obey most of the rules most of the time. If not, people will violate each other's rights to such an extent that anarchy will prevail. Different societies develop mechanisms to ensure social order in different ways. In the United States, behavior control rests on a number of formal mechanisms, such as a written constitution; local, state, and federal laws; and an elaborate system of police, courts, and penal institutions. Many small-scale, technologically simple societies have less formal (but no less effective) means of controlling behavior. Regardless of the specific methods used, one thing is certain: Every society has a system for coercing people to obey the social rules, and these are called *social control systems.*

Again, knowing the means that culturally different people rely upon for maintaining social order is important for managers of international workforces. To maintain order and good working relationships among employees, corporations operating abroad are likely to be more successful by using local mechanisms of social control rather than imposing those that work effectively in the home office.

SUPERNATURAL BELIEF SYSTEMS　All societies have a certain degree of control over their social and physical environments. People in all societies can understand and predict a number of things. For example, a dense, heavy object when dropped into a lake will sink to the bottom; if I have $5 and give you $2, I will have $3 left; the sun always rises in the east and sets in the west. However, we cannot explain or predict with any degree of certainty many other things: Why does a child develop a fatal disease, but the child's playmate next door does not? Why do tornadoes destroy some houses and leave others unharmed? Why do safe drivers die in auto accidents and careless drivers do not? Such questions have no apparent answers, because they cannot be explained by our conventional systems of justice or rationality. Therefore, societies develop *supernatural belief systems* for explaining these unexplainable occurrences.

The way people explain the unexplainable is to rely on various types of supernatural explanations such as magic, religion, witchcraft, sorcery, and astrology.

Religions and other supernatural belief systems affect the conduct of business by shaping attitudes about work, savings, consumption, efficiency, and individual responsibility. To illustrate, Euro-American Christianity, as it is embodied in the Protestant ethic, emphasizes hard work, frugality, and getting ahead for the sake of glorifying God. The Islamic religion, although not hostile to capitalism, places greater emphasis on the individual's responsibility to the society, including charity to the poor and ensuring that profits are made only through fair business dealings rather than through fraud, deceit, or usury. And another world religion, Hinduism, places emphasis on spiritual goals rather than on economic or professional accomplishments. At the very least, global businesspeople must be sensitive to these broad divisions in how people's values and work practices are affected by their religious traditions.

Thus, despite the great variety in the details of cultural features found throughout the world, all cultures have a number of traits in common. This basic anthropological principle, known as *cultural universals*, can be an important tool for helping global businesspeople become sensitive to and appreciate culturally different business environments. Greater empathy for cultural differences—a necessary if not sufficient condition for increased knowledge—can be attained if we can avoid concentrating solely on the apparent differences between cultures but appreciate their underlying commonalities as well. In other words, we will be less likely to prejudge or be critical of different practices, ideas, or behavior patterns if we can appreciate the notion that they represent different solutions to the same basic human problems facing all cultures of the world, including our own.

Cultural Change

All cultures experience continual change. Any anthropological account of a culture is merely a snapshot view at one particular time. Should the anthropologist return several years after completing a cultural study, he or she would not find exactly the same situation, because no culture remains completely static year after year. Although small-scale, technologically simple, preliterate societies tend to be more conservative (and thus change less rapidly) than modern, industrialized, highly complex societies, it is now generally accepted that, to some degree, change is a constant feature of all cultures.

Students of culture change generally recognize that change occurs as a result of both internal and external forces. Mechanisms of change that emerge within a given culture are called *discovery* and *invention.* Despite the importance of discovery and invention, most changes occur as a result of borrowing from other cultures, a process known as *cultural diffusion.* The importance of cultural borrowing can be better understood if viewed in terms of economy of effort: Borrowing someone else's invention or discovery is much easier than discovering or inventing it all over again. Anthropologists generally agree that a substantial majority of all things, ideas, and behavioral patterns found in any culture had their origins elsewhere. Individuals in every culture, limited by background and time, can get new ideas with far less effort if they borrow them. This statement holds true for our own culture as well as other cultures, a fact that Americans frequently tend to overlook. Because so much cultural change is the result of diffusion, it deserves a closer examination. Although cultural diffusion varies from situation to situation, we can identify certain generalizations that hold true for all cultures.

First, cultural diffusion is a *selective process.* Whenever two cultures come into contact, each does not accept everything indiscriminately from the other. If they did, the vast cultural differences that exist today would have long since disappeared. Rather, items will be borrowed from another culture only if they prove to be useful and/or compatible. For example, we would not expect to see the diffusion of swine husbandry from the United States to Saudi Arabia because the predominant Muslim population has a strong dietary prohibition on pork. Similarly, polyandry (the practice of a woman having two or more husbands at a time) is not likely to be borrowed by the United States because of its obvious lack of fit with other features of mainstream American culture. Successful international marketing requires an intimate knowledge of the cultures found in foreign markets to determine if, how, and to what extent specific products are likely to become accepted and used in the ways in which they were intended.

Second, cultural borrowing is a two-way process. Early students of change believed that contact between "primitive" societies and "civilized" societies caused the former to accept traits from the latter. This position was based on the assumption that the "inferior" small-scale societies had nothing to offer the "superior" civilized societies. Today, however, anthropologists would reject such a position because it has been found time and again that cultural traits are diffused in both directions. For example, Native Americans have accepted a great deal from Europeans, but diffusion in the other direction also has been significant. It has been estimated that those crops that make up nearly half of the world's food supply today (such as corn, beans, squash, sweet potatoes, and even the so-called Irish potato) were originally domesticated by Native Americans. Native Americans have given the world articles of clothing such as woolen ponchos, parkas, and moccasins, not to mention American varieties of cotton, a material used widely throughout the world for making clothing. Even the multibillion-dollar pharmaceutical industry in the Western world continues to produce and market commercial drugs first discovered by Native Americans, including painkillers such as cocaine and Novocain, anesthetics, quinine, and laxatives. This concept that cultural diffusion is a two-way process should help global leaders be more receptive to the idea that the corporate culture, as well as the local culture, may change. The local culture may, in fact, have a good deal to offer the corporate culture, provided the corporate culture is open to accepting these new cultural features.

Third, frequently borrowed items are not transferred into the recipient culture in exactly their original form. Rather, new ideas, objects, or techniques

Cultural diffusion is responsible for the greatest amount of culture change in all societies.

are usually reinterpreted and reworked so that they can be integrated more effectively into the total configuration of the recipient culture. In other words, once a cultural element is accepted into a new culture, it may undergo changes in form or function. Pizza is a good example of how a cultural item can change form as it diffuses. Pizza, which diffused from Italy to the United States in the late 19th century, has been modified in a number of significant ways to conform to American tastes. It is unlikely that its Italian originators would recognize a pizza made of French bread, English muffins, or pita bread and topped with pineapple, tuna, clams, or jalapeno peppers. An understanding that cultural diffusion frequently involves some modification of the item is an important idea for those interested in creating new product markets in other cultures. To illustrate, before a laundry detergent—normally packaged in a green box in the United States—would be accepted in certain parts of West Africa, the color of the packaging would need to be changed because the color green is associated with death in certain West African cultures.

Fourth, some cultural traits are more easily diffused than others. By and large, technological innovations are more likely to be borrowed than are social patterns or belief systems, largely because the usefulness of a particular technological trait is more immediately recognizable. For example, a man who walks five miles each day to work quickly realizes that an automobile can get him to work faster and with far less effort. It is much more difficult, however, to convince a Muslim to become a Hindu or an American businessperson to become a socialist. The idea that some components of culture are more readily accepted than others should at least provide some general guidelines for assessing what types of changes in the local culture are more likely to occur. By assessing what types of things, ideas, and behavior have been incorporated into a culture in recent years, strategic planners are in a better position to understand the relative ease or difficulty involved in initiating changes in consumer habits or workplace behavior.

While all cultures are dynamic, some of the change that occurs in organizational cultures is intended and purposeful—that is, it is planned. Decades ago, Kurt Lewin emphasized that planned change required an awareness of the particular problem and a plan to address it (Lewin, 1947). It necessitates action on the part of the organization—often the management—to initiate and manage the change process. Planned change is goal oriented rather than occurring spontaneously, fortuitously, or developmentally. Business anthropologists routinely work with organizations on matters related to planned change: to understand the issues organizations face, suggest possible solutions, implement the changes, and evaluate the effectiveness of the changes. Sometimes anthropologists offer their recommendations based on independent research or based on their familiarity, experience, and leadership in particular areas of organizational activity. In other instances they collaborate with organizational decision makers on projects to facilitate teamwork and problem solving, to investigate product development issues, to promote healthy supplier interactions, or to enhance customer expectations, among others. Planned change has some of the elements of invention (since it must fit the unique circumstances of the business situation) and some elements of cultural borrowing (since knowledge of other similar situations outside the organization might be adapted for the situation at hand).

Of course, organizations—like individuals—often find change difficult. In fact, organizational members at any level may resist a new corporate initiative as in this manufacturing example:

> We've been through I don't know how many hours of training where they say, "I don't care what it takes. We won't send out cars that are below our quality standards." Then we get back on the line and the first thing they say is, "No, we don't have time to stop the line and solve this problem. We have to keep going." So what kind of message is that sending? (Briody, Trotter, and Meerwarth 2010: 100)

This example represents a type of resistance known as a cultural contradiction. The ideal scenario was presented during a training session and then disregarded later on the plant floor. If the resistance is not addressed, employees may become jaded and managers may lose credibility. Fortunately, cultural processes known as *enablers* can address, or at least mitigate, such forms of resistance. For example, empowering employees, following standardized work, rebalancing the work pace, or cultivating work ethic and pride are some possible enablers that could speed up the process of organizational-culture change. Change must be planned and implemented carefully for the resistance to be overcome (i.e., stopping the line) and for the results to be successful (i.e., improved quality standards).

People from All Cultures Are Ethnocentric

All cultures, to one degree or another, display ethnocentrism, which is perhaps the greatest single obstacle to understanding another culture. *Ethnocentrism—* literally being "culture centered"—is the tendency for people to evaluate a foreigner's behavior by the standards of their own culture, which they believe is superior to all others. Because our own culture is usually the only one we learn, we take our culture for granted. We typically assume that our behavior is correct and all others are wrong, or at least very strange. The extent to which ethnocentrism pervades a culture is clearly seen in our history textbooks. Consider, for example, the historic event of the Holy Wars between the Christians and the Muslims during the Middle Ages. In our textbook accounts of the wars, we refer to the Christians as crusaders and the Muslims as religious fanatics. Yet, if we read the Islamic accounts of these same wars, the terms *crusaders* and *fanatics* would be reversed.

Sometimes our own ethnocentrism can startle us when we find ourselves in a different cultural setting. A particularly revealing episode occurred when an American visited a Japanese classroom for the first time. On the wall of the classroom was a brightly colored map of the world. But something was wrong: right in the center of the map (where he had expected to see the United States) was Japan. To his surprise, the Japanese did not view the United States as the center of the world.

Ethnocentrism prevents us from seeing that other people view our customs as equally strange and irrational. For example, people in the United States think of themselves as being particularly conscious of cleanliness. As a nation we probably spend more money per capita on a whole host of commercial products designed to make ourselves and our environments clean, hygienic, and odor free. Yet a number of practices found in the United States strike people in other parts of the world as deplorably unclean. To illustrate, whereas most Americans are repulsed by an Indonesian who blows his nose onto the street, the Indonesian is repulsed by the American who blows his nose in a handkerchief and then carries it around for the rest of the day in his pocket; the Japanese consider the American practice of sitting in a bathtub full of dirty, soapy water to be at best an ineffective way of bathing and at worst a disgusting practice; and East Africans think that Americans have no sense of hygiene because they defecate in rooms (the bathroom) that are frequently located adjacent to that part of the house where food is prepared (the kitchen).

All people in all societies are ethnocentric to some degree regardless of how accepting or open-minded they might claim to be. Our ethnocentrism should not be a source of embarrassment because it is a by-product of growing up in our society. In fact, ethnocentrism may serve the positive function of enhancing group solidarity. On the other hand, ethnocentrism can contribute to prejudice, contempt for outsiders, and intergroup conflict. Although it is a deeply ingrained attitude found in every society, it is important that we become aware of it so that it will not hinder us in learning about other cultures. Awareness of our own ethnocentrism will never eliminate it but will enable us to minimize its more negative effects. It is vital for businesspeople to refrain from comparing our way of life with those of our international business partners. Instead, we should seek to understand other people *in the context of their unique historical, social, and cultural backgrounds.*

Cultures Are Integrated Wholes

Cultures should be thought of as integrated wholes: Cultures are coherent and logical systems, the parts of which to a degree are interrelated. Upon confronting an unfamiliar cultural trait, a usual response is to try to imagine how such a trait would fit into one's own culture. We tend to look at it ethnocentrically, or from our own cultural perspective. All too frequently we view an unfamiliar cultural item as simply a pathological version of one found in our own culture. We reason that if the foreign cultural item is different and unfamiliar, it must be deviant, strange, weird, irrational, and consequently inferior to its counterpart in our own culture. Our interpretation, with its unfortunate consequences, is the result of pulling the item from its proper cultural context and viewing it from our own perspective. It is also the result of being unable to see the foreign culture as an integrated system.

When we say that a culture is integrated, we mean that it is an organized system in which particular components may be related to other components, not just a random assortment of cultural features. If we can view cultures as integrated systems, we can begin to see how particular cultural traits fit into the integrated whole and, consequently, how they tend to make sense within that context (see Figure 1-1). Equipped with such an understanding, international businesspeople should be in a better position to cope with the "strange" customs encountered in the global business arena.

The notion of integrated culture helps us to understand why culturally different people think and behave the way they do. However, we should avoid taking the concept too literally. To assume that all cultures are perfectly integrated, we would have to conclude that every idea or behavior is both absolutely rational and morally defensible, provided that it performs a function for the well-being of the society. However, believing in the general validity of the integrated nature of culture does not require that we view all cultures as morally equivalent; not all cultural practices are equally worthy of tolerance and respect. Some practices (such as the genocide perpetuated by Stalin, Hitler, or the Bosnian Serbs) are morally indefensible within any cultural context. To be certain, cultural anthropologists have sometimes been overly nonjudgmental about the customs of people they study. But, as Richard Barrett has suggested, "The occasional tendency for anthropologists to treat other cultures with excessive approbation to the extent that they

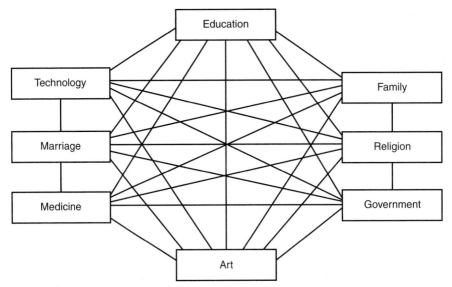

FIGURE 1-1   *The various parts of a culture are all interrelated to some degree.*

sometimes idealize them, is less cause for concern than the possibility that they will misrepresent other societies by viewing them through the prism of their own culture" (Barrett, 1991: 8).

The notion of integrated culture has several important implications for global businesspeople. When we understand that the parts of a culture are interrelated, we will be less likely to view foreign cultures ethnocentrically. Rather than wrenching a foreign cultural item from its original context and viewing it in terms of how well it fits into our own culture, we will be reminded to view it from within its proper cultural context. This concept allows us to understand more fully why a particular cultural item is found in a society, even if it violates our sense of personal decorum or morality.

Corporations Also Have Cultures

Just as societies, tribes, religious communities, and neighborhoods all have cultures, so too do corporations. Shared values, behavior patterns, and communication styles all help the employees of a firm, from the janitor to the CEO, both feel and express a common identity. A corporate culture, in other words, helps ensure that people at all levels of the organization are pulling together in the same direction. Successful corporate cultures manage to integrate *symbols* (such as a corporate logo), *legends* (stories about past successes and failures), *heroes* (influential managers from the past), *communication patterns* (language and nonverbal cues), *shared values* (what the organization stands for and believes in), *patterns of social interaction* (expected forms of behavior between those of different statuses and roles), and *shared experiences* (such as working together on successful projects). The process of developing and maintaining a healthy corporate culture involves a number of distinct activities including:

- establishing trust and respect as a foundation for workplace interaction and collaboration
- identifying and building on a common work ethic among employees in pursuit of organizational goals
- setting clear expectations, soliciting input, gaining consensus, and resolving conflict
- documenting the essential organizational features, including "lessons learned," and integrating them into everyday practice
- making the culture visible to employees on a regular basis so that behavior and expectations are aligned (i.e., "walking the talk")
- orienting new employees to their work tasks, colleagues, and the corporate culture generally.

Having a well-defined and explicit corporate culture not only increases efficiency but it also contributes to overall competitiveness (Barney 1986). When a formerly domestic corporation decides to globalize its operations, it needs to pay attention to globalizing its culture as well. A corporate culture that works well for employees in Atlanta may need to be at least partially redefined by the national culture of Indonesia, where it is now conducting some of its manufacturing. This certainly does not mean that a corporation should jettison its corporate culture when operating abroad. Rather, it means that hitherto domestic companies need to modify their cultures to accommodate local cultural realities. It is, in other words, not possible for a corporation to export its culture wholesale to Indonesia and expect local workers to check their own cultures at the door each morning.

Successful multinational corporations (MNCs), as they have expanded their overseas operations, have developed somewhat localized versions of their original corporate cultures. As McCune (1999) illustrates, when Wal-Mart, the largest retailer in the United States at the time, opened its first discount store in Germany, it found that some features of its corporate culture (first developed in Bentonville, Arkansas) were not warmly embraced by their German employees. Workers had no difficulty with company cheers such as "Who's Number One? The Customer!" However, they balked at applying Wal-Mart's "ten-foot rule," which required all employees to greet any customer within a 10-foot radius. This rule is not enforced among Wal-Mart employees in Germany because both employees and customers place a high value on their privacy when they are shopping. Thus, Wal-Mart had the good sense to realize that it would be counterproductive to allow its corporate culture to supersede the local German culture. Instead, Wal-Mart permitted a local variation of the corporate culture that was more compatible with local German culture. What is important to realize is that neither version of the corporate culture sacrifices the overarching cultural principle that the "customer is number one!"

Philippe d'Iribarne (2002) provides two detailed case studies (one of a combined Italian–French microelectronic company headquartered in Geneva and the other a French food company located in Mexico) showing how Western corporate cultures can promote supportive communities of highly motivated workers by building upon deep-seated local cultural values. In Morocco, Islamic norms and values were combined with Total Quality Management values to transform SGS-Thomson's factory culture, whereas in Mexico, norms and values regarding family and the pursuit of a higher moral purpose were combined with the traditional corporate model of Danone of France. In both cases, it was not the imposition of a foreign corporate culture over local cultural values. Rather, organizational excellence was achieved by integrating local cultural values and behavior patterns into the Western corporate culture. These two case studies demonstrate the fact that cultural differences are not *de facto* obstacles to creating efficient production facilities. In both situations the company managers (1) took the time and energy to understand local cultural realities, and (2) were willing to adapt their management practices and corporate cultures to the local cultural context in Morocco and Mexico.

CULTURAL DIFFERENCES IN BUSINESS: CHALLENGES AND OPPORTUNITIES

This book is written with the primary objective of integrating the insights and findings of cultural anthropology with the practice of global business. When focusing on the nature of cultural differences, we cannot avoid pointing out the many pitfalls awaiting the naïve (culturally uninformed) businessperson ready to engage the global marketplace. In fact, at times, the reader might be overwhelmed with the daunting number of cultural differences that can result in needless misunderstandings (and a lack of success) when marketing, negotiating, or managing abroad. The purpose of focusing on cultural differences is not to discourage the reader from entering the realm of global business, but rather to educate the reader to (1) understand the cultural features different from one's own, (2) use that knowledge to alter one's own behaviors so as to meet one's professional objectives more effectively, and (3) assist organizations and individuals in developing solutions to the cultural problems they encounter.

Thus, the more knowledge we have about our culturally different business partners, the more likely we will avoid cross-cultural misunderstanding. We are not suggesting that we eliminate, or even reduce, the number of the cultural differences by having you either (1) give up your own culture, or (2) force your own culture upon others. Rather, it is important to recognize cultural differences, learn about them, and also understand that cultural differences provide opportunities for *individual* and *organizational synergy.* When people from two different cultures work cooperatively in an atmosphere of mutual understanding and respect, the outcome can be more productive than either group working independently. This can be illustrated by a U.S. manufacturer of cell phones wanting to expand its markets into Africa. One effective strategy for obtaining a larger market share of cell phones is for the U.S. firm to create an ongoing dialogue between its international marketing department, its new product development department, and the local African sales representatives in cities such as Lagos, Nigeria, Nairobi, Kenya, and Dakar, Senegal. The local sales force knows the local needs, which professions can be served best by cell phones, which features are most important, and what people would be able to afford. These local salespeople would know that local fishermen would profit handsomely by having the capacity to contact various restaurants and fish markets via cell phone while they head back to port with their day's catch. These fishermen would not need all of the "bell and whistles" found on many cell phones, but rather an inexpensive way to communicate to their customers while they are several miles out at sea. Once the local fishing industry has been identified as a potential new market, the R&D people can develop an inexpensive phone that would meet the needs of the fishermen. Thus by pooling their different areas of expertise, the company and the local African sales representatives can develop new products more effectively to expand the cell phone market.

It is also important to understand that cultural differences can be used as assets rather than liabilities when MNCs form task-oriented teams based on cultural diversity. It has long been known that culturally diverse groups (provided that all members understand and respect the cultural perspectives of one another) perform tasks better than culturally homogeneous groups. For example, in experiments conducted by Warren E. Watson and his colleagues (1993), socially and culturally diverse work groups out-performed more homogeneous ones when the tasks were open-ended and the goal was to generate as many creative solutions as possible. Thus, if managed successfully, cultural diversity within an organization can be an asset rather than a potential liability, that is, something that must be eliminated from the corporate structure as quickly as possible.

CROSS-CULTURAL SCENARIOS

Read the following cross-cultural scenarios. In each mini-case study, a basic cultural conflict occurs among the actors involved. Try to identify the source of the conflict and suggest how it could have been avoided or minimized. Then see how well your analyses compare to the explanations in Appendix A.

1-1   Bernice Caplan, purchaser for women's apparel for a major U.S. department store, had just taken over the overseas accounts. Excited and anxious to make a good impression on her European counterparts, Bernice worked long, hard hours to provide information needed to close purchasing contracts in a timely manner. Stefan, one of her Dutch associates in Amsterdam, sent an urgent message on May 1 requiring information before the close of day on 6/5. Although Bernice thought it odd for the message to be marked URGENT for information needed over a month away, she squeezed the request into her already busy schedule. She was pleased when she had whipped together the information and was able to fax it by May 10, three full weeks before the deadline. She then placed a telephone call to Stefan to make sure that he had received the fax and was met with an angry, hostile response. The department store not only lost the order at the agreed-upon cost, but the Dutch office asked that Bernice be removed from their account.

Where did Bernice go wrong?

1-2   Pierce Howard, a California winemaker, was making a sales presentation to a large distributor in Shanghai, China. As part of his presentation, Pierce mentioned that he thought that his wines would be well received in China because they were very popular in Japan, and, after all, the two countries had a great deal in common. From this point on in the presentation, the Chinese lost interest in Pierce and his line of California wines.

How can you explain this situation?

1-3   Howard Duvall, an up-and-coming accountant with a New York–based firm, was on contract in Mombasa, Kenya, for three months to set up an accounting system for a local corporation. Because he had never been out of the United States before, he was interested in learning as much as possible about the people and their culture. He was fascinated by the contrasts he saw between the traditional and the modern, relations between Africans and Europeans, and the influence of the Arabic language and the Muslim religion. Every spare moment, he had the company's driver take him to see the interesting sights both in town and in the rural villages. To document the sights for friends back home, he brought his 35 mm camera wherever he went. Although Howard was able to get a number of good pictures of game animals and buildings, he became increasingly frustrated because people turned their backs on him when he tried to take their pictures. Several people actually became quite angry.

What advice could you give Howard?

1-4   In what was considered a "hostile takeover," a U.S. corporation purchased a regional wine-producing vineyard in Limoges, France, in a strategic maneuver to enter the European market. Frank Joseph, a human resource specialist, was sent to Limoges to smooth the ruffled feathers of the vineyard's workers. Along with videos and propaganda on the merits of working for a Fortune 500 corporation, Frank also brought to Limoges a number of company logo items. In what was intended as a goodwill gesture, he presented the workers with T-shirts, ball caps, ink pens, and coffee cups to take home to their families. Over the next several weeks, Frank never saw any of the company's logo items being worn or used by the workers. Instead, the workers were uncommunicative toward him and at times even hostile.

Why was Frank treated in this manner?

1-5   A U.S. fertilizer manufacturer headquartered in Minneapolis decided to venture into the vast potential of third-world markets. The company sent a team of agricultural researchers into an East African country to test soils, weather conditions, and topographical conditions to develop locally effective fertilizers. Once the research and manufacturing of these fertilizer products had been completed, one of the initial marketing strategies was to distribute, free of charge, 100-pound bags of the fertilizer to selected rural areas. It was believed that those using the free fertilizer would be so impressed with the dramatic increase in crop productivity that they would spread the word to their friends, relatives, and neighbors. Teams of salespeople went from hut to hut in those designated areas, offering each male head of household a free bag of fertilizer along with an explanation of its capacity to increase crop output. Although the men were very polite, they all turned down the offer of free fertilizer. The marketing staff concluded that these local people were either uninterested in helping themselves grow more food and eat better, or so ignorant that they couldn't understand the benefits of the new product.

What was ethnocentric about this conclusion?

2

■ ■ ■

Lenses for Understanding Culture and Cultural Differences

Whether you are a manager engaged in implementing a new work process, an evaluator charged with examining the effectiveness of an intervention, or a market researcher seeking innovative ways of capturing new consumers, you will confront cultural issues in your work. As a manager, you may discover that certain groups within your home organization are reluctant to adopt the new work process developed in Germany. In fact, you have heard people comment, "Over my dead body!" As an evaluator, you are worried that the intervention worked better with virtual workgroups rather than those that were located in the same facility. You know your boss will not be pleased with these results because this intervention was her initiative. As a market researcher, your career mobility and your organization's long-term survival are dependent on figuring out how to attract younger female shoppers to your lingerie products, which compete head on with Victoria Secret. Oh, and you are supposed to do this when the economy is flat!

There are cultural aspects to all of these issues. Businesspeople need ways of accessing the internal workings of culture and using those insights when problem solving. There are many ways of learning about culture—through direct experience, observation, comparison with other situations, discussions with cultural experts (e.g., the young female lingerie shoppers), case studies and research reports, artifacts—the list goes on and on. Of course, anthropologists do this work for a living and become quite adept at unlocking explanations for viewpoints, assumptions, beliefs, and behavior—even those occurring under conditions of rapid change. Nevertheless, it is possible for those with an open mind, an interest in people, a desire to learn, and a focus on addressing the issues to be quite successful. This chapter focuses on four lenses that are helpful in teasing out cultural insights in global business settings: contrasting values, context, metaphors, and change.

CONTRASTING VALUES

It is not unusual for anthropologists to speak of people from different cultures as having different sets of assumptions or different value systems. A *value system* represents what is expected or hoped for in a culture, not necessarily what actually occurs. Values deal with what is required or forbidden, what is judged to be good or bad or right or wrong. Thus, values represent the standards by which behavior is evaluated. If communication and understanding between people from different cultures is to be successful, each party must understand the value assumptions—or cultural starting points—of the other. Unfortunately, our own values, the result of cultural conditioning, are so much a part of our consciousness that we frequently fail to acknowledge their existence and consequently fail to understand that they may not be shared by people from other cultures. When that occurs, cross-cultural cues can be missed, communication can become short-circuited, and hostilities can be generated. To maximize our chances of understanding the cultural environment of international business, it is imperative that we examine cultural values—theirs as well as our own.

Parades both celebrate and reinforce ethnic identity.

Any attempt to analyze values is bound to be a tricky business at best. Part of the difficulty stems from the inherent bias in analyzing one's own culture (e.g., national, organizational, occupational). Because we are all influenced to some degree by the experiences of our own culture, any attempt to describe that culture inevitably will be distorted. Equally vexing is the enormity of the task. Moreover, whenever we make statements about the nature of our culture, we are (or may be) implying that other cultures possess the opposite traits. For example, to say that people in the United States place a high value on the individual is to imply that other cultures—such as Tanzanians—place a higher value on the group. Similarly, to say that people who graduate from Princeton are really smart and creative can imply that other university graduates are not as sharp or talented. Such comparative statements presuppose that we are dealing with unified, monolithic cultures. In actual fact, the many cultures of the world cannot be sorted out into neat and tidy categories due to internal variation in demographics, attitudes, and belief systems, to name a few. The United States is a case in point. It has been labeled a "melting pot" though a more apt characterization might be a "salad bowl," whereby the individual subcultures retain their own identity and integrity. While acknowledging the difficulties inherent in generalizing about values in such heterogeneous cultures as Tanzania and the United States, Princeton and a small public university, or Yahoo and Google, contrasting value patterns are both possible and valuable. Indeed, the dual processes of making generalizations and comparisons are imperative if we are to enhance our understanding of other cultures as well as our own.

A value-orientation approach for understanding cultural differences was developed by Florence Kluckhohn and Fred Strodtbeck and their colleagues in the 1950s. Their research, which took place in Zuni, Navajo, Spanish-American, Mormon, and Texan communities, has served as the foundation for much of the cross-cultural and international business research since then. This approach assumed that certain universal problems and conditions face people in all societies, and that there are only a limited number of solutions to these problems. Although all potential solutions to these universal problems are present in every society, one solution tends to be preferred by most members of a particular culture. As social scientists, Kluckhohn and her colleagues believed that these different value orientations could be operationalized and presented in a questionnaire format. Once sufficient numbers of questionnaires were administered in a particular culture, dominant value orientations could be identified. Kluckhohn and Strodtbeck (1961: 11) put forth five universal problems (posed as questions) for which all cultures must find solutions:

1. *Human nature orientation:* What is the character of innate human nature? Potential options include innately good, innately bad, or a combination of the two.
2. *Man–nature orientation:* What is the relation of man to nature? Potential options include mastery over nature, subjugation to nature, or harmony with nature.
3. *Time orientation:* What is the temporal focus of human life? Is time directed to the past, present, or future?

4. *Activity orientation:* What is the modality of human activity? Do people value an individual's accomplishments or his or her innate personal traits?
5. *Relational orientation:* What is the modality of man's relationship to other men? Is individualism more highly valued than commitments and obligations to the wider group such as family, neighborhood, or society?

Although published over a half-century ago, the value orientations of Kluckhohn and Strodtbeck have relevance for international business. For example, a society that believes that humans are essentially good would tend to emphasize training and development programs because workers are seen as changeable; societies that view humans as essentially evil, on the other hand, would emphasize recruiting the right workers for the right jobs because employees are not likely to change after being hired. In "doing societies," which emphasize individual accomplishments, employees should be rewarded for maximizing their work, whereas in "being societies," which emphasize personal characteristics and social relationships, employees should be rewarded for being fair-minded, thoughtful, and good team players. Or, in highly individualistic societies, hiring should be conducted on the basis of experience, past performance, competence, and education, whereas in more collectivist societies, it would be appropriate to consider the social relationship of the job candidate to others in the firm.

Other scholars have built upon this value-orientations model. In their classic textbook, which essentially launched the eclectic field of intercultural communication, John Condon and Fathi Yousef (1975) added an additional 20 dimensions to Kluckhohn's original five by looking at such variables as gender (equality vs. male dominance), authority (democracy vs. authoritarianism), social mobility (high vs. low mobility), and formality (low vs. high levels of informality). Dutch social scientist Geert Hofstede (1980, 1991, 2001) derived five major dimensions of cultural values from his large-scale study of IBM, which employed people from all over the world. His study involved the use of large amounts of questionnaire data in 53 national cultures. Hofstede was able to rank these cultures along the following dimensions:

- individualism–collectivism (the degree to which individual vs. group interests prevail)
- uncertainty avoidance (the degree of tolerance of change and ambiguity)
- power distance (the degree of inequality)
- masculinity–femininity (the degree of differentiation in gender roles)
- long-term vs. short-term orientation (an emphasis on the future compared to the past and the present).

Based on organizational studies in Denmark and the Netherlands, Hofstede also discovered six dimensions associated with organizational culture (e.g., process oriented vs. results oriented, loose control vs. tight control) (Hofstede, 1991, Hofstede, 2001). Many other researchers have examined values cross-culturally (Brake, Walker, and Walker 1995; Wilson and Dalton 1996). One of the more recent studies was carried out by Global Leadership and Organizational

Behavior Effectiveness (GLOBE) researchers who gathered data from managers representing 951 organizations in 62 national cultures. Their goal was to understand the relationship between culture and societal, organizational, and leadership effectiveness (House et al. 2004; Chhokar, Brodbeck, and House 2007). They identified nine dimensions of national culture as well as six major leadership styles (e.g., performance oriented, team oriented, autonomous).

The contrasting values approach provides one mechanism for understanding how cultures differ on a variety of key cultural attributes or dimensions. It is alternately known as dimensional, bipolar, or culture-general research. This approach entails an exploration of cross-cultural similarities and differences on key dimensions (e.g., individualism–collectivism). Those dimensions are expressed as two poles along a continuum (e.g., from individualism to collectivism). Cultures fall somewhere along that continuum (e.g., the United States is more individualistic, while China is more collectivistic). The approach is also considered culture-general because comparisons can be made across a large number of cultures. The research design relies on survey questionnaires, scores, scales, and relative rankings, which are analyzed quantitatively.

Key strengths of the bipolar, dimensional approach lie "in its clarity and consistency" and in "juxtaposing one culture against another to facilitate cross-cultural comparisons" (Fang 2005–06: 72). It is designed to help you understand the value *preferences* of people from different cultural groups. It enables you to see how your cultural values compare with other cultural values on a number of important dimensions. It also gives you a set of "hooks" on which you can hang (and better understand) the various cultural traits that you may encounter. This framework assumes that cross-cultural awareness can take place only when you view other cultural values in relation to your own. Because cultural values lie behind breakdowns in cross-cultural communication, such an approach can help you diagnose and, it is hoped, avoid potential miscommunications. We now explore four of these dimensions: the individual–collective, equality–hierarchy, change orientation, and time orientation.

The Individual–Collective Dimension

All cultures must ask and answer the following question: To what extent should people pursue their own individual activities and agendas rather than contribute to the success and well-being of the larger group, such as family, neighborhood, clan, team, or company? Some national cultures such as the United States, Canada, Great Britain, and the Netherlands, and organizational cultures such as General Motors and General Electric, place a high value on individualism. These cultures emphasize the worth and dignity of the individual over the group, independence rather than interdependence, and relatively few social obligations. Other national cultures such as Guatemala, Japan, and Taiwan, and organizational/institutional cultures such as Kaiser Permanente (the largest health care system in the United States) or an Israeli kibbutz, tend to emphasize the larger group. These cultures encourage people to put the interests of the group above their own, maintain strong ties and obligations to group members, and value long-term social relationships above short-term accomplishments. The individual–collective dimension can be summarized as follows:

Individual-Oriented Cultures	**Collective-Oriented Cultures**
Individuals are major units of social perception	Groups are major units of social perception
Explain others' behavior by personal traits	Explain others' behavior by group norms
Success attributed to own ability	Success attributed to help from group
Self-defined as individual entity	Self-defined in terms of group
Know more about self than others	Know more about others than self
Achievement for one's own sake	Achievement for benefit of group
Personal goals over group goals	In-group goal over personal goals
Value self-assuredness	Value modesty
Value autonomy and independence	Value interdependence
Fear dependence on others	Fear ostracism
Casual connections to many groups	Strong connections to a few groups
Few obligations to others	Many obligations to others
Confrontation is acceptable	Harmony is expected
Task completion is important	Relationships are important

HOW INDIVIDUALISM–COLLECTIVISM PLAYS OUT IN INDIVIDUAL-ORIENTED CULTURES

- The ideal of the individual is deeply rooted in the social, political, and economic institutions of such societies as the United States and England. The individual is considered to be the source of moral power and totally competent to assess the effects of his or her own actions, and is expected to be responsible for those actions. In the United States, the Bill of Rights protects people against infringement of their individual rights by the state, thus allowing them to express their ideas freely, practice whatever religion they choose, assemble freely, and generally control their own lives to as great a degree as possible.
- Family ties tend to be *relatively* unimportant. That is not to say that in the United States the family is unimportant in any absolute sense, for the family remains the primary group to which most Americans have their strongest loyalties. Nevertheless, when compared with other cultures, Americans divide their time and emotional energy between family and a wider variety of social groupings, including school, workplace, labor union, friends, place of worship, and a host of voluntary organizations. Moreover, the constant preoccupation with self has resulted in the truncation of extended family ties, reducing the notion of family to its smallest possible unit—the nuclear family.
- The concept of individualism is instilled from an early age in the United States by constant encouragement of children to become self-sufficient. Children are taught to make their own decisions, clarify their own values, form their own opinions, and solve their own problems.

Children are encouraged to make decisions for themselves in highly individualistic societies.

- The aim of education is not to serve God, country, or family but to enable individuals to maximize their human potential—or in the words of the U.S. Army recruiting campaign, "Be all that you can be!"
- Individuals, not groups, are evaluated for the work they do and compensated accordingly.

HOW INDIVIDUALISM–COLLECTIVISM PLAYS OUT IN COLLECTIVE-ORIENTED CULTURES

- People tend to identify or define themselves primarily as members of a group rather than as individuals. When asked "Who are you?" most Americans would give their name, profession, and where they live, probably in that order. When asked the same question in Swaziland or Kenya, for example, a person is likely to give his name, his father's name, and his extended family (which may number in the hundreds of people).
- Property, such as land or livestock, is controlled by the larger group rather than being individually owned. Whereas Americans *own* property (to the extent that they have total control over it), people in collectivist societies have only limited rights and obligations to property that is ultimately controlled by the larger group.
- Basic life choices, such as who you will marry or what profession you will follow, are not made exclusively, or even primarily, by the individual. For example, marriages in some parts of the world are arranged by parents and other influential members of the two family groups involved.
- Collectivist societies have a strong sense of responsibility to the group (e.g., country, family, company). In Asian cultures, if an individual does not give his or her best effort, it is seen as letting down the entire group; in other words, both success and failure are "team affairs."

ROOTS OVER MONEY

The strength of social relationships in collectivist cultures can create hiring difficulties for global firms. While on a short-term assignment to Venezuela, Harry Dalton, an upper-level manager for a U.S.-based multinational corporation, was extremely impressed with the performance of one of the local managers. In fact, Harry was so impressed that he offered him a job in the home office in Chicago, which involved a promotion, a handsome increase in salary, and a generous moving allowance. But, much to Harry's surprise, the Venezuelan thanked him but turned down the job offer. Harry began to think that he had seriously misjudged this man's intelligence. What Harry did not realize, however, was that the Venezuelan manager was making a perfectly intelligent career decision. Coming from a collectivist society, Venezuelans tend to first consider the needs of their family or organization before considering their own self-interest. Being offered a promotion and higher salary would not be the most compelling reason for taking a new position. Rather, the Venezuelan manager would think primarily about the interests of extended family members, many of whom probably would not want him to move. Then the employee would consider the interests of the local company, which probably needs him to continue working in Caracas. People are not always motivated by individual benefits when deciding to take a new job.

IMPLICATIONS FOR BUSINESS WITHIN COLLECTIVIST CULTURES

1. In highly individualistic societies such as the United States, it makes sense to hold out incentives to individuals as a way of motivating them. But in collectivist cultures, such as Japan, one's primary responsibility is to one's work group, not one's own professional advancement. Thus, to single out an individual member of a Japanese work team for praise is likely to embarrass the individual and demoralize the others on the team.
2. Be aware of the need to build long-term relationships. If building long-term relationships is the only way to do business with people in collectivist societies, then Americans will need to spend time and energy nurturing these relationships.
3. Be careful about using the pronoun *I*. Often Americans use the pronoun *I* much more frequently than they use the word *we*. People from collectivist societies sometimes get the impression that Americans are "loose cannons" (John Wayne types, shooting from the hip) and are speaking for themselves rather than the organizations they represent.
4. Do not discount family, tribal, or national loyalties in other cultures, for they may be much stronger than your own.
5. Use third parties to make contacts and introductions.
6. Be aware that while nepotism is generally frowned upon in individualistic societies, it may be considered both functional and ethical in collectivist societies.
7. Communicate respect for the wider good (e.g., environment, whole society) rather than simply the good of the organization. Collectivist cultures tend to be more publicly conscious.
8. Emphasize your own sense of loyalty and that of your company, because loyalty and the meeting of obligations are important in collectivist cultures.

A COLLECTIVE APPROACH FOR SMALL BUSINESS ENTREPRENEURS

Collectivism can be harnessed to improve business outcomes. Microfinance has been a successful strategy assisting low-income entrepreneurs—particularly in developing markets—to launch their own businesses (Helms 2006). The entrepreneur typically receives a small loan of a couple hundred dollars which pays for equipment, materials, and other start-up costs. Many institutions and organizations provide microfinance including the World Bank Group, foundations, private funds, banks, and commercial investors.

One model of microfinance uses foundation support to create a rotating loan belonging to the community, an approach that is aligned with collectivist traditions in the Andes. The Chijnaya Foundation, named for an Altiplano community of 800 in southern Peru (Bolton 2010), helps communities in the highlands work on projects and business ventures that lead to long-term sustainability and improved "cultural and economic well-being" (http://www.chijnayafoundation.org/chijnaya-foundation-purpose-and-promise). The first loans were made in 2006 for about $250 per household to build animal shelters to protect cattle from the harsh weather. "The economy of Chijnaya is based on cheese. The shelters increase the productivity of milk from the cattle. The milk is processed into cheese in the communally owned cheese factory," stated anthropologist Ralph Bolton, President and CEO. Fifty households received the micro loans, purchased the building materials together (to get a better rate), built the shelters, and paid back the loans with 2 percent interest at the end of the year. Bolton commented, "That first group increased their cash income by 40 percent in one year."

Microfinance has come under criticism recently because the micro loans are not always paid back. Chijnaya has not had this problem. The 100 percent repayment of the first-year recipients enabled another group of households from the community to participate in the program the following year. Since 2006, the microfinance program has spread to 10 other communities, with more planned for 2011. For some key reasons, this pattern of recycling the money has enjoyed a 100-percent repayment rate on almost 400 loans to date. First, the foundation provides funding to an association within the community, rather than to individuals. Bolton pointed out, "We do this as a group enterprise." Indeed, the funding belongs to the association. Second, each recipient provides documentation and signs for the loan. Third, both current recipients and next-in-line recipients apply pressure, as necessary, to ensure that the loans are repaid so that future funding is available. Finally, there is strong interest within the community to continue working with the foundation since the recipients have improved their income stream as a result of the loans.

The Equality–Hierarchy Dimension

The equality–hierarchy dimension, which is also referred to as power distance, raises the following question: How should people with different levels of power, prestige, and status interact with one another—equally or unequally? Those national cultures that emphasize the equality polarity such as Canada, Sweden,

Australia, and the United States, or organizational cultures such as industrial research labs, tend to minimize power and status differences. Power tends to be more diffused, people in higher positions can be questioned, and subordinates want their superiors to consult with them and be accessible. This egalitarian orientation leads to relatively informal relations between people of high and low status, a general disregard of protocol, and a high level of delegation of authority. At the other end of the continuum—represented by such countries as Malaysia, Panama, and the Philippines, or subcultures such as airline pilots or the military—people expect that status and power hierarchies will be maintained. In fact, hierarchical inequalities are seen as essential for the culture's well-being because they satisfy a need for structure, order, and security. People at the higher levels of the hierarchy are treated with great deference by those lower down the ladder. People in authority should not step out of their privileged roles, bosses should not be questioned, and there is little or no delegation of authority. This dimension can be represented in the following way:

Egalitarian Cultures	**Hierarchical Cultures**
Low-status differences	High-status differences
Power diffused to many people	Power concentrated with few people
Delegation of authority	Little delegation of authority
Informal social relations	Formality in social relations
Minimum deference for superiors	Maximum deference for superiors
Superior can be questioned	Superior cannot be questioned
Little respect for old age	Great respect for old age
Mechanisms to redress grievances	No mechanism to redress grievances

Alfons Trompenaars and Charles Hampden-Turner (1993) represent this dimension by using a series of triangles illustrating varying degrees of social distance. Hierarchical societies are represented by tall triangles (with a small base and relatively long sides) in which the distance between those at the top and those at the bottom is considerable. More egalitarian societies, on the other hand, are represented by very flat triangles in which there is relatively little social distance among the various levels of the society.

HOW EQUALITY–HIERARCHY PLAYS OUT IN EGALITARIAN CULTURES

- Downplaying status differences, an important theme running through American culture, has its roots in our nation's early history. By moving onto the American frontier, the early settlers gave up much of the social structure's formalities and rigidities found in Europe. The hard work required for survival on the frontier was hardly conducive to the preservation of pomp and circumstance. Hard work also made social mobility possible.
- Early Americans developed much fewer formal customs of dress, speaking, etiquette, and interpersonal relationships than found among their European ancestors.

To a large extent, this informality and reticence to "stand on ceremony" persists to the present time, institutionalized in phrases such as "dress casual" or "casual Fridays."

- Americans assume that informality is a prerequisite for sincerity. They become uncomfortable when faced with the type of ceremony, tradition, and formalized social rules found more widely throughout Europe. Moreover, they are likely to feel uneasy when others treat them with too much deference.
- Authority figures—such as clergy, professors, and supervisors—are often called by their first names rather than their official title and last name.
- In many egalitarian societies, informality (for example, de-emphasizing status differences) is reflected in the structure of everyday language. The distinction between the formal and informal *you*, found in such languages as German and French, requires speakers to make linguistic choices that reflect the social status and role of the people being addressed. In contrast, the English language makes no such distinctions.
- Authority figures, such as supervisors or college professors, are allowed to admit that they don't have all the answers. They will not lose respect because they admit fallibility.

HOW EQUALITY—HIERARCHY PLAYS OUT IN HIERARCHICAL CULTURES

- Upper-status people are expected to maintain their high status and prestige at all costs. Don't expect to see Queen Elizabeth of England wearing Levi's in public or the King of Malaysia running through Kuala Lumpur in his jogging outfit.
- Languages are structured in such a way as to ensure that one's relative status is reflected in the very construction of a sentence.
- High-status people are expected to be addressed by their formal title followed by the last name ("Hello, Dr. Evans") rather than the first name ("Yo, Stan").
- Children defer to their parents, younger defers to older, women defer to men, employees defer to employers, students defer to teachers, sellers defer to buyers, and everyone defers to the head of state.
- Professors (or highly respected authorities) would give a false answer rather than admit they don't know.
- Social rank in hierarchical organizations is displayed in a number of subtle ways, including size of office and presence of an administrative and /or technical assistant.

IMPLICATIONS FOR BUSINESS WITHIN HIERARCHICAL CULTURES

1. In egalitarian cultures such as the United States, it is expected that high-status people will play down their superior rank. In hierarchical cultures, people need to know from the outset what your status is so that they will know how to interact with you in an appropriate fashion. Thus, communicate your status, authority, credentials, expertise, and the like, but without arrogance or boasting.
2. The decision-making process takes longer in egalitarian cultures where all levels are asked for input. In hierarchical cultures, decisions are made more rapidly because some measure of consensus is not expected from all levels.
3. It is not particularly wise or productive for a manager from an egalitarian culture to play down the organizational hierarchies in other countries. The boss is the boss and should be treated as such.
4. A boss does not appreciate having his or her decisions or judgments called into question. You exercise your democratic inclinations at your own peril.

5. Pay attention to different levels of social status when dealing with people. Don't expect that lower-status people in your organization will be able to negotiate or conduct business with those of higher status.
6. Don't assume that all people have equal access to information.
7. Use high-status individuals (third parties) as your agents, contacts, and intermediaries.
8. Expect that there will be a greater level of tension in everyday interactions between high- and low-status people (or between young and old or between men and women).
9. Realize that subordinates expect to be closely supervised, will smile more frequently, and will repress negative emotions.

"CHIPPING" AWAY AT GENDER-BASED HIERARCHIES

Gender roles affect other cultural traditions in business and leisure such as golf. Nicole Laflamme, an attorney in Québec, often played golf with clients and colleagues. One weekday afternoon after a tournament, she and her three male colleagues sat down in the lounge of a private golf club to have a drink. The manager of the club appeared.

Manager: "What are you doing, Madame?"
Laflamme: "What do you mean?"
Manager: "You're not allowed in this room."
Laflamme: "I'm part of a tournament. I'm with my colleagues. What do you mean?"
Manager: "Well, you are a woman."

Laflamme had broken the rules; she had inadvertently entered the male-only lounge. Golf clubs, like many other institutions, had rules based on the presumption that men worked outside the home (while women did not), and that men needed special areas within the club should they want to build or solidify business relationships or conduct business. Club membership was held by the male head of household.

In the early 1990s, a ladies' golf champion at another club sought legal help from Laflamme. This client faced similar issues, including where she was allowed to socialize in the club (due to her gender) and restricted tee times (i.e., not Wednesdays or early Saturday mornings when male members had priority). The client reported feeling like a "second-class citizen." When her club decided to offer its wives full membership, this client purchased a share, only to discover that she would also have to pay an entrance fee of $30K Canadian. The client's response was "No way!" given her many years of membership (through her husband), and her success in winning numerous prizes and trophies for the club. (Her elder son would not be subjected to the entrance fee if he were to become a full member.) She was told, "This is a private club. If you don't like the rules, you don't have to stay" (Nicole Laflamme, personal communication).

Unlike in the United States or Great Britain, saying it was a private club did not halt the dispute (see, for example, Crouse 2011). Laflamme and the ladies' golf champion took the case to the newly formed Québec Human Rights Tribunal.

(continued)

While the tribunal did not have legal authority to enforce its decisions, it had the ability to declare an action discriminatory, and set damages. The defense, replete with economic arguments, consisted of attorneys who were senior members of the same club as Laflamme's client. Laflamme won. With victory in hand, she turned her attention to her own golf club. It was only after the airing of a television documentary exposing her club's discriminatory practices that its membership rules changed (http://archives.radio-canada.ca/sports/golf/clips/11730/). Other clubs followed over the better part of a decade so that by the early 2000s, golf clubs in Québec had instituted gender-neutral membership policies. Hierarchies can and do change—in this case in response to a confluence of factors including a significant narrowing of the gap between men and women in educational attainment and labor force participation rates, and changing views of male and female roles. As the status of women in Québec changed, so too did the gender hierarchy within the golf clubs, which in turn affected the strong relationship between business and golf and hierarchies in the business world generally.

The Change Orientation Dimension

This change orientation dimension incorporates a mix of elements related to uncertainty, ambiguity, risk, structure, flexibility, and change. It has been discussed widely in the literature, albeit from different perspectives and by using different sets of terms. Condon and Yousef (1975: 99–102) discuss significant components of the dimension under the heading of "mutability;" Brake and colleagues (1995: 68–69) use the "order versus flexibility" dichotomy as part of their model; and Wilson and Dalton (1996: 15–17) use the terms "dynamic" and "stable." Hofstede (1980, 1991, 2001) uses the phrase "uncertainty avoidance" to refer to the lack of tolerance for ambiguity and the need for formal rules and high-level organizational structure. For him, this dimension indicates the extent to which a culture conditions its members to feel either comfortable or uncomfortable in unstructured, ambiguous, and unpredictable situations. We prefer the label change embracing–change fearing because it emphasizes the notion of change and removes the double negative (low to high uncertainty *avoidance*).

   Cultures differ in the degree to which they can tolerate ambiguity, cope with uncertainties, and adapt to the future. Change-embracing cultures (i.e., low uncertainty avoidance) tend to be more tolerant of unorthodox opinions, are comfortable with fewer rules and simpler organizational structures, and are more relativistic in their beliefs, philosophies, and religions. National culture examples include Singapore, Denmark, Hong Kong, and the United States, while start-ups, investment banks, Internet companies, and consulting businesses represent organizational-culture examples. Change-fearing cultures (i.e., high uncertainty avoidance) are at the other end of the continuum. They try to minimize unstructured situations as much as possible by (1) maintaining strict laws and regulations, (2) providing safety and security measures, (3) adhering to absolute truths, and (4) rejecting unorthodox ideas. Greece, Portugal, and Japan are illustrative national-culture examples, along with public sector bureaucracies and large corporations. Critical components of this dimension include:

Change-Embracing Cultures	Change-Fearing Cultures
Willingness to live day-by-day	Greater anxiety about the future
Less emotional resistance to change	More emotional resistance to change
More risk taking	Less risk taking
Willingness to change employer	Tendency to stay with same employer
Hope for success	Fear of failure
Little loyalty to employer/partners	Considerable loyalty to employer/partners
Sometimes rules can be broken	Rules should not be broken
Conflict is natural and to be expected	Conflict is undesirable
Initiative of subordinates encouraged	Initiative of subordinates discouraged
Differences are tolerated	Differences are considered dangerous
Low stress	High stress
Little emotional expression	Emotional expression is acceptable
Superordinates may say "I don't know"	Superordinates have all the answers
Less formal organizational structures	Formal organizational structures

There is considerable variability across cultures in terms of the extent to which people feel that behavior should follow formal rules. In change-fearing cultures, behavior is rigidly prescribed, either with written laws or unwritten social codes. Even if individuals within such cultures occasionally break the rules, they generally believe that it is a good thing that the rules exist. In short, people feel anxious in the absence of formal regulations. At the other polarity, change-embracing cultures also have rules and regulations, but they are considered more of a convenience than an absolute moral imperative. People in such cultures can live comfortably without strict conformity to social rules and, in fact, often appreciate their freedom to "do their own thing." In terms of engaging in negotiations, people from change-fearing cultures are not very good negotiators because the outcome of the negotiations is never predictable. People from change-embracing cultures are much more comfortable in negotiating situations in which the outcome is not a foregone conclusion.

Anthropologist Kathleen Gregory-Huddleston was interested in how technical professionals in the computer industry conceptualized job opportunities and career paths in California's Silicon Valley. She focused on one particular aspect of this cultural system—computer firm growth from "start-up" through maturity. Start-ups represent a change-embracing culture. Gregory-Huddleston found that start-ups were intense entrepreneurial work environments where everyone was "on critical path" (1994: 127) and focused on a single purpose. Team spirit was high, as was the risk of failure. Impromptu parties marked the achievement of internal goals and stock options were an important incentive. By contrast, mature firms are more likely to be at the change-fearing end of the continuum. In her study, Gregory-Huddleston found that they exhibited a greater degree of formality. Their organizational structure was "more clearly defined, complex, and stable" (p. 127) compared with the start-ups that did not even have a Personnel Department. Mature firms did not support or reward entrepreneurial behavior to the same extent as the start-ups. Indeed, they were considered more secure and bureaucratic and had little immediate risk of failure.

Gregory-Huddleston also described the conflict that emerged between "oldtimers" (or "pioneers") and "newcomers" (or "settlers") as computer start-ups grew and matured. The organizational culture underwent a shift following an Initial Public Offering. Oldtimers reacted negatively to the increasing number of new company policies, red tape around salary, hiring, project scheduling (not on the weekends), and product maintenance (rather than under-the-gun innovations). One oldtimer commented, "It keeps getting duller and duller around here" while a newcomer acknowledged that newcomers were characterized as "plod[ding] along like Clydesdale engineers" (p. 129). Similarly, newcomers were frustrated by oldtimers' expectations of working overtime and "setting impossibly short targets for [product] release" (p. 129). She recommended ways of reducing this kind of subcultural conflict:

- Large, established firms can encourage entrepreneurial activity through incentives (e.g., profit sharing, reduction of red tape).
- Large firms can develop creative strategies for preserving the informality of start-ups.
- Oldtimers can try to accommodate the values and requirements of operating large firms, or simply exit them.
- Efforts can be made by all parties to create a new organizational culture through common experience.
- Entrepreneurs can move out of established firms into new ventures that become part of the wider industrial base.

The culture embracing–culture fearing change dimension has particular relevance for the fast-paced global economy of the 21st century. The increasing use of the Internet is radically changing the way we do business today. If the world's budding entrepreneurs are to be successful in today's electronic business culture, they will have to make decisions quickly, and not always with all the information at their fingertips. In other words, they will need to learn how to do business in an environment filled with uncertainty and risks. Entrepreneurs in such change-fearing cultures as Greece or Portugal are likely to be at a marked disadvantage when competing in the new economy with those from change-embracing cultures such as the United States where businesspeople see value in trying but failing, because even in failure, there is something to be learned. A failed American business person filing for bankruptcy, although hardly a hero, is at least seen as an entrepreneurial risk taker. By contrast, in change-fearing cultures, filing for bankruptcy is a sign of a flawed character. Let's take a look at the relationship between this dimension and workplace attitudes and behavior.

Entrepreneurial start-up businesses, such as the many housed in the Tech Town area of Detroit, require initiative, creativity, hard work, measured risk-taking, and perseverance.

HOW ORIENTATIONS TO CHANGE PLAY OUT IN CHANGE-EMBRACING CULTURES

- Employees/partners are willing to have their pension funds invested in the stock market rather than in a low-interest-bearing money market account.
- Employees/partners are more willing to experiment with new techniques and procedures.
- Employees/partners are not as threatened by workers from other countries as are those from change-fearing cultures.
- Employees/partners are better able to function in meetings with a loose agenda.
- Employees/partners have relatively little loyalty to employers because they do not depend on the company for security.
- Employees/partners have a preference for a broad set of guidelines rather than a formal set of rules and regulations.
- Bosses, professors, and other authority figures are not reluctant to say, "I don't know the answer to that question." (But, they will take the initiative to find out the answer.)
- Employees/partners are more likely to function effectively in work teams.
- Leaders are more likely to be innovative, creative, and approachable.

HOW ORIENTATIONS TO CHANGE PLAY OUT IN CHANGE-FEARING CULTURES

- Employees/partners would prefer to keep their pension funds in a safe, low-interest-bearing account (or under the mattress).

- Employees/partners are less likely to try something new because the results might be highly unpredictable.
- Employees/partners are likely to resist the hiring of immigrants or others seen to be "outsiders."
- People feel much more secure with a highly structured set of policies, rules, and regulations. Moreover, they have little tolerance for bending the rules under any circumstances.
- Employees/partners generally have a high level of loyalty to their employers and expect the same in return. Barring significant economic and/or political turmoil, relatively little job turnover will occur.
- Fewer members of the workforce are willing to travel abroad for overseas assignments.
- Employees/partners prefer a manager whom they perceive to be competent and whose authority cannot be questioned.
- Employees/partners are not always comfortable working in problem-solving teams.
- Leaders are not likely to be innovative or approachable.

IMPLICATIONS FOR BUSINESS WITHIN CHANGE-FEARING CULTURES

1. Build into your proposals and decisions as much predictability about the future as possible, so as to minimize any anxiety.
2. Anticipate and reward your employees/partners for their loyalty to the organization or venture.
3. Make modest proposals for change, not radical ones.
4. Be careful not to appoint or recommend managers who are too close to the age of most individuals in the organization or venture.
5. Provide structured work experiences that are likely to produce successful outcomes to help overcome the inherent fear of failure.
6. Make certain that organizational and partnership guidelines (rules/regulations) are in place, explicitly stated, and followed.
7. Avoid being too unorthodox in your opinions and recommendations.
8. Expect people to be highly rigid during negotiations. Whatever proposal you put on the negotiating table should contain built-in protections that will make the future somewhat more predictable.
9. Do not have unrealistic expectations about your employees/partners' personal initiative, creativity, or ability/willingness to work in teams.
10. Be aware of the fact that most people are not likely to appreciate a manager who delegates authority.

The Time Orientation Dimension

A major component of any constellation of values is how a particular culture deals with time. We consider this time dimension from four specific perspectives:

1. The importance of a precise reckoning of time
2. The degree to which a culture uses sequential or synchronized time
3. Whether a culture is past-, present-, or future-oriented
4. The busyness factor.

PRECISE VERSUS LOOSE RECKONING OF TIME   For those cultures that reckon time precisely, such as Switzerland and the United States, time is seen as a tangible commodity that must be used efficiently. To ensure this, people are expected to make schedules, establish timetables, and meet deadlines. Much like money, time can be saved, spent, or wasted. In the United States, where punctuality is highly valued, the relationship between time and money is summed up in the expression "Time is money." At the opposite end of the spectrum, in such places as the Middle East and South America, people take a looser, more relaxed approach to time. Schedules and deadlines are seen more as expressions of intent rather than obligations. Rather than reacting to the arbitrary positions of the hands on a clock, people are more likely to respond to social relationships that are occurring in the present. People from cultures with relaxed notions of time see those who deal with time very precisely as being rude because they are willing to cut off social relationships for the sake of keeping their next appointment. The time dimension can be represented in the following way:

Precise Reckoning of Time Cultures	**Loose Reckoning of Time Cultures**
Punctuality	Little punctuality
Rigid schedules	Loose schedules
Time is scarce/limited	Time is plentiful
"Time is money"	Social relationships

*Most Americans tend to take time
very seriously.*

Even though people from most cultures understand the meaning of clock time (hours, minutes, and seconds), each culture has its own vocabulary of time and its own pace of life. With increased business relations between the United States and Mexico, many U.S. businesspeople are becoming keenly aware of the differences in how these two cultures deal with time. The "*mañana* syndrome is basic to Mexican business" (Jessup and Jessup 1993: 34). Jeff Lewis has spent most of his life in Mexico—growing up there in an expatriate family, and now raising his own family there. He states, "I often tell newly arrived foreigners (to Mexico) that while it literally means tomorrow, it actually means NOT TODAY." He gives the following simple example: "When calling the cable company for a service call, the answer I got was that they would send a technician *mañana*. The technician did not arrive the next day, but rather three days later." Day-to-day working situations require great patience since there is less attention to deadlines. Lewis offers an example that has a direct impact on job performance:

> On a number of occasions, I would request information from co-workers and subordinates in order to prepare a report for upper management. It would be clear that I needed the information by 9:00 a.m. on a particular day. Often the information requested would not arrive by the appointed hour, but rather at the end of the same day, causing me to have to spend late hours preparing the final report.

Lewis also points out that the degree of the "*mañana* syndrome" varies geographically. "The northern part of the country is much more U.S. in its focus, its way of doing business, and its adherence to schedules and deadlines. As you move farther south, this way of doing business becomes much less prevalent."

Many cultures tend toward precise reckoning of time or loose reckoning of time. India is interesting because punctuality and rigidity of schedules are largely "situational, fluid, and player dependent" according to anthropologist Anulekha Roy. Let's say that you were given a 10:00 A.M. appointment by an accountant at an Indian bank. How long you wait for that appointment is a function of the type of bank, whether the accountant is tied up with another matter, the age of the accountant, the accountant's perception of your role, and your nationality, among other factors. In other words, you could experience an on-time appointment under one set of circumstances, and a lengthy wait on a different occasion. In the event that the accountant is occupied when you arrive, "Be prepared to accept the fact that it will take time," warns Roy. It is also possible to have a less timely appointment if you are dealing with a government bank rather than a private bank, if you get an older accountant rather than a younger one, if you requested the meeting as an individual rather than as a "company's representative," or if you are Indian rather than a Westerner. Should you find yourself experiencing an unexpectedly long delay, Roy suggests, "This is a negotiated situation and you can push." She advises letting the accountant know your time constraints beyond which you will need to reschedule.

Sequential versus Synchronized Time   In some respects, time speaks more plainly than words, for time conveys powerful messages about how people relate to the world and to each other. Cultures also tend to do things sequentially (one thing at a time) or synchronically (a number of things at the same time). This dichotomy between sequentially and synchronically oriented societies uses terms suggested by Trompenaars and Hampden-Turner (1998: 126–28). However, others have used different terminologies to refer to the same phenomenon. For example, Brake and colleagues (1995: 50–51) use the terms *single focus* and *multifocus*, whereas years earlier anthropologist Edward Hall (1976: 14–18) spoke of *monochronic time* (M-time) and *polychronic time* (P-time). The person from a sequential, or M-time, culture conceives of time as a straight, dotted line with regular spacing. Tasks are routinely accomplished one at a time, meetings have highly structured agendas, and schedules are rigidly followed. Because everything has its own time and place for the sequential thinker, any changes in the normal sequence are likely to produce anxiety. In such sequentially oriented societies as Great Britain, the United States, and the Netherlands, one should never jump ahead of others waiting in line. According to Trompenaars and Hampden-Turner, "In the Netherlands you could be the Queen, but if you are in a butcher's shop with number 46 and you step up for service when number 12 is called, you are still in deep trouble...(after all) order is order" (1998: 126).

Those people in sequentially oriented societies would argue that proceeding in a straight line is reasonable because it is orderly, efficient, and involves a minimum of effort. However, this type of straight-line thinking may not always be the best way of doing something, because it is blind to certain efficiencies of shared activities and interconnections. Sometimes juggling a number of different tasks at the same time may in fact be the most time efficient. Continuing with the butcher shop analogy, Trompenaars and Hampden-Turner cite the example of the shop in Italy (a more synchronically oriented society) where the butcher unwraps and slices an order of salami for one customer and then yells out, "Anyone want salami before I rewrap it?" Even though each customer is not served in order, the whole process is more efficient because it involves far less unwrapping and rewrapping of the various types of meat.

Thus, the person from a synchronically oriented society (P-time) conducts a number of activities in parallel, without being thrown off his or her rhythm. By way of contrast, those people that are sequentially oriented (M-time) envision a crucial path from which they do not want to deviate. Both approaches to time are usually so well ingrained in people that a person of one style will have difficulty when interacting with a person accustomed to the opposite style. To illustrate, a New Yorker is likely to think a salesclerk in Buenos Aires is extraordinarily rude when she is writing up his sales order while talking on the phone, drinking a diet cola, and flirting with another customer. Someone from a synchronically oriented society, however, will think that his American colleague (who is talking on the phone) is rude because the American does not greet him when entering his office, for it is considered a serious slight not to be greeted even while still talking on the phone. The differences between those who are sequentially oriented (M-time) and synchronically oriented (P-time) can be summarized as follows:

Sequentially Oriented Cultures	Synchronically Oriented Cultures
One task at a time	Multiple tasks at a time
Concentration on task	Easily distracted
Schedules taken very seriously	Plans change often and easily
Many short-term relationships	Long-term social relationships
Time is a threat	Time is a friend

PAST, PRESENT, AND FUTURE ORIENTATIONS   A third aspect of the time dimension concerns the extent to which people focus on the past, the present, or the future. To be certain, all three alternatives must be recognized, but as Kluckhohn and Strodtbeck (1961) argued, one time orientation is likely to predominate. Past-oriented societies regard previous experience and events as the most important and, in fact, use the past as a guide to the present. Traditional wisdom that has been passed down from previous generations is given a primary emphasis. Because the elders are the link with the past, they are afforded the highest level of deference in the present. Events in such societies are seen as circular or recurring. Consequently, the tried-and-true solutions to problems are the ones most likely applied to present-day problems. In such cultures, the leaders are expected to carry the vision of the past into the present and future.

Present-oriented societies tend to emphasize spontaneity, immediacy, and experiencing each moment to its fullest. According to this perspective, people do not do things because they reflect a glorious past or will bring about some gain in the future. Rather, people do things because of the inherent pleasure they will derive in the here and now. This perspective on time can be summed up in the adage "Take care of today, and tomorrow will take care of itself." Because people with a present orientation typically believe that their lives are controlled by external forces (such as fate or luck), they have developed a number of ways of appreciating the simple pleasures of daily activities. Business organizations in such present-oriented societies formulate short-term plans, allocate resources based on present demands, and train their personnel to meet current goals.

People from future-oriented societies believe that it is far more important to trade off short-term gains in the present for more long-term benefits in the future. One does not engage in activities today for the sole reason of benefiting from the immediate rewards, but rather from the potentially greater benefits that will be realized in the future. For example, rather than buying a caramel macchiato from Starbucks every day, you could put your money in a savings account and buy an iPad at the end of the year and have money left over for lots of apps and iTunes. In the event of premature death, future-oriented parents are willing to pay life insurance premiums today so that their dependent children are protected from financial catastrophe. People from the United States, Canada, and a number of European countries believe that they have a good deal of control over their lives and can to some degree influence the course of future events. Business organizations in those cultures plan work and resources to meet long-term goals that will be directed to future needs. They may also be in a hurry to get things done so that they can move on and tackle other things.

The American view of the future—which, it is believed, can be controlled from the present—is relatively short term. American businesspeople tend to emphasize gains in the immediate future, not the distant future. Other societies have much deeper conceptions of the future. For example, in Japan it is not at all unusual for a couple to take out a 100-year mortgage on a house. Moreover,

---

HOW FAST SHOULD THE CLOCK MOVE?

Americans get impatient for change. In 1992, Poland, like other countries in Eastern Europe, was moving to market economic systems with the help of international agencies. To privatize its housing system, it received a $350 million loan; anthropologist Ruth Sando and her colleagues at Fannie Mae (a U.S. government enterprise backing U.S. mortgages) were brought in to provide technical expertise. The complexities were enormous: provide the Poles with a technical knowledge of banking, set up a financing structure for them, help them learn how to handle risk associated with mortgage lending, train the bank staff—in short, engage in institution building. If Fannie Mae was not successful, hundreds of millions of dollars would be at risk.

Sando framed the problem in this way: "Americans look at the task, develop a timeline, and get to work" (Ruth Sando, personal communication). Sando's boss ended her speech at the start of the assignment in Poland with the Nike slogan—"Just do it!"—a phrase consistent with the economic "shock therapy" approach developed by U.S. economic advisors guiding the Polish government on its path to capitalism. Yet, a fundamental cultural difficulty revolved around the concept of time—particularly in planning initiatives. The project plan devised by the Americans was overly ambitious in that it "didn't include time for difficulties on the ground," stated Sando. Americans are "very action-oriented and our business organizations do not put a value on the planning process…(which) can be a real weakness in American business at home as well as abroad." There had been little planning taking into account the country's political instability, the hyperinflation, or the simple fact that there were no laws on the books around land ownership and transfer. "We were not naïve about how hard it would be, but (about) how long it would take," she recalled. Sando believed that if there had been local input during the planning process, and if the plans had taken into account all the variables involved, the project goals and timeline would have been more realistic. It took years for the project to be considered a success, far longer than originally planned.

Japanese companies are likely to include projections for the next two centuries in their business plan, not just for the next decade, as is typical in Europe and the United States. The notion of a future-oriented society can become meaningful only when we realize that some societies have a very truncated view of the future. According to John Mbiti, many traditional African societies have essentially a two-dimensional notion of time, "with a short past, a present, and virtually no future" (1969: 17). Because African time is composed of a series of events that are experienced, the future must be of little meaning because future events have not yet occurred. Mbiti supports his argument with linguistic data from the Gikuyu and Kikamba languages of Kenya. Both languages contain three future tenses covering a period not exceeding two years from the present. If future events do not fall within this shallow range, virtually no linguistic mechanism can conceive or express them. Given these linguistic structures, it is safe to assume that speakers of these East African languages have little or no interest in those things that might occur in the distant future.

THE BUSYNESS FACTOR   Some recent research in the United States focuses on an aspect of time that links America's precise reckoning of time, with its emphasis on sequential time and short-term time orientation. It is the concept of busyness as described by anthropologists Charles Darrah, James Freeman, and Jan English-Lueck. Busyness is about "our hectic days." While it involves fitting "everything into the scarce time available," it also involves managing commitments at work and home and developing coping strategies (2007: 4–5). One of their study participants (a mom) described a list of 21 chores for the day:

> I had to do a written letter to the day care this morning telling them how Nicole's gastroenterologist appointment went yesterday because I'm a little concerned that this is the ninth week and I don't want the day care to do anything drastic like say, "Oh, we can't take her because you can't figure this out." I needed to go to the bank; I did that. I need to pick up a particular test that they want to do for Nicole from the laboratory. I need to get an oil change. I've got to get gas in the car. I gotta get chlorine for the pool. I need to order some fruit for the party, for Angela's birthday party. I need to go get some high-fiber foods for Nicole because we're going to try that with her, and then I need to write a thank-you note to someone who gave us a gift the other day. Pick up some photography. See, it's a lot of little stuff, and Humberto (her husband) just doesn't do all that little stuff, and not all of it needs to be done. (2007: 117–18)

This mom is organizing her day by the set of activities that she would like to accomplish; putting items on the chore list helps to create the day's structure. She appears to be motivated by her list. You can almost feel the drive behind her words as she outlines what she needs to do. There is a sense that she needs to get on it—that there is no time to waste. All of the chores on the list are tied to the present or near-term future. Some of the items are time-limited (e.g., the birthday party) while others may have a longer time horizon (e.g., oil change). Yet, she seems to be filling up her entire day with these chores even though she has admitted that "not all of it needs to be done." It is almost as if her life is jam-packed with tasks, activities, and obligations requiring completion. Of course the unintended effect is that her life comes to be defined by its busyness.

HOW TIME ORIENTATION PLAYS OUT IN PRECISE/M-TIME CULTURES

- People pay close attention to their watch, tend to divide time into very precise units, and are frequently fully scheduled or overbooked.
- People tend to eat meals because "it's time to eat," though they may sometimes eat on the run.
- Business deadlines are taken very seriously.
- People move rapidly.
- Meetings start pretty much on time, usually no later than five minutes after the designated time.
- People do one thing at a time, rather than a number of things at the same time (though since the advent of electronic devices, multitasking has increased).
- People tend to emphasize getting contracts signed and then moving on to some new endeavor.

HOW TIME ORIENTATION PLAYS OUT IN LOOSE/P-TIME CULTURES

- Few people pay close attention to the clock.
- People eat because of the "need to share food," rather than because of the position of the hands on the clock.
- Business deadlines are hoped for, but people will not get overly upset if something prevents the deadline from being met.
- People move at a more leisurely pace.
- Meetings start after an appropriate amount of time is devoted to socializing.
- People do many things at the same time.
- A greater emphasis is placed on building social relationships rather than on completing the task on time.

HOW TIME ORIENTATION PLAYS OUT IN PAST-ORIENTED CULTURES

- People have a great concern for history and origins of their families, businesses, and social institutions.
- Employees are motivated by examples from the "golden past."
- Predecessors and older people are looked to as role models. Even though they may not have had the most recent formal education, their wisdom and experience are highly valued.
- Business hosts will want to share their cultural history with you (via museums, monuments).

HOW TIME ORIENTATION PLAYS OUT IN PRESENT-ORIENTED CULTURES

- People live in the here and now and look for immediate gratification.
- Everything is evaluated in terms of its immediate impact.
- People are not particularly effective at deferring gratification or planning for the future.

The tempo of life and business in Santiago, Chile, is more leisurely and relaxed compared with the hurried pace and tight scheduling of time in much of North America.

HOW TIME ORIENTATION PLAYS OUT IN FUTURE-ORIENTED CULTURES

- People tend to be enthusiastic planners.
- There is a considerable willingness to defer present gratification for even more gratification later on.
- People are generally optimistic about progress in the future.
- People place a high value on being youthful, because the young have more of a future than the more senior members of the society.

HOW TIME ORIENTATION PLAYS OUT IN BUSY CULTURES

- People try to keep themselves organized through short-term planning.
- Days are filled with activities that help them manage their obligations.
- Busy people find satisfaction in achieving what they set out to do.
- Getting things done is the goal and reflected in the old adage: "If you want something done, give it to a busy person!"

IMPLICATIONS FOR BUSINESS WITHIN LOOSE/P-TIME CULTURES

1. Suppress the urge to get things done quickly (because "Faster is better" and "Time is money"). Be willing to spend time building long-lasting relationships.
2. Do not show impatience. You may be viewed as untrustworthy and as someone who wants to cheat your business partners.

3. Become more flexible in your scheduling and broaden your concept of what is an acceptable range of tardiness.
4. Be aware that higher-status people can keep lower-status people waiting, but the opposite is not true.
5. Do not be put off when business associates do more than one thing at a time. Be prepared to be in several different conversations at the same time.
6. Understand and respect local traditions and long-term commitments.
7. Use role models and situations from the past as ways of motivating your employees.
8. Sell the reputation of your company and its success over time.

CONTEXT

Context is a second lens for understanding cultural similarities and differences. It is a communication concept developed by anthropologist Edward Hall to differentiate across and within cultural groups. He defines context as "information surrounding an event" (1989: 6). Cultures can be compared on a scale ranging from high context to low context. Hall stated it this way:

> A high-context (HC) communication or message is one in which most of the information is either in the physical context or internalized in the person, while very little is in the coded, explicit, transmitted part of the message. A low-context (LC) communication is just the opposite; i.e., the mass of the information is vested in the explicit code (language). (1976: 91)

The concept of context provides a different kind of insight into culture than can be derived from a contrasting values approach. Though it too reflects dimensional polarity—where each end of the continuum stands in opposition to the other—it is based on communication behavior. Communication exchanges, whether verbal or written, are readily observable. Once observed, it is easier to figure out how to respond appropriately to the situation.

One way to think about communications is in terms of directness (see Chapter 4 "Linguistic Style" section). High-context communications are indirect and understated, and sometimes ambiguous. The emphasis is largely on the non-verbal aspects of the exchange. People in high-context cultures or situations seem to know what the other person is thinking, feeling, or expecting. Few words are necessary to express the messages being conveyed. Moreover, they do not "get to the point quickly" but instead, "talk around the point...think[ing] intelligent human beings should be able to discover the point of a discourse from the context, which they are careful to provide" (Hall 1983: 63). Many high-context business communications are not written down because the information is shared verbally. By contrast, low-context communications are direct and open, and presented in a logical format. They are also more explicit and precise than high-context communications. Verbal and written exchanges are highly structured, detailed, and specified. "...The listener knows very little and must be told practically everything" (1989: 184). You cannot count on information being conveyed, or being conveyed accurately in a business environment. Therefore, much communication is painstakingly prepared in written form—whether through memos, posters, e-mails, and the like—and then distributed.

Cultures around the world range from high to low context. Asian, Arabic, and Latin cultures are considered higher context than northern European, Canadian, and U.S. cultures. High- and low-context communication is correlated generally with the collectivism–individualism dimension of culture (Gudykunst and Kim 2003) and with the P-time/M-time orientation (Gannon and Associates 1994). Members of high-context cultures have extensive information networks and close relationships with family, friends, and coworkers, and clients with whom they work. They typically share a set of common goals—personal or work-related—and routinely expect, exchange, and store in-depth information about each other. Members of low-context cultures do not share information as easily in their relationships with others. Indeed, many of their relationships are not long lasting, but rather transitory. Members of low-context cultures need quite a bit of background information to function effectively. Goals in low-context cultures tend to be individually defined; even within a large corporation, individual employees typically have their own interests at heart.

Hall's work on context applies in many circumstances beyond national-culture differences. For example,

> Twins who have grown up together can and do communicate more economically (HC) than two lawyers in a courtroom during a trial (LC), a mathematician programming a computer, two politicians drafting legislation, two administrators writing a regulation, or a child trying to explain to his mother why he got into a fight. (1976: 91)

Twins, no matter what their national culture, engage in high-context communications because they have shared a life together. "A high-context individual will expect his interlocutor to know what's bothering him, so that he doesn't have to be specific" (1976: 113), according to Hall. On the other hand, an American boss might shift from the "high-context, familiar form of address to the low-context, formal form of address" to indicate frustration, annoyance, or displeasure (1989: 7) such as, "Hey, what you been up to?" versus a concise and controlled "Good morning." A similar shift might occur in the example of the mother responding to the child who got into a fight and his mother. "Individuals use low- and high-context messages depending on their relationship with the person with whom they are communicating" (Gudykunst and Kim 2003: 72), as well as on the specifics of the situation at hand.

Knowing the contextual preferences of the cultural group with whom you are interacting is relevant, useful, and important information. If your client is German (low context), he or she is likely to want detailed design specifications, comprehensive test results, and robust sales forecasts. Expect to spend time pouring over the numbers and reviewing the issues in depth. If your client is Mexican (high context), he or she is likely to want to begin building a business relationship with you. Expect to spend some time in conversation on a variety of general topics unrelated to business prior to focusing on the technical details of your new product. In a

If a relationship has been established, even occasional collaborators can pick up where they left off.

similar way, if your client is an American with whom you have done business in the past, your interaction is likely to have some high-context elements (e.g., recall of shared experiences, knowledge of best processes and procedures to employ). If your client is an American with whom you have never done business, your communication style will be low context. You will need to provide appropriate background information on your idea or proposal, identify possible goals, and discuss options for maximizing success.

METAPHORS

Criticisms have been leveled at the dimensional or contrasting values approach (and to some extent the context approach). One criticism is that it assumes cultural homogeneity (Tung and Verbeke 2010: 1266). In other words, if a culture is identified as individualistic, hierarchical, or long-term time oriented, that designation is said to apply across the board to all cultural members. The "either/ or" cultural dimension approach has no room for what Tony Fang calls "both/ and" orientations such as long term and short term, or individualist and collectivist (2005–06: 75). When talking about the United States, the dimensional approach emphasizes individualism, even though American culture also consists of cooperative and collective endeavors (e.g., group projects, team sports).

Rosalie Tung has pointed out that assumptions of homogeneity can lead to "results that mask or confound the phenomena under investigation" (2008: 45). When intra-cultural variation is ignored or overly simplified, it becomes impossible to capture the richness or complexity of the culture.

Another criticism of the dimensional, bipolar approach is that it does not offer fine-grained, in-depth description and insight into a national culture, organizational culture, or subcultural group. Some cultural groups have similar scores on dimensional attributes. Martin Gannon and his colleagues report that national cultures such as the United States, Germany, England, New Zealand, and Australia exhibit similar scale values and rank orderings in the large quantitative dimensional studies that have been conducted (2005–06). Yet, we all know that these cultures are distinctive in their own right on a number of cultural traits.

Metaphoric analysis is an alternative to the dimensional approach. Metaphors are content rich and culture-specific so they help to clarify how cultural groups differ. A simple example of a metaphor is "time is money." Metaphors use the attributes of one item or phenomenon (money) to describe or explain a different item or phenomenon (time). Typically that second element is less tangible than the first. Metaphors create an image that captures the essence and vividness of that particular phenomenon (Ortony 1975). Gareth Morgan pointed out, "certain features are emphasized and others suppressed in a selective comparison" (1980: 611). Thus, "time is money" can be understood to mean that time is valuable, and indeed has a monetary value associated with it. Such a metaphor would be used in M-time cultures where it is believed that time is earned, spent, saved, and wasted.

Metaphors can be used to uncover the cultural content of any given group, though, as Martin Gannon points out, they are "just a first step in attempting to understand a specific culture" (2009: 282). They enable the exploration of behaviors, attitudes, beliefs, values, and expectations as an integrated whole; a reasonably holistic understanding of a cultural group can be derived through an apt metaphor. Thus, metaphors can be employed as a "frame of reference" for understanding culture (Gannon et al. 2005–06: 45). A metaphor is for the anthropologist what a hypothesis is for a physicist. After empirical testing, one can decide whether the metaphor works and enables an accurate and appropriate understanding of the culture. For example, Clifford Geertz (1973) used the metaphor of the cockfight to reveal the intricacies of Balinese culture, while Susan Montague and Robert Morais examined success models in U.S. culture through both football games and rock concerts (1976). Metaphors are often identified using a combination of techniques including ethnographic methods (e.g., observation, participant observation, interviews), questionnaires, and documentary materials. They are often validated through discussions with cultural experts or insiders.

Metaphoric analysis did not take off, however, until Martin Gannon and his associates published *Understanding Global Cultures: Metaphorical Journeys Through 17 Countries* (1994). They selected three to six characteristics of a particular metaphor to apply to each of the nations. For example, the metaphor for France was French wine; they described the culture of France in terms of the key features of wine (e.g., purity, classification, composition). They illustrated Nigeria using the metaphor of a marketplace with its diversity, social dynamism, and the balance of tradition and change. Metaphors have been applied beyond national-culture settings. For example, Gannon's most recent book (with Pillai 2010) includes metaphors for clusters of nations (e.g., the Chinese family altar), and continents such as Australia, while an edited volume by anthropologists Elizabeth Briody and Robert T. Trotter, II uses metaphors to highlight the evolving culture of organizational partnerships (2008).

The cultural insights from metaphoric analyses have applicability for global business. Let's take a look at one industry–university partnership that was in its fourteenth year at the time a case study on it was published. Anthropologist Julia Gluesing and her colleagues participated in and described the longstanding relationship between Ford Motor Company, Visteon Corporation, and Wayne State University (2008). The purpose of the partnership was to offer a master's degree program for working engineers that would cross the disciplinary boundaries between business and engineering and prepare the engineers for working globally. Since the partners were central to the U.S. automotive industry, the metaphor for the partnership was a "high-performance automotive test track" (2008: 126). The test track represented the intersection of business and academic values (see Figure 2-1) that would lead to winning outcomes for the partners (e.g., class projects yielding a high return on investment for Ford and Visteon; tuition revenue and research access to the automotive partners for Wayne State). It focused

> attention on teamwork, on learning the specific skills, and on blending the diverse talents that are necessary to drive well under difficult conditions while keeping the car on the road, overcoming unexpected obstacles, recovering from mistakes, continuing to push to the finish with inoperable or damaged parts, and winning. (2008: 139)

The metaphor both described the cross-cultural adaptability among the partners that was a necessary part of their collaboration and represented a set of guidelines and clear direction for the partners to follow. Similarly, it specified and documented the positive "win-win" outcomes that were essential to the partnership's longevity. Thus, the metaphor reflected both the actual state and the ideal state of the partnership.

Metaphors also have the potential to assist in the process of planned cultural change. Gannon (2001) used the metaphor of the traditional British house, a "durable, long-lived entity based on tried, tested and historically successful designs" (2001: 238), to capture the essence of Great Britain. He expanded upon the metaphor to describe how the house was built (a submetaphor for growing up British) and living within the house (a submetaphor for being British). Intervention strategies for planned change can target attributes associated with the traditional British house metaphor. For example, when engaging in

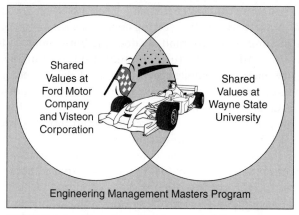

FIGURE 2-1 *Metaphors, like the test track for a program directed at automotive managers, can convey key values.*

organizational change in Great Britain, interventions can target the "acceptance of tradition," an important attribute of the metaphor. Gannon suggested three intervention strategies:

- Identify relevant tradition(s) within the organization.
- Demonstrate how the planned change builds on the relevant tradition(s).
- Involve people in the change process to ensure their approval and support of the change.

CHANGE

Gannon's example of the traditional British house offers a nice transition into a discussion of change. Metaphoric analysis has been evaluated in terms of its strengths and weaknesses (Gannon 2009). Metaphors do a better job than dimensions in exposing the internal workings of a particular culture or subcultural group. They can be called up on demand to improve cultural sensitivity or to propose solutions to practical problems. They do not mask intra-cultural variation in the way that dimensional studies do. Metaphors also have the virtue of being easy to remember. However, scholars have pointed out the imprecision, ambiguous meaning, and poor reliability of metaphors in interpretation and communication (Ramsay 2004), as well as the confusion and vagueness associated with the metaphor's boundaries (Ortony 1975). Metaphors also do not lend themselves as readily to cross-cultural comparison because of their culture-specific nature.

Both the dimensional and metaphoric approaches are effective under conditions of stability. However, globalization continues to exert pressure on the pace and extent of change worldwide (Friedman 1999; Lewellen 2002; Spindler and Stockard 2007). Novel and rapidly evolving conditions are an ongoing part of our lives. The Arab Spring comes to mind, as does the burgeoning of text messaging among teenagers, and multicultural immigration in Europe. In business environments, new energy companies are being created, private sector organizations are changing hands, and virtual partnering arrangements are solidifying. And, any of these circumstances and situations could morph into new forms before you could catch your breath. Fluidity, transparency, and mobility are affecting the who, what, when, where, and why of our thoughts and actions.

Change is embedded within the concept of cultural dynamics. Tony Fang views national culture as a product of the "dynamic interplays" between nationality, region- or ethnic-specific groups, organization- or industry-specific groups, and global culture (2005–06: 86–87). He offers an example of changing expectations among businesspeople in the large urban cities of southern Brazil. São Paulo, Curitiba, and Porto Alegre have more exposure to global business and foreign direct investment than does the northern region of Brazil. These southern cities are becoming more M-time in orientation, with greater emphasis on planning and adherence to schedules, while their northern neighbors retain their P-time orientation. Several examples in this book emphasize this shift in time orientation, including the example offered by Jeff Lewis in this chapter.

The concept of negotiated culture has been applied to newly formed business organizations. Anthropologist Mary Yoko Brannen and Jane Salk introduced this concept to explain the evolving relationship between the German and Japanese sides of a joint venture located in Germany. They found that national-culture characteristics were important in guiding how both partners responded to events in the factory. However, these characteristics were unable to explain the ways in which the plant's organizational culture changed over time. Brannen and Salk discovered that the partners negotiated and accommodated each other's expectations using four different methods (2000: 478):

- Compromise by one group (e.g., Japanese managers not expecting their counterparts to socialize with them outside of work; German managers forgoing vacations in the first two years)
- Meeting in the middle (e.g., meetings were longer and more frequent for the Germans and shorter and less frequent for the Japanese)
- Innovating something new for both groups (e.g., use of English with allowances for native-language discussions)
- Division of labor to minimize need for further negotiation with each partner in charge of certain factory departments.

This view of culture as a "dynamic and ongoing process of social negotiation" (p. 480) can be adopted in a variety of business arrangements involving employees, clients, partners, and consumers.

It is important to be alert for signals of change. As new groups, communities, and organizations are forming, it is not always possible, nor advisable, to rely on past models to explain a new entity or phenomenon. Facebook is a case in point. It capitalized on a change in technology (people were online a lot) and values (people wanted the ability to stay connected and fewer barriers to those connections) to produce both a method for connecting people and a culture associated with it. It also brought to the forefront some interesting cultural dilemmas about access (e.g., Do you "friend" your mother? What about your little brother? What about someone you do not know?) with which users had to cope. By being astute observers of the world around us, we have a reasonable chance of spotting a change (or a confluence of change elements), conceptualizing it, examining it, and figuring out how to tap into it for the benefit of individuals, organizations, and societies.

Anthropologist Martin Ortlieb has proposed two parameters tied to change in the business world. Each parameter, representing opposing ends of a scale, is a way of conceptualizing culture.

- *Slippery culture* can be characterized as distinct, finite, linked with place, and timeless. It is "something that is 'just' hard to define and difficult to pin down." Ortlieb states that business decision makers have traditionally adhered to the slippery-culture mentality, meaning that they believe that culture can be managed once it is recognized and understood. Their belief system, an important part of their managerial role, is that once you grasp what the culture is, any problem with it "can be fixed, in a best-case scenario, once and for all" (2009: 187).
- *Emergent culture* can be found at the other end of the spectrum and described as "inherently shifting and elusive yet perceptible" (p. 186). This view of culture is seen as continually evolving, though it remains identifiable and recognizable. Ortlieb indicates that anthropological researchers working in business endeavors are aligned with the emergent culture orientation. These anthropologists retain an openness to the world around them, a capacity to engage, learn, and document. Their research projects and methods uncover constantly changing user needs, expectations, and practices that are used to shed light on new business opportunities.

These two bookend concepts represent distinctive—even competing—orientations to culture. Those ascribing to the slippery culture orientation seem to want to hold on to their models or beliefs about what *is* and deal with any issues associated with it. In other words, they seem to want to make their past approaches and initiatives their models for the future. If we were to put ourselves in the shoes of these decision makers, we too would be seeking solutions to problems and would probably want to minimize the disruption to the organization and its work processes and procedures. However, they appear to be more reactive than proactive since they are fully grounded in the present.

By contrast, those aligned with the emergent view of culture seem more comfortable with the nature and pace of change in today's globalizing world. They appear to want their work to be as complete, up to date, and accurate as possible so that it can bridge the interface between the user/customer community and organizational decision makers. They seem to be looking forward into the future, rather than backward; they seem to face change head on, rather than resist it.

Ortlieb describes the changing conceptualization of culture at Yahoo, aided by its anthropological researchers. With this change in conceptualization from slippery to emergent, came changes in business practices. For example, Yahoo product development was originally done in the United States, with rollouts to the rest of the world. After the creation of regional business centers, new products were tested outside the United States with adaptations made. "It was the idea of fixing the cultural context: like fixing a technical bug, like flipping a switch, the cultural issue could be sorted. If it weren't, then several iterations would eventually approximate an acceptable local solution…" (p. 200). As the market expanded and Yahoo became a global brand, Yahoo's internal processes had to keep pace. Global requirements gathering, performed by the research staff, have become the norm. "Products that resonate in substance, form, and/or positioning with local concepts and needs will perform better than clumsy adaptations of foreign concepts that do not ring true locally and which everybody in the local target audience recognizes as such" (p. 201).

Yahoo has advanced along the scale toward the emergent view of culture as evident in the value it now places on these new global research models, methods, and input. Yahoo seems to have learned to listen and respond appropriately to internal researcher input. At the same time, the researchers undoubtedly have become increasingly proficient in making compelling arguments to Yahoo's leaders. This change within Yahoo's own culture has positioned it to be highly responsive to its customers, and the changing connectivity environment, worldwide. The concept of an emergent culture reflects both the changing mindset among managerial leaders (an evolution in the organizational culture) and changing customer dynamics (the ongoing transformation in the external environment).

THE ELUSIVE CANADIAN JUICE CUSTOMER

Understanding emergent culture from the customer perspective can be a tricky undertaking. For example, why would a juice brand that is highly successful in the United States have a minimal market presence in Canada? In light of such different marketplace performances, Robert Morais' firm conducted research in Canada that asked such questions as: What are the best ways to understand Canadian customers and their ongoing cultural evolution? How culturally different can Canada be from the United States? Do any of the factors linked with product success in the United States resonate with Canadians?

Researchers have argued that Canadian cultural values and themes are distinctive, contrasting remarkably with those of the U.S. (Lipset 1986, 1990; Adams 2003). "Canada is interesting because, as a U.S. resident, you feel you are close to the culture—but, you can be far from understanding it" (Robert Morais, personal communication). The U.S.-based juice manufacturer assumed that the Canadian market was like the U.S. market. For example, U.S. juice advertising

(continued)

and packaging for this product was used in the Canadian market with few, if any, modifications. Morais, an anthropologist, noted that life stresses (e.g., of work, family) dominated the conversation in a series of focus groups conducted in Canada. The stresses described by Canadians were also a salient pattern in U.S. life. In the United States, many people counterbalance their stress through movements like "slow food," "simplicity," "eco-friendly," and similar trends. He wondered if his client's juice brand could be connected to a stress-reducing cultural movement in Canada. Given that both Canadians and Americans feel stress in their lives, he speculated whether there were similar stress-reducing cultural movements in Canada, and if his client's juice brand could be connected to them.

At the time of this writing, these questions were not yet answered. Nevertheless, Morais' openness to the evolving Canadian market and his comparative U.S.–Canadian framework put him that much closer to discovering and making sense of Canadian customer expectations and preferences. Exploration of these issues would provide targeted insight into the dynamics of Canadian juice customers, as well as their connectedness with their U.S. neighbors.

CONCLUSION

In this chapter, we have outlined four lenses through which understanding and problem solving in global business settings might occur. This framework, derived from the work of many scholars over the past 40 years, raises important questions that need to be answered when encountering and working within a new and different culture. These questions include the following:

1. What are the key attributes distinguishing people who belong to an individualistic culture compared with a collectivist culture?
2. Do people with different levels of power and prestige treat one another equally or unequally?
3. How do cultures differ in terms of taking risks, tolerating ambiguity, and needing relatively little organizational structure?
4. How precisely do people from different cultures deal with time?
5. What strategies might be employed in conducting a business meeting when members of both high-context and low-context cultures are interacting for the first time?
6. What metaphor and its associated attributes could reveal the culture of an organization that you have worked with during your career?
7. What are some indicators of an emergent culture when two teams begin working on a project together?

This chapter should serve only as a starting point when interacting cross-culturally. To be certain, there are other dimensions and aspects of culture that could have been discussed but were not owing to limitations of space. Moreover, we must keep in mind that these dichotomies, images, and descriptions are not a precise description of reality. There are no cultures that embody absolutely all the traits associated with any of these basic polarities of equality and hierarchy or M-time and P-time. Cultures are composed of unique combinations of traits that can be portrayed, but which will surely change over time. We trust that the four lenses presented here will remind you to make the most of your powers of observation and comparison, analytic talents, and problem-solving abilities to work effectively with your global business colleagues and partners.

CROSS-CULTURAL SCENARIOS

Read the following cross-cultural scenarios. In each mini-case study, a basic cultural conflict occurs among the actors involved. Try to identify the source of the conflict and suggest how it could have been avoided or minimized. Then see how well your analyses compare to the explanations in Appendix A.

2-1 Bill Nugent, an international real estate developer from Dallas, had made a 2:30 P.M. appointment with Mr. Abdullah, a high-ranking government official in Riyadh, Saudi Arabia. From the beginning things did not go well for Bill. First, he was kept waiting until nearly 3:45 before he was ushered into Abdullah's office. When he finally did get in, several other men were also in the room. Even though Bill wanted to get down to business with Abdullah, he was reluctant to get too specific because he considered much of what they needed to discuss sensitive and private. To add to Bill's sense of frustration, Abdullah seemed more interested in engaging in meaningless small talk rather than dealing with the substantive issues concerning their business.

How might you help Bill deal with his frustration?

2-2 Tom Young, an up-and-coming executive for a U.S. electronics company, was sent to Japan to work out the details of a joint venture with a Japanese electronics firm. During the first several weeks, Tom felt that the negotiations were proceeding better than he had expected. He found that he had very cordial working relationships with the team of Japanese executives, and they had in fact agreed on the major policies and strategies governing the new joint venture. During the third week of negotiations, Tom was present at a meeting held to review their progress. The meeting was chaired by the president of the Japanese firm, Mr. Hayakawa, a man in his mid-forties, who had recently taken over the presidency from his 82-year-old grandfather. The new president, who had been involved in most of the negotiations during the preceding weeks, seemed to Tom to be one of the strongest advocates of the plan that had been developed to date. Also attending the meeting was Hayakawa's grandfather, the recently retired president. After the plans had been discussed in some detail, the octogenarian past president proceeded to give a long soliloquy about how some of the features of this plan violated the traditional practices on which the company had been founded. Much to Tom's amazement, Hayakawa did nothing to explain or defend the policies and strategies that they had taken weeks to develop. Feeling extremely frustrated, Tom then gave a strongly argued defense of the plan. To Tom's further amazement, no one else in the meeting spoke up. The tension in the air was quite heavy, and the meeting adjourned shortly thereafter. Within days the Japanese firm completely terminated the negotiations on the joint venture.

How could you help Tom understand this bewildering situation?

2-3   As an organizational consultant from Detroit working with a Mexican company, Christine Shaver has been traveling to Mexico City every other week for months to help her client improve its marketing. On this occasion, Christine scheduled a three-day trip, during which she planned to meet with a number of employees. But on the first day of scheduled meetings, she was informed that everyone would be leaving work at 2:00 P.M. because it was a fiesta day. She was beside herself because she had come all the way to Mexico just to have her first day of work cut short. As it turns out, Christine's Mexican colleagues failed to understand why she was so upset.

What was behind this misunderstanding?

2-4   Jennifer Ellis, vice president of a North Carolina knitwear manufacturer, was sent by her company to observe firsthand how operations were proceeding in their Korean plant and to help institute some new managerial procedures. Before any changes could be made, however, Jennifer wanted to learn as much as possible about the problems that existed at the plant. During her first week, she was met with bows, polite smiles, and the continual denial of any significant problems. But Jennifer was enough of a realist to know that manufacturing operations always have some problems. So after some creative research, she uncovered a number of issues that the local manager and staff had not acknowledged. None of the problems was particularly unusual or difficult to solve, but Jennifer was frustrated that no one mentioned them. "If you don't acknowledge the problems," she complained to one of the Korean managers, "how do you expect to be able to solve them?" And then just today when a problem was finally brought to her attention, it was not mentioned until the end of the workday when there was no time left to solve it.

How could you help Jennifer understand the dynamics of this situation?

2-5   For the past three years, Ned Ferguson had served quite successfully as the manager of a U.S.-owned manufacturing company in Taiwan. Shortly after Ned's arrival in Taipei, he instituted a number of changes in plant operations that increased both production and worker satisfaction. However, within the last several months, a series of what seemed to Ned to be unrelated incidents had occurred. First, there had been a fire in the warehouse, which fortunately was contained before too much damage had been done. On the following day, the wife and two children of the local plant supervisor were killed in a spectacular automobile accident. Finally, within the past several weeks, there had been a rash of minor accidents on the assembly line; such situations were quite uncharacteristic of the plant's excellent safety record. Ned heard that rumors were running rampant about the plant being cursed by evil spirits. Moreover, he knew that absenteeism had increased dramatically. To try to deal with these problems, Ned called together his chief supervisors. His American staff recommended that some experts from the insurance company come in to review the safety procedures, which, they argued, would show the workers that the company was taking their safety needs seriously. But the Taiwanese supervisors considered this step to be inadequate and instead suggested that a local religious priest be brought in, during company time, to pray for the workers and ward off any evil forces. Ned and his U.S. staff thought that such an action would do nothing but give official company support to superstition. The meeting ended without any substantial agreement between U.S. and Taiwanese supervisors.

How would you explain this basic cultural conflict?

3

■ ■ ■

Communicating across Cultures

The Nonverbal Dimension

Imagine that you are walking into an engineering meeting in the United States involving both Americans and Japanese. You know that this group has been working together for several months and that the Japanese will be in the United States for one week. It is your first meeting with them. You find an empty seat along one wall, sit down, and look around. Things somehow seem different.

The first thing you notice is that the Japanese visitors are grouped together on one side of the large U-shaped table. Several of them are already seated at the table, while others sit in a row of chairs behind them. They are positioned so that they can see both the large screen used for projection at the front of the room, and anyone coming through the door. The Americans are standing and talking to each other on the side of the room near the door. You are thinking that they will have to take their seats opposite the Japanese because there is no other place for them to sit.

Then you see the chief engineer and a designer that you met a long time ago on an earlier project. The chief engineer takes his seat about halfway down the American side of the table. Eventually the designer sits down too—several seats from where you are sitting. In walks another person you recognize—nice guy. He is talking with one of the Japanese businessmen as they make their way over to the Japanese side. They sit down next to each other opposite the chief engineer. Hmm...that's interesting.

There are not many women present. In fact, there are none among the Japanese visitors. You do note that there are three other females, two of whom you recognize though you do not know their names. They are dressed in "business casual," as are their male counterparts. Interestingly, all of the Japanese are wearing suits and ties. As you are trying to sort through everything you have seen, your thoughts are interrupted as the chief engineer welcomes everyone to the meeting.

The use and arrangement of space are examples of nonverbal communication, or communication without words. Both the configuration of the space and the behaviors taking place within it offer important clues about what is happening culturally. Watching only from the sidelines, the American newcomer figured out that this gathering was not an ordinary business meeting—at least not for her. She correctly perceived that the table divided attendees into two groups—the guests and the hosts. She noted that there was almost no interaction between the two groups prior to the start of the meeting. Style of dress distinguished the two groups: the Japanese were dressed more formally than the Americans. Finally, she was aware of the gender composition among meeting participants.

But there were unanswered questions: Why were people grouped the way they were given that the meeting was happening on U.S. soil? What kinds of people got to sit at the table? Why was the chief engineer sitting in the middle on his side of the table? Was there a reason that the Japanese were located farther away from the door? She had every sense that these questions were just the tip of the iceberg.

The participants in this meeting were communicating with each other in many ways before the meeting began. They were enforcing group boundaries through their arrangement of the space. They were paying attention to their own rules of politeness—the Americans by agreeing to Japanese preferences for seating arrangements, and the Japanese through their more formal dress. The seating arrangement would soon become clear: Those seated in the middle of each side of the U-shaped table were the most senior leaders, followed by their direct reports and others in descending order of rank on either side and behind them. As for "nice guy"—he turned out to be the bilingual interpreter for the Japanese.

THE NATURE OF NONVERBAL COMMUNICATION

Communication takes place in two ways: (1) through nonverbal communication, or what anthropologist Edward Hall refers to as the "silent language" (1959), and (2) through language in which using words and other vocalizations are combined to produce mutually understood meanings. In Chapters 3 and 4, we examine the nature of communication in international business and how communication problems can develop when people communicate, or attempt to communicate, across cultures. Successful communication in the international business environment requires an understanding of both nonverbal and verbal expressions.

Nonverbal communication is responsible in its own right for the majority of messages sent and received as part of human communication. In fact, it has been suggested on a number of occasions that only about 30 percent of communication between two people in the same speech community is verbal in nature. People rely heavily on nonverbal cues in international business situations, particularly when they lack the language skills for communicating in that context.

Even though some nonverbal cues function in similar ways in many cultures, considerable differences in nonverbal patterns can result in breakdowns in communication in a cross-cultural context. The literature is filled with scenarios of how a misreading of nonverbal cues leads directly to cross-cultural friction.

The need to master the nonverbal repertoire of another culture—in addition to gaining linguistic competence—increases the challenge of working successfully in an international business setting. Yet, people who know the nonverbal cues of another culture are more likely to experience successful interactions and be better positioned for building relationships with members of that culture.

Types of Nonverbal Communication

Research in nonverbal forms of communication began in earnest in the second half of the 20th century. Like any relatively new field of study, what constitutes the subject matter of nonverbal communication has not always met with widespread agreement. Classifications of nonverbal behavior among some of the earlier writers vary from the threefold scheme of A. M. Eisenberg and R. R. Smith (1971) to the typology of John Condon and Fathi Yousef (1975: 123–24), which includes 24 categories. Despite the many alternative ways of categorizing the domain of nonverbal communication, the following topics are found widely in the literature:

- Facial expressions (smiles, frowns)
- Hand gestures
- Walking (gait)
- Body posture
- Proxemics (space usages)
- Touching
- Gaze
- Olfaction (scents or smells, such as perfume)
- Color symbolism
- Artifacts (such as business cards, cell phones)
- Dress
- Hairstyles
- Cosmetics
- Time symbolism
- Graphic symbols
- New technologies and visual media
- Silence

Two broad categories of differences emerge in nonverbal expression: (1) the same nonverbal cue that carries with it very different meanings in different cultures, and (2) different nonverbal cues that carry the same meaning in different cultures.

Often the same gesture has different, or even opposite, meanings. Hissing, for example, used as a somewhat rude way of indicating disapproval of a speaker in U.S. society, is used as a normal way to ask for silence in certain Spanish-speaking countries and as a way of applauding among the Basuto of South Africa. In U.S. society, protruding one's tongue is an unmistakable gesture of mocking contempt, whereas in traditional China it is an expression of embarrassment over a faux pas. The hand gesture of putting one's index finger to the temple communicates "he is smart" in the United States but also means just the opposite—"he is stupid"—in certain Western European cultures.

In contrast, the same message can be sent in various cultures by very different nonverbal cues. To illustrate, in the U.S. and most Western European societies, the nonverbal cue for affirmation (i.e., signifying yes or agreement) is nodding the head up and down. However, affirmation is signaled among the Semang of Malaya by thrusting the head forward sharply, in Ethiopia by throwing the head back, among the Dyaks of Borneo by raising the eyebrows, among the Ainu of northern Japan by bringing both hands to the chest and then gracefully waving them downward with palms up, and by rocking the head from shoulder to shoulder among the Bengali servants of Calcutta (Jensen 1982: 264–65).

At times, nonverbal communication is expressed in similar ways around the world. There are commonalities in presenting at formal business meetings, for example, regardless of location or organization. The presenter typically stands in front of the group to speak. That position establishes the presenter as the focus of attention, and often, a source of authority. Indeed, we talk of a presenter having "a command of the audience." The presenter can use his/her physical stance and role to gather nonverbal feedback from those present (e.g., disagreement conveyed through frowns, lack of understanding conveyed through raised eyebrows) and then act on it to enhance his/her delivery. PowerPoint slides can be used for a better and easy understanding of the topic being discussed; later, the slides can be shared electronically with attendees. Finally, the speaker may ask the audience for comments and questions that are addressed either during, or immediately following, the formal presentation. Thus, PowerPoint slides serve as a visual mechanism to share information and generate discussion.

Potential Pitfalls in Studying Nonverbal Communication

A variety of difficulties appear in studying nonverbal communication in the global business environment. First, there is the potential hazard of overgeneralization. We frequently hear references made to such geographical areas as the Middle East, Latin America, or sub-Saharan Africa. However, it is important to keep in mind that there is wide variation in nonverbal communication in such locales. In sub-Saharan Africa alone, there are more than 40 independent nation-states and approximately 750 different linguistic communities that speak mutually unintelligible languages. Yet, we cannot count on uniformity even within a single speech community, for even here there are likely to be internal variations in nonverbal communication patterns, depending on such variables as class, gender, education, occupation, and religion. For example, many of Edward Hall's insightful conclusions on Arab nonverbal communication (discussed subsequently) are based on the observations of middle- and upper-class males, largely students and businesspeople. Arab females would not very likely conform to the same patterns of nonverbal communication as the Arab males that Hall describes. Thus, it is advisable to exercise some caution when generalizing even within a single culture or speech community.

A second potential obstacle is the unwarranted assumption that within any given speech community, all nonverbal cues are of equal importance. Some nonverbal patterns may be rarely used and imperfectly understood, whereas others are more universally understood and taken more seriously.

A third possible pitfall lies in overemphasizing the differences in nonverbal communication patterns across cultural groups. Although we focus on the great variety of nonverbal patterns found throughout the world, many nonverbal similarities also exist among different speech communities. The problem, of course, for the international businessperson is to distinguish between them.

Finally, we should avoid thinking that the consequences of misunderstanding nonverbal cues are always catastrophic. To be certain, misreading some nonverbal cues can lead to the misinterpretation of social meanings, which in turn can result in serious breakdowns in communication and even the generation of hostility. Many other nonverbal cues, on the other hand, have no such dire consequences, and instead cause only minor irritations or even amusement. Having said this, however, we should also realize that the more we know about the nonverbal cues found in the international business environment, the greater will be our chances of successful communication and the achievement of our personal and professional objectives.

BUSINESS INTRODUCTIONS

Nonverbal behaviors are associated with business introductions. Knowing the proper greeting and parting rituals can facilitate business interactions. In this section, the focus is on introductions among businesspeople that are face-to-face.

Greetings and partings are complicated. They consist of numerous nonverbal actions all packed into one event. For example, facial expressions, posture, touching, and eye contact can play some role in business introductions. These actions may occur almost simultaneously—say, a smile accompanied by a handshake—or sequentially, in which the exchange of business cards occurs after the verbal introductions. In addition, greetings and partings can be difficult if one is unfamiliar with local etiquette. A case in point is India, where people often use a form of noncontact. They place their palms together at chest level with fingers extended upward and say the word *Namaste* or *Namaskar* (depending upon locale) which means "good day". This form of salutation is used when meeting or saying goodbye to a person of a different age, status, or gender. Americans working in India may use this form of greeting, though a handshake is becoming increasingly common in international business.

Greetings can be awkward when people meet on subsequent occasions. There may be confusion about which form of greeting or parting to use. For example, in Mexico it is quite common to shake hands when getting introduced to someone for the first time. If a strong business relationship develops over time, the handshake is likely to be abandoned in favor of an *abrazo* ("hug") for males, or a kiss on the cheek when a female is involved. It is sometimes difficult to know when the transition occurs. According to anthropologist Laura Corrunker, "As an American, you want your Mexican colleagues to know that you know the differences regarding greetings, but you don't want to assume that the relationship has become familiar and informal. I struggled with this often when I was in Mexico." Thus, it is not always possible to know with 100-percent certainty how to participate in a greeting ritual. When in doubt, err on the side of formality. An American businessman could be caught off guard by an *abrazo*, though the reaction by the Mexican counterpart is likely to be a wide smile.

In parts of Asia, introductions are accompanied by two nonverbal processes that initiate an interaction: business card exchange and bowing; bowing may also occur at the end of a conversation. Although Westerners, in a very general sense, understand the meaning attached to these processes, they are complex. The notes from a participant in a Japanese cross-cultural training session revealed the following:

> The last thing that we did before the training was over was to practice exchanging business cards and practice bowing. When you hand someone a business card, you would say, "My name is..." or "*Watashi-no-namae wa....*" Then there are two things you can say. One is, "It's the first time we're meeting." A second thing that you could say is, "Pleased to meet you." I practiced bowing and giving my business card with one other person and found it quite difficult. I wasn't sure if you bowed first and then gave the business card later.

Business Card Exchange

Business cards belong to a type of nonverbal communication called artifacts. It turns out that the business card exchange precedes bowing. The reason is relatively straightforward. The business card helps the Asian businessperson to learn your title or position within a firm. Armed with this information, the Korean businessperson is able to understand your rank or position relative to him or her (Kohls 2001). The Japanese businessperson uses this information to determine how deferential to be (Hall and Hall 1987). Deference appears not only in how deeply one bows, but also in the tenor and content of the subsequent discussion. These kinds of considerations matter because hierarchy is an important dimension of these Asian cultures. Indeed, hierarchy was also at work in this chapter's opening example of a meeting between some Japanese and Americans; the most senior Japanese executive sat in the middle of his side of the table surrounded by his subordinates.

Appropriate business card exchange follows a number of rules. When giving or receiving a business card, you hold it on the corners with both hands. It is important to make sure the wording can be read by the recipient as he/she takes the card. Koreans and Japanese who are dealing with Americans typically have one side of their business cards printed in English. The giver says his or her name, and may say the firm's name as well. As you take a business card, take the time to read it. In both cultures, it is appropriate to make facial expressions that give some indication

Business card exchange provides information, demonstrates respect, and establishes hierarchy.

of recognition or admiration based on what you have read on the business card. No matter how many people you might be introduced to, use the same level of care when exchanging cards. If at a meeting, it is considered appropriate to place all the cards on the table in front of you so that they are aligned with the seating arrangement. It is not a good idea to write on a business card in the presence of the giver.

Bowing

Bowing is a type of nonverbal communication associated with posture. Once you have exchanged business cards, you and your new colleague will bow to each other; sometimes a handshake will follow. In both Korea and Japan, reciprocal bowing is determined largely by rank. In fact, the depth of their bows reveals the relative social status of two communicators (the deeper the bow, the lower the status). In Korea, the two individuals bow slightly to each other; normally it is the lower-ranked person who bows first. In Japan, when bowing deeply, it is conventional to lean slightly to the right to avoid bumping heads. The person of lower status is expected to initiate the bow, and the person of higher status determines when the bow is completed. People of equivalent status are expected to bow at the same depth while starting and finishing at the same time. As H. Befu relates, this synchronization is an important feature:

> The matter of synchrony, in fact perfect synchrony, is absolutely essential to bowing. Whenever an American tries to bow to me, I often feel extremely awkward and uncomfortable because I simply cannot synchronize bowing with him or

her...Bowing occurs in a flash of a second, before you have time to think. And both parties must know precisely when to start bowing, how deep, how long to stay in the bowed position, and when to bring their heads up. (1979: 118)

Bowing also occurs in Japan as a form of greeting without the exchange of business cards. As an indication of how pervasive bowing is in Japan, Elizabeth Würtz states that the McDonald's website in Japan uses videos showing bowing men on the introductory page and bowing females on the contact page (2005: 285), while Helmut Morsbach reports that "some female department store employees have the sole function of bowing to customers at department store escalators" and that many Japanese "bow repeatedly to invisible partners at the other end of a telephone line" (1982: 307).

Americans are not expected to know all of the ritual subtleties associated with business introductions if they have not had experience in these cultures. Indeed, Koreans and Japanese may simply shake hands with the Americans—particularly in partnering situations in which they meet on an ongoing basis. However, those from the host culture will appreciate the willingness and interest by their guests to learn about their culture. Those efforts will go a long way in establishing a positive impression between American businesspersons and their Asian counterparts.

Gift Giving

Gift giving also belongs to a type of nonverbal communication called artifacts. It is important in many cultures and functions to promote and solidify social connections. Gift giving in a business, rather than personal, context often occurs as a way to create a strong, positive image as part of business introductions. S. J. Yoon points out that if an initial meeting between a Korean and an American firm takes place in Korea, a gift may be presented at the first meeting. If a series of meetings are planned, the gift giving may occur at the last meeting. Moreover, "If one of the parties is not prepared to give one (at some meeting), the party may bring a gift at the next meeting," according to Yoon.

A gift is presented after those in attendance have introduced themselves. The giver typically presents it to the highest-status person present, such as a team leader, manager, or executive. The gift may or may not be opened immediately. If it is opened right away, the giver might provide an explanation of what the gift is (e.g., a particular handicraft, a product of a particular region). One business consultant from Michigan routinely takes pins and tie tacks made of Petosky stone (a rock of fossilized coral and the state stone of Michigan) for his Brazilian clients. Another consultant took packages containing several varieties of nuts to Brazil. This gift had the virtue of widespread appeal and could be shared easily in an office environment.

Wiboon Arunthanes and his colleagues developed a cross-cultural gift giving model that provides guidance to global businesspeople about gifts. They compared high- and low-context cultures with giver and recipient views of gift giving. When the giver and recipient are from a high-context national culture (e.g., Turkey, Spain),

Gift giving can help establish and/or cement business relationships.

gift giving is viewed as a "must." When the giver and recipient are from a low-context national culture (e.g., Canada, Switzerland), gift giving is optional. When the giver is from a high-context culture and the recipient is from a low-context culture, the recipient "may feel very reluctant to accept a gift and even offended if it is an expensive one…and probably will be quite concerned with legal and ethical issues" (1994: 48). When the reverse pattern applies and the recipient is from a high-context culture and the giver is from a low-context culture, gifts "will be fully expected" but "the giver tends to underestimate and downplay the importance of giving business gifts" (p. 48).

There are sensitivities around business gift giving. Decades ago, Marcel Mauss (1923) suggested that gift exchange was based on expectations of return. Bronislaw Malinowski (1922: 176–91) talked about "gifts and countergifts" along a continuum from a "pure gift" in which no return is expected, to "gifts returned in economically equivalent form," to trade for "mutual advantage." Business gift giving does not serve as a "pure gift." Instead, it functions as a way to build or reinforce business relationships, typically in anticipation of a future for the relationship. In Korea, "If the business relationship grows deeper and more mature over time, the gift giving may be used to symbolize long-term friendship," and thus be viewed with great importance, according to S. J. Yoon.

In China a gift carries long-term social obligations within *guanxi*, one's set of interpersonal connections. Such relationships involve the reciprocal exchange of favors and gifts that are mutually beneficial. Andrew Millington and his colleagues investigated supplier relationships in a sample of manufacturing firms from the United Kingdom in China. They found that gifts were small and given at the time of Chinese holidays, and that companies distinguished between gift giving and dining on the one hand, and "under-table" or "back-door dealings" on the other. One of their interviewees stated,

> We strive to get good relationships with the supplier through frequent contact, often of the social kind: lots of dinners, going out in order to make sure any problems can be swiftly solved on the basis of these friendship dealings. Guanxi is to sort out minor problems and to have the relationship run smoothly, based on trust and without too much lengthy administration—but if the fundamentals of quality and price are not there, merely guanxi will not hold up the relationship. (2005: 262)

Nevertheless, *guanxi* relationships are sometimes perceived by Westerners as nepotistic or corrupt. Care must be taken to ensure that the gift is legal and ethical or else the business relationship may be adversely affected.

INTERACTIONS AMONG BUSINESSPEOPLE

Business interactions among individuals and organizations begin at the time of first communication—whether that communication involves an e-mail, face-to-face meeting, conference call, or some other means. Business introductions are a preliminary part of business interactions. If all goes well, business relationships grow through subsequent contact. In this section, the focus is on interactions among businesspeople once the business introductions have taken place.

Many different domains of nonverbal communication affect the quality, effectiveness, and longevity of business interactions. A thorough discussion of all aspects of nonverbal communication would take us beyond the scope of this book. To convey the importance of nonverbal communication in an international business context, we examine some domains that have important effects on inter-personal communication and global business practice. Included in this section are body posture, gaze, facial expressions, hand gestures, dress, proxemics, and new technologies and visual media.

Body Posture

The way that people hold their bodies frequently communicates information about their social status, religious practices, feelings of submissiveness, desires to maintain social distance, and sexual intentions, to mention only some areas. When communicating, people tend to orient their bodies toward others by assuming a certain stance or posture. A person may stand over another person, kneel, or "turn a cold shoulder"; in each case, something different would be communicated by the body posture. Postural cues constitute very effective signs of a person's inner state as well as his or her behavioral expectations of others.

When people are interacting in a cross-cultural environment, sharp differences can be seen in terms of what postures are taken and what meanings they convey. For example, in the United States, we stand up to show respect; in certain Polynesian cultures, people sit down. We frequently lean back in our chairs and may even put our feet on our desks to convey a relaxed, informal attitude, but the Swiss and Germans would think such a posture rude. For many people, squatting is the most normal position for relaxing, yet for the typical American it seems improper, "uncivilized," or at least not terribly sophisticated.

Sometimes we can inadvertently choose a body posture that will have disastrous results. Condon and Yousef describe such a case:

> The British professor of poetry relaxed during his lecture at Ain Shams University in Cairo. So carried away was he in explicating a poem that he leaned back in his chair and so revealed the sole of his foot to an astonished class. To make such a gesture in a Moslem society (where the foot is considered the filthiest part of the body) is the worst kind of insult. The Cairo newspapers the next day carried banner headlines about the student demonstration which resulted, and they denounced British arrogance and demanded that the professor be sent home. (1975: 22)

This same meaning was seen on the global stage on two high-profile occasions at the start of the 21st century. In 2003, the statue of Saddam Hussein was dramatically pulled down in Baghdad with the help of a U.S. tank. As a nonverbal gesture of pure cultural insult, Iraqis in the street began pounding the fallen statue with their shoes. Five years later in 2008, an Iraqi reporter hurled shoes at President George W. Bush during a news conference in the palace of Prime Minister Nuri al-Maliki located in Baghdad's Green Zone. The reporter said, "This is a farewell...you dog!" in Arabic.

How we position ourselves when communicating with another person is also culturally variable. To turn one's back on someone is a clear nonverbal indicator in the United States (and in many other societies as well) of an unwillingness to converse at all. But the degree to which two people are expected to face one another in normal conversation is not the same in all cultures. Even though two white, middle-class Americans have no difficulty conversing while walking next to each other with an occasional turn of the head, Edward Hall found it to be a major problem when attempting to walk and talk in this fashion with an Arab friend (1966: 160–61). While they walked, the Arab stopped to face Hall each time he spoke. Because many Arabic cultures insist on a high degree of eye contact when conversing, conversants must be facing one another directly. Hall soon discovered that to talk while walking side by side without maintaining intense eye contact was considered rude by the Arab's standards. This example illustrates not only how body stance or position communicates different messages but also how two domains of nonverbal communication—body position and gaze—are intimately interconnected.

Gaze

All cultures use gaze (eye contact) as a very important mechanism for communicating nonverbally. John Heron (1970: 244) refers to gaze as "the most fundamental primary mode of interpersonal encounter," for it is where two pairs of eyes come together "that people actually meet (in the strict sense)." Unlike other forms of nonverbal communication, gaze is particularly salient because it is so noticeable. As Phoebe Ellsworth notes,

> For a behavior that involves no noise and little movement, it has a remarkable capacity to draw attention to itself even at a distance.... People often use a direct gaze to attract another person's attention in situations where noise or gesticulation are inappropriate. The fact that we expect others to be responsive to our gaze is illustrated by our exasperation when dealing with people who have learned immunity to the effects of a stare, such as waiters. (1975: 5–6)

The communicative function of the eyes has not escaped poets and essayists, for as Ralph Waldo Emerson wrote, "One of the most wonderful things in nature is a glance of the eye; it transcends speech; it is the bodily symbol of identity" (cited in Champness 1970: 309). The eyes are, in fact, such a powerful force for interpersonal interaction that it is impossible not to communicate through visual behavior; that is, if we maintain eye contact with someone, we are communicating just as much as if we avoid eye contact.

Although some aspects of eye communication are partially controlled by physiology, such as pupil dilation, much of the meaning attached to gaze and gaze avoidance is culturally determined. Like many other forms of learned behavior, gaze can be affected by early childhood socialization, as exemplified by infants who are carried on their mothers' backs and thus have little contact with the mothers' faces. In later life, cultures tend to be extremely efficient at instilling certain values concerning gaze or its avoidance. Yet whenever it may be internalized, how,

The direct intense gaze is a sign of attentiveness and respect in some societies, whereas in others it is threatening and hostile.

when, and to what extent people in different cultures use gaze as a communication mechanism vary widely.

One of the best scientifically controlled studies of eye contact in a number of different cultures was conducted by O. M. Watson (1970) among foreign-exchange students in the United States. Pairs of students were invited into a laboratory and asked to talk on any subject in their native language while being observed from a one-way screen. Watson found that the highest levels of gaze were recorded for Arabs and people from Latin America, and the lowest levels were found among Indians and northern Europeans. These findings lend credence to the earlier statement made by Edward Hall that "Arabs look each other in the eye when talking with an intensity that makes most Americans highly uncomfortable" (1966: 161). In such cultures, a lower degree of eye contact (such as might be found in the United States) can be viewed as impolite, inattentive, insincere, and aloof.

There are also differences in the use of eyes to send and receive messages. Charles Mitchell tells of an American businesswoman who had developed a good working relationship (over the telephone) with a British colleague working in London:

> All went well until the American traveled to London to meet face-to-face with her British colleague to sign a research and development contract. The first meeting did not go well. "There was something that did not seem right," she says, "Throughout the presentation none of the Brits, not even the guy I had developed a phone relationship with, would look us in the eye. It was like they were hiding something. After a lot of internal discussion, we decided to sign the contract, but many of us still felt uneasy.... It almost ruined the relationship and sunk the deal." (2000: 5)

On the other hand, many societies teach their children to avoid direct eye contact in general or in specific social situations. Michael Argyle and Mark Cook report that among the Wituto and Bororo Indians of South America, both parties in a conversation must avoid direct eye contact by looking at some external object while talking (1976: 29). In Japan, rather than looking a person straight in the eyes, one should focus the gaze somewhat lower, around the region of the Adam's apple (Morsbach 1982: 308). The Navajo define eye contact so negatively that they have as part of their folklore a mythical monster named He-Who-Kills-With-His-Eyes who serves to teach Navajo youngsters that to stare can actually kill another person. In many parts of sub-Saharan Africa, direct eye contact must be avoided when addressing a person of higher-status. When we interact in an international business context with people from such cultures, we must realize that our insistence on maintaining a relatively high level of gaze could be interpreted as threatening, disrespectful, haughty, or insulting.

Rules for eye contact in public places also vary from one culture to another. "In small towns in India, people do not see foreigners often, so they stare at them. Seeing somebody so different is a novelty" according to anthropologist Anulekha Roy. To gaze at a foreigner is not considered rude by local standards. Indeed, "They do not even realize that the foreigner will feel uncomfortable." By contrast, in the United States, staring openly at someone in a public place is considered rude and an infringement on one's privacy. Instead, Americans practice what Erving Goffman (1963) refers to as "civil inattention," a very subtle practice whereby people give others just enough eye contact to acknowledge their presence but at the next moment withdraw that eye contact so they are not singled out as an object of particular curiosity. When two people are walking toward each other, civil inattention permits eye contact up to approximately eight feet before the eyes are cast downward as they pass, or as Goffman puts it, "a kind of dimming of lights" (1963: 84). Like so many other aspects of nonverbal behavior, civil inattention is such a subtle social ritual that most middle-class Americans are barely aware of it. Nevertheless, it remains an important nonverbal behavior that regulates interaction in the United States.

Hand Gestures

Until the mid 20th century, the systematic study of hand gestures had gone largely unnoticed. Nonverbal communication in general and hand gestures in particular have long been considered a trivial aspect of communication, especially in the Western world. Because we are told that language (the capacity to use words to symbolize) is the hallmark of our humanity, we tend to consider all other forms of communication as pedantic and unimportant. But human communication is greatly enriched by the nonverbal component. According to Susan Goldin-Meadow (2003) using hand gestures can assist us in thinking "by reducing cognitive effort," and in fact, speakers are likely to increase the number of speech errors when they cannot use hand gestures. Also, the very meaning of words can, in fact, change, depending on the accompanying hand gestures. Randall Harrison (1974: 135) offers an illustration from the English language. The words "Just let me say..." when used with the gesture of the hand up, palm facing the addressee, are likely to mean: "Wait, let me say...." These same words with the gesture of the hand out and palm facing downward would most likely imply: "Let me tell you how it really is." Finally, to utter these words with the hand out and palm facing upward would mean "It seems to me...." Thus, these three different palm orientations can provide three quite different meanings to the same words. Obviously, words are nearly indispensable for the communication of facts, but without hand gestures the human communication process would be mechanical and less capable of subtle nuances.

    The use of fingers, hands, and arms for purposes of communicating varies considerably from one culture to another. Some cultures (e.g., those located in southern Europe and the Middle East) employ a wide variety of gestures frequently and with considerable force and purposefulness. The half-jocular notion that Italians would be unable to express themselves if their hands were tied behind their backs is more than a vulgar stereotype. Based on research conducted on Italian and Jewish immigrants in New York City, David Efron (1941) found that Italians used broad, full-arm gestures with relative frequency. At the other extreme, some indigenous Indian groups in Bolivia use hand gestures very sparingly because the cool highland climate requires them to keep their hands under shawls or blankets (Jensen 1982: 266). Still other cultures, like our own and those found in northern Europe, illustrate a middle position and tend to be more reserved in their use of gestures. These cultures place a higher value on verbal messages and no doubt consider excessive gesturing to be overly emotional, nonrational, and socially unsophisticated.

Proficiency in nonverbal communication is essential if one hopes to become competent in a particular culture. Through the process of socialization, young children learn nonverbal communication, including hand gestures. For those of us who are exposed to cultures at an older age, the task requires observation, relationship skills, and perseverance. Martin Meissner and Stuart Philpott experienced the "language of manual gestures" first hand as they described their field work with sawmill workers in British Columbia, Canada:

> Some of the meanings (of the gestures used in the mills) became apparent from the context or consequences. Others were shouted to us over the shoulder and eventually explained at lunch time. The repertory was enlarged, during breaks, in conversations with a group of sawyers...Questions and jokes were of course also specifically directed to us, and we were usually at a loss for the quick and effective answer which the situation demanded. We used crude sketches and written descriptions to record signs at the time of observing their use. (1975: 291, 293)

They discovered that the workers used more than 200 gestures only when in the mill, and not in the lunch or coffee areas. Moreover, their analysis showed that these gestures were used only when high levels of noise (from the equipment) were combined with specific elements of the production process (e.g., rapid work cycles, workers spatially separated, workers confined to a fixed work station). Meissner and Philpott's work has the double virtue of documenting their process for learning the gestures, and describing the circumstances that led to the proliferation of gestures they recorded.

Andrew Molinsky and his colleagues designed a study to examine the relationship between length of stay in a foreign location and gesture recognition accuracy. They had an actor perform 28 nonverbal gestures—most of which were hand gestures. Study participants had to decide if these gestures were commonly used in the United States or not. Examples of a common American gesture included "thumbs-up" and "thumbs-down" gestures, a gesture indicating quotation marks, an "I can't hear you" gesture in which the person cups his left hand around his left ear, and a "phew" gesture in which the person wipes his brow from left to right (2005: 385–86). Molinsky and his colleagues found that the longer a nonnative was in the United States, the greater the accuracy in recognizing American gestures. Their work illustrates the importance of nonverbal gestures in cultural adaptation.

Unlike verbal communication, which is usually well documented in structure and meaning, the nonverbal aspects of communication in most language communities are very infrequently described; when they are, those descriptions are usually superficial and incomplete. One of the rare exceptions is the study conducted by Desmond Morris and colleagues (1979) of 20 major gestures found in Western Europe. Data were collected from 40 localities, using 25 languages, in 25 different countries. A sizable number of these gestures, used and understood widely in contemporary Europe, are also used and understood in the United States. There is, for example, general consensus in both the United States and Western Europe about the meaning of crossed fingers (good luck), the contemptuous nose thumb, and the sexually insulting forearm jerk. Given our strong European heritage, many European gestures have survived the Atlantic crossing. Yet, despite these similarities on both sides of the Atlantic, far more gestures that have little or no meaning in the United States are used commonly in Europe. Morris and his associates cite the following hand gestures, which are widely used in Europe but have little meaning to the average American:

- The *eyelid pull* (the forefinger is placed below one eye, pulling the skin downward and thereby tugging on the lower eyelid)—meaning "I am alert" or "Be alert" in Spain, France, Italy, and Greece.
- The *chin stroke* (the thumb and forefinger, placed on each cheek bone, are gently stroked down to the chin)—meaning "thin and ill" in the southern Mediterranean area.
- The *earlobe pull* or *flick* (the earlobe is tugged or flicked with the thumb and forefinger of the hand on the same side of the body)—a sign of effeminacy found predominantly in Italy, meaning "I think you are so effeminate that you should be wearing an earring."
- The *nose tap* (the forefinger in a vertical position taps the side of the nose)—meaning "Keep it a secret."

Different cultures can use quite different gestures to signify the same idea. Beckoning for someone to come into your office can be done in a variety of ways. In many parts of Europe, you extend your arm outward, palm down, and fingers curled as if you are scratching something. By contrast, in the United States, the palm is extended upward as you move your curled fingers back and forth. The movement of the fingers in both the European and American models signals to the person to move toward your office. Michaela Safadi and Carol Ann Valentine point out that the Saudis use the palm-up gesture more so than other Arab-speaking cultures that use the palm-down gesture (1990: 281). Americans have a second option when beckoning to a child or lower-status person: palm up with only the index finger elongated and moving forward and backward. According to Roger Axtell, the beckoning index finger would be considered impolite in places such as Malaysia and in parts of the Balkans since it is a gesture used to call animals (2007: 23). Because the human hand is such a precision instrument, and since communication patterns are so arbitrary, a vast array of alternative hand gestures can convey any given idea.

Cross-cultural misunderstandings can also occur when a single hand gesture has a number of different meanings in different parts of the world. For example, most people in the United States know that to signify that something

---

A MYRIAD OF MEANINGS BEHIND "THUMBS UP"

The thumbs-up gesture is interesting because it has multiple meanings attached to it. There is a broad, global consensus that it is a positive symbol; it generally means "OK" or "fine" and is interpreted that way in many parts of the world. However, this gesture is associated with numbers: in Germany it means "one" and in Japan "five." Alternately, in Nigeria, it is considered a rude gesture. An analysis of this gesture in Brazil by anthropologist Joel Sherzer was especially revealing. Sherzer was able to link the thumbs-up gesture (TUG) to seven kinds of interactions (1991: 191–92). He found that the meaning of the gesture was a function of the particular social context as in these situations:

- "To signify 'positive,' 'good,' or 'OK' with or without (words)…In a game of tennis, one man hits a clear winner. His opponent responds by making the TUG."
- As a response to a correction, "A informs B that her car headlights are on. B says *'obrigado'* (thank you) and makes the TUG".
- "As a request for permission to perform an action in a wide variety of situations…A man wants to cross the street even though the light is against him. He makes the TUG to a car moving toward him. The car stops for him, and he crosses the street."

Thus, the thumbs-up gesture is culturally complex. It represents a mix of global consensus, between-culture differences, and within-culture differences all wrapped up in one.

---

is OK or good, one raises one's hand and makes a circle with the thumb and forefinger. In fact, Roger Axtell reports that Milton Bradley Company conducted a survey to identify the most well-known American gestures prior to the introduction of its game Guesstures. "The O.K. sign had 98 percent recognition, greater than any other gesture" (2007: 12–13). However, this same hand gesture means "zero" or "worthless" to the French, "money" to the Japanese, "male homosexual" in Malta, and a general sexual insult in parts of South America.

Another example—and one that had some serious diplomatic repercussions—is the clasped-hands-over-the-head gesture made famous by Soviet Premier Khrushchev on his visit to the United States in the 1960s. Interpreted by Americans as an arrogant gesture used by victorious prizefighters, it was used by Khrushchev as a gesture of international friendship.

Facial Expressions

The face, perhaps the single most important part of the body for channeling nonverbal communication, is particularly rich in its potential for communicating emotional states. Next to speech, the face is the "primary source of giving information" (Knapp 1972: 68–69). In English and in most other languages as well, only a handful of words refer to specific facial expressions (e.g., *smile, frown, grimace, squint*); human facial muscles, however, are so complex that literally hundreds of different facial expressions are possible. The face is, in fact, so central to the process of communication that we speak of "face-to-face" communication, and English speakers to some extent—and Japanese to a far greater degree—speak of "losing face" in certain embarrassing situations.

There is little question about the importance of the face as a source of nonverbal communication. The face is capable of conveying emotional, attitudinal, and factual information in short periods of time. In addition, the question of facial expressions has been central to the nature-nurture debate surrounding all nonverbal communication. Unlike every other form of nonverbal communication—which tends to be largely culture bound—a substantial body of literature claims that some facial expressions may be innate human traits, regardless of cultural context. Charles Darwin (1872) was the first to propose the notion of certain universal facial expressions, an idea also supported by F. H. Allport (1924) and Paul Ekman, Wallace V. Friesen, and Phoebe Ellsworth (1972). All these researchers have attempted to demonstrate that certain emotions are expressed by the same facial expressions in widely diverse cultures, including isolated, preliterate cultures having little contact with the Western world. Some researchers have traveled the globe in search of remote tribal groups that have facial expressions identical to our own. For example, I. Eibl-Eibesfeldt (1971) contends that all people give a rapid "eyebrow flash" when greeting someone (the eyebrows are instantaneously raised and then lowered). Although this research is not exhaustive, the wide global distribution of this particular facial movement strongly suggests that the behavior is inborn. Moreover, children who were born blind and deaf exhibit the normal repertoire of facial expressions, which would tend to eliminate the possible explanation that the expressions were acquired through the process of learning (Eibl-Eibesfeldt 1972).

The nature-nurture question has not been settled, and others contend that facial expressions are culture bound. R. L. Birdwhistell (1963) advances the position that facial expressions do not have universal meanings but are instead the result of cultural, not biological, inheritance. To substantiate this position, one has only to examine the variations in smiling behavior throughout the world. Weston LaBarre (1947: 52) distinguishes between two well-described cultures in the southwest Pacific—the Papuans, known for their wide use of smiling, and the Dobus, where "dourness reigned." Geoffrey Gorer (1935: 10) reports that in certain parts of Africa, laughter and smiling are used to express surprise, wonder, and embarrassment, not amusement or happiness. Morsbach (1982: 307) suggests that, although a sign of joy in Japan, smiling can also be used to hide displeasure, sorrow, or anger, and the trained observer should be able to distinguish between these two types of smiling. J. V. Jensen (1982: 265) contends that in some Asian cultures smiling is a sign of weakness, and it is for this reason that teachers avoid smiling in class lest they lose control over their students. Thus, it would appear that, despite the fact that all people smile, the meanings attached to this particular facial expression vary widely.

In some parts of the world, it is considered highly desirable to maintain an expressionless face. Nowhere is this ideal more widely adhered to than in Japan, which no doubt accounts for the contention by many Westerners that the Japanese are "inscrutable." According to Morsbach,

> Self-control, thought of as highly desirable in Japan, demands that a man of virtue will not show a negative emotion in his face when shocked or upset by sudden bad news; and if successful, is lauded as *tiazen jijaku to shite* (perfectly calm and collected), or *mayu hitotsu ugokasazu ni* (without even moving an eyebrow).... The idea of an expressionless face in situations of great anxiety was strongly emphasized in the *bushido* (way of the warrior) which was the guideline for samurai and the ideal of many others. (1982: 308)

This ideal of masking one's emotions is well supported by research conducted by K. Shimoda, M. Argyle, and R. Ricci-Bitti (1978). English, Italian, and Japanese judges were asked to read or "decode" the nonverbal facial expressions of performers from these three cultural groups. All three sets of judges had the least accuracy reading the facial expressions of the Japanese performers, a result explained by the lack of negative facial expressions.

Another factor that tends to produce cultural differences is that facial expressions are filtered through one's culturally learned display rules. Our culture teaches us what we should feel and how we should show it. It might be appropriate to intensify a felt emotion because it is socially expected, such as a display of exaggerated pleasure over receiving a Christmas present that was not particularly attractive or desirable. On other occasions, it might be socially appropriate to deintensify, or de-emphasize, an

Differences in facial expressions may suggest the need for further inquiry.

A SMILE IS NOT JUST A SMILE

Smiles don't always indicate happiness. Christopher Engholm relates a personal experience that illustrates the meaning of a smile in China:

> One morning, standing in front of our hotel in Korla, a desert town in the Xinjiand province of China, a United Nations consultant and I saw a tractor-wagon, loaded with masonry rock, hit a ditch and dump its contents upon its driver.... Our hotel concierge ran over to examine the situation and gave us the lowdown with a toothy smile: "He dead for sure. Hit his head very hard, I think." We stood there horrified at his seeming indifference, until we remembered that his smile was a shield to protect us—the honored foreign guests—from being disturbed by the event. (1991: 134)

---

emotion, such as repressing one's delight over winning a large pot in a poker game. In some situations, a culture requires one emotion to mask another, as exemplified by the runner-up in a beauty contest who is expected to suppress her own disappointment by showing happiness for the winner. And, Morsbach (1982: 307) reminds us that the Japanese often mask their sorrow or anger by laughing and smiling. Thus, these socially learned display rules of intensification, deintensification, and masking can modify facial expressions from one cultural context to another. If, in fact, cultural learning can affect how and to what extent messages are sent by facial expressions, it behooves international businesspeople to become familiar with this critical aspect of nonverbal communication.

Dress

Royal weddings are big business—big international business. The wedding of Prince William and Kate Middleton in London on April 29, 2011, was expected to generate £50 million in revenue from food, hotels, souvenirs, and attractions on the day of the wedding alone, "kick-starting a tourism bonanza that is set to last a decade" (Gordon 2011). Indeed, there are hopes for billions of dollars in revenue from the wedding (Ridgwell 2011).

One of the topics covered by the media was dress: of the wedding party, guests, and onlookers. Fashion writers from the United States (as well as other countries) wrote reviews of what women were wearing at the royal wedding, in much the same way that they often describe (in excruciating detail) the gowns and jewelry of the female nominees at the Academy Award ceremony. While the outfits that surfaced at the wedding were seen by the foreign press as generally tasteful and appropriate for a British royal wedding, much attention was paid to the wide variety of prominent hats—in many shapes and sizes—worn by female attendees at the royal wedding. Indeed, American media drew upon many analogies to describe these hats, and their first cousins, the fascinators, which are made of feathers, ribbons, and flowers and stick in one's hair. Many of these headpieces were considered over-the-top and likened to a giant salmon, alien appendage, lampshade, cow catcher, salad plate, bait, tea cozy, and uterus and fallopian tubes, to name a few.

Yet, this fascination with dress—particularly hats and fascinators—was tinged with disparagement. These mocking descriptions show no willingness or ability to recognize the strong tradition and meaning behind such accessories. Since hats are routinely part of the British female costume, they function to define and distinguish British from American couture. In Britain, hats complete an outfit, drawing attention to the wearer and signaling the wearer's style and status. In America, hats are viewed (mostly) as some combination of unnecessary, impractical, or silly, with some exceptions (e.g., church attendance among African American women, female attendance at the Kentucky Derby). Thus, hats play a central role in differentiating British and American women when formally dressed. Belittling these highly individualized accessories has the effect of creating an "in-group/out-group" categorization in which the Americans clearly view themselves as part of the "in-group."

What is behind the way people dress? Clothing and other accessories represent important symbols of cultural identity. They serve to distinguish groups of people based on occupation, gender, age, socio-economic status, and club or association affiliation (e.g., soccer leagues and clubs, Girl Scouts/Girl Guides, hospital volunteers), among others. They signal belonging to or participation in a particular national culture (American tourists wearing shorts and baseball caps and carrying cameras in Europe), organizational culture (uniforms worn by fast-food employees) or subculture (Orthodox Patriarchs of Constantinople and Russia in

Fashion and attire often fail to translate across borders.

clerical garb). Thus, identity through dress is double-sided: it enables the wearer to be recognizable as a member of a particular group, and it functions to knit group members together as part of a common community.

Sometimes dress becomes the subject of debate. Anthropologist Ann Jordan discovered tensions over dress among the staff at a large hospital in Riyadh, Saudi Arabia. She reported that "some Saudis believe that female nurses in scrubs should wear scrub uniforms with long sleeves, so that their arms will not be exposed, and that they should veil" (Jordan 2008: 188). Scrubs are the outfits consisting of tops and pants worn by medical personnel; the term originated from the process of "scrubbing" for surgery. "Those opposing the long sleeves won out because of concerns about long sleeves coming in contact with the sterile field during medical procedures," stated Jordan. Interestingly, Jordan found that female physicians, nurses, and other medical specialists who were Muslim had more flexibility in what they wore inside the hospital compared to other public places. Some women inside the hospital opted to cover their faces while others did not (Jordan 2008). All were able to replace the *abayah* (the long, loose black robe that is a required covering for females in public) with a lab coat and long skirt or long pants.

There have been cultural changes in dress over time. Clothing protocol in American business organizations underwent a fairly dramatic change in the second half of the 20th century. A key pattern was the more formal the dress, the higher the status of the individual. Senior leaders routinely wore business suits and ties— "gray pinstripe on the East Coast" according to anthropologist Frank Dubinskas (1988: 185). Entry-level professionals or support staff wore jacket and tie, or shirt

---

TAKE A LOOK AT THAT *ABAYAH!*

When anthropologist Ann Jordan takes a group of American female students to Saudi Arabia, she has them purchase an inexpensive, conservative *abayah* and headscarf online before departure. Once on location, the students, dressed in their own *abayahs*, quickly note the variation in this traditional form of dress worn by Saudi women. Some are hand embroidered. Some are decorated with sequins and beads along the edges of sleeves or on the back. Others may be trimmed in some color, or reveal a design beneath the outer layer. Such decoration makes the traditional dress for Saudi females less conservative. Indeed, *abayahs* can be very stylish and cost thousands of dollars—a far cry, Jordan points out, from the undifferentiated "garbage bag that Westerners often perceive" (Ann Jordan, personal communication). "*Abayah* watching" provides clues about the current political climate, regional differences in this form of cultural expression, and location-specific variation (e.g., university setting, government building). Once women enter their homes or places of employment, and if they are in the presence of only women and appropriate male relatives, they remove their *abayahs* until they move back into the public eye. "*Abayah* watching is one way to learn a little about Saudi culture, as well as just being a fun activity," stated Jordan.

and tie (for males) and dresses or skirts and blouses (for females). The dress of mid-tier professionals varied, tending to be more formal if one were interacting with higher-ranking managers—say, at a meeting. By the late 1980s, "business formal" attire began transitioning to "business casual." It seemed to coincide, at least in the larger corporations, with the demise of highly visible indicators of executive status (e.g., executive dining rooms), the transformation of office secretaries into administrative assistants, and the widespread usage of personal computers by salaried and executive employees.

Proxemics

How people use space in their interactions with others is another "silent language" that must be understood to achieve clear communication within global business settings. This area of nonverbal communication is known as the study of *proxemics*, a term introduced by anthropologist Edward Hall, most notably in his book *The Hidden Dimension* (1966). In this section we focus on both personal space and organizational space, drawing on examples from around the world.

Although earlier researchers had developed similar concepts to Hall's notion of personal space (Sommer 1959; Kuethe 1962; Little 1965), his observations and theories are clearly presented and rich in cross-cultural insights. Hall's major contribution to our understanding of intercultural communication has been to demonstrate that people follow predictable cultural patterns when establishing distance between themselves and others. How close a person gets to another in normal conversation depends on the nature of the social interaction, but in all cases the specific magnitude of the distance is dictated by *cultural* norms.

An important part of Edward Hall's (1966) typology of proxemics is his delineation of four categories of distance based on his observations of middle-class Americans:

1. *Intimate distance:* Ranging from body contact to 18 inches, a distance used for love-making, comforting, and protecting, at which olfactory and thermal sensations are at their highest.
2. *Personal distance:* From 18 inches to four feet, depending on the closeness of the relationship. At this distancing mode people have an invisible "space bubble" separating themselves from others.
3. *Social distance:* From four to 12 feet, a distance used by acquaintances and strangers in business meetings and classrooms.
4. *Public distance:* From 12 to 25 feet, at which the recognition of others is not mandatory and the subtle shades of meaning of voice, gesture, and facial expression are lost.

Although the specific distances described apply to middle-class Americans, all cultures have accustomed their people to feel comfortable at a specific distance. What is appropriate distance for one cultural group might appear to be "crowding" to another, or "standoffish" to a third. For example, operating within Edward Hall's category of personal space, most middle-class Americans choose for normal conversations a distance of approximately 20 inches, with minor variations depending on gender and level of intimacy. For certain cultural groups in South America and the Caribbean, the normal conversational distance is in the range of 14 to 15 inches. And for certain cultures in the Middle East, that distance is as small as nine to ten inches. These appreciable differences should make it painfully obvious just how important an understanding of proxemic variables is to effective intercultural communication. To stand 20 inches from a Saudi Arabian, although normal for an American, communicates reserve, unfriendliness, and a sense of superiority. Yet when the Saudi moves closer, to establish what for him is a more comfortable conversational distance, the typical American interprets it as pushy or aggressive. Because of these culturally produced perceptions of space, Americans, when conversing with South Americans or Middle Easterners, may find themselves continually backpedaling in an attempt to maintain their 20-inch distance as their foreign acquaintances continue to move closer. Although both conversants are simply trying to establish the normal conversational distance as determined by their cultural upbringing, considerable misunderstandings can occur.

Proxemic patterns are so important for cross-cultural communication largely because they represent such a subtle and frequently overlooked form of nonverbal communication. Each culture develops its own set of rules and uses of space, which like other aspects of culture are learned, but learned in an unconscious manner. It would be hard to find anyone in the United States who could testify that while growing up his or her adult role models explicitly taught him or her to maintain a conversational distance of 20 inches. Nevertheless, according to the findings of Edward Hall and others, middle-class Americans have learned what "proper" distance is, and they have learned it with remarkable consistency.

There is variation in space usage within national cultures. Personal or individual attributes affect the use of space. Children play on playgrounds. Millionaires live in big expensive homes. Conductors walk the aisles of trains, and

---

THE "RIGHT" DISTANCE

Anthropologist Conrad Kottak says this about differences in personal space usage:

> The world's cultures have strikingly different notions about displays of affection and about matters of personal space. When North Americans talk, walk, and dance, they maintain a certain distance from others—their personal space. Brazilians, who maintain less physical distance, interpret this as a sign of coldness. When conversing with a North American, the Brazilian characteristically moves in as a North American "instinctively" retreats. In these body movements, neither Brazilian nor North American is trying consciously to be especially friendly or unfriendly. Each is merely executing a program written on the self by years of exposure to a particular cultural tradition. Because of different ideas about proper social space, cocktail parties in international meeting places such as the United Nations can resemble an elaborate insect mating ritual as diplomats from different cultures advance, withdraw, and sidestep. (2004: 88)

tuk-tuk drivers, operating their three-wheeled vehicles (in places like Honduras and Thailand), weave in and out of traffic. Native Americans may live and work on reserves (in Canada) and reservations (in the United States). Students are found in classrooms—often sitting, while their teachers are there too, but usually standing.

In another example, spatial differentiation is created to accommodate gender differences in the medical profession. The weekly resident and intern meeting took place in a big hall at a large hospital in Riyadh, Saudi Arabia. Anthropologist Ann Jordan accompanied the head physician to this meeting. Upon arrival, she noted that the female interns and residents sat on one side of the hall while the males sat on the opposite side. This gender separation made sense to Jordan given what she knew about Saudi culture (Jordan 2011). What was somewhat surprising, however, was that the head physician—a male—chose to sit with Jordan on the female side of the hall. She asked him to explain why he sat with the women. He replied that he was their mentor and teacher and had to help both female and male physicians. Consequently, he could sit with the female interns. One lesson to draw from this example is that cultures have roles that link together culturally distinct and/or disparate groups. This head physician served as a bridge in the training of medical professionals within a particular spatial context.

As the world has been globalizing, there has been a growing commonality in business office environments. Two key spatial patterns are associated with business discussions in many places around the world. One pattern is the conference room, which typically accommodates several clients or colleagues. A second pattern is the use of an individual's office when only a few clients are involved; typically, there is a table around which people can sit—situated away from the occupant's desk or work station.

There is variation, of course, for which an awareness of proxemics is valuable. An attorney's office in Santiago, Chile, will have a desk against the wall but "usually, small conference tables or coffee tables are there—around which people can talk, have coffee, and discuss business," according to anthropologist Ken Erickson. An ambience is created for the purpose of building business relationships. The business encounter has a quality of informality, though there is adherence to particular cultural rules regarding the use of space. Erickson reports

> Many smaller business office buildings in Santiago are converted old residences, walled, with outside space for discussion and meetings, as well as formal, fairly standard conference rooms. Offices are shared; bosses tend to meet people outside their own (boss's) offices, in the conference room, around a table in the patio. If the company has many employees, you don't eat where you conference, and you don't conference in the canteen. But you may talk business after a nice lunch. Wine will be served—Chilean.

Contrast that kind of business environment with German business culture in which there is a strong value of privacy and personal space. A preference for closed doors while working is one way in which this preference is expressed.

Moreover, Germans become uncomfortable when someone moves his or her office chair closer to adjust the social situation. "There is great sensitivity about not moving or rearranging things in another office, acknowledging boundaries, and asking for permission when traversing boundaries" according to anthropologist Joerg Schmitz. As in many business contexts, there are a range of options for office environments. While private offices are common, so are double offices (*Doppelbüros*) in which two people share an office, often with the desks facing each other. This kind of office arrangement is more common among mid-level management. Schmitz points out that German companies have experimented with open office space (*Grossraumbüros*): "It may be a testament to the prevailing preference for 'privacy' that those office arrangements do not get great reviews." As reported in a Swiss-German newspaper on April 27, 2010, a study found that employees do better in small, individual offices rather than open office arrangements (http://www.tagesanzeiger.ch/wirtschaft/konjunktur/Schlechte-Noten-fuers-Grossraumbuero/story/11770162).

Regardless of whether we encounter a preference for open doors or closed doors, or flexible or inflexible office arrangements, space usage is likely to have different meanings in different cultures, which can influence the nature of the international business relationship.

THE IMPORTANCE OF WALLS

Workspace is important around the world, though its meaning can differ by occupation and national culture. The head of General Motors Research and Development (GM R&D) encountered resistance to open office environments (cubicles) both in the established research facility in Warren, MI and in the newer laboratories in Bangalore, India. "One reason our team was called in was because the Bangalore researchers kept putting in requests for headsets (to block ambient noise) and more one-on-one space for interacting with others," reported anthropologist Tracy Meerwarth. This research executive asked his anthropologists to help him understand and manage the issue.

Common themes across the two labs included a shared set of workspace requirements such as a workspace free of acoustical and visual distractions. To be productive, researchers emphasized the importance of privacy and "heads-down" (quiet) work (Meerwarth et al. 2008b), in addition to the ability to engage in problem-solving discussions with other researchers. Their researcher model of workspace was at odds with most other groups within the corporation where frequent and regular interaction was the norm and where workspace consisted of cubicles.

There was an interesting difference distinguishing the Warren and Bangalore researchers. The Bangalore researchers were much more likely than the Warren researchers to view private offices, which they called "cabins," as a

(continued)

key status symbol. Cabins were an important recruiting and retention tool in that they represented "hierarchy, power, and cultural symbolism in Bangalore's highly-competitive industrial-research market" stated Meerwarth. Warren researcher comments did not reflect a significant focus on status, but rather emphasized the importance of "getting the work done," according to Meerwarth's colleague Wendy Bartlo, also an anthropologist. One insight from this project was that workspace in Bangalore played a role in shaping its organizational culture and in reinforcing themes of hierarchy and status within Indian society generally.

Workspaces should be designed with the work tasks in mind to maximize productivity. Walls and doors help researchers concentrate and collaborate without disturbing others.

New Technologies and Visual Media

People communicate with each other nonverbally through visual media. Drawings, paintings, cartoons, photographs, video, and film are among the most well-established forms of visual expression. Sending photographs to friends and loved ones is one way to communicate the importance of relationships while architectural drawings provide visual and numerical guidelines for the construction of a home, building, or city park. Other examples of visual media include PowerPoint slides, flow charts, electronic drawings and gestures, and application-sharing technologies. These forms of visual media enable both the compilation of ideas, recommendations, and timelines as well as the launch of creative "real-time" brainstorming to achieve work objectives.

Websites make use of visual media including animation, photographs, and images to generate audience interest in products and services. Elizabeth Würtz conducted a cross-cultural analysis of visual communication on McDonald's websites. She found five different strategies used to communicate messages. One strategy involved the use of animation. In high-context cultures, there was a significant amount of animation and the portrayal of people who were moving (e.g., people dancing or jumping in China and Chile). By contrast, in low-context cultures, animation was minimal, and people were shown in relaxed situations (e.g., listening to music on the Swiss-German site and in Scandinavia). Another strategy involved the design of the websites. Scandinavian sites were "tabular and functional" while the Asian sites had a "montage/layer-upon-layer approach" (2005: 293). In general, the websites in high-context cultures used more imagery than text.

Anthropologist Susan Squires has been involved with three different projects for three different companies related to video technologies. Her research is less about cultural differences and more about cross-cultural similarities. In the mid-1990s, her work at Andersen Consulting (now Accenture) focused on employee attitudes toward and use of videoconferencing on personal computers. In 1999–2000, Squires explored mobile phone needs and preferences for Ericsson— including a videophone—in a three-country telecommunications study. In her current research, she is exploring Apple iPhone user interest in the videophone once again—this time through FaceTime video calling.

When survey participants were asked about these different video technologies, they reacted favorably to them. However, the observational data demonstrated that users rejected these technologies when asked to use them. In the videoconferencing study, they would either turn off the video option or remove the video window from their computer screen soon after the simulation began, "much to the chagrin of the engineers helping with the simulation observations" (Squires 2005: 83). Forty percent of the participants assigned to the video package indicated discomfort in being "on camera" since it was possible to see the context in which that person was working (e.g., in a messy office, at home). In the videophone study, study participants in the United Kingdom, for example, expressed concerns "about etiquette ('When would it be alright to turn the video part off?'); privacy ('What if I want to call in sick to work and my boss wants to see how sick I look?'); and security ('What about telemarketers? I don't want them to see me.')" (2005: 86). Finally, only 8 percent of iPhone users also use FaceTime video calling so "It's still not being adopted," stated Squires. Neither videoconferencing nor videophone has gotten the traction that was anticipated. But there was an interesting twist in this would-be technology. Study participants in the videophone project asked Squires if the videophone could be turned around and made into a camera phone. "The answer was 'Yes' and now cameras are on every phone!"

Dane Archer wanted to capture nonverbal behaviors through film. Such media captures actions and experiences that are often difficult, if not impossible, to describe in verbal or written form. Archer discovered that nonverbal behaviors could be "performed, illustrated, modeled, taught, and explicated to cultural outsiders" (1997: 98). One goal in his 28-minute documentary video *A World of Gestures: Culture and Nonverbal Communication* was to create a visual "archive" that could teach specific gestures as well as make viewers aware of cultural differences. Because viewers are able to see nonverbal behaviors in action, they can learn the subtleties of the gestures and sometimes even some of the conditions under which they are used. In addition, viewers can often compare and contrast what they observe with those forms of nonverbal communication with which they are familiar. In that sense, film and video reveal cultural differences to viewers—often quite effortlessly.

Film is a core technique in consumer research because it enhances the discovery of cultural insights. A film clip documents what actually happens in the particular situation such as how people use products and services or the conditions under which they use them. It not only portrays the context in full visual detail, but also allows viewers to imagine themselves as part of that context. Indeed, film can be a compelling form of evidence for understanding products and services in the broader social milieu.

A MOVING PICTURE IS WORTH A THOUSAND WORDS

Anthropologist Ken Erickson and his colleagues routinely use video in their consumer work to capture consumer behavior and highlight key findings. One project they did for Boeing, which manufactures airplanes, was to document how people with limited mobility managed to get into and out of their seats, or how they managed to use the restroom. Special needs among the traveling public has been an important and growing initiative at Boeing, and at airlines such as Japan Airlines (JAL), which has expressed concern about the interior spatial design of planes for its rapidly-aging Japanese population. Erickson's research team "flew along" with, interviewed, observed, and filmed passenger experiences in four different locations: the United States, China, India, and Chile.

At one moment in the film clip during their final presentation, a U.S. participant with mild cerebral palsy struggled to fasten his seatbelt. Stabilizing the right side of the seatbelt with his right hand, he attempted to use his left hand and push the left side of the seatbelt into the slot. After three tries over the course of 29 seconds, he completed the task. With a heavy sigh a few seconds later,

(continued)

he muttered an expletive. His relief was palpable. "One of the Boeing directors immediately interrupted the presentation." "He asked that the video be sent as soon as possible to Boeing's seat contractor so that it could get started on some new design ideas" (Ken Erickson, personal communication). The researchers later learned that the last time seatbelts were re-designed was in 1964!

Some in the air travel business told the researchers that design and service changes for the disabled were an expense that they could not easily afford. "How many of our customers," Erickson paraphrased, "would really benefit from such design changes?" Yet, Boeing's design team was energized by the compelling film clip of the recalcitrant seat belt. Boeing's focus on universal design (i.e., design changes that benefit everyone) was consistent with an increasingly progressive American attitude vis-à-vis the disabled. Boeing has responded to the cost argument in this way:

> These design changes will have an impact on everyone, for two reasons. First, because everyone who is now able-bodied will, at some time in his/her life, experience some physical change or limitation—a broken arm, a case of arthritis, body changes due to illness, or even a reduction in hearing ability. Second, designing for special needs often benefits able-bodied people too.

The film made the difference by revealing the challenges faced by the disabled—an aspect of culture that is often hidden from view.

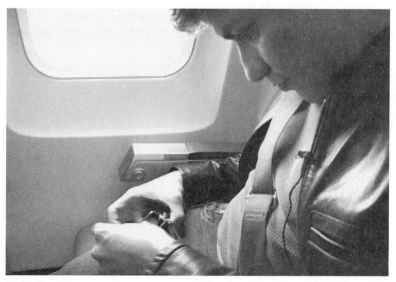

Video footage can capture consumer use, often illustrating the unexpected.

One mode of nonverbal communication among those who do not know each other's language(s) involves drawing. It is fairly common to see designers and/or engineers expressing themselves through hand-drawn sketches. A Brazilian engineer commented, "It works best face-to-face. The (Japanese) guys help you even if the subject is new to you. They explain with drawings. If you remove a pencil from his [*sic*] hands, he can't work very well (given the language barrier)." Another Brazilian working on the same product program with the Japanese stated, "Their English isn't as good as ours. We realize we must be very clear with them. We use drawings. Now we are doing well." These statements reveal the bidirectionality of this form of nonverbal communication: Brazilians and Japanese use drawings to communicate with each other. Technical drawings represent a singularly important, if not principle, way in which ideas are exchanged when written or spoken languages are not shared. As such, drawings are a realistic alternative to language. However, drawings may have a key shortcoming: they may be only a partial communication strategy if they require additional explanation. Under such circumstances, designers and engineers may pull in bi- or multilingual colleagues to serve as impromptu interpreters to facilitate understanding.

Oftentimes, anthropologists focus their attention on cultural differences. They seek to describe and explain what is distinctive about a particular cultural group, in comparison with one or more other cultural groups. This example emphasizes cross-cultural similarities as Brazilian and Japanese product development personnel try to bridge a gap in their ability to transmit information and insights to each other. The drawings, a form of nonverbal communication, become a "workaround" strategy enabling them to launch their collaboration and establish a foundation for a shared, emergent culture.

CONCLUSION

The United States is a highly literate society that tends to emphasize the verbal channel of expression. Most Americans, if forced to think about it at all, see the spoken word as the primary carrier of meaning. They are much less likely to give much credence to the nonverbal aspects of communication. As important as language is to facilitating intercultural communication within a global business setting, it is only a first step to intercultural understanding. Of equal importance is the nonverbal dimension, which we all rely on but only vaguely recognize. Now that we have examined several of the more common modes of nonverbal communication in some detail, it would be instructive to look at some of the more salient features of nonverbal communication in general.

1. Nonverbal communication is largely a learned, or culturally transmitted, phenomenon. Although some convincing evidence shows that certain limited aspects of

nonverbal communication are universal (e.g., the expression of emotions through smiles, frowns, eyebrow flashes), the great majority of nonverbal cues, and the meanings attached to them, vary from culture to culture.

2. The comparatively new field of nonverbal communication studies has not been able to describe comprehensive systems of nonverbal communication for a single-speech community as linguists have done for language. We do not have, at least not yet, a grammar specifying the rules for constructing nonverbal messages. Nor are nonverbal dictionaries available that might provide, in reference book fashion, the meaning of a particular nonverbal cue.

3. Many nonverbal cues are sent and received despite our best intentions to do otherwise. Whereas language is every bit as effective for masking our true feelings as it is for expressing them, much of nonverbal communication is beyond our purposeful control. We can smile when we are unhappy, and to that extent we can purposefully control some nonverbal cues, but we cannot control our blushing when embarrassed, perspiring when nervous, or pupil dilation when frightened.

4. Because some nonverbal communication is beyond the individual's control, it is not uncommon to find a noticeable lack of fit between a person's words and his or her nonverbal messages. For example, in response to the question "How are you?" a person might respond "Fine" while at the same time sending a number of nonverbal messages (such as sullen tone of voice, downcast eyes, and a frown) that totally contradict the upbeat verbal response. Research indicates that when a discrepancy occurs between the verbal and the nonverbal, the observer will most likely believe the nonverbal (Burgoon, Buller, and Woodall 1989: 9–10).

5. Nonverbal behavior is by and large unconscious—to a much greater degree than with language. We send nonverbal messages spontaneously without giving much thought about what hand gestures we are choosing to punctuate our words, how far we are from someone else's mouth in normal communication, or how long we maintain eye contact. Because so much of our nonverbal behavior is operating on the unconscious level, seeking clarification of a misunderstood nonverbal cue becomes nearly impossible. Although we can ask someone to repeat a sentence, we would be quite unlikely to ask someone to explain what he or she meant by a half smile, a particular posture, or a sudden movement of the head.

6. Based on past research, strong evidence indicates that women are able to read nonverbal cues better than are men. Judith Hall, reviewing 52 gender-related studies, found that 75 percent showed a significant female advantage (1978). Using the PONS (Profile of Nonverbal Sensitivity) test, Robert Rosenthal and his colleagues found an even greater female advantage than the earlier studies (1979: 80–84).

Although much has been made of the distinction between nonverbal communication and language, the two forms are in fact inextricably interconnected. To ignore the nonverbal behavior and learn just the spoken language would be as unreasonable as doing just the opposite. An understanding of both modes is necessary to reveal the full meaning of an intercultural event. Being able to read facial expressions, postures, hand gestures, gaze, and space usage, among others, increases our sensitivity to the intricacies of cross-cultural communication so necessary for success in the global business arena. To really know another culture, we must be able to hear the silent messages and read the invisible words.

CROSS-CULTURAL SCENARIOS

Read the following cross-cultural scenarios. In each mini-case study, a basic cultural conflict occurs among the actors involved. Try to identify the source of the conflict and suggest how it could have been avoided or minimized. Then see how well your analyses compare to the explanations in Appendix A.

3-1   Lily Feenan, an associate in an internationally known architectural firm in Philadelphia, was assigned to head up a project designing public housing units in Nairobi, Kenya. With a small team of colleagues, Lily spent about three months designing and preparing the schematics for a large, nine-building project consisting of over 200 separate units. The various units were laid out in much the same way that public housing units would be designed in Philadelphia, Atlanta, or Chicago—that is, with two bedrooms, a large bathroom, a living room, and dining area with an adjoining open kitchen. Once completed, the units were rented (with substantial government subsidies) to needy families. Unfortunately, many of the new residents, while grateful to live in new housing with modern conveniences, were not at all satisfied with one particular design feature shared by all of the units in the project: every unit came with a dining room which opened up into the kitchen.

How could local Nairobi residents possibly take issue with an open kitchen design?

3-2   George Gomez, a Boston banker, was assigned for several weeks as a trouble-shooter in the Rome office. To facilitate his adjustment to the Italian banking system and to assist with translation, the branch manager suggested George work with Maria Fellini, a bilingual employee of the bank. Maria, like George, was single and in her early thirties; she lived with her widowed mother. Maria invited George to their home for dinner. When George arrived, he brought a large bouquet of chrysanthemums for Maria's mother as a token of his appreciation for her hospitality. Maria answered the door, greeted George, and took the flowers into the kitchen. But for the entire evening, neither Maria nor her mother mentioned anything about the flowers. George felt that perhaps he had done something inappropriate, or maybe they were just not appreciative.

What went wrong?

3-3   Andy Ross, an electrical engineer for a Chicago firm on a contract with the Turkish government, had been living with his wife Nancy in Istanbul for several months. When Andy had to spend several weeks in Ankara, he thought it was a good opportunity to combine business with pleasure. Because he was entitled to some vacation time, he decided to travel leisurely to Ankara by car with Nancy to spend some time in rural Turkey and get a better feel for village life. Living in Istanbul had been very enjoyable, because both Andy and his wife had found it to be a sophisticated and interesting European city. But when traveling in the outlying regions, they began to feel uneasy for the first time since coming to Turkey because the local people seemed hostile. On their second day out of Istanbul, they stopped in a small coffeehouse that they had heard was a focal point of social activity in rural Turkey. But shortly after arriving, they sensed that they were not welcome. People stared and stopped talking to one another. They could not understand why people were so hostile, particularly since people seemed so friendly in Istanbul.

What explanation might you offer Andy and Nancy?

3-4   Aware of the enormous interest the Japanese have in the game of golf, a U.S. sports equipment manufacturer decided to explore the possibilities of a joint venture with a Japanese firm. Three representatives from each firm met in San Francisco to work out the details of the proposed venture. After the six men were introduced to one another, they were seated at opposite sides of a large conference table. In an attempt to show the Japanese their sincerity for getting down to the task at hand, the Americans took off their jackets and rolled up their sleeves. Then one of the Americans said to his counterpart across the table, "Since we are going to be working together for the next several days, we better get to know each other. My name is Harry. What's your name?" The joint venture never did take place.

What went wrong?

3-5   Steve Reichs was on a month-long assignment at his company's office in Pusan, Korea. Wanting to catch the attention of his supervisor who was standing across the room, Steve "crooked" his index finger at him in an innocent gesture to have him come closer. Not only did Steve get his supervisor's attention, he so infuriated his boss that Steve came very close to being sent back to the home office.

What was the problem?

4

■ ■ ■

Communicating across Cultures

Language

Business organizations, like other social systems, require effective communication to operate efficiently and meet their objectives. International business organizations require effective communication at a number of levels. The firm must communicate with its workforce, customers, suppliers, and host-government officials. Effective communication among people from the same culture is often difficult. But when attempting to communicate with people who do not speak English—and who have different ideas, attitudes, assumptions, perceptions, and ways of doing things—one's chances for miscommunication increase enormously.

All cultures have their own set of ideal standards for appropriate communication. The process of communicating across cultures can be short-circuited when at least one party assumes that its communication standards are universally understood. Even when the cross-cultural communication takes place using the same language, there are a number of parameters that can lead to misunderstandings or even a breakdown in the dialogue. For example, is the speaker the appropriate person to be delivering the message? Is the addressee the appropriate person to be receiving the message? Is the content of the message mutually understood by both parties? Is the message being sent and hopefully received in the appropriate social context? Is it the right time for the message to be received successfully? Is the message being sent according to the appropriate medium (e.g., face to face, telephone, written letter, e-mail, text messaging)? Is the style of the message (e.g., formal/informal, direct/indirect) appropriate for the situation? What impact does the choice of words, tone of voice, and use of nonverbal cues have on the recipient? And, is the location of the communication (e.g., an office, restaurant, taxi, golf course) appropriate for the message?

THE IDEAL OF LINGUISTIC PROFICIENCY IN GLOBAL BUSINESS

If international business people are to succeed, there is no substitute for an intimate acquaintance with both the language and the culture of those with whom one is conducting business. In fact, because of the close relationship between language and culture, it is virtually impossible not to learn about one while studying the other.

Consider this example. Isuzu Motors Ltd. requested a meeting with its strategic alliance partner General Motors (GM) in the United States to resolve criteria issues related to brakes. About 20 people were present. Three were Japanese speakers, four were bilingual English-Japanese, and the remainder spoke only English. One issue concerned the "operating forces relative to gradient that complied with FMVSS." The U.S. Federal Motor Vehicle Safety Standards required 112.5 lbs. of force for its parking brake when the light-duty truck was parked on a 20 percent grade (slope). Isuzu had a proposal to meet this requirement. A discussion ensued between the GM park brake expert (Donald), the interpreter (Dan), two integration engineers (Len and James), and a general assembly engineer (Mary).

Donald (appearing extremely upset):	How would 110 lbs. be acceptable from a spec (specification) perspective?
Dan (conferring first with the Isuzu brake engineers):	It's a stiff requirement and if it fits within the bounds, you are acceptable.
Donald:	The legal limit is 112. If you design to 110, and if you can guarantee that every vehicle is less than 112 (then that's fine), but there's no safety factor.
Dan (conferring first with the Isuzu brake engineers):	With 112 and Isuzu's design, the outer limit of the variation would be 110.
Len:	So your question is, what is their nominal target value?
Donald:	What are you going to design to?
Len:	90.
Donald:	No, they (Isuzu) said they would *shoot for* 90.
James:	There must be a thousand statements like this in the criteria…What we need to do is say, 'OK. We understand each other,' and then move forward.

If they say 110, they'll do 110. The program will fail if not. We're in a partnership. We believe it and we move on. We will have an opportunity to validate their design. Conformity is our problem in the plants as much as theirs.

Donald: That's what we're talking about. We wouldn't do that. We know if the legal limit is 112, when we get into production (in the plant), we won't have a legal truck...Who's going to live with it if it doesn't work? Me!...We would design to 110 if it was 120, and we would design to 90 if it was 112.

James: How do you know they won't target to 90?

Donald: The translation yesterday was that they would *shoot for* 90.

Dan: Isuzu's process is flexible...Both sides have to be flexible. I know it's a legal requirement, but they (Isuzu) have a plant in the U.S...Isuzu feels...(He stopped suddenly and looked at Donald who seemed to be smiling). We're working hard here. You gave me the impression that you're not going to take me seriously.

Donald: OK. Go on. Go on.

Dan: In GM, we design to 90 and we go to 110. Isuzu looks at it the other way. 110 is the worst case. They design to the worst outer, which is 110. This is the worst case scenario. So it's the reverse of what we do. Nominal is 90 lbs. This is just a different philosophy.

Mary: They do the same thing with fasteners. We start with a joint and make a fastener fit the joint. Isuzu starts with a fastener and makes it fit the joint. They end up with a lot less variation. It is the reverse of what we would do.

James: I'm going to record your objection, Donald, and then we will have to move on.

Language plays a vital role in helping people understand each other. Without some ability to communicate, business ventures cannot be successful. In this strategic alliance, language differences were managed in two important ways. First, both firms selected at least some employees with language skills in both English and Japanese. Isuzu employees also took English-language classes. Second, "language interpreting" by designated employees was a routine part of the alliance's work activities; these employees have been referred to as "bridge individuals" or "linking pins" because of their bilingual, and sometimes multilingual skills (Harzing, Köster, and Magner 2011). The interpreters were frequently called upon (and sometimes called away from their usual job responsibilities) to provide real-time assistance in facilitating communication between English and Japanese speakers. Their language skills were in high demand by both sides.

The passage reveals the difficulties that the alliance encountered despite having the two strategies in place. On the one hand, Dan's interpreting skills were excellent; he was the skillful conduit for detailed information between the Japanese and English speakers. On the other hand, we read that while Donald understood the words that Dan used—the interpretation of what the Japanese said—he was not convinced of the value of the meaning. Indeed, there was a deeper issue going on involving a distinction between how the Japanese and American engineers dealt with design requirements. The Japanese engineers' cultural models of engineering were so different to be incomprehensible to Donald. A glimpse of this close relationship between language and culture becomes evident with Dan's statement "This is just a different philosophy." The language and culture connection is solidified further as Mary offers an example of how differently the two groups deal with fasteners.

Those with foreign language skills are primed to perform relationship-building functions in global business environments. Not only was Mary able to serve as a check on Dan's interpreting, but she was also able to jump in to support Dan in his quest to help convince Donald of the merits of the Japanese approach. After all, Mary had the benefit of listening to the discussion in Japanese, the way Dan interpreted the Japanese discussion, and Donald's response to Dan's interpreting. Mary also served another useful purpose: to help restore some degree of objectivity and neutrality to the discussion. Her statement to Donald was straightforward and matter-of-fact, in contrast to Donald's ethnocentric attitude and Dan's judgmental response to it. Those with language skills serve as bridge builders. They are able to move the work along and help overcome the miscommunication, misunderstanding, and cultural "disconnects" that emerge. This popular strategy is one of many that global firms and partnerships use to deal with the language barrier (Harzing, Köster, and Magner 2011).

Most of the explanations offered for not learning to speak another language appear transparent and designed to justify past complacency and/or ethnocentrism. For example, we frequently hear that U.S. firms doing business abroad need not train their overseas personnel in a second language because English is rapidly becoming the international language of business. After generations of assuming that our goods and services were so desirable that the rest of the world would come to us, we now find ourselves in a highly competitive world marketplace with greater linguistic parity. English is now just one of the major languages of world trade and the mother tongue of only five percent of the world's population. One message from the brake example above is the importance of foreign language skills—particularly for technical specialists such as engineers. These individuals will be in a better position to understand the language and conceptual approaches of their global partners compared with those who have not had such exposure.

A host of other arguments has also been advanced to justify a monolingual approach to international business. For example, it has been suggested that Western businesspeople can avoid the time and energy needed to learn a second language by hiring in-country nationals who are well grounded in the local language and culture. Yet, the more people that have the appropriate foreign language proficiency on a given business venture, the better. Moreover, any interpretation works best when the interpreter's abilities match the situation. The interpreter was both familiar with the Japanese language and with engineering concepts, positioning him to combine both knowledge sets for the benefit of the venture. Others have argued that a second language is not practical because most international businesspeople do not remain in the host country for more than a year or two. It has even been suggested that becoming proficient in a second language could actually hinder one's career advancement, because spending so much time out of the home country, would keep one out of the organization's political mainstream. Yet, making *any* effort to learn the language of your partner will be useful in global business endeavors. It will enable you to participate more actively in the discussions, and help you build relationships with your partners faster and more effectively. In addition, having such experiences helps you to adapt to the next set of circumstances you will face both at home and abroad.

Despite these and other arguments (or perhaps post facto rationalizations), the simple fact remains that a fundamental precondition of any successful international business enterprise is effective communication. Whether dealing with international sales, management, or negotiations, the Western businessperson who must rely on translators is at a marked disadvantage. International business, like any business, must be grounded in trust and mutual respect. What better way to gain that trust and respect than by taking the time and energy to learn someone else's language?

These arguments should be ample justification for Western businesspeople to have second-language competence, but we can add three other compelling reasons as well. First, as Benjamin Lee Whorf (1956: 212–14) has suggested, the only way to really understand the *worldview* (a system of categories for organizing the world) of another culture is through its language. Second, the experience of learning a second language is beneficial in the learning of third and fourth languages, so that the time spent today learning Spanish will facilitate the learning of Chinese or Arabic in the future. Third, learning another language (and culture) is the best way to gain a fuller appreciation of one's own language (and culture). With all

---

TO SPEAK OR NOT TO SPEAK PIDGIN

What language should visitors speak when engaging in business and commerce in Cameroon, a coastal country in central and western Africa? The official languages of the country are French and English (although there are a few hundred indigenous languages as well), so the answer might be readily apparent. Anthropologist Adam Koons noted that "Cameroonians would be happy to speak to me in either English or French" depending on whether it was the anglophone or francophone region. However, he quickly discovered that many locals spoke Pidgin English throughout the country; Pidgin is a simplified language composed of two or more languages and spoken as a second language. With the help of colleagues, friends, and a Peace Corps Pidgin manual, he managed to become somewhat proficient in Pidgin in a couple of months.

One day, Koons was in francophone Douala, Cameroon's largest city. He was making some purchases in a store that he had used periodically for a long time, and had always received a serious and impersonal response. When he heard Pidgin being spoken, he switched to Pidgin. Suddenly, everyone became friendly and accommodating. Even though most people speak formal French, they often feel more comfortable in Pidgin, and speak it among themselves. "There was a complete change in attitude toward me" (Adam Koons, personal communication).

In speaking what the locals speak, the nature of the relationship with them changes. It suggests an interest in them, in their culture, and in their preferred language. Indeed, it makes it possible to "speak to them on their own terms." Engaging with locals in this way, Koons stated, "offers a whole other level of acceptance," a valuable asset in business, trade, and commerce.

---

these cogent arguments in favor of second-language proficiency, one cannot help noticing the general lack of attention foreign-language competence has been given by Western business and educational organizations.

There are, of course, exceptions to this general rule of neglecting second-language learning. The CEO of a major American manufacturer strongly urged new managing directors of Brazilian operations to learn Portuguese, reflecting on his own experience in the role. Even though the hours spent working with a tutor would cost the new managing director valuable time away from normal duties, the CEO felt this would be time well spent, especially since the role required meeting with workers, dealers, customers, and government officials.

The United States has been called, only half-jokingly, the "land of the free and the home of the monolingual." One is hard pressed to name another country in which a higher percentage of its native-born population speaks only one language. While the data vary from country to country, it is generally agreed that approximately half of the general population of the European Union and 70 percent of its student population between the ages of 15 and 24 have functional proficiency in a second language, as compared to less than 10 percent of U.S.

citizens. The United States is the only country in the world where it is possible to earn a university education without attaining functional literacy in a second language. Not only can it be done, but in actual fact, most university graduates in the United States never master a second language. Since 1960, the Modern Language Association of America has been tracking enrollments in languages other than English in U.S. institutions of higher education. The ratio of enrollments in modern languages per 100 total enrollments has plummeted from a high of 16.5 percent (1965) to 8.6 percent (2009) (Furman, Goldberg, and Lusin 2010:18). In general there is much less attention to language requirements. The existing instructional programs in foreign languages, from elementary school through the university, are largely voluntary, short term, superficial, and often the first to be cut when budgets are trimmed. In the current era of globalization, the need to understand other languages has become more critical than ever before because what we don't know can hurt us.

Yet, even for those firms that take seriously the multilinguistic environment of international business, many hazards lie along the way. The literature is filled with examples of problems U.S. firms have had in their international advertising campaigns because of sloppy translations. For years the Pepsi Cola Company used the highly successful slogan ("Come Alive with Pepsi") in all of its advertising in the United States. With this domestic success, the company decided to use this slogan in its advertising in South East Asia. But the only way that the slogan "Come Alive with Pepsi" could be translated into the local

If you want to communicate effectively in the global marketplace, there is no substitute for the hard work it takes to learn another language.

language was "Pepsi brings your dead ancestors back from the grave." This faux pas caused a lot of snickers, but didn't increase sales of their carbonated beverage. In other instances of imprecise translations (Slater 1984), U.S. firms have advertised cigarettes with low "asphalt" (instead of tar), computer "underwear" (instead of software), and "wet sheep" (instead of hydraulic rams). As amusing as these examples may seem, such translation errors have cost U.S. firms millions of dollars in losses over the years, not to mention the damage done to their credibility and reputations. Moreover, companies have gotten themselves into trouble when their product names have not translated well into foreign markets. According to Ricks (1999: 38–42), electronics firm Olympia attempted to market a photocopy machine named "Roto" in Chile only to learn later that the word *roto* means broken in Spanish. A female employee of Coca-Cola hired to hand out samples of Fresca soft drink in Mexico was met with considerable laughter by the local people, for whom the word *fresca* means lesbian. And, European companies have tried to sell products with unappealing names in the United States, including "Zit" (a European chocolate and fruit dessert), "Super Piss" (a Finnish product for unfreezing car door locks), and "Bum" (a Spanish potato chip).

In all these examples, it is clear that the translators knew the language, but they still sent unintended messages. Even though they knew the meanings of all the words used and the grammatical rules for putting them together, communication was nevertheless short-circuited. One way to reduce the possibilities of sending the wrong message is to use back translation, whereby one person translates a document and then a second person translates the translated version back to the original language. Although not perfect, back translation provides a valuable check against sending unintended messages.

Not only do businesses face formidable problems when translating from one language into another, but confusion can also occur between two groups that ostensibly speak the same language. We often hear this comment: "Fortunately, we are being transferred by the company to London, so we won't have a language problem." It is true that they will not have to master a totally new language, complete with grammar, vocabulary, and sound system. But it is equally true that there are a number of significant differences between British and American English that can lead to confusion and misunderstandings. In some cases, the same word can have two very different meanings on either side of the Atlantic. The U.S. businessman in London will be in for quite a jolt when his British counterpart, in a genuine attempt to pay a compliment, refers to the American's wife as "homely," because in the United States the word means plain or ugly, but in the United Kingdom it means warm and friendly. And how many times has the term "table an item on the agenda" led to needless confusion and acrimony at joint British and American business meetings? Why? Because for the British "to table an agenda item" means to give it top priority by moving it to the top of the agenda, while in the United States it means to postpone the

WORDS MATTER WHEN MARKETING ABROAD

During the late 1990s, CARE, a global humanitarian organization dedicated to fighting poverty, partnering with the U.S. Centers for Disease Control and Prevention (CDC), developed a water treatment product with a chlorine base that would sterilize drinking water. When introducing this product to communities in western Kenya, Care personnel approached village leaders and sought their advice on marketing it. Staff and village leaders came up with a locally appropriate spelling for the product as a way to promote local ownership and use. The bottles were labeled *Klorin*, a term that was consistent and compatible with local language use. Words are extraordinarily important in this kind of social marketing because it "promotes self-determination, dignity and self-respect" (anthropologist Adam Koons, personal communication). Moreover, the newly labeled product was viewed as home-grown rather than imposed by some global organization. After 12 months, production was turned over to the private sector. *Klorin* was produced by a locally owned Kenyan firm and sold in shops, at kiosks, and at fairs. The labeling contains pictographic instructions, locally designed for maximum comprehension. The project was presented in the 2001 Global Health Conference and was identified by CDC as a "best practice." All of the CARE projects in western Kenya were eventually given *local names* to promote and reinforce immediate ownership and comprehension.

Marketing a water treatment product in Kenya required the use of language that enabled local residents to view the product as home grown rather than imposed by foreign organizations.

agenda item indefinitely. And imagine the look on the American businessman's face when his female British counterpart asks him for a "rubber" (an eraser) or invites him to "knock her up" (stop by her house).

LINGUISTIC DIVERSITY

What do we mean by language? A *language* (a universal found in all cultures of the world) is a symbolic code of communication consisting of a set of sounds (phonemes) with understood meanings and a set of rules (grammar) for constructing messages. The meanings attached to any word by a language are totally arbitrary. For example, the word *cat* has no connection whatsoever to that animal the English language refers to as cat. The word *cat* does not look like a cat, sound like a cat, or have any particular physical connection to a cat. Somewhere during the development of the English language, someone decided that the word *cat* would refer to that particular type of four-legged animal, whereas other languages symbolized the exact same animal by using totally different words. Language, then, consists of a series of *arbitrary* symbols with meanings that, like other aspects of culture, must be learned and that, when put together according to certain grammatical rules, can convey complex messages.

Since languages are arbitrary symbolic systems, it is not surprising that there is enormous linguistic diversity on the face of Earth. While there is no universal agreement about the exact number of languages in the world, most linguists would estimate it to be about 5,500. It is generally recognized that there are about 750 languages spoken in sub-Saharan Africa, more than 150 on the subcontinent of India, and approximately 700 in the single country of Indonesia. However, these estimates should be kept in their proper perspective. As Kenneth Katzner has suggested,

> A single statistic tells a great deal: Of the several thousand languages of the world, fewer than 100 are spoken by over 95 percent of the earth's population. One language, Chinese, accounts for 20 percent all by itself, and if we add English, Spanish, Russian, and Hindi, the figure rises to about 45 percent. German, Japanese, Arabic, Bengali, Portuguese, French and Italian bring the figure to 60 percent....When we realize that the last five percent speak thousands of different languages, it is clear that the great majority of these languages are spoken by tiny numbers of people... (1975: viii–ix)

A major difficulty of trying to determine the exact number of languages in the world is that linguists don't always agree as to where to draw the boundaries between linguistic groups. Mutual unintelligibility is frequently used as the criterion for distinguishing between language groups. If people can understand one another, they speak the same language; if they can't, they don't. Yet, as is all too obvious, this criterion is hardly ironclad because there are varying degrees of intelligibility. Despite the fact that we cannot determine with absolute certainty the precise number of languages in the world today, the fact remains that the variety of

TABLE 4.1 Major Languages of the World

Language	Primary Country	Number of Speakers
Chinese	China	1,213,000,000
Spanish	Spain/South America	329,000,000
English	United Kingdom/ United States	328,000,000
Arabic	Worldwide	221,000,000
Hindi	India	182,000,000
Bengali	Bangladesh	181,000,000
Portuguese	Portugal/Brazil	178,000,000
Russian	Russia	144,000,000
Japanese	Japan	122,000,000
German	Germany	90,000,000

Source: The World Almanac and Book of Facts 2010 (New York, NY: World Almanac Education Group, 2010, p. 721).

languages throughout the world is vast (see Table 4.1). And despite the claims by some U.S. businesspeople that English is widely used in international business, this enormous linguistic diversity in the world must be of concern to any businessperson attempting to compete in an increasingly interdependent marketplace.

Many people from developed countries tend to divide the great variety of cultures found in the world today into two categories: advanced civilizations like their own and so-called primitive cultures that are frequently based on small-scale agriculture or hunting-gathering and have simple systems of technology. In keeping with this bipolar thinking, it is popularly held that technologically-simple societies have equally uncomplex or unsophisticated languages. In other words, we frequently think that "primitive people" have "primitive languages." Yet anthropological linguists tell us that this is not the case, for technologically simple people are no less capable of expressing a wide variety of abstract ideas than are people with high levels of technology.

To illustrate this point, consider the Navajo language spoken by Native Americans living in Arizona and New Mexico. When compared with English, the Navajo language is no less efficient in terms of expressing abstract ideas. All we can say is that the two linguistic systems are different. It is true that Navajo does not have certain grammatical distinctions commonly found in English, as anthropologists Ralph L. Beals, Harry Hoijer, and Alan R. Beals have noted:

> The Navajo noun has the same form in both the singular and the plural—there are no plural noun endings (such as the -s of books or the -en of oxen) in Navajo. Similarly, the third-person pronoun of Navajo is singular or plural and nondistinctive in gender: it can be translated he, she, it, or they, depending on the context. Finally, we find no adjectives in Navajo. The function performed by the English adjective is in Navajo performed by the verb. (1977: 513)

Yet, in another area of structure, the Navajo language is considerably more precise than English. As Peter Farb reminds us, it is impossible for a Navajo speaker simply to say, "I am going" (1968: 56). Rather, considerably more information will be built into the verb form. For example, the verb stem would indicate whether the person is going on foot or by horseback, wagon, boat, or airplane. If the Navajo speaker is, in fact, going on horseback, she or he then must choose another verb form that will specify if the horse will walk, trot, gallop, or run. Moreover, the verb form chosen will also indicate if the speaker is "preparing to go," "going now," "almost at one's destination," or a number of other options. To be certain, the English speaker can convey the same information, but to do so would require a vast quantity of words. The Navajo language can provide an enormous amount of information by the proper use of a single verb form.

The central point is this: Despite the fact that the Navajo and English languages are very different, we can hardly conclude that one is any more efficient than the other at expressing a wide variety of abstract ideas. All cultural groups have symbolic systems that are, by and large, equally efficient at sending and receiving verbal messages. Such an understanding on the part of the international businessperson should serve as an important reminder that English is not inherently superior to the language of those with whom one is doing business and whose language one is learning.

LANGUAGE AND CULTURE

A fundamental tenet of anthropological linguistics is that there is a close relationship between language and culture. It is generally held that it is impossible to understand a culture without taking into account its language; and it is equally impossible to understand a language outside of its cultural context. Yet, despite the close connection between language and culture, we should not think of the relationship as being complete or absolute. Some societies share common cultural traditions but speak mutually unintelligible languages. On the other hand, societies with quite different cultures may speak mutually intelligible languages. Nevertheless, culture influences language and language influences culture in a number of ways.

The Influence of Culture on Language

Perhaps the most obvious relationship between language and culture is seen in vocabulary. The vocabularies of all languages are elaborated in the direction of what is considered adaptively important in that culture. In industrialized societies, the vocabularies contain large numbers of words that reflect complex technologies and occupational specialization. The average speaker of standard American English knows hundreds of technological terms, such as *carburetor*, *microchip*, and *bulldozer*, as well as a myriad of terms designating occupational specialties, such as *accountant*, *philosopher*, *teacher*, *clerk*, and *thoracic surgeon*, because technology and professions are focal concerns in U.S. culture. Thus, standard American

English enables Americans to adapt most effectively to their environment by providing a conceptual lexicon most suited to U.S. culture.

It is equally true for nonindustrialized societies that those aspects of environment and culture that are of special importance will be reflected in the vocabulary. The Koga of southern India have seven different words for *bamboo*, an important natural resource in their tropical environment, yet have not a single word for *snow* (Plog and Bates 1980: 209). The pastoral Nuer of the Sudan, whose everyday lives revolve around their cattle, have words in their language that enable them to distinguish between hundreds of types of cows, based on color, markings, and configuration of horns. This elaborate vocabulary is an indication of the central economic and social role that cattle play in their society (Hickerson 2000: 157–58). The Inuit complex classification of types of snow is a classic example of the close connection between language and culture. Whereas the typical New Yorker has a single word for *snow*, the Inuit have a large number of words, each designating a different type of snow, such as drifting snow, softly falling snow, and so on. Even though the New Yorker can express the same ideas with a number of modifiers, the Inuit view snow as categorically different substances because their very survival requires a precise knowledge of snow conditions. Whether we are looking at the Koga, the Nuer, or the Inuit language, the point remains the same: In all languages, points of cultural emphasis are directly reflected in the size and specialization of the vocabularies. In other words, a language will contain a greater number of terms, more synonyms, and finer distinctions when referring to features of cultural emphasis.

Although it is frequently more difficult to find points of cultural emphasis in large, highly differentiated societies, one area of cultural emphasis in the United States is sports. To illustrate, Nancy Hickerson (2000: 165) reminds us that standard American English contains a number of colloquialisms that stem from the popular sport of baseball:

1. He made a grandstand play.
2. She threw me a curve.
3. She fielded my questions well.
4. You're way off base.
5. You're batting 1,000 (500, zero) so far.
6. What are the ground rules?
7. I want to touch all the bases.
8. He went to bat for me.
9. He has two strikes against him.
10. That's way out in left field.
11. He drives me up the wall.
12. She's an oddball (screwball, foul ball).
13. It's just a ballpark estimate.

These baseball expressions routinely appear in American commerce—in business meetings, commercial interactions, and even in marketing and advertising. Often the importance of "winning the game" is emphasized, where "the game" may refer to meeting sales targets, improving product quality, or enhancing customer satisfaction.

In some parts of the world the influence of culture on language is a very deliberate political process. In France, the *Académie française*, created by Cardinal Richelieu in 1635, has served as a form of "language police," protecting the French people from having to accept foreign words into their language. The Internet revolution of the 1990s has spawned a number of words from English that have been incorporated directly into many world languages. For example, nouns like the "Web," "spam," and "virus" and verbs like "surf," "chat," and "boot" have been adopted in their original English form by many language communities. But this is not so much the case with the French. The recommended word for the World Wide Web is not *le Web* or *le Net* but rather *la Toile* (the spider's web). The French prefer to use the term *pirate informatique* (literally, IT pirate) rather than the English word "hacker" for someone who breaks into computer systems illegally. For many terms and phrases, the cognates of English words are recognizable such as *un message texte* or *un texto* (text message), *les medias sociaux* (social media), *les applications* (apps), and *virtuel* (virtual). However, sometimes the recommended French translation does not gain traction. The Académie française chose the word *courriel* for the English word "e-mail" but *un mail* or *un message électronique* are typically used. Nevertheless, the Académie française tries to fulfill its mission of protecting the French language and helping it to evolve in ways that help it retain its distinctive French character.

The Influence of Language on Culture

We have just seen how languages tend to reflect cultural emphases. On the other side of the linguistic coin, however, some linguists have posited that language may actually influence certain aspects of culture. Language, they suggest, establishes the categories on which our perceptions of the world are organized. According to this theory, language is more than a system of communication enabling people to send and receive messages with relative ease. Language also establishes categories in our minds that force us to distinguish those things we consider similar from those things we consider different. And because every language is unique, the linguistic categories of one language will never be identical to the categories of any other. Consequently, speakers of any two languages will not perceive reality in exactly the same way. Edward Sapir was one of the first linguists to explain how language tends to influence our perceptions:

> The fact of the matter is that the real world is to a large extent unconsciously built up on the language habits of the group. No two languages are ever sufficiently similar to be considered as representing the same social reality. The worlds in which different societies live are distinct worlds, not merely the same world with different labels attached. (1929: 214)

Along with the amateur linguist Benjamin Lee Whorf, Sapir developed what has been referred to as the *Sapir–Whorf hypothesis*. This hypothesis, dealing with the relationship between language and perception, states that language is not merely a mechanism for communicating ideas but is the shaper of ideas. While there is no consensus among scholars concerning the exact nature of the relationship between language and perception, most cultural linguists agree that people from different cultural groups do not see the world in exactly the same way. For example, Lera Boroditsky (2009) has demonstrated how even frivolous aspects of language, like grammatical gender, can have significant effects on perception. In many languages, such as the romance languages, nouns are classified as either masculine or feminine, which means that nouns belonging to different genders are treated differently. In French, for example, speakers must use the proper gender-related pronouns and adjectives depending on the gender of the noun. To illustrate, in a language that designates the word "sofa" as masculine, to say "My sofa is old" requires that the words "my," and "old" be used in their masculine form so as to agree with the masculine noun "sofa." In French one would say, *Mon canapé est vieux*. If referring to a "table" or an "aunt" (which are both feminine nouns), the pronoun and adjective would need to have feminine endings. Under certain circumstances, verb endings also must agree with gender. The contrast between "He arrived" vs. "She arrived" makes this point: *Il est arrivé* compared with *Elle est arrivée*.

Boroditsky asked the question: Does treating words as either masculine or feminine make speakers think of sofas and uncles as masculine (having the traits of males) and tables and aunts as feminine (having the traits of females)? In one of many studies Boroditsky asked German and Spanish speakers to describe the characteristics of objects having opposite gender assignments. To illustrate, she asked them to describe a "key," the word for which is masculine in German and feminine in Spanish. In describing a key, German speakers used such words "heavy," "hard," "jagged," "metal," and "serrated," while Spanish speakers used such words as "lovely," "intricate," "golden," "little," "shiny," and "tiny." And, when asked to describe an expansion bridge, which is feminine in German and masculine in Spanish, German speakers used such descriptors as "beautiful," "elegant," "fragile," "pretty," and "slender," while Spanish speakers used such words as "big," "strong," "dangerous," "sturdy," and "towering." Boroditsky concluded by saying that "apparently even small flukes of grammar, like the seemingly arbitrary assignment of gender to a noun, can have an effect on people's ideas of concrete objects in the world" (2009).

The implications of the Sapir–Whorf hypothesis for the international businessperson are obvious. The hypothesis states that linguistically different people not only communicate differently but also think and perceive the world differently. Thus, by learning the local language, the international businessperson will acquire a vehicle of communication as well as a better understanding of why people think and behave as they do.

Language Mirrors Values

Besides reflecting its worldview, a language also reveals a culture's basic value structure. For example, the extent to which a culture values the individual, as compared to the group, is often reflected in its language or linguistic style. The value placed

Owing to the different, and seemingly arbitrary, assignment of gender to nouns in the German and Spanish languages, German speakers would describe this expansion bridge as "beautiful," "elegant," "fragile," and "slender," while Spanish speakers would use such words as "strong," "dangerous," "sturdy," and "towering."

on the individual is deeply rooted in the American psyche. Most Americans start from the cultural assumption that the individual is supreme and not only can but should shape his or her own destiny. That individualism is highly valued in the United States can be seen throughout its culture, from the love of the automobile as the preferred mode of transportation to a judicial system that fiercely protects the individual rights of the accused. Even when dealing with children, Americans try to provide them with a bedroom of their own, respect their individual right to privacy, and attempt to instill in them a sense of self-reliance and independence by encouraging them to solve their own problems. In business settings, individuals (rather than teams) are rewarded for their specific contributions to a project. Individuals are expected to be entrepreneurial and independently minded. Individuals build their own careers, often changing jobs frequently as they climb the career ladder. (For a more thorough discussion of this basic value difference, see Chapter 2.)

Owing to the close interrelatedness of language and culture, values (such as individualism in the United States) are reflected in standard American English. One such indicator of how our language reflects individualism is the number of words found in any American English dictionary that are compounded with the word *self*. To illustrate, one is likely to find in any standard English dictionary no fewer than 150 such words, including *self-absorbed*, *self-appointed*, *self-centered*, *self-confident*, and *self-supporting*. The list of English terms related to the individual is significantly larger than one found in a culture that places greater emphasis on corporate or group relationships.

In the United States, individual happiness is the highest good. In such group-oriented cultures as Japan, people strive for the good of the larger group such as the family, the community, or the whole society. Rather than stressing individual happiness, the Japanese are more concerned with justice (for group members) and righteousness (by group members). In Japan the "we" always comes before the "I" whereas in the American workplace, people have to be reminded that "There is no 'I' in 'TEAM.'" As John Condon states, "If Descartes had been Japanese, he would have said, 'We think, therefore we are' " (1984: 9).

An important structural distinction found in Japanese society is between *uchi* (the in-group) and *soto* (the out-group), or the difference between "us" and "them." This basic social distinction is reflected in the Japanese language. For example, whether a person is "one of us" or "one of them" will determine which conversational greeting will be used, either *Ohayo gozaimasu*, which is customarily used with close members of one's in-group, or *Konnichiwa*, which is more routinely used to greet those outside one's inner circle. O. Mizutani (1979) conducted an interesting experiment outside the Imperial Palace in Tokyo, which is a favorite place for jogging. Dressed like a jogger, he greeted everyone he passed, both other joggers like himself and nonjoggers, and noted their responses. Interestingly, 95 percent of the joggers greeted him with *Ohayo gozaimasu* (the term reserved for in-group members), whereas only 42 percent of the nonjoggers used such a phrase. He concluded that the joggers, to a much greater degree than the nonjoggers, considered him to be an in-group member because he, too, was a jogger.

Group members in Japan don't want to stand out or assert their individuality because, according to the Japanese proverb, "The nail that sticks up gets hammered down." In Japan the emphasis is on "fitting in," harmonizing, and avoiding open disagreement within the group. People in the United States express their individualism in exactly the opposite way by citing their proverb "The squeaky wheel gets the grease." If Japanese must disagree, it is usually done gently and very indirectly by using such passive expressions as "It is said that..." or "Some people think that..." This type of linguistic construction enables one to express an opinion without having to be individually responsible for it in the event that others in the group might disagree.

How language is used in Japan and the United States both reflects and reinforces the value of group consciousness in Japan and individualism in the United States. The goal of communication in Japan is to achieve consensus and promote harmony, whereas in the United States it is to demonstrate one's eloquence. Whereas language in Japan tends to be cooperative, polite, and conciliatory, language in the United States is often competitive, adversarial, confrontational, and aimed at making a point. The Japanese go to considerable length to avoid controversial issues that might be disruptive; Americans seem to thrive on controversy, debate, argumentation, and provocation, as is evidenced by the use of the expression "just for the sake of argument." Moreover, the Japanese play down individual eloquence in favor of being good listeners, a vital skill if group consensus is to be achieved. Americans are not particularly effective listeners because they are too busy mentally preparing their personal responses rather than paying close attention to what is being said. Thus, all these linguistic contrasts between Japan and the United States express their fundamentally different approaches to the cultural values of "groupness" and individualism.

LINGUISTIC STYLE

Not only do the thousands of world languages have different structures (grammar, vocabulary, and syntax), but they also have different *linguistic styles*. For example, cultures vary in terms of how explicitly they send and receive verbal messages. In the United States, effective verbal communication is expected to be explicit, direct, and unambiguous. Good communicators are supposed to say what they mean as precisely and straightforwardly as possible. North Americans like to "tell it like it is," "get down to brass tacks," "lay their cards on the table," and avoid "beating around the bush." A great emphasis is placed on using words powerfully and accurately, and silences, even short ones, are anxiety-producing. Communication patterns in some other cultures are considerably more ambiguous, inexact, and implicit. In some Eastern cultures, such as Japan or China, where there is less emphasis on words, people tend to derive more meanings from nonverbal cues and the general social context. It is not that words are unimportant in Eastern cultures, but rather that the words are inseparably interrelated to social relationships, politics, and morality. Given this more holistic approach to communication, its purpose in many Eastern cultures is not to enhance the speaker's individuality through the articulation of words but rather to promote harmony and social integration. In such societies one is expected to be sensitive to subtle contextual cues and to not assume that critical information will always be verbalized.

This cautious approach can be seen in the general suppression of negative verbal messages. As a result, politeness and the desire to avoid embarrassment often take precedence over the truth. This approach, at least in part, explains why Eastern cultures have so many nonverbal ways of saying "no" without directly or unambiguously uttering the word. Needless to say, this practice has caused considerable misunderstanding when North Americans try to communicate with the Japanese. To illustrate, the Japanese in everyday conversation frequently use the word *hai* (yes) not necessarily to convey agreement, but rather that they understand what is being said.

When negotiating with Asians, it is important to understand that "yes" is not always an affirmative response. Before taking "yes" for an answer, one must ascertain if in fact it was merely a polite response that really meant "no."

Japanese people tend to be much less direct in their discourse than North Americans.

Asian businesspersons, for example, are not likely to say "no" directly to a proposal but rather will reply in ways that are synonymous with "no." To illustrate, Engholm (1991: 115–16) suggests a number of ways that Asians say "no" without coming right out and saying it. In response to a Westerner's question: "Has my proposal been accepted?" an Asian businessperson is likely to reply in a number of different ways:

> **The conditional "yes":** "If everything proceeds as planned, the proposal will be approved."
> **The counter-question:** "Have you submitted a copy of your proposal to the Ministry of Electronics?"
> **The question is criticized:** "Your question is difficult to answer."
> **The question is refused:** "We cannot answer this question at this time."
> **The tangential reply:** "Will you be staying longer than you originally planned?"
> **The "yes, but ... " reply:** "Yes, approval looks likely, but...." The meaning of "but" could mean "it might not be approved."
> **The answer is delayed:** "You will know shortly."

Direct and indirect styles of communications often lead to misunderstandings and miscommunications. Many North Americans view a person who is being indirect as tricky, deceptive, and of questionable integrity. At best, Westerners consider indirect communication to be a waste of their time. On the other hand, those from implicit cultures see the explicit communication styles of North Americans to be rude, course, and insensitive. The longer one is an active participant in a high-context culture where directness is not a salient trait, the better one will be able to assess particular reactions. However, for those who have limited familiarity or experience with such situations, anthropologist Cathleen Crain has developed some useful coping strategies to deal with potential instances of "misperceived" agreement. To launch an initiative in South East Asia, Crain commented, "We expect people won't agree until they say, 'Here are the next steps.' If we are unclear, we will ask, 'Is it time to consider next steps?' If they say, 'Yes, and I need to talk with others,' then they are not ready. If they say, 'Yes, we can plan now,' then they are ready to commit." It is important to listen and observe such business interactions carefully to pick up clues of agreement and disagreement. One also can seek the counsel of a trusted local about the readiness of the individual or group to make a decision.

In these same high-context societies that rely on relatively indirect messages, it is not unusual to leave sentences unfinished or to tolerate intermittent periods of silence. Whereas most Westerners try to make their point as quickly and straightforwardly as possible, many Eastern cultures value silence as a major element of their rhetorical styles. Silence allows Japanese communicators, for example, to gain a better feel for their partners, and for this reason, they are not reluctant to let long silences develop during negotiations or business meetings. These silences, unfortunately, are frequently misunderstood by Westerners; they tend to assume a lack of understanding, and therefore interrupt the silence by reiterating their point once, or by moving on to a new agenda item.

In certain Asian societies, which rely on rhetorical ambiguity, successful communication depends on sensitivity to the nonverbal context. Other speech communities, such as certain Arabic cultures, are equally imprecise, but for exactly the opposite reason. These societies engage in overassertion, exaggeration, and repetition. In many Arabic-speaking cultures, certain common ending words are meant to be emphasized; frequently certain pronouns will be repeated to dramatize the message fully; highly graphic metaphors and similes are common; and it is not unusual to hear an Arabic speaker use a long list of adjectives to modify a single noun for the sake of emphasizing the point.

When Arabs and North Americans are compared on a continuum of understatement and overstatement, Arabs are considerably more likely to overstate the case than are North Americans. What would be an assertive statement to a North American might appear to be weak and equivocating to an Arab. Even though verbal threats are commonplace in the Arabic language, they tend to function more as a psychological catharsis than as an accurate description of the speaker's real intentions. It should be kept in mind that this rhetorical feature of linguistic overassertion is just another form of verbal ambiguity or inexactness because it fails to send direct, precise messages.

CULTURAL STUFFINESS?

Languages also vary in terms of the level of formality and verbosity required in certain communication situations. For example, the French businessperson uses a highly convoluted closing when writing a business letter. Whereas the American will routinely use the single word "sincerely," the Frenchman is likely to close with such statements as "We beg you to receive, Sir, the expressions of our devoted sentiments," or equally wordy, "I beg you to accept, Gentlemen, with my anticipated thanks, the expression of my distinguished sentiments" (Keegan and Green 1997: 95).

In addition to the level of explicitness, another aspect of linguistic style deals with turn-taking between speakers. As Engholm and Rowland remind us, these differences in timing can cause problems:

> Brazilians frequently have two people talking at once in a conversation, with almost no pauses. Americans sometimes have brief pauses between speakers and sometimes have a little overlay of speakers. If you are speaking with people from a culture that has many verbal overlays, such as the Brazilians, you may have to be more assertive if you want to participate in the conversation. If you are speaking with people from a culture with more verbal pauses, you may have to learn to pause more often to make sure others get a chance to speak. When talking with a Japanese, it is typical for Americans to wait just long enough to become uncomfortable and then begin speaking again. The Japanese person, however, has remained silent to show respect for the speaker or the comment, and by the time he feels it is appropriate to say something, the American is already speaking again. The result is that we end up monopolizing conversations. (1996: 81–82)

Another culturally-variable dimension of linguistic style involves the very *quantity* of messages sent and received. To illustrate, using Condor tracking software, the Visteon Corporation, a global automotive supplier, noticed that e-mail communication to and from France was five times greater than the other 26 countries with which it conducted business. According to anthropologist Julia Gluesing, "It did not matter what the part was—a heater, radiator, hose—the team servicing France was communicating a lot more, so the structure of their network was different." Gluesing spent time educating the global sales manager about French national culture, communication patterns, and linguistic style. The global manager also spent time in France learning about French culture and language. In the end, the global manager understood that "A part is not a part; it comes with a communication relationship" (Julia Gluesing, personal communication).

The global manager's team had to engage in much more communication with the French, compared with the Americans. The expectations for communication content and communication frequency were different. Julia Gluesing continued,

"You have to be customer-focused and understand the communication patterns when working virtually." This culture-specific communication pattern with the French had gone unnoticed until it was made explicit through Condor's social-network visualizations. As a result, the global manager had a new insight about how to redistribute the work load of her team. The time and effort required for appropriate interactions between her team and the French customers would now be taken into account.

Differences in linguistic style frequently can be observed in the same speech community between men and women. For example, lack of social power and even submissiveness can be observed in female speech patterns in the United States and a number of other places in the world. According to Robin Lakoff (1975, 2004), Julia Wood (1994), Deborah Tannen (1990), and Chevis Kramer (1974), women in the United States speak less forcefully than men, as evidenced by their more frequent use of qualifiers ("It may just be my opinion, but...") or the practice of following a declarative statement with a question (such as "Isn't it?" or "Wouldn't you agree?"). In some cases, women in the United States end their sentences with a rising intonation, suggestive of a question. In all three of these situations, women are perceived as not speaking with authority because these stylistic features implicitly seek confirmation of their ideas.

These, then, are just some of the differences in linguistic style found throughout the world. A thorough discussion of all of the dimensions of linguistic style would be beyond the scope of this book. But we can appreciate some of the more important aspects of the topic by contrasting the linguistic styles of two very different languages, English and Japanese (see Table 4.2).

TABLE 4.2 Communication Styles: Differences between English and Japanese

Japanese	English
1. Emphasizes "we" (group)	1. Emphasizes "I" (individual)
2. Formal	2. Informal
3. Importance of rank	3. Emphasizes equality
4. Group consensus	4. Individual opinion
5. Cooperative	5. Competitive
Compromise	Adversarial
Conciliation	Win
6. Polite	6. Argumentative
7. Avoid Controversy	7. Express controversial issues
8. Unemotional	8. Emotional
9. Indirect	9. Direct
10. Patience	10. Impatience

(continued)

TABLE 4.2   *(Continued)*

Japanese	English
11. Suspicious of words	11. Emphasizes words
12. Tolerates silence	12. Abhors silence
13. High context	13. Low context
14. Better at listening	14. Better at speaking
15. Emphasizes form	15. Emphasizes content
16. Qualified statements	16. Positive, assertive statements
17. Prefers a set agenda	17. Prefers free-form discussion
18. Controlled nonverbal cues	18. Exaggerated nonverbal cues
19. Lower decibel level	19. Higher decibel level
20. More passive role	20. More assertive role
21. Avoids dominating	21. Likes to dominate
22. Little eye contact	22. Relatively high eye contact
23. Relationship oriented	23. Task oriented
24. Willing to learn English	24. Less willing to learn Japanese
25. Opens with apology/flattery	25. Opens with a joke
26. "Yes" means "I hear you"	26. "Yes" means "I agree"
27. Don't like public praise	27. Like public praise
28. Long pauses between speakers	28. Little or no pause between speakers
29. Emphasis on business cards	29. No great emphasis on business cards
30. Slower pace of speech	30. Faster pace of speech

Source: This list of differences draws heavily upon Alan Goldman, *For Japanese Only: Intercultural Communication with Americans* (Tokyo: The Times of Japan, 1988).

LANGUAGE AND SOCIAL CONTEXT

The understanding of linguistic differences in international business can be further complicated by the fact that people frequently speak several different languages or different forms of the same language, *depending on the social situation*. Bilingualism (or multilingualism) is the most obvious form of situational language use, for a person may speak one language at home, another language at work, and still another language in the marketplace. But people who speak only one language also switch styles of language. For example, the expressions college students use when speaking to one another in the dormitory are noticeably different than the forms of expression they use when they are conversing with their ministers, grandparents, or professors. Levels of formality between speakers, relative status, and gender and age of the speakers can frequently determine what is said and how it is said.

The form of the English language used by these teenagers from the United States with their minister is quite different from the form they use with their close friends.

Depending on who is addressing him, a man could be referred to as "Dr. Allen," "Richard," "Dick," "Sir," "Sweetheart," "Doc," or "fella," among others. It is not likely that his wife or mother would address him as "Dr. Allen," nor is it likely that the nurses at the hospital would refer to him as "Dick" or "fella." Moreover, the same person may use different terms of address in different social situations. His wife may address him as "Dick" at the dinner table, "Sweetheart" while making love, and "Richard" if they are engaged in an argument.

People in the United States are addressed by either (FN) first name (Richard) or by (TLN) title and last name (Dr. Allen), depending on the level of formality and relative social status between the speakers. In the American English context, there are only three possible combinations of address between two people: (1) reciprocal use of TLN, as in the exchange "Hello, Professor Davis" and "Good evening, Mrs. Bolton," (2) reciprocal use of FN, as in the exchange "What's happening, Jack?" and "Not much, Norm," and (3) nonreciprocal use of TLN and FN, as in the exchange "Good morning, Dr. Graves" and "Hello, Ricky." The first two exchanges—both reciprocal—imply relatively equal status between the speakers. The first situation indicates a formal, non-intimate relationship, whereas the second situation indicates an informal, more intimate relationship. Unlike the first two cases, the third case (TLN/FN) is indicative of marked status inequality, either differences in age (children and adults) or differences in rank within an organization (teacher and student; executive and administrative assistant; surgeon and nurse).

SILENCE CAN BE GOLDEN

Social context is an important factor in how people communicate, or even whether they communicate at all. Construction superintendent Justin Clark had just been transferred to Saudi Arabia for two years to supervise the building of new state-of-the-art oil rigs for the Saudi government. Upon moving into their rented house, Justin and his wife Lorna discovered several things that needed repair. The landlord, very happy to have rented the house on a two-year lease, was very prompt in responding to their request for repairs. However, when he arrived, Justin was not home, and the landlord entered the house without speaking or acknowledging Lorna's presence. The repairs proceeded under the landlord's supervision. Lorna was insulted and felt that the landlord's behavior was rude and disrespectful. Since she was the one home at the time, she thought the landlord should have at least greeted her.

Actually, according to Saudi Arabian culture, the landlord was treating Lorna politely and with respect. Because her husband was absent, it would have been considered an invasion of her privacy to speak to Lorna.

In the Javanese language, every speech situation (not just terms of address) requires the speaker to make choices that reflect the relative social status of the person being addressed. Before a word is uttered, the speaker must choose one of three basic linguistic styles: the plain, the fancy, and the elegant. In addition, the Javanese speaker can use special terms known as *honorifics*, which enable the speaker to express minute gradations of social respect within each of these three styles. As Farb has noted, "He has no choice but to inform his listener exactly what he thinks of him—because the style he selects reveals whether he considers the listener worthy of low speech, the middle-ground fancy speech, or elegant speech, with or without honorifics" (1974: 44).

SOME ADDITIONAL COMPLICATING FACTORS

To function effectively in any language community, it is necessary to know not only the formal structure of the language (vocabulary and grammar, for example), but also how it is used in different social situations. We have seen that what is said and how it is said can vary depending on the gender, age, or relative social status of the speakers. To further complicate the learning of another language, most languages, for a variety of cultural reasons, employ certain nonstandard forms such as slang, euphemisms, acronyms, proverbs, verbal dueling, and humor, and all have various conversational taboos.

Slang

Slang is a form of casual or playful language comprised typically of short-lived phrases and figures of speech, which often substitute for more standard terms for the sake of added raciness, humor, or irreverence. This definition should not lead us to conclude that slang is the language of the common people. Instead, slang should be viewed as the speech of those who consider themselves to be part of a particular subgroup within the wider linguistic community. In cities like New York, we are likely to hear such expressions as "recessionista" (a woman who manages to dress stylishly while sticking to a strict budget during hard economic times), "nonversation" (a completely worthless conversation, wherein nothing meaningful is communicated, typically occurring at parties or singles bars), and "Lehman Sisters" (wives and/or girlfriends of recently unemployed Lehman Brothers' executives who bonded to share their collective, unexpected fall off the socioeconomic ladder after Lehman Brothers collapsed in 2008). Jazz musicians, computer buffs, teenagers, prostitutes, psychologists, and truck drivers are just several subgroups within the United States that have their own slang. The importance of slang, whether we are referring to the speech of truck drivers or Princeton undergraduates, is that it helps determine who is a member of an in-group and who is not.

Businesspeople, too, have their own slang, which they use within their own in-groups. Such expressions as "dead in the water" (*inoperative*), "take no prisoners" (*harsh*), "red tape" (*complicated procedures*), and "bottom line" (*net profit*), among many others, are used daily by American businesspeople. These examples of slang present two important problems for the person trying to learn a second language. First, slang increases the possible variations of expressions in any given speech community. Second, since many slang words are used for only several years before disappearing or becoming incorporated into the standard form of the language, keeping up with current slang trends is difficult.

SPEAK PLAINLY

When communicating across cultures, it is best to avoid using jargon, slang, or euphemisms. Terence Brake, Danielle Walker, and Thomas Walker remind us (in a dialogue between an American and his potential business partner from India) that, although they might seem innocuous, these irregular forms of the English language can cause problems:

"I've been reviewing the materials you gave me, Mr. Nehru. You have a real cash cow here. Excellent."

First of all, is Mr. Nehru going to have any idea what a "cash cow" is? And if Mr. Nehru is a Hindu, isn't it possible he might take offense to the use of "cow" in this context? (1995: 174).

Euphemisms

Behavioral and verbal taboos exist in all known societies; that is, certain categories of words should be avoided in normal, polite parlance. In many—but certainly not all—cases, the prohibited words are associated with sexual relations and everyday bodily functions such as menstruating, urinating, and defecating. Whatever words may be deemed to be taboo by a language, it is a fairly arbitrary process, for a word prohibited in one speech community may be perfectly acceptable in another. Taboo words are dealt with through the use of *euphemisms*—that is, by substituting a bland, vague, or indirect expression for one thought to be too direct, harsh, or blunt. In the English language, for example, the subject of death is so unpleasant that we have developed an entire system of euphemisms to avoid dealing with the subject in a direct way. People don't die, they "pass away." Those in charge of burials are no longer undertakers but are now "funeral directors." Corpses are not buried in graves, but rather the "dearly departed" are "interred" in "memorial parks." Hearses, which clearly are single-purpose vehicles, are now euphemistically called "coaches."

The 21st century has ushered in a whole new collection of euphemisms. For example, because Iraq was in "material breach" of United Nations' resolutions on disclosing "weapons of mass destruction," the United States government engaged in a "pre-emptive strike" to bring about "regime change" with "minimal collateral damage" for the sake of enhancing "homeland security." And, when the occupation of Iraq failed to keep control of certain Iraqi cities, the world witnessed the "re-Bathification of Falluja," a clever euphemism for handing the city back to the very people the war was designed to replace.

Even though the English language has more than its share of euphemisms, this practice of substituting vague words for more precise ones can be found to some degree in all languages. Again, the existence of taboo words and euphemisms presents yet another obstacle to second-language learning for the international businessperson. The learner must become familiar with the prevailing value system of the particular speech community to understand which topics can be dealt with in a direct and straightforward manner. Without such an understanding, knowing when to use a bland expression and when not would be impossible.

Verbal Dueling

In certain speech communities and under specified conditions, people are encouraged to engage in *verbal dueling* (competitive communication), in which the speakers are more concerned with asserting their dominance than with imparting information. One particularly well-documented example of verbal dueling from our own society is an institutionalized form of an insult contest played by urban black adolescent males—"playing the dozens." This form of verbal dueling begins when one player insults a member of the opponent's family, in most cases his mother. Although the person whose family member has been disparaged can choose not to play, in most cases he will retort with a counter-insult of his own. These insulting verbal thrusts and parries will continue until the participants get bored or someone emerges victorious, with both participants being incited by an attentive audience.

In some cases verbal dueling can be carried out at a national level. According to Ehud Ya'ari and Ira Friedman (1991), all three of the major players in the 1991 Gulf War (Iraq, Kuwait, and Saudi Arabia) used an archaic rhetorical art form to exchange insults over the airwaves. This traditional form of verbal dueling, known as *hija*, dates back to biblical times; warriors (such as Goliath) would loudly ridicule their opponents while boasting of their own prowess. This ancient literary tradition of "cursing in verse" was based on the notion that one could gain a supernatural advantage by insulting one's adversaries in rhyme. The *hija* form of verbal dueling—which has its own format, meters, and rhyming patterns—begins with boastful self-praise and then proceeds to vitriolic insults. Immediately after the Iraqi invasion of Kuwait in August 1990, the Saudi, Iraqi, and Kuwaiti television stations broadcast hours of uninterrupted *hija* poetry, praising themselves while berating the opposition. The content of the dueling poets was scathing. To illustrate, because the allied forces included some women, the Iraqi *hija* poets ridiculed the Saudis for hiding behind the skirts of women, a direct and unequivocal insult to their virility. On the other side, Saudi *hija* poets composed brutal verses that accused Saddam Hussein of attacking his neighbors at night, of being ungrateful for the help given him in his earlier efforts against the Iranians, and, the ultimate insult, of being a Jew.

Both of these forms of verbal dueling—whether they are found in a Philadelphia ghetto or the Persian Gulf—are examples of nonstandard forms of language use that must be understood if the second-language learner is to appreciate fully the subtleties of the communication patterns in the global marketplace.

Humor

Humor is another aspect of language that tends to confuse the new-language learner. No known cultures lack humor, but what is perceived as being funny varies enormously from one culture to another. In some cultures, like the British and American, humor is used in business meetings, and business presentations often start with a humorous anecdote. In other cultures, however, business is considered no joking matter. It is not unusual at international business conferences, particularly in Asia, to hear the interpreter say, "The American is now telling a joke. When he finishes, the polite thing to do is to laugh." Often jokes are told in an international business context when, in fact, it is inappropriate to use humor in such situations. But, even if humor is appropriate, the meaning of the joke or humorous story is frequently lost because it doesn't translate well from one culture to another.

Humor does not often translate well from one culture to another.

Jokes are difficult to understand because they contain a good deal of information about the culture of the joke teller. To "get" the joke, the listener must understand these pieces of cultural information and how they are combined to make something funny. The long-standing joke in the United States about lawyers is a case in point. "Why do lawyers not have to worry about sharks when they vacation at the beach?" The answer: "Professional courtesy." To appreciate the humor, the listener would have to know several pieces of cultural information about the United States: (1) Sharks have been known to attack Americans while swimming; (2) lawyers in the United States have the reputation of preying on people; and (3) members of some professions in the United States give special considerations to other members of their profession. Assuming that the listener does understand these culture-specific pieces of information, he or she still needs to appreciate the idea that humor is found in ridiculing an entire profession of people. Asians, however, with their strong traditions of Buddhism and Confucianism, place a high value on politeness and face-saving for others and would find little to laugh about in this type of sarcasm or parody.

HUMOR DOES NOT TRANSLATE WELL

Looking for a distributor of its products in Germany, a large Baltimore hardware manufacturer was invited to present a demonstration of its product line to a reputable distributor in Frankfurt. Wanting to make the best possible impression, the company sent its most promising young executive, Fred Wagner, who spoke fluent German. When Fred first met his German hosts, he shook hands firmly, greeted everyone with a friendly *Guten Tag,* and even remembered to bow the head slightly as is the German custom. Fred, a very effective public speaker, prefaced his presentation with a few humorous anecdotes to set a relaxed and receptive atmosphere. However, he felt that his presentation was not very well received by the German executives. In fact, his instincts were correct; the German company chose not to distribute Fred's hardware products.

Even though Fred thought he had done his cultural homework, he made one particular tactical error. Fred did not win any points by trying to set an informal, relaxed atmosphere by telling a few jokes. Although this may be an acceptable approach for an after-lunch speech at the Baltimore Rotary Club, it was viewed as quite inappropriate in a German business setting, because it was too informal and unprofessional.

Conversational Taboos

Communicating in a business context, whether we are managing, selling, or negotiating, requires a certain amount of small talk before the business at hand actually takes place. All linguistic communities have certain topics of conversation, known as *conversational taboos*, that are considered inappropriate in either polite society or in a business context. When Americans deal with one another for the first time, the small-talk conversation usually starts off with topics that are fairly innocuous, such as the weather, sports, or some noncontroversial aspects of the physical environment. Such topics as religion or politics are usually scrupulously avoided because they are likely to be contentious. Other topics are avoided because they are considered to be too personal and thus off limits, particularly in initial meetings. These include such topics as health, the health of family members, how much one earns, the cost of personal possessions, and personal data such as age, weight, or sexual preference.

Just as with other aspects of culture, what is an appropriate topic of conversation varies from one group to another. Some cultures, such as German and Iranian, do not share our American taboos on discussing politics; in fact, they often think of Americans as being intellectual lightweights for avoiding such topics. In many parts of the world that place a high value on group and family (such as South America), inquiries about the well-being of a family member is considered quite appropriate. People from a number of cultures do not appreciate discussing topics that may be historically embarrassing, such as World

War II for the Germans and Japanese or illegal immigration into the United States for Mexican businesspeople. Because of the enormous cultural variation on taboo topics, the best advice to follow is (1) do your homework beforehand, and (2) take your cue from the other person by allowing him or her to initiate the discussion.

INFORMATION AND COMMUNICATION TECHNOLOGIES IN THE 21ST CENTURY

The revolution in information technology (IT)—which started in the early 1990s—has had profound consequences on the way humans communicate in the 21st century. Most "20-somethings" today often fail to realize how their parents communicated just a generation ago. Back in the "dark ages" of the 1980s, people could send and receive messages by writing letters, speaking either face-to-face or via such technology as the telephone, telegraph, the radio, or television. It was just several decades ago that the Internet and cell phones began to emerge as the communication technologies of choice. When viewed from this narrow time frame, the changes in the number of ways of communicating at our disposal today have revolutionized information delivery and how we produce and consume it. At the same time IT has transformed our social and professional lives. Many IT commentators argue that the new technologies of e-mail, online discussions, networking websites, and high-speed information diffusion will lead to more informed, engaged, and influential global business people. Others, however, contend that the communications revolution may instead spawn a population of impressionable, impersonal, superficial, and easily manipulated people. While the impact of the Internet and cell phone technology on society is still widely debated, one thing is certain: the new 21st century technologies are powerful vehicles for change in the way humans communicate and share information.

Text messaging has had a particularly important impact on the way people are communicating in the 21st century. Because it is less expensive to "text message" than to actually speak on one's cell phone, many messages today lack both intimacy and specific details. Because the typical cell phone screen accommodates only about 160 characters, text messaging encourages blandness, brevity, and superficiality. On the other hand, it does encourage creativity in devising such shorthand symbols as "gr8," "2moro," and "4ever" (for an entire online dictionary of chat acronyms and texting shorthand, see http://www.netlingo.com/acronyms.php). According to MobiThinking, an online research organization that tracks the growth of mobile Web devices, in February 2011 there were 5.3 billion users of mobile devices, or 77 percent of the world's population (http://www.mobithinking.com/). Moreover, 6.1 trillion messages were sent worldwide in 2010, a number which is expected to grow to 10 trillion by 2013. The leader in handheld communication devices is China, whose people send about four times as many text messages as do people living in the United States. This greater popularity in

Texting has become an increasingly common form of communication.

IT'S ALL ABOUT TEXT CHAT

New technologies create new interactions and cultural rules. As a way to enhance TV viewing, social television systems now enable social interaction among TV viewers in different locations. These systems are known to build a greater sense of connectedness among TV-using friends. One field study focused on how five friends between the ages of 30–36 communicated while watching TV at their homes. The technology allowed them to see which of the friends were watching TV and what they were watching. They chose if and how to communicate via social television—whether through voice chat or text chat. Voice chat was initiated through a remote by a friend calling another who was already online; TV speakers conveyed the audio conversations. Text chat was enabled by typing messages using a keyboard, which then appeared on the TV screen for a friend who was online.

The study produced six voice chats and 43 text chats (containing 1,287 text messages), indicating an overwhelming preference for text over voice. Users offered two key reasons for favoring text chat (Huang et al. 2009: 589–90). First, text chat required less effort and attention, and was more enjoyable than voice chat. One study participant reported: "You don't feel like you have to be waiting on the other person's response." Second, study participants viewed text chat as more polite. Another indicated, "I felt with the text I wasn't really obligating them to give me all their attention. If I send them a text, they can look at it and send it back to

(continued)

me at their discretion…with the voice chatting…they have to give you a lot more attention."

Written communication is being adapted for use with new communication technologies. "Text chat is a way of initiating an interaction. It leaves open the possibility of building on the initial message, and thus building the relationship" (anthropologist Crysta Metcalf, personal communication). At the same time, the emerging cultural rules associated with it do not obligate the recipient to respond, respond fully, or respond immediately. The fact that text chat was the favored communication mode over voice chat parallels the popularity of texting over phone usage, particularly among younger age groups. Businesses need to understand these cultural rules, not just the technologies, to communicate effectively in a changing world.

China is due, at least in part, to the nature of the Chinese language. Because in Mandarin Chinese the names of numbers sound very similar to certain words, it is possible to send the message "I love you" by simply typing in the number 520 or "Drop dead" by using 748. Moreover, in China leaving voicemails is considered both rude and humiliating to the sender, whose message must be left with a machine. Using text messages enables both senders and recipients to save face by eliminating the human voice.

In addition to allowing us to communicate quickly, often, and inexpensively with virtually anyone in the world, our 21st century technologies, such as the World Wide Web, have profound implications for the way we define the words in our language. In pre-Internet times, the hard copy dictionary has always served as the final authority for what a word means and how it is used. The authors of dictionaries (lexicographers) traditionally have arrived at their definitions by carefully analyzing as many examples as possible of how a particular word is used. While some complex words found in any standard desk dictionary can have as many as nine or ten possible uses, even these definitions fail to cover all possible usages. According to lexicographer Erin McKean (2009: 16), a recent study showed that in a set of randomly chosen passages from modern fiction, 13 percent of the nouns, verbs, and adjectives were used in ways not found in large desk dictionaries. The major shortcoming of the traditional dictionary is that there is limited space available to give only a sampling of how words are used. There are, in other words, many more contemporary usages that never make it into a standard dictionary because of the limitations of physical space.

The beauty of the Internet, however, is that there are virtually no space limitations. As a result, it is possible for 21st century lexicographers to define words by including every conceivable example of the word's use. These examples could be generated electronically not only from literature, non-fiction writing, and newspapers, but also from websites, blogs, and social networking sites. In fact, this is what the online dictionary called http://www.wordnik.com/ is currently doing—text-mining every available example of how a particular word in used in everyday standard English and then including these examples, along with the definition, on the near infinite space of the www. Such a capability will, no doubt, enable translators to determine the meaning of words more accurately in their translations across languages.

CONCLUSION

It has been estimated that there are some 5,000 mutually unintelligible languages in the world today. Some of them have hundreds of millions of speakers, whereas some have only hundreds. Yet, despite the diversity in the size of different linguistic communities, no languages are inherently more efficient at expressing a wide range of ideas than others. Thus, there is no reason for English-speaking businesspeople to harbor a linguistic superiority complex.

Learning a language requires time, hard work, and dedication on the part of the learner, and a sense of commitment on the part of the employer. Even after one masters the vocabulary, grammar, and syntax of a second language, engaging in verbal miscommunication is still possible, even likely, for several reasons. First, it is frequently impossible to translate some ideas from one language into another without a loss of some meaning. Second, some languages rely more on the explicit spoken word, whereas others rely more on the use of nonverbal cues and communication context. Third, people frequently speak different forms of the same language, depending on the social situation in which the communication takes place. Finally, to further complicate communication, all languages, to some extent, use nonstandard forms such as slang and euphemisms.

Yet, despite the formidable task that learning a second language is for most people, many good reasons justify the effort. Learning a new language or the host language

- Builds rapport and sets the proper tone for engaging in business worldwide.
- Shows interest and goodwill and signals an intent to build relationships in the new cultural environment.
- Can play a major role in adjusting to culture shock because efficient communication can (1) minimize the frustrations, misunderstandings, and aggravations that face the linguistic outsider, and (2) provide a sense of safety, mastery, and self-assurance.
- Facilitates learning other languages.
- Helps you understand your own language(s) better.

In addition to all these cogent reasons, perhaps the best reason for learning a second language is that it enables the learner to get "inside" another culture. Communicating effectively—which is so essential to the conduct of business affairs—involves more than a proficiency in sending and receiving messages. Effective communication requires an understanding of how people think, feel, and behave. In short, it involves knowing something about the cultural values, attitudes, and patterns of behavior, and one of the best ways to gain cultural awareness is through a culture's language.

CROSS-CULTURAL SCENARIOS

Read the following cross-cultural scenarios. In each mini-case study, a basic cultural conflict occurs among the actors involved. Try to identify the source of the conflict and suggest how it could have been avoided or minimized. Then see how well your analyses compare to the explanations in Appendix A.

4-1   Stan Gorelick, an engineer for a Chicago-based international construction company, was working on a two-year building project in Montevideo, Uruguay. After several months on the job, Stan attended a cocktail party reception his firm was hosting for some of the local subcontractors. Upon entering the formal cocktail party about 30 minutes after it started, Stan greeted several groups of people with a cheerful "Hola!" (Hello) and headed for the bar. Soon, Stan noticed that some of the attendees seem to be upset with him.

What did he do wrong?

4-2   While working for a Philadelphia bank in Kuala Lumpur, Malaysia, Claire Roberts met, quite unexpectedly, one of her female colleague at a shopping mall one weekend. The local Malaysian colleague was accompanied by her five-year-old daughter. Claire was so taken by the girl's beauty that she patted the girl on the head while commenting to the mother what a gorgeous child she had. Much to Claire's surprise, however, the mother responded by saying that the girl was not very pretty at all and then abruptly left.

What had Roberts done? She was simply trying to pay the woman's daughter a compliment.

4-3   Wendy Robinson, a vice president for marketing for a California cosmetic company, has been sent by her company to France to select a new sales manager for the Paris area. After sitting through a sales presentation (which included numerous historical and literary references) given by one of the leading candidates, Wendy wondered why this person had been so highly recommended. While trying to concentrate on the candidate's presentation, Wendy questioned whether the candidate was compensating for his lack of technical knowledge by including excessive literary and historical references.

Could there be another explanation?

4-4   Mark Watson, an enthusiastic fast-track executive with a manufacturing company from Minneapolis, was sent to Bangkok to set up a regional sales office. Within several days of arrival, Mark set up a number of appointments to interview perspective employees. Although his interviews with male candidates were reasonably successful, the female candidates were not responding very positively. In fact, the first several female candidates withdrew their applications after the first interview.

What was Mark doing that was turning off the female candidates?

4-5   Lars Jansson, a recent Harvard MBA and one of his organization's most innovative planners, was assigned to the Stockholm office for a two-year period. Lars had been looking forward to the transfer. He had learned some Swedish as a child because his paternal grandparents were from Sweden; he was glad to be getting back to his "roots." Lars was also looking forward to getting to know his Swedish colleagues on a personal level. During the third week there, an opportunity to socialize presented itself after the weekly planning meeting concluded. Anders Pettersson, a person about Lars' age, engaged Lars in conversation. They shook hands and exchanged some pleasantries. Lars asked Anders if he had any children. Anders replied that he has two daughters and a son. Lars asked if he lived in a house or apartment. Anders said that he owned a condo in central Stockholm. Then Lars said, "Wow! I looked for a place there but the condos I saw were really expensive." Anders said nothing and started gathering his things to leave. Lars continued, "Hey, I just read about the fluctuating interest rates. How are you dealing with those?" Anders appeared distant and uncommunicative and said, "Sorry, but I have to go now."

What did Lars do wrong?

5

■ ■ ■

Negotiating across Cultures

In a very general sense, the process of negotiating is absolutely fundamental to human communication and interaction. If we stop to consider it, we are negotiating all the time. We negotiate with our spouses, children, coworkers, friends, bosses, landlords, customers, bankers, neighbors, and clients. Because negotiating is such an integral part of our everyday lives, it becomes largely an unconscious process because we do not spend a lot of time thinking about how we do it. As with so many other aspects of our behavior, the way we negotiate is colored by our cultural assumptions. Whether we are effective negotiators or not, our culturally conditioned negotiating framework, expectations, and styles are largely operating at an unconscious level.

Because the act of negotiating is so central to our lives, we frequently fail to define it. Those who write about the process of negotiation, on the other hand, do define it—sometimes in excruciating detail—but fail to agree on a common definition. But, as Robert Moran and William Stripp (1991: 71–72) remind us, the common theme running through all definitions of *negotiation* is that two or more parties, who have both common and conflicting interests, interact with one another for the purpose of reaching a mutually beneficial agreement. Some scholars have categorized the negotiation process into three phases— pre-negotiation, negotiation, and post-negotiation—in an effort to understand the importance of the context, interactions, and activities as the negotiations evolve (Weiss 1993; Kumar and Worm 2004). Distinctions also have been drawn between the "up front" discussions among negotiating partners as well as the "constant and ongoing negotiation" over the course of a business relationship (Teegen and Doh 2002: 751). In this book, we use the term *negotiating* to refer to the period prior to implementation of some initiative agreed to by the negotiating partners. If negotiations are happening for the first time, the negotiating period is the time when business relationships are formed and decisions are made about whether to work together toward some goal. If the negotiating partners have worked together in the past, relationships will be rekindled during the negotiating period and new projects targeted for attention.

When negotiating within our own culture, it is possible to operate effectively at the intuitive or unconscious level. However, when we leave our familiar cultural context and enter into negotiations with those from other cultures, the scene changes dramatically and different challenges appear. There may not be the same shared values, interests, goals, ethical principles, or cultural assumptions between the negotiating parties. As we demonstrated in previous chapters, different cultures have different values, attitudes, morals, behaviors, and linguistic styles, all of which can greatly affect the process and outcome of our negotiations. An ever-increasing body of literature has developed documenting the differences in cross-cultural negotiating styles (see, e.g., Lewicki, Weiss, and Lewin 1992; Tinsley and Pillutla 1998; Weiss 2006). To illustrate, Kam-hon Lee and his colleagues gathered videotaped and questionnaire data on Chinese and American executives participating in simulated buyer–seller business negotiations. The executives reviewed their own videotaped interactions. They noted periods of tension, rated the intensity of the tension, and offered insights to account for it. The Americans reported more tension overall. They indicated that the Chinese kept revisiting issues, "returning to ground we already covered," or continued to emphasize that "there were more issues to discuss" (2006: 638). It would have been useful for the Americans to know that their negotiating partners categorized and framed the negotiations differently than they did. The Chinese pattern was consistent with a holistic approach to problem solving—a pattern that contrasted with the American sequential approach in which issues were compartmentalized and dealt with one by one.

Researchers Jeanne Brett and Tetsushi Okumura (1998) studied the effects of culture on the process of negotiating between Japan and the United States. They found that the basic value differences of individualism versus collectivism (see Chapter 2) were reflected in differential levels of self-interest in the negotiation process. The more individualistic Americans (who come from a culture where the definition of self is less dependent on group membership) are more likely to emphasize their own personal self-interests when negotiating. The Japanese, by way of contrast, are more likely to suppress their personal self-interests in favor of the interests of the group and the importance of honoring their social obligations. Moreover, the direct versus indirect way of communicating (see Chapter 4) that distinguishes Japanese and Americans can affect the process of negotiations. In general, the Japanese tend to communicate much more indirectly than Americans; that is, they leave much information unstated about their expectations, positions, and priorities. Americans, on the other hand, state their positions very explicitly and expect those on the other side of the table to do likewise. Consequently, the Japanese negotiators are able to understand the priorities of the Americans, but the opposite is not true. Americans conclude (erroneously) that the Japanese are sneaky and covert, and the Japanese conclude (equally erroneously) that their American counterparts are not very intelligent because they cannot understand the subtle and indirect messages that the Japanese are sending.

In some cases the very vocabulary of negotiating can have different meanings in different cultures. In the Persian language (spoken in Iran) the word "compromise" is defined differently than it is in English. To the Iranian, "to compromise" means only to surrender one's own principles, not, as it means in the English-speaking world, to reach a settlement agreeable to both parties. For Americans, in particular, a "willingness to compromise shows morality, good faith and fair play" (Herbig and Kramer 1991: 21). Moreover, the term *mediator* also has a negative connotation in the Persian language, referring to an unwanted intruder, rather than someone whose function is to broker a mutually agreed-upon settlement. According to Fisher, Ury, and Patton (1991: 33–34):

> In early 1980, U.N. Secretary General Waldheim flew to Iran to seek the release of American hostages. His efforts were seriously set back when Iranian national radio and television broadcast in Persian a remark he reportedly made on his arrival in Tehran: "I have come as a *mediator* to work out a *compromise*." Within an hour of the broadcast his car was being stoned by angry Iranians.

Many cultural differences already discussed in earlier chapters can influence the flow of negotiations. The relative emphasis placed on formal versus informal styles of discourse, for example, can lead the very formal Swiss negotiators to avoid joking, getting on a first-name basis, or taking off their jackets and loosening their ties during negotiating sessions. Or, when negotiating with change-fearing cultures (i.e., those scoring high on uncertainty avoidance), one can be relatively certain that their negotiators will be adverse to divulging information, proposing new approaches, or increasing the risk of uncertainty. Moreover, cultural factors can influence the type of written agreement each side is seeking in a cross-cultural negotiation. Some cultures, such as the United States, strive to bring about a written contract that takes into account as many detailed eventualities as possible. The French or the Chinese, by way of contrast, are more likely to insist on a much less detailed contract, one that tends to emphasize the more generalized relationship between the two parties.

Thus, as is obvious, we cannot negotiate across cultural lines without being conscious of how the basic features of different cultures can influence the negotiation process. In this chapter, our aim is to analyze the cross-cultural negotiation process, because by heightening our awareness of some of the potential pitfalls, we may become more effective international negotiators.

THE NATURE OF CROSS-CULTURAL NEGOTIATION

Effective negotiation does not involve bludgeoning the other side into submission. Rather, it involves the more subtle art of persuasion, whereby all parties feel as though they have benefited. There is no simple formula for success; each situation must be assessed as part of its own unique set of circumstances. The successful negotiator must choose the appropriate strategy, project the correct personal and organizational images, do the right type of homework, ask the most relevant questions, and offer and request the appropriate types of concessions at the right time. Negotiating within one's own culture is sufficiently difficult, but the pitfalls increase geometrically when one enters the global arena.

Being a skilled negotiator in any context entails being an intelligent, well-prepared, creative, flexible, and patient problem solver. International negotiators, however, face an additional set of problems and obstacles not ordinarily encountered by domestic negotiators. As we have tried to establish, one very important obstacle to international negotiations is culture. Because culture involves everything that people have, think, and do, it *will* influence or color the negotiation process. The very fact that usually one party in a negotiation will travel to the country of the other party establishes a foreign negotiating setting for at least one party. Indeed, this "strangeness" can be a formidable barrier to communication, understanding, and agreement.

There are other challenges as well. The literature over the past four decades has identified a number of characteristics of global business negotiations that set them apart from domestic negotiations. For example, global negotiation entails working within the confines of (a minimum of) two different and sometimes conflicting legal structures. Unless the negotiating parties can both understand and cope with the differing sets of laws, regulations, policies, and political authorities, a joint international contract may be governed by two or more legal/political systems. Another barrier may be the extent to which government bureaucracies in other countries exert their influence on the negotiation process, a problem not always understood by Westerners whose governments are relatively unobtrusive in business negotiations. A third factor unique to negotiating global contracts is the existence of different currency systems that can vary in relative value over the course of the contractual period. Moreover, since all governments seek to control the flow of foreign and domestic currency across their borders, negotiated contracts often depend on the willingness of those governments to make currency available. Finally, global negotiations are vulnerable to the sometimes volatile, or at least unpredictable, geopolitical realities. Sudden changes in governments, the enactment of new legislation, wars or internal revolutions, and even natural disasters can disrupt global business negotiations either temporarily or permanently. For example, the disintegration of the Soviet Union, the U.S. invasion of Iraq, and the earthquake and tsunami affecting the Fukushima Nuclear Plant in Japan had far-reaching implications for business negotiations (as well as ongoing business activities worldwide). Although we recognize the importance to international negotiations of these obstacles (e.g., different legal structures, interference by government bureaucracies, geopolitical instability), our discussion of global business negotiation will focus on the cultural dimension.

It should be apparent by now that success in negotiating global business contracts requires a deep understanding of the culture of those on the other side of the table. The reason for this cultural awareness, however, is not for the purpose of bringing the other side to its knees—to make them do what we want them to do—nor is it to accommodate them by giving up some of our own strongly adhered-to principles. Rather, an appreciation of the important cultural elements of the other side is essential if one is to get on with the business at hand so that all parties concerned can feel as though they are better off after the negotiations than before. Moreover, it is equally the responsibility of both sides to understand each other's cultural realities. International negotiation is a two-way street, with both sides sharing the burden and responsibility of cultural awareness.

WHERE TO NEGOTIATE

Earlier we defined *negotiation* as a process between individuals and organizations who share some common interests and who stand to benefit from bringing the process to a successful conclusion. Both sides have a stake in the outcome, so it stands to reason that the place of negotiations could be on the home turf of either party or in a neutral environment. The selection of a site for the negotiations is of critical importance because there are a number of advantages to negotiating in your own backyard. In the world of international diplomatic negotiations, the question of where a summit meeting will occur is taken very seriously because it is assumed that the location will very likely affect the nature and the outcome of the negotiations. The business negotiator who travels abroad is confronted with an appreciable number of problems and challenges not faced by those who negotiate at home. Let's consider some of the difficulties encountered when negotiating abroad.

First, and perhaps most important, the negotiator abroad must adjust to an unfamiliar environment during the days, weeks, or even months of the negotiations. This adjustment involves getting used to differences in language, foods, pace of life, and other aspects of culture. The negotiator who is well prepared will make a relatively smooth and quick adjustment, yet not without moments of discomfort, awkwardness, and general psychological disorientation. Time and effort must be spent learning about the new environment, such as getting to the location where the negotiations will be held, figuring out how to access local communication systems, or simply locating the rest room. For those who are less well prepared, the adjustment process may be so difficult that there is little energy left for the important work of negotiating.

Second, the business negotiator cannot avoid the deleterious effects of jet lag. Even for those international travelers who heed all conventional wisdom concerning minimizing jet lag (e.g., avoiding alcohol, eating certain foods), an intercontinental flight will nevertheless take its toll on their physical condition. Thus, the traveling negotiator is not likely to be as rested or alert as his or her counterparts who do not have to cope with jet lag.

Third, the negotiator has little or no control over the setting in which the discussions take place. The size of the conference room, the seating arrangements, and the scheduling of times for both negotiating and socializing are decisions made by the host negotiating team. The side that controls these various details of the process can use them to its own advantage.

Jet lag can be a disadvantage when negotiating abroad.

Fourth, the negotiator working in an unfamiliar cultural environment is hampered further by being physically separated from his or her business organization and its various support personnel. Frequently, before negotiators can agree to certain conditions of a contract, they must obtain additional information from the home office. Those negotiating at home have a marked advantage over the traveling negotiator because it is always easier to get a question answered by a colleague down the hall than dealing with time differences or relying on telephone, e-mail, or express mail delivery.

Finally, negotiators working on foreign soil are under pressure to conclude the negotiations as soon as possible, a type of pressure not experienced to the same degree by those negotiating at home. The longer negotiations drag on, the longer the negotiator will be away from the other operations of the office that need attention, the longer his or her family and social life will be disrupted, and the more it will cost the firm in terms of travel-related expenses. Given these very real pressures, negotiators working abroad are more likely to make certain concessions that they might not make if they were negotiating at home.

It would appear that negotiating abroad has a number of distinct disadvantages as compared with negotiating at home, including the hassle of an unfamiliar cultural setting, uncertain lines of communication with the home office, lack of control over the negotiating setting, and considerable expenditure of both time and travel funds. There is little doubt that, given the choice, most Western businesspeople would opt to conduct their negotiations at home. Yet, more often than not, Westerners are attempting to sell their products and ideas abroad. And if the potential international customers are to learn about these products or services, it is essential that Westerners go to them. Moreover, in many parts of the world, particularly in developing areas, potential customers from both the private and public sectors have limited resources for traveling. Thus, in many cases, if Westerners desire to remain competitive in the global marketplace, they have no choice other than to do their negotiating on foreign soil.

EFFECTIVE STRATEGIES FOR INTERNATIONAL NEGOTIATORS

In keeping with the conceptual nature of this book, this chapter does not attempt to list all the do's and don'ts of negotiating in all the cultures of the world. Such an approach—given the vast number of features found in each culture—would be well beyond the scope of this book and certainly beyond any single individual's capacity to comprehend. Whereas some works have taken a country-by-country approach to international negotiating (Kennedy 1985; Moran and Stripp 1991), here we focus on certain general principles of cross-cultural negotiating that can be applied to most, if not all, situations. This chapter does not provide a cookbook-style guide for avoiding negotiating faux pas in all the major cultures of the world, but it does draw upon some of the best practices of successful intercultural negotiators.

Avoid Cultural Cluelessness

One could not have read the preceding chapters without predicting our first effective strategy for global negotiations: a warning against underemphasizing (or worse yet, ignoring) the cultural/linguistic features of those on the other side of the table. By now we should be well aware of the fact that people from different cultures have different ways of thinking, perceiving, behaving, evaluating, and communicating. People from the *same* culture, who differ in age, class, religion, education, and experience, often have difficulty understanding one another. But when negotiating with people from very different cultural backgrounds, the chances of misunderstanding increase enormously.

To be certain, negotiators from other cultures have different, sometimes radically different, cultural assumptions than our own. It is vitally important that we are aware of how some of our own normal statements, which make perfect sense from our cultural perspective, may be incomprehensible to, or perceived negatively by, those with whom we are negotiating. In Table 5.1, you will find some typical statements made by American negotiators, the U.S. values they represent, and how those values differ from those in other cultures with whom U.S. negotiators frequently interact.

This list represents just a small sample of the statements that might be made by a typical U.S. negotiator operating exclusively under his or her cultural assumptions. No one is suggesting that one set of values is any better than the other. And certainly no one is suggesting that U.S. negotiators give up, or even temporarily suspend, their cultural values. However, unless one is aware of the cultural value preferences encapsulated in one's own culture (and how they

TABLE 5.1 Different Value Assumptions: United States and Elsewhere

Statements of U.S. Negotiators	U.S. Value Assumption	Alternate Value Assumption
"Yes, I can make that work."	Individualism	Collectivism
"Just call me George."	Informality	Formality
"This is my best and final offer."	Competition	Cooperation
"Let's take one item at a time."	Monochronic	Polychronic
"I don't want to beat around the bush."	Directness	Indirectness
"Let's get down to business; after all, time is money."	Precise time	Loose time
"Let me run this past my CEO, who, by the way, is only 28 years old."	Egalitarian	Hierarchical

contrast with those on the other side of the table), one will not be in the best position to communicate in a fashion most likely to lead to a win-win conclusion.

Moreover, what we know, or think we know, about our own culture is not necessarily perceived in the same way by culturally different people. In other words, we may see ourselves as holding a particular value but then describe that value in only the most positive ways. Those looking at us from the outside, however, are more likely to see some of the negative implications of that value as well. Having a realistic view of how others view us can help avoid cultural cluelessness. Even cultures that share many of the characteristics of American culture, such as those in Western Europe, may still tend to have a mixed view of attributes Americans value about themselves.

Concentrate on Long-Term Relationships, Not Short-Term Contracts

If there is one central theme running through the literature on global business negotiations, it is that the single most important consideration is building relationships over the long run rather than focusing on a single contract. At times, U.S. businesspeople have been criticized for their short-term view of doing business. Some feel that they should not waste time; they should get in there and get the contract signed and get on to other business. If the other side fails to meet its contractual obligations, the lawyers can sue. Frequently, this approach carries with it the implicit analogy of a sports contest. Negotiating across cultures is like a football game, the purpose of which is to outmaneuver, outmanipulate, outsmart, and generally overpower the other side, who is seen as the opponent; the wider the margin of victory, the better. But conventional wisdom, coupled with the experience of successful negotiators, strongly suggests that international business negotiating is not about winning big, humiliating the opposition, making a killing, and gaining all the advantages. Rather, successful international business

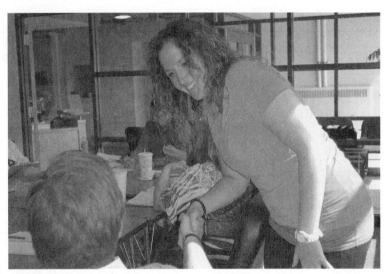

Taking the time to get to know people as individuals can improve outcomes during and after negotiations.

negotiating is conducted in a cooperative climate in which the priorities of both sides are met and in which both sides can emerge as winners. It is only under these circumstances that a business relationship will have a chance of lasting well into the future.

To be certain, considerable variation exists throughout the world in terms of why people enter into business negotiation in the first place. In some societies, such as our own, businesspeople may enter into negotiations for the sake of obtaining the signed contract. Other societies, however, view the negotiations as primarily aimed at creating a long-standing relationship and only secondarily for the purpose of signing a short-term contract. While there are differences within any given culture, Jeswald Salacuse points out that a signed contract represents *closing* a deal for many Americans, while for Asians, signing a contract is seen as *opening* a relationship (1991: 60). Indeed, the "essence of the deal" for Asians is the relationship and not the contract (1998: 5). Even though relationship building may not conform to the typical American's time frame, the inescapable truth is that because relationships are so important in the global arena, negotiations are unlikely to succeed without them.

Building relationships requires that negotiators take the time to get to know one another. Frequently, this involves activities—eating, drinking, visiting national monuments, and playing golf—that strike the typical American as being outside the realm of business and consequently a waste of time. This type of ritual socializing, however, is vital because it represents an honest effort to understand, as fully as possible, the goals, values, interests, and opinions of the negotiators on the other side. Trust is a critical ingredient in negotiation and a key success factor.

CONTRACTS AND RELATIONSHIPS

Most businesspeople are aware of the importance of relationships in Japanese national culture, but cultural sensitivity sometimes conflicts with other business objectives. A global technology company with headquarters in the United States worked with a number of firms to manage its IT departments. As this company streamlined and standardized its work processes, it has required its employees to become more systematic in how they engaged in business negotiations, and more standardized in terms of the presentation of the contract at the outset of discussions. This policy was certainly influenced by the North American context with its preference for contracts, but was also a response to "fact-based" decision making (e.g., cost reduction, minimization of losses, anticipated benefits).

Resistance to these new policies that reduced negotiator discretion emerged. There was "pushback" from the Japanese employees of this global company who argued that "Japan is different," meaning that the one-size-fits-all standard should not apply to Japan. They preferred getting to know one's partners, customers, and business associates as a critical first step in launching new business initiatives, products, or ventures. headquarters was reluctant to accept the advice of its Japanese employees and continued to insist that the company must conduct business the same way worldwide.

This global technology company encountered two sources of tension: national culture (American vs. Japanese) and approach (standardization vs. customization). Currently, the company expects that the Japanese firms will adapt to its centralized and standardized approach. It appears willing to risk some loss of business to gain the benefits of standardization. One lesson from this example is that it is important to face such trade-offs openly, after exploring alternatives.

For example, any firm dealing with a Chinese firm would do well to show its "sincerity and commitment...to gain the Chinese partner's trust" because trust seems to be the "ultimate predictor for success of business relations in China" (Fang, Worm, and Tung 2008: 167–68). Similarly, Mohammad Elahee and Charles Brooks advocate building trust relationships, not only between firms, but also among the individuals representing those firms. One of their interviewees sums it up this way:

> The most effective way for a foreigner to negotiate effectively is to develop a network of personal relationships within the company or group of people with whom they are going to negotiate. This should be done long before the negotiation begins. Established personal relationships are an absolute requirement for successful [business] negotiations in Mexico (2004: 403).

Negotiating partners do not have to have completely similar priorities, goals, and values because it is possible to disagree in a number of areas and still have a good working relationship. According to Rajesh Kumar and Verner Worm, conflict during negotiations does not necessarily produce "dysfunctional outcomes" (2003: 279). In their study involving Northern European and Chinese businesspeople, outcomes were dependent on the quality of the negotiators' pre-existing relationships. What we take away from such studies on negotiation is that both parties need to be willing to identify their shared interests while working at reconciling their conflicting interests in a spirit of cooperation and mutual respect. This twofold task, which is never easy to accomplish, has the very best chance of succeeding if a relationship built on trust and mutual respect has been established between the negotiating parties.

Another aspect of the negotiation process that is likely to create concern pertains to the continuity of participation of the negotiators in the venture. Large multinationals located in the United States often include senior executives, attorneys, and other specialists as part of the negotiation team. Legal expertise, for example, is viewed as essential in the preparation of a written contract to guide the new business relationship. However, once an agreement is reached and the contract signed, the legal work is largely completed. The attorneys return to headquarters to tackle new assignments and are unlikely to have future contact with any of the negotiators—whether from their own organization or that of their negotiating partner. That kind of change can cause significant disruption within the fledgling venture. Relationships that are built during the pre-negotiating and negotiating phases are no longer available to the partners in the same way. The trust and cooperation so necessary for success take a hit when team members exit. One way to address this issue is to plan for and retain a high proportion of the negotiating team after contract signing. The venture will launch more easily and ramp up more quickly with a critical mass of pre-existing relationships from among the negotiating partners.

Focus on the Interests behind the Positions

After the parties in a negotiation have developed a relationship, both sides typically set forth what they want to achieve from the negotiations. In a collaborative partnering arrangement, the parties are likely to indicate their hopes and expectations for a particular project or initiative. They may propose project roles, suggest monetary and personnel contributions for themselves and their counterparts, identify a time frame, and float anticipated outcomes. In a buyer–seller relationship, discussions are likely to focus on product and service attributes such as cost, quality, and market demand. For example, from a seller's perspective, the proposal may involve selling a certain number of sewing machines at x dollars per unit. From the perspective of the purchaser, it may involve receiving a certain number of sewing machines within a month's time at x minus $30 per unit. Effective global negotiators will look behind those positions for the other party's underlying expectations. Often the position of one side is in direct opposition to the position of the other side. If the negotiators focus just on the positions themselves, they will not likely resolve or reconcile their differences. However, by looking beyond the positions to the basic expectations that gave rise to those positions in the first place, it is often possible to find creative solutions to satisfy both parties.

The need to distinguish between a *position* and the *requirements underlying the position* has been effectively illustrated by Dean Allen Foster (1992: 286–87). The representative of a U.S. telecommunications firm had been negotiating with the communications representative from the Chinese government. After months of relationship building and discussing terms, the finalization of the agreement appeared to be in sight. At the eleventh hour, however, the Chinese representative raised an additional condition that took the American by surprise. The Chinese representative argued that since they were about to embark on a long-term business relationship between friends, the U.S. firm should give its Chinese friends a special reduced price that it would not give to other customers. The problem with this request was that the U.S. firm had a strict policy of uniform pricing for all countries with which it did business.

If we look at this situation solely in terms of the positions of the two parties, it would appear to be an impasse. For anything to be resolved, one party would have to get what it wanted, whereas the other would have to abandon its position. But, by understanding the basic requirements behind the positions, both sides have more room to maneuver so that a win-win situation can result. The Chinese position was based on two essential requirements or expectations: (1) to get a lower price, thus saving money, and (2) to receive a special favor as a sign of the American's friendship and commitment to the relationship. The position of the U.S. firm was grounded in the principle of uniform pricing. By looking at the situation from the perspective of *underlying expectations* rather than positions, it now became possible to suggest some alternative solutions. The U.S. negotiator offered another proposal: to sell the Chinese some new additional equipment at a very favorable price in exchange for sticking with the original pricing agreement. Such an arrangement met all the requirements of both parties. The Chinese were saving money on the new equipment, *and* they were receiving a special favor of friendship from the U.S. firm. At the same time, the U.S. company did not have to violate its own policy of uniform pricing. In this example, a win-win solution was possible because the negotiators concentrated on the expectations behind the positions rather than on the positions themselves. Once the negotiators were willing to look beyond a prepackaged, nonnegotiable, unilateral position for having their own requirements met, they could explore new and creative ways of satisfying each other.

Understanding the interests behind a position requires insight and creativity as Jeswald Salacuse (2003: 98) reminds us:

> In one negotiation between Bechtel, an international construction firm, and a foreign manufacturing corporation for the construction of an electrical cogeneration plant, the foreign negotiators insisted that if the plant did not operate at a specific standard, Bechtel would have to dismantle the entire plant and take it away. Bechtel was unwilling to make the guarantee. As the negotiations appeared to disintegrate, Bechtel negotiators understood that the real interest of the foreign corporation was

not in having a cogeneration plant, but in having a reliable supply of electricity. They therefore proposed that, if the plant were defective, Bechtel would take it over and run it, provided that the purchaser agreed to buy all of the electricity it produced. Ultimately, the two sides struck a deal on this basis.

Avoid Overreliance on Cultural Generalizations

The central theme of this book has been that success in any aspect of global business is directly related to one's knowledge of the cultural environment in which one is operating. Simply put, the more knowledge people have of the culture of their business partners, the less likely they will be to misinterpret what is being said or done, and the more likely their business objectives will be met. Communication patterns, both linguistic and nonverbal, need to be mastered as well as the myriad of other culture-specific details that can get in the way of effective intercultural business communication. But just as it would be imprudent to place too little emphasis on cultural information, being overdependent on such knowledge is equally inadvisable.

Identified cultural patterns represent only possible *tendencies* at the negotiating table. As Paul Herbig and Hugh Kramer suggest, "No two humans belonging to the same culture are going to respond in exactly the same way" (1991: 20). Not all Middle Easterners engage in verbal overkill, and not all Japanese are reluctant to give a direct answer. If we tend to interpret cultural generalizations too rigidly, we run the risk of turning the generalizations into cultural stereotypes. We may chuckle when we hear heaven defined as the place where the police are British, the cooks are French, the mechanics are German, the lovers are Italian, and it's all organized by the Swiss; conversely, hell is defined as the place where the cooks are British, the mechanics are French, the lovers are Swiss, the police are German, and it's all organized by Italians. Such cultural stereotypes can be offensive to those being lumped together uncritically, but they can be particularly harmful in the process of global business negotiations because they can be wrong. Sometimes negotiators on the other side of the table do not act the way the generalization would predict.

To be certain, peoples' negotiating behavior is influenced by their culture, but there may be some other factors at work as well. How a person behaves may also be conditioned by such variables as education, biology, or experience. To illustrate, a Mexican business negotiator who has an M.B.A. from the Wharton School may not object to discussing business at lunch, as most other Mexicans might. We should not automatically assume that all Mexicans will act in a stereotypical way. Given this particular Mexican's education and experience, he or she knows how to behave within the U.S. frame of reference. It is therefore important that we move beyond cultural stereotyping and get to know the negotiators on the other side not only as members of a particular cultural group but also as individuals with their own unique set of personality traits and experiences.

Be Sensitive to Timing

Timing may not be everything, but in global negotiations it certainly can make a difference between success and failure. As pointed out in Chapter 2, different cultures have different rhythms and different concepts of time. In cultures like our own, with tight schedules and a precise reckoning of time, it is anticipated that business will be conducted without wasting time. But in many parts of the world, it is not realistic to expect to arrive one day and consummate a deal the next before jetting off to another client in another country. While the more likely scenario involves spending what may seem like inordinately long periods on insignificant details, frustrating delays, and unanticipated postponements, it has the potential to reap significant benefits. Bringing the U.S. notion of time into a global negotiation will invariably result in either frustration or the eventual alienation of those with whom one is negotiating.

As a general rule, global negotiations, for a number of reasons, take longer than domestic negotiations. We should keep in mind that McDonald's engaged in negotiations for nearly a decade before it began selling hamburgers in Moscow. In another situation, a high-level salesperson for a U.S. modular office furniture company spent months negotiating a deal in Saudi Arabia. He made frequent courtesy calls, engaged in long discussions on a large number of topics other than office furniture, and drank enough coffee to float a small ship. But the months of patience paid off. His personal commission (not his company's profit) was in excess of $2 million! The lesson here is clear. A global negotiator must first understand the local rhythm of time and, if it is slower than at home, exercise the good sense to be patient.

Sometimes the American insistence on negotiating contracts as quickly as possible (after all, "time is money") can subvert the negotiating process altogether. In a well-publicized case involving a subsidiary of the ill-fated Enron Corporation, a negotiated contract to sell electricity to a state-operated power company in India was eventually canceled by the government on the grounds that it was concluded too hastily. Suspicious of attempts to speed up negotiations, Indian officials concluded that the public interest was not being adequately protected (Salacuse 2003). Rushing into deals or concluding them in a hurried manner can send the wrong signals to one's partner or to the stakeholder groups with which that partner is connected.

Another important dimension of time that must be understood is that some times of the year are better than others for negotiating internationally. All cultures have certain times of the year when people are preoccupied with social or religious concerns or when everything having to do with business simply shuts down. Before negotiating abroad, become familiar with the national calendar. To illustrate, do not plan any global deal making with the Taiwanese on October 10, their national day of independence; or with the Japanese during "Golden Week" when most people take a vacation; or anywhere in the Islamic world during Ramadan when Muslims are more concerned with fasting than with negotiating. Any attempt to conduct negotiations on these holidays, traditional vacation times, or times of religious observance will generally meet with as much success as a non-American

Just like us, businesspeople around the world try to avoid doing business during their important holidays.

might have trying to conduct business negotiations in the United States during the week between Christmas and New Year's Day.

Still another consideration of time has to do with the different time zones between one's home office and the country in which the negotiations are taking place. Owing to these different time zones, an American negotiating in Manila cannot fax the home office in New York and expect an answer within minutes, as might be expected if the negotiations were taking place in Boston. If at 4:00 P.M. (Manila time) a question is raised that requires clearance or clarification from the home office, an answer will not be received until the next day because in New York it is 3:00 A.M. Thus, attempting to operate between two distant time zones can be frustrating because it tends to slow the pace of the negotiations.

Remain Flexible

Whenever entering an international negotiating situation, the Western negotiator, despite the best preparation, will always have an imperfect command of how things work. In such an environment, some of the best-laid plans frequently go unexecuted. Schedules change unexpectedly, government bureaucrats become more recalcitrant than predicted, and people don't follow through with what they promised. When things do not go as expected, it is important to be able to readjust quickly and efficiently. To be flexible does not mean to be weak; rather, it means being capable of responding to changing situations. Flexibility involves avoiding the all-too-common malady known as "hardening of the categories."

The need for remaining open and flexible has been well illustrated by Dean Allen Foster (1992), who tells of a U.S. businessman trying to sell data-processing equipment to a high-level government official in India. After preparing himself thoroughly, the American was escorted into the official's office for their initial meeting. Much to the businessman's surprise, seated on a nearby sofa was another gentleman who was never introduced. For the entire meeting, the host-government official acted as if the third man were not there. The businessman became increasingly uncomfortable with the presence of this mystery man who was sitting in on the negotiations, particularly as they discussed specific details. After a while, the businessman began having paranoid delusions. Who was this man listening in on these private discussions? He even imagined that the man might be one of his competitors. Ultimately, he became so uncomfortable with this situation that he lost his capacity to concentrate on the negotiations and eventually lost the potential contract. Here was a perfect example of a negotiator who was unsuccessful because he could not adjust to an unfamiliar situation. In India, as in some other parts of the world, it is not unusual for third parties to be present at negotiations. They may be friends, relatives, or advisors of the host negotiator, invited to listen in to provide advice—and perhaps a different perspective. Unaware of this customary practice in India, this U.S. negotiator began to imagine the worst until it had irreparably destroyed his capacity to focus on the negotiations at hand.

Flexibility was a key to success for the U.S. firm P.T. Essex, a subsidiary of the drug manufacturer Schering Corporation. It set out to negotiate a land purchase in East Java where it hoped to build a new manufacturing facility. The negotiations were lengthy and multifaceted in that they involved several stakeholders (e.g., Essex, Indonesian governmental entities, peasant landowners), and a series of issues (e.g., building networks into the community, making an offer, furnishing payment). The firm expanded its networks, working with local officials to understand and address key local concerns. Richard Reeves-Ellington, Essex's U.S. manager and an anthropologist, followed appropriate conventions for meeting and interacting with the locals. Essex also reviewed its intended offer with two local officials from the village and got their support. Yet, after several meetings, no agreement was reached even though the peasant landowners indicated they were not seeking higher payments for the sale of their land.

Reeves-Ellington asked one of the village officials if "other, nonmonetary issues...might be blocking progress in the negotiations" (2009: 399). Two concerns emerged which were tackled in succession. First, the villagers wanted to purchase *hadj* tickets (for the pilgrimage to Mecca to which Muslims aspire) with the money they would receive from Essex, but tickets were difficult to obtain. Reeves-Ellington had to persuade a reluctant Essex of the value of the tickets as part of the offer, and then get Essex to figure out how it might acquire them. Essex's Javanese lawyer singlehandedly convinced the home office that the purchase of the tickets "was a stroke of genius and should be done" (p. 401). He argued that villagers needed a critically important reason—such as going on a *hadj*—to sell their land; attending a *hadj* would improve both the villagers' status within the community and their chances for long-term success because they would be viewed as more trustworthy and pious. Essex accepted this argument and then turned its attention to acquiring the tickets. It ended up using its own local and international networks, which ultimately led to contact with the Minister of Religion, who made the tickets available.

The second concern related to the peasants' tie to the land. The peasants believed that if they sold their land, they would break their spiritual bond with it—given their particular belief system. Possible solutions to address this issue flowed back-and-forth between Reeves-Ellington and village officials. Essex initially proposed allowing the peasants to use some of the land for farming after the land sale. However, village officials, local lawyers, and ministry leaders rejected this proposal since it would allow "de facto squatters' rights" (p. 403). Eventually, the collaborative effort resulted in two solutions. First, some of the land would be available for public use under the supervision of village officials, though that amount would be reduced over time. "It's their culture and they know how to make it work," pointed out Reeves-Ellington, who nicely summed up Essex's respect for its Javanese negotiators. A second solution promised priority consideration in hiring at the new Essex manufacturing facility for those agreeing to sell their land. The purchase offer, the land-use proposal, and the *hadj* tickets were offered to the villagers as a package, which they accepted shortly thereafter.

This example highlights the importance of flexibility throughout the negotiation process. Flexibility helps negotiating partners address the complexity and adapt to each other's cultural circumstances. Remaining flexible has another advantage as well. Flexibility creates an environment in which creative solutions to negotiating problems can emerge. We said earlier that negotiations should be win-win situations, whereby both sides can communicate their basic requirements and interests, rather than just their positions, and then proceed to brainstorm on how best to meet the needs of both sides. A win-win type of negotiation is most likely to occur when both sides remain flexible and open to exploring nontraditional solutions.

Prepare Carefully

It is difficult to imagine any undertaking—be it in business, government, education, or athletics—where advanced preparation would not be an asset. Nowhere is this truer than in the arena of global negotiating where the variables are so complex. There is a straightforward and direct relationship between the amount of preparation and the chances for success when engaging in global deal making. Those who take the rather cavalier attitude of "Let's go over and see what *they* (the other side) have to say" are bound to be disappointed. What is needed is a substantial amount of advanced preparation. In addition, the would-be negotiator needs to seek answers to important questions concerning his or her own objectives, bottom-line position, types of information needed as the negotiations progress, an agenda, and accessibility of support services, to mention a few. These and many other questions need to be answered *before* getting on the plane.

Vivian Sheer and Ling Chen (2003) identified successful strategies used by Chinese and Western negotiators (a mix of Americans, British, Canadians, and Germans). Both groups emphasized the importance of researching market conditions as well as anticipating risks and problems that might occur during negotiations. In addition, the Chinese looked into the reputation of the Western firm as well as

Much preparation for international negotiations can be done via computer.

its competitors. They also focused considerable effort on planning the agenda and presentation materials. The Westerners conducted research on the power structure of Chinese organizations by tapping into their own Chinese networks and hiring locals. They also researched Chinese policy generally. The lesson here is that it is important to start with as full an understanding as possible of circumstances and constraints associated with your negotiating partner. The availability and portability of the Internet and social media now put vast quantities of information into virtually anyone's hands. Failure to prepare adequately will have at least two negative consequences. First, it communicates to the other side that you do not consider the negotiations sufficiently important to have done your homework. Second, ill-prepared negotiators frequently are forced into making certain concessions that they may later regret.

A basic part of preparing for negotiations is self-knowledge. How well do you understand yourself, the assumptions of your own culture, and your own goals and objectives for this particular negotiation? If you are part of a negotiating team, a number of questions must be answered: Who are the team members? How have they been selected? Is there general consensus on what the team hopes to accomplish? Is there a proper balance between functional skills, cross-cultural experience, and negotiating expertise? Is there a division of labor for tasks such as note taking, serving as a spokesperson, or making local arrangements? Has there been sufficient time for discussions of approaches and frameworks, likely scenarios, priorities, and strategies and counterstrategies?

A particularly important area of preparation has to do with getting to know the negotiators on the other side of the table. At the outset, it must be determined if the organization is the appropriate one with which to be negotiating in the first place. Once that has been decided, it is important to know whether its negotiators have the authority and responsibility to make decisions. Having this information *before* the negotiations begin can eliminate the possibility of long delays stemming from the last-minute disclosure that the negotiators on the other side really cannot make final contractual decisions. Once involved in the negotiating process, it is important, as a general rule, to get to know the other team's negotiators as people rather than simply as members of a particular culture.

"THE BEST LAID PLANS ..."

Even the best preparation can fail—especially in a cross-cultural context—so problem-resolution skills are especially important. Mary Beauregard found herself in an awkward situation with a new trainer she had hired to deliver cross-cultural training on Mexico to American automotive engineers. The two worked together to develop the workshop materials. Beauregard emphasized her expectations for a "nuts-and-bolts approach" given that the participants were eager to begin addressing the issues they were facing with their Mexican counterparts. The trainer seemed more than agreeable to the proposed approach.

Following introductions, the workshop began. Beauregard reported a set of behaviors that were completely unexpected:

> I watched Dr. García (a pseudonym) take our well-thought-out slides and move them to a side table...he reached into his briefcase and produced a packet of worn, typewritten slides, with misspelled words and incorrect grammar. He then began a presentation on the sociological and anthropological background of culture. Although his intentions were good, he was rapidly losing twenty-two engineers...During the morning break, I delicately asked Dr. García what in the world he was doing. His explanation revolved around setting a foundation for the concepts we were going to be covering, which he had previously agreed to present in a much more hands-on manner...I politely asked him to discontinue his lecture and to get to our slides and the agreed-upon format. When we reconvened, he went back to his old slides, completed his lecture, and finally got down to business about forty minutes later (Beauregard 2008: 85).

Beauregard recovered from this setback in two ways. First, she spoke with the trainer and learned that he had his own ideas about what Americans needed to know about Mexicans. She also discovered that he only wanted to provide the best for the client. Second, she arranged a three-way debriefing with the trainer and her client to outline how future training sessions would be presented. The trainer, responding both to the client's dissatisfaction with the poor evaluations on the opening lecture, and the potential for many future workshops in the United States and Mexico, agreed to conduct future workshops according to the original plan.

This example highlights some of the difficulties encountered in cross-cultural negotiations despite significant planning, preparation, and the best of intentions. It points to the emergent and delicate nature of the relationship between the parties—a relationship that was not yet characterized by *confianza* (trust) or an open and candid exchange of ideas. Over time, however, Beauregard's relationship with the trainer blossomed and resulted in a highly successful multiyear partnership.

Learn to Listen, Not Just Speak

The style of oral discourse in the United States is essentially a very assertive one. Imbued with a high sense of competition, most Americans want to make certain that their views and positions are presented as clearly and as powerfully as possible. As a consequence, they tend to concentrate far more on sending messages than on receiving them. Many Westerners treat a discussion as a debate, the objective of which is to win by convincing the other party of the superiority of their position. Operating under such an assumption, many Americans concentrate more on their own response than on what the other party is actually saying. They seem to have a stronger desire to be heard than to hear. Although public speaking courses are quite common in our high schools and colleges, courses on how to listen are virtually nonexistent. Because effective listening is a vital component of the negotiating process, Westerners in general, and Americans in particular, are at a marked disadvantage when they appear at the negotiating table.

If the best negotiator is the well-informed negotiator, then active listening is absolutely essential for understanding the other side's positions and interests. The understanding that comes from active listening can have a positive persuasive effect on your negotiating partners in at least three important ways. First, it can convince your negotiating partners that you are knowledgeable and thus worthy of entering into a long-term relationship. Second, the very fact that you made the effort to really hear what they were saying will, in almost every case, enhance rapport and trust. Third, by listening to and reflecting on your negotiating partner's point of view, you will be better equipped to identify the common ground between the different points of view, be able to problem solve more generally, and achieve more of your negotiating objectives.

Listening offers insight into underlying positions.

Developing good listening skills may be easier said than done. Nevertheless, some general guidelines, if followed, can help improve your ability to grasp oral messages more effectively:

1. Be aware of the phenomenon that psychologists call *cognitive dissonance*, the tendency to discount, or simply not hear, any message that is inconsistent with what you already believe or want to believe. In other words, if the message does not conform to your preconceived way of thinking, it is possible to dismiss it subconsciously. It is important to actively hear *all* messages—those with which you agree and those with which you do not. You do not have to agree with everything being said, but it is important to hear the message so that you will then be in a position to seek creative ways of resolving whatever differences may exist.
2. Listen to the whole message before offering a response. Focus on understanding rather than interrupting the message so that you can give a rebuttal/response. Since no one likes to be cut off before he or she is finished speaking, it is vital for the effective negotiator to practice allowing other people to finish their ideas and sentences.
3. Concentrate on the message rather than the style of the presentation. It is easy to get distracted from what is being said by focusing instead on how it is presented. No matter how inarticulate, disorganized, or inept the speaker might be, try to look beyond those stylistic features and concentrate on the content of the message.
4. Learn to ask neutral, open-ended questions that are designed to allow the speaker to elaborate on a particular point. Examples include: What kinds of strategies do you use? How can we improve the process? What are your thoughts on addressing this issue?
5. Be conscious of staying in the present. All people bring into a negotiation session a wide variety of "baggage from the past." It is tempting to start thinking about yesterday's racquetball game with a friend, this morning's intense conversation with your boss, or the argument you had with your spouse at breakfast, but to do so will distract you from actively hearing what is being said.
6. Consider the possibility of having a friend or close associate serve as an official listener whose job it is to listen to the other side with another set of ears. Such a person can provide a valuable new perspective on what is being conveyed and can also serve as a check on your own perceptions.
7. In almost all situations, taking notes will help you become a more effective listener. Provided you don't attempt to record every word, selective note taking can help highlight key points. Not only will note taking help document the messages, but when the speaker notices that you are taking notes, he or she, in all likelihood, will make a special effort to be clear and accurate.

As difficult as it may be, Western businesspeople, particularly Americans, need to develop active listening skills if they are to become effective global negotiators. Acquiring this skill is becoming increasingly more difficult because, as linguist Deborah Tannen (1998) has suggested, the adversarial nature of communication in the United States has escalated so sharply that we have become an "argument culture." Active listening entails suspending, at least temporarily, one's highly competitive notion about winning the debate, and instead, strive for full understanding of what is being said on the other side of the bargaining table. It involves getting past the other party's accent, thought process, or linguistic style and focusing on what message is being transmitted. Since it is impossible to disguise

Note taking signals interest and serves as a memory aid.

an honest and energetic effort to understand what the other party is saying, an inevitable by-product of active listening is the creation of greater empathy and rapport, two vital ingredients of successful global negotiations.

Act Ethically and with Integrity

We find that the world is becoming more heterogeneous, fast-paced, and complex, due in large part to globalization. If we are to succeed in such a world, creating and nurturing long-term relationships built on trust with our global business partners is essential. There is nothing particularly complicated or mysterious about building trust, nor are there any simple shortcuts. Trust develops only when people act with integrity—which means being honest with oneself and with others, keeping promises, and accepting responsibility for one's actions. Acting with integrity involves standing behind your words and commitments no matter how convenient it might be to do otherwise. In short, integrity is the bedrock on which trust relationships are built.

Integrity also means not violating the ethical standards of one's own culture, firm, or self, or those of your global partner. While ethical breaches may provide a short-term economic gain, acting ethically at home and abroad remains the best strategy for building long-term, sustainable business relationships. At the same time, it is important to be aware, particularly in global contexts, that your negotiating partner may hold different ethical standards. Often these differences are rooted in history, tradition, practices, and laws. Ethical questions, like cultural values in general, are addressed differently in different parts of the world.

To illustrate, the Foreign Corrupt Practices Act prohibits U.S.-based corporations from giving money to government officials in exchange for contracts—in other words, engaging in bribery. Although this type of *quid pro quo* is outlawed by the U.S. Congress, it is considered an acceptable form of business practice in some of the more collectivist cultures found in Asia, Africa, and the Middle East. In such societies, the benefits reaped by government officials taking a *quid pro quo* is justified on the basis that (1) it is a traditional way of meeting communal obligations by redistributing wealth to certain segments of the population, and (2) it supplements the low salaries of civil servants. The cross-cultural relativity of ethics is also seen in the issue of employee "whistle-blowing." In the United States, an employee is usually on the ethical "high ground" when exposing illegal activities of his or her employer. In more collectivist societies, such as Peru or Japan, whistle-blowing is discouraged because it violates the higher value of loyalty to the group (i.e., corporation).

Awareness of each other's ethical standards is critical not only in negotiations, but also in any subsequent business that results. Before entering into negotiations, it is important to be aware of the ethical and legal requirements of your country and organization, and issues that are likely to arise with your negotiating partner. A business relationship can break down, perhaps catastrophically, if both parties' ethical standards are not understood and if no agreement is reached on the ethical standards that will be observed. The Sullivan Principles and the United Nations Global Compact are among many documents providing guidance on corporate social responsibility. They represent voluntary initiatives that support such values as human rights, equal and fair employment practices, implementation of employee training programs, abolition of child labor, and environmental sustainability (Sethi and Williams 2000; Williams 2004). Organizations seeking to work together can use these documents as a way to gauge each other's commitment to and generate discussion surrounding business ethics.

Another way to test the congruence of ethical standards is to ask your negotiating partner some basic questions, and be prepared to answer similar questions in return. Choosing the appropriate tone, timing, and phrasing for such questions is often delicate and challenging. Some questions may need to be explored outside the negotiation room and in other ways (e.g., due diligence, plant visits). Questions could cover your negotiating partner's current business activities, as well as the potential business arrangement in which you might work together.

- What current labor practices and conditions does your negotiating partner face?
- What are the environmental rules in your negotiating partner's country/countries of operation? What environmental practices will your partnership venture use?
- How does your negotiating partner handle quality issues or customer complaints related to products or services?
- What position does your negotiating partner take on copyright and patent infringements?
- How might you and your negotiating partner problem solve around the issue of payment to public officials?

Understanding your partner's constraints and interests is contingent, in part, on asking basic questions and exploring common ground.

- What are the requirements for disclosure and accounting governing your potential relationship?
- What are the tax practices to which any transactions must adhere?
- What ethical standards will be followed in advertising?

The Reeves-Ellington example of the East Javanese villagers (discussed earlier in the chapter) shows the importance of exploring questions and developing creative solutions that are consistent with both parties' ethical standards. The village officials made clear to Essex that allowing villagers to use the land after it was sold would not work out long term; current practice made it difficult to evict squatters. However, Essex and the villagers were able to come up with a plan that all parties could find consistent with their legal and ethical practices. Indeed, taking the time to address these issues in advance reduces the risk of disastrous misunderstandings that may have consequences beyond failure of the business relationship and put reputations—or even lives—at risk. Acting ethically and with integrity is good for a healthy relationship with your negotiating partner and the communities and governments with which you will be dealing. It is also critical to your career and the long-term success of your organization around the world.

THE USE OF INTERPRETERS

Knowing as much as possible about the language and culture of the people with whom you are doing business matters. Speaking the language of your business partner gives you an enormous advantage in that it enhances rapport and allows you to understand more fully their thought patterns, assumptions, beliefs, and expectations. However, negotiators are not always proficient in the language spoken by their negotiating partners. Greeting a partner in his/her language is typically viewed favorably as is engagement in informal conversations (should the U.S. negotiator have the appropriate language skills). Such actions symbolize a general willingness for the U.S. negotiator to step out of his/her comfortable cultural milieu and into some other cultural space (though it might only be momentary if it is restricted to *Muy buenos días* [Good morning]). Moreover, these kinds of interactions can begin to build a bridge of understanding between the negotiating partners, and lay a foundation for the important work of relationship development.

At the same time, when deciding on which language to use in the negotiation, do not be guided by the principle that a little knowledge is better than none at all. In other words, unless you are extremely well versed in a foreign language, do not try to negotiate in that language directly; rely instead on the services of a competent interpreter. Even if you have a relatively good command of the language, working through an interpreter may be helpful because it allows you more time to formulate your response. On the other hand, use of an interpreter has certain disadvantages, such as increasing the number of people involved, increasing the costs of the negotiations, and serving as a barrier to the two sides really getting to know one another (see Chapter 4).

When considering the use of a linguistic intermediary in cross-cultural negotiations, it is important to distinguish between a translator and an interpreter. Although both roles are aimed at turning the words of one language into the words of another language, the *translator* usually works with documents, whereas the *interpreter* works with the spoken word in a face-to-face situation. Translators have the luxury of using dictionaries and generally are not under any great time constraints. Interpreters, on the other hand, must listen to what is being said and then instantaneously translate those words into the other language. Interpreting is a demanding job, because it requires constant translating, evaluating, and weighing the meaning of specific words within the specific social context. A good interpreter not only will need to be aware of the usual meaning of the words in the two languages but also must consider the intent of the words and the meanings of the nonverbal gestures.

When selecting an effective interpreter, it is important for that person both to be intimately knowledgeable of the two languages, and have technical expertise in the area being negotiated. For example, although a U.S. university professor of Spanish literature may have an excellent command of the language, he or she may not be particularly effective at translating scientific terms, engineering concepts, statistical results, or highly technical data on something like weaving equipment. It is this type of shortcoming that could lead an interpreter to translate the term *hydraulic ram* into the term *wet sheep*. Because of these special demands, language interpretation is more exhausting—and may be less accurate—than language translation.

The use of an interpreter involves placing an additional person between the two primary negotiators. Therefore, one should take a number of precautions to ensure that the interpreter clarifies communication rather than obscures it.

- Spend sufficient time with the interpreter to get to know one another before the negotiations begin. Review your own notes, slides, and technical terms and phrases that may cause misunderstandings. When the interpreter understands your goals and expectations, he/she can represent your interests to the other side and be on the lookout for valuable information.
- Ask the interpreter to go over the important nonverbal cues you will need to be aware of when negotiating.
- Make certain that the interpreter is located at the proper place at the negotiating table so he or she can be most effective.
- Have the interpreter apologize for your inability to speak your negotiating partner's language.
- Insist that the interpreter translate small segments of information rather than waiting until the end of a long, complex chain of sentences.
- Help the interpreter by speaking slowly, clearly, and using active rather than passive verbs.
- Direct your comments to your negotiating counterpart, rather than to the interpreter.
- Plan your words carefully so as to avoid ambiguities, slang, jokes, or other expressions that do not translate well.
- Pause momentarily between sentences to provide a little more time for the interpreter to do his/her job.
- Use carefully prepared graphics when possible. Encourage the use of spontaneous drawings and sketches to help get a point across. A picture, figure, or chart really can be worth a thousand words.
- Recognize that "side conversations" among a few people are likely to occur during the negotiations. Such discussions can be potentially valuable when they clarify concerns or lead to the development of new questions. However, if they come to dominate the negotiations, it is probably time to take a break.
- Ask the interpreter to offer an explanation when either side's negotiating team is engaged in a "huddle"—discussing an issue, sharing a story or joke, or examining new documents or electronic communications. A simple statement from the interpreter is a courteous way of keeping all present informed about what is going on.
- Submit complicated questions to the interpreter in writing to enable ease of translation.
- Check periodically for comprehension by asking your negotiating partners to paraphrase back to you their understanding of your major points.
- Give interpreters periodic breaks to recharge their intellectual batteries because interpreting is an exhausting job.
- Confirm all important negotiations in writing so as to avoid misunderstandings.
- Treat interpreters with respect and acknowledge them as the highly qualified professionals that they are. The purposeful development of cordial relations with your interpreter can only help facilitate the process of communication at the negotiating table.

THE GLOBAL NEGOTIATOR

We have examined, in a very general way, some of the problems and challenges of negotiating abroad. This chapter is not intended to be a cookbook for the would-be global negotiator. Rather, it is offered as a set of general guidelines for those who find themselves negotiating across cultures. Bear in mind that no two negotiating situations are exactly alike, but most of the strategies suggested here are applicable to whatever type of cross-cultural negotiating session one might imagine. We have suggested that global negotiators should (1) avoid cultural cluelessness, (2) concentrate on building long-term relationships rather than short-term contracts, (3) focus on the interests that lay behind the positions, (4) avoid overdependence on cultural generalizations, (5) develop a sensitivity to timing, (6) remain flexible, (7) prepare carefully ahead of time, (8) learn to listen effectively, (9) act ethically and with integrity, and (10) know when and how to use interpreters.

A major theme running through the contemporary literature is that, because negotiating across cultures involves mutual interdependence between the parties, it must be conducted in an atmosphere of mutual trust and cooperation. Quite apart from your position on the issues that are being negotiated, maintaining a high degree of personal respect for those on the other side of the table is critical. Even though your negotiating partners are likely to view the world very differently than you, always approach them with respect and with a willingness to learn. Do not try to reform them at the negotiating table in the hopes that they will eventually be more like you, for the simple reason that it will *not* work. On the other hand, do not go overboard in the other direction by "going native;" most people tend to be suspicious of anyone imitating their gestures or behaviors. The soundest advice is to learn to understand and respect cultural differences while retaining one's own. This spirit of mutual respect and cooperation has been cogently expressed by Salacuse:

> At times the two sides at the negotiating table are like two persons in a canoe who must combine their skills and strength if they are to make headway against powerful currents, through dangerous rapids, around hidden rocks, and over rough portages. Alone they can make no progress and will probably lose control. Unless they cooperate, they risk wrecking or overturning the canoe on the obstacles in the river. Similarly, unless global deal makers find ways of working together, their negotiations will founder on the many barriers encountered in putting together an international business transaction (1991: 164).

CROSS-CULTURAL SCENARIOS

Read the following Cross-Cultural Scenarios. In each mini-case study, a basic cultural conflict occurs among the actors involved. Try to identify the source of the conflict and suggest how it could have been avoided or minimized. Then see how well your analyses compare to the explanations in Appendix A.

5-1   Within the past decade, Ray Cisneros had worked hard to become the top salesperson for the entire West Coast district of his company which manufactures and distributes vinyl floor coverings. When his company received an invitation to make a marketing presentation to a large distribution firm in Santiago, Ray's Hispanic background, fluency in Spanish, and excellent sales ability all made him the logical choice for the assignment. Ray had set up an appointment to make his presentation the day after he arrived since it would take about 13 hours (with a brief layover) to get there from Los Angeles. But upon arrival, the marketing representative of the host firm, who met him at the airport, told him that the meeting had been arranged for two days later so that Ray could rest after the long trip and have a chance to see some of the local sights and enjoy their hospitality. Ray tried to assure his host that he felt fine and was prepared to make the presentation that day. Ray could see no good reason not to get on with the business at hand. Eventually, the marketing representative (somewhat reluctantly) intervened on Ray's behalf, and the meeting was reset for Ray's original appointment time. But once the meeting began, Ray noticed that the Chilean executives never really got beyond the exchange of pleasantries. Finally, the vice president in charge suggested that they meet again the next afternoon. Ray was feeling increasingly frustrated with the excruciatingly slow pace of the negotiations.

How could you help Ray gain some clarity on this cross-cultural situation?

5-2   Larry Ligo, an art dealer from Florida, was in some intense business negotiations with a Brazilian firm. At the meeting many differing opinions were discussed, and at times the exchanges became somewhat heated. This intensity was exemplified by the Brazilians, who tapped Larry on the shoulder or arm each time they expressed an opinion. The repeated taps began to make Larry angry. In fact, he wondered whether the Brazilians were trying to pick a fight. The next time Larry was touched on the arm he impulsively jerked his arm away. The Brazilians were surprised by Larry's response. After that Larry sensed that the discussion was not progressing smoothly.

Why?

5-3   Frank MacDougall had been chosen to set up a branch office of his engineering consulting firm in Seoul, Korea. Although the six engineering consultants who would eventually be transferred to Seoul were Americans, Frank was interested in hiring local support staff. He was particularly interested in hiring a local person with excellent accounting skills to handle the company's books. He was confident that he would be able to find the right person for the job because his company was prepared to offer an excellent salary and benefits package. After receiving what he considered to be several excellent leads, he was surprised to be turned down by all four prospective candidates. They were very appreciative of being considered for the position, but all preferred to stay with their current employer. Frank just couldn't understand why all four Koreans chose to pass up an increase in salary and fringe benefits.

How would you explain this situation to Frank?

5-4   Roger Brown, marketing vice president for a Seattle-based lumber company, was making a sales presentation to a plywood wholesaler in Tokyo. Roger had just proposed what he considered to be a fair price for a large shipment of first-quality plywood. Much to his amazement, the three Japanese executives did not respond immediately but rather sat across the table with their hands folded and their eyes cast downward, saying nothing. Fifteen seconds passed, then 30, and still no response. Finally, Roger became so exasperated that he said with a good deal of irritation in his voice, "Would you like for me to repeat the offer?" From that point onward, the talks were stalled.

What advice would you give Roger for future any interactions with the Japanese?

5-5   Steve Lee, an executive with a Hartford insurance company, was sent to Kuwait immediately after the 1990 Gulf War to investigate damage claims to several hotels his company had insured. Back in the States, Steve had the reputation of being extremely affable and sociable. The day after Steve arrived in Kuwait City, he met with Mr. Said, the manager of one of the insured tourist hotels. His previous telephone conversations with Said were upbeat and had led him to expect that Said was interested in getting the claims settled quickly and efficiently. His initial meeting with Said went extremely well, with both men agreeing on most of the issues discussed. At the end of that first meeting they shook hands, and to emphasize the depth and sincerity of his goodwill, Steve grasped Said's hand with two hands and shook vigorously. For reasons that Steve never understood, the subsequent meetings with Said were never as cordial and friendly as that first meeting.

What explanation might you give to Steve?

6

■ ■ ■

Partnering across Cultures

PARTNERSHIP BASICS

Partnering is at the heart of global business and partnerships are the vehicle for bringing people, ideas, resources, and energy together. Partnering requires the participation of at least two parties in the pursuit of some shared goals and objectives.

In this chapter we take a broad perspective on partnering and partnerships. Partnerships may be viewed as "organizations," though their structure varies from one-on-one relationships between an entrepreneur and a supplier, to a network that consists of people filling several different roles, to a formal, legal entity such as a joint venture that draws on resources from parent firms. A large corporation might partner with two suppliers to develop a new composite material for sports equipment. An entrepreneur might partner with a family business to market and sell jewelry over the Internet. A consulting organization might partner with a client firm to help make its organizational culture more effective or augment its consumer base. Colleagues with different skill sets might partner to develop a crisis-management plan for their company. Representatives from several firms might work with a federal agency on the development of noncompetitive technologies. Thus, partnerships may take a variety of forms depending on mutual interests, the availability and experience of the key personnel, the contribution of resources, and the urgency and scale of the effort.

Partnerships come with fundamental challenges—which often lead to conflict. Most partnerships fail due largely to cultural and organizational differences among the partners. Some of the obstacles to success include: status and power differences, intergroup dynamics, insufficient time spent in building trust relationships, knowledge flows and constraints on learning, misconceptions about the partner(s), inadequate effort and energy, and differences in management styles (see, e.g., Olie 1990; Meschi 1997; Jamali 2004; Thompson and Perry 2006). When the partners operate within the same organization as colleagues or team members, they share a common organizational culture, though they may come from different disciplinary backgrounds, have a range of expertise and experience, and be associated with particular functional areas. Contrast that situation with a partnership between a university and a community, a consultant and a global organization with offices in multiple locations around the world, or two organizations representing two different industries with headquarters in two different countries. Typically, as the cultural complexities increase, so too do the challenges.

Effective partnerships operate with the principle of collaboration at their core. They involve an ability to work together and problem solve. Participants in effective partnerships have built strong, healthy relationships with one another, many of which are associated with high levels of cooperation, commitment, and trust. Participants have worked hard to maintain the synergy that they have developed. Without a strong relational base, it would not be possible to sustain the partnership indefinitely. In this book, we use the partnership definition coined by Elizabeth Briody and Robert T. Trotter, II: "Collaborative arrangements, in which participants enter into relationships, combine their resources, time, and expertise through the various roles they play, and work toward the creation of new knowledge, products, and services" (2008: 7, 196).

Increasing numbers of individuals, groups, organizations, and institutions are engaging in an array of partnering arrangements to take advantage of opportunities in many parts of the globe. New partnerships are proliferating in concert with the break-neck speed of globalization. This chapter is designed to assist you both as an individual and/or as a member of some larger organizational entity. One of our goals is to raise awareness about the impact of culture and cultural differences on partnering and partnership performance generally. A related goal is to focus attention on the domains of relationships and problem solving. Knowledge of and experience in these domains can help guide your interactions and work activities in partnering situations. We begin with one of the most common activities associated with partnerships: meetings.

MEETINGS AS OPPORTUNITIES FOR COLLABORATION

What are meetings? They are clearly an essential part of business—a key way to meet people, gather information, exchange ideas, and get projects and initiatives started. In fact, they have been described as "communication events" (Schwartzman 1993: 39). Meetings can be helpful in moving things along so that progress is made toward work goals and objectives. A lot of people spend a lot of time in meetings—not to mention all the pre- and post-work associated with them. Many people view meetings as so routine and integral to work that they often take them for granted.

Should this book devote any attention to meetings? Is there a need to understand meetings with colleagues, clients, and business partners—potential or actual—who work in different locations or organizations? The answer to these questions is a resounding: *Yes!* Meetings are a critical area of cultural difference.

The lines between meetings and discussions are often blurred and both need to be taken seriously.

While meetings enable people to share ideas, plan strategies, announce decisions, and an array of other functions, culture affects how meetings are conceptualized, managed, and integrated into the business context.

Meetings and National-Culture Differences

As with other dimensions of culture, people typically assume that the way they do something is universal—until they are exposed to an alternative. Let's take a look at this field notes excerpt in which a bilingual German marketing specialist identifies differences in meeting goals and attributes compared with a group of Americans with whom he is working.

> I have had such a terrible morning (that) I'll have to tell you about it. It's just so frustrating! … There are a lot of meetings that are completely unorganized with no purpose. You will get a call on the day of the meeting that the meeting will last from 9:00 until 5:00 and it is about a particular topic. The agenda will be distributed in a second VME (voice mail) and then you find that your name is on the agenda. You are supposed to say something about a particular topic and you are totally not prepared so you look stupid. Then, no one takes minutes. The meeting consists of statements of opinion by single (individual) people. If a conclusion is made, no one follows it. This is a very inefficient way to work with each other. In Europe, we have meetings that are scheduled many months in advance. They tell you what type of meeting it will be and some of the issues of those meetings so that they can plan far ahead in time. Four weeks before a particular meeting, you can try to get on the agenda. The organizer will ask you what decision you want made. A one-pager is required. You must turn this in 48 hours before the meeting takes place so people know exactly what you will

be discussing. At the meeting, decisions get made and someone takes minutes. After the meeting is over, someone reviews the draft minutes and they get sent out and there is no more discussion.

National-culture differences in meeting styles have been identified as an important focus of attention. Pamela Sheppard and Bénédicte Lapeyre have described such differences between the British and the French. The British use meetings for "debate for those who take part in and are affected by a decision. Everyone is expected to make some sort of contribution, whatever its quality, and not necessarily in their specialist area. They are not regarded as interruptions from real work" (1993: 35). By contrast, the attributes of a French business meeting parallel many of the elements of German meetings portrayed in the excerpt above.

> In France meetings called by the manager will follow an established format with a detailed agenda. The purpose is for briefing and coordination rather than a forum for debate or decision making. People will come well-prepared for the contribution they are expected to make…Kicking ideas around, floating a few trial balloons is relatively uncommon…. (p. 35)

Moreover, when differences in meetings become apparent to attendees of different national backgrounds, misunderstandings can occur.

Working globally requires quick learning and rapid adjustment to unfamiliar conditions. It is helpful to know something about the national culture in which the meeting is scheduled because the meeting style will encompass cultural elements that feature prominently in the national culture. For example, in German national culture, leaders hold high status and command significant authority. Accordingly, the leader performs a central role in German meetings.

Looking for clues in how a meeting is run will help you figure out ways to interface effectively with meeting participants. Ask yourself these questions when participating in a meeting with those from a different national culture:

- Who is doing the talking—a leader, a select group of participants, or all the participants?
- Can anyone present material or offer ideas?
- Whose views seem to matter?
- Does anyone keep the meeting moving along?

The answers to these questions will enable you to identify the roles that meeting participants play, the amount of planning associated with the meeting, the extent to which the agenda is followed, and what occurs at the end of the meeting.

Meetings and Organizational-Culture Differences

While it is helpful to know the nationalities of meeting participants—particularly those who are the meeting hosts—other factors are at play in structuring meeting goals, in presenting content, and in the interactions that occur. Indeed, there is significant variation in the function, management, and significance of meetings within any given national culture. Variation in meetings is evident within a firm's supply chain, between a firm and its partners, or within a firm's departments. Indeed, characteristics of an organizational culture are reflected in an organization's meeting style.

Elizabeth Briody examined differences in meeting styles among organizations working together on global ventures. Her work demonstrated that organizational culture played a more important role than national culture in shaping the business practice of meetings (Briody, Cavusgil, and Miller 2004). One three-way partnership she studied involved two American organizations and one German organization. She discovered not only that the two American organizations employed distinctive meeting styles, but that the Americans who worked for the German organization held the same expectations about meetings and exhibited the same behavior during meetings as their German counterparts.

Meeting attributes, such as the *purpose of meetings,* differentiated these three partnering organizations. For the German organization, the purpose of meetings was to make decisions. For one of the American organizations, the purpose was to reach consensus—a core theme in its organizational culture. For the other American organization, meetings were used to present, discuss, and debate the issues. A second attribute, the *amount of time allocated to meetings,* also was a point of contrast. Time in meetings was kept to a minimum in both the German organization and in one of the American organizations. However, in the other American organization, much of the workweek was spent in meetings—with reports as high as "30 hours a week." When this American organization was criticized for its meeting patterns, one of its members commented, "It's interesting why the Germans…do not think that we are working when we are in a meeting." Indeed, the organizational culture of this American organization equated meetings with work. A third attribute, *meeting content and format*, also varied among the three organizations. Meeting content and format were pre-determined in the German organization where there was a high value on structure and order. In one of the American organizations, the content of the meeting evolved; it was possible to add a meeting agenda item prior to or during the meeting. In the other American organization, the content was "focused" and directed toward the key issues that required resolution.

Now let's examine meeting attributes of another partnership that Briody studied involving General Motors Truck Group (GMTG) and Isuzu Motors Ltd. GMTG preferred free-flowing dialogue on technical issues and opportunities to engage in problem solving during its meetings with Isuzu. It considered brainstorming, on-the-spot discussions, and debate appropriate meeting behaviors. GMTG believed that meeting format should be flexible enough to accommodate exploration of new issues. At the same time, meetings could be venues for crystallizing or reinforcing "joint" decisions on which the partners agreed.

Isuzu's actions indicated a strong preference for solving technical issues within its own organization, rather than attempting to solve them during a meeting. It sought to generate consensus in-house, with a presentation of the results to GMTG in as complete a form as possible. Isuzu valued being well informed and prepared. It preferred to receive feedback, questions, and presentation material prior to its meetings with GMTG. Isuzu expected a pre-planned and structured approach to discussions with its partner.

An excerpt from Briody's field notes documents a discussion that occurred immediately following introductions during a two-day meeting in Japan. The meeting was conducted in English, though side conversations occurred in both Japanese and English.

> (The Isuzu program manager) went over the agenda and asked if there were any questions. (The GMTG program manager) said, 'We would like to spend time with the vehicles today or tomorrow and drive the vehicle if possible—maybe during lunch.' (The Isuzu program manager) started smiling and said, 'This is a late request.' (GMTG's chief engineer) said, 'We have concerns and we need to let (the GMTG program manager) see what the vehicle is like.' (The GMTG program manager) said, 'Also, we could give an update on where we are relative to Contract Signing (a milestone in GMTG's product development process).' (The Isuzu program manager) said, 'When?' (The GMTG program manager) responded, 'Maybe at the end of the Planning section?' At this point, (the interpreter) turned to me (Briody) and said, 'We have been into the meeting for six minutes and there have already been two surprises. The Japanese aren't very good with surprises.'

Leaders played a prominent role in Isuzu and GMTG. Both program managers engaged in a dialogue that reflected tensions about power and authority. The GMTG program manager presented the requests conditionally: "we would like … if possible—maybe during lunch" and "we could give…." However, his tone of voice, supplemented by a statement by GMTG's chief engineer, left no doubt about what GMTG expected. GMTG used its clout to insist on full compliance with its "requests."

The flow of the exchange showed an Isuzu program manager on the defensive. Although he invited comments on the prepared agenda, he did not anticipate the response he got. Isuzu program-level meetings formalize what has already been accomplished. Such meetings are not planned with the flexibility to accommodate on-the-spot requests, which can have a negative effect on the meeting's overall success. Had the Isuzu program manager known that GMTG wanted to drive the prototype vehicle, he could have ensured that it was ready to be taken on the road. In the end, the Isuzu program manager was pushed to integrate two new items into an already-full agenda, and direct a few engineers to work that morning so that the prototype would be ready for GMTG's noontime drive. The balance of power had shifted, at least temporarily, to the GMTG side of the partnership.

Lessons Drawn from Meetings

The cultural patterns embedded in meetings offer insights for understanding expectations, assumptions, and behavior in organizational and/or partnership settings. A first obvious lesson is that there is significant *variation in how meetings are structured and executed.* Meeting styles reflect and are reflective of the cultures of the meeting participants. In this section, we have emphasized the influence of both national culture and organizational culture on the character of meetings, though meeting styles also may reflect the impact of subcultural groups or the composition of meeting participants (e.g., females, new hires). Learning as much as possible about how to prepare for the meeting, how it is likely to proceed, and what follow-up tasks are typical will reduce the misunderstandings and level of frustration, and increase the likelihood of success.

A second lesson is that meetings reveal *differences in power and status* within each individual organization, and among the participating organizations. Meetings illustrate different views of hierarchy and the role of leader, the degree of balance achieved between guests and hosts, and the strategies used by individuals and organizations to attain their goals. Clues about who must be persuaded, and the best ways to approach the task of persuasion, are embedded in meeting protocols and behaviors. Discovering and operating on the basis of such clues can lead to improved meeting outcomes.

A third lesson is that meetings represent *important interactions* among individuals, groups, and organizations. They symbolize the possibilities of what might be, as well as the realities of what actually is. Meetings launch collaborations, bringing people together to accomplish certain goals. They are a playing field on which relationships are formed and/or strengthened, or weaken and/or fail. Taking the time to build relationships with meeting attendees during breaks, meals, after work, and on other occasions helps to shape the interactions in a positive way and facilitate goal achievement.

Power and status are often evident in seating position, discussion content, and agenda control.

One other important lesson is that meetings can be *highly volatile events* from which attendees can learn. They are part of a person, a community, and/or an organization's identity and practices. Problems arise when individuals, groups, or organizations decide to work together and do not realize that their approaches differ, or may even be incompatible. Meeting participants may not be able to articulate precisely what the differences are, but they will be able to express their annoyance and dismay over the way others run meetings. Raising awareness of such differences is a critical first step in understanding how the differences may be accommodated. Establishing a common meeting style, as a follow-up, will begin the process of helping disparate individuals, groups, and organizations create a shared foundation or platform for collaboration.

DECISION-MAKING MODELS TO ADVANCE THE PARTNERSHIP WORK

Decision making is another critical element of partnership activity and partnership success. It is the process of arriving at some determination or conclusion related to partnership goals and objectives. Partnership decision making represents judgments about specific aspects of the work: What tasks need to be done? Who should be involved? When should the tasks be completed? How should they be carried out? Where will the money come from? Under what circumstances will additional data be gathered? Decisions crosscut all partnering activities. As such, they are critical to the achievement of goals and overall partnership performance.

Decision Making and Cultural Differences

Just as meetings reflect cultural differences, so too does decision making. Partnership participants may hold different views of decision-making roles. For example, some may consider decision making a largely collaborative endeavor, while others may see it as the responsibility of the highest-ranking leaders. Partnership participants also may have different conceptions of how decision making should proceed. Some may find that significant time should be spent in gathering and discussing input from all parties, while others may be more comfortable making the call quickly on the advice of key subject matter "experts."

There seems to be an increasing sensitivity to decision-making differences as more individuals and organizations are engaged in global business endeavors. Decision-making dilemmas are a key source of conflict and a major impediment to partnership success. The individual's role is highlighted frequently in management (Segil 1996; Kalmbach and Roussel 1999; Spekman and Isabella 2000). However, the linkages between organizational culture and decision making have not been fully explored. Recent attention has been directed to the composition of the work group—including its diverse knowledge and skill base—as a way to improve decision making (Shachaf 2008).

Decision-making issues appear front and center as individuals and organizations attempt to plan and carry out partnering work. Frustration often occurs as people begin to realize that their partners do not conceptualize the decision-making process in the same way that they do. Partnership participants may also learn about decision-making differences through reading, cross-cultural training, or discussions with those who have lived and worked abroad. Generally speaking, decision making tends to be viewed as a characteristic of national culture. People often refer to the groups involved by their nationality, rather than singling out any other characteristic (e.g., their gender, organization). For example, Americans are said to tally up their votes compared to the Japanese who make decisions based on group consensus.

Decision Making and Organizational-Culture Differences

It turns out that decision-making processes vary enormously within any given national culture. They are a reflection of such factors as the people and organizations involved (including their role and status) and the importance and urgency of the decisions under consideration. Elizabeth Briody has researched decision-making processes in two different partnerships involving six different organizations. Each of the six organizations had its own distinctive decision-making model. Moreover, each organization was characterized by a particular key relationship (i.e., peer, superior–subordinate), and a cultural principle or theme that permeated work-related values and behavior. Attributes of each organization are described in Table 6.1.

MAJORITY PREFERRED AT SMALL CAR GROUP The Small Car Group decision-making model can be described as majority preferred. It was a cross between "majority rule," in which attempts are made to foster as much consensus as possible, and "leadership rule" in which the leader plays a significant role in directing decision making (see also de Tocqueville 1835: 254–70). Small Car Group employees expected to contribute their ideas to unit operations via information sharing and debate. There were frequent and continuous efforts to "pitch" both technical and business-related ideas in the hope of generating "buy-in" from the appropriate leader(s) and organizational members. Thus, the key relationship was between a given individual and any potential "allies" that the individual was able to influence. Alliance formation was the key cultural principle, with some alliances carrying more weight than others. For example, if the relevant leader(s) agreed with a particular proposal, there was a greater likelihood that the proposal would be accepted and the decision made. These alliances varied in duration, some lasting only as long as it took to get a particular decision made.

100 PERCENT CONSENSUS AT SATURN Saturn employees indicated that they made and expected to make their decisions based on 100 percent consensus. They respected the viewpoints of their Saturn colleagues as they worked together to arrive at the best possible solutions. Arriving at unanimous consent could take considerable

TABLE 6.1 Selected Organizational-Culture Differences on Two GM Vehicle Programs

	Small Car Group (based in the United States)	Saturn Corporation (based in the United States)	Adam Opel AG (based in Germany)	GM Truck Group (based in the United States)	GM do Brasil (based in Brazil)	Isuzu Motors Ltd. (based in Japan)
Decision-Making Model	Majority preferred	100 percent consensus	Leadership driven	Individual empowerment	Collaboration	Single voice of authority
Key Relationship	Individual to potential allies, particularly leaders	Intra-group, including leader	Leader to subordinates	Individual alone, with input from others as needed	Peers	Leader to subordinate, with some input from others
Key Cultural Principle	Alliance formation	Equality	Hierarchy	Individualism	Interdependence	Harmony

time and energy. However, Saturn employees used two strategies to enable their decision-making model. First, employees adhered to the rule of thumb that if someone was 70 percent comfortable with a proposed decision, he/she must be 100 percent committed to it. Second, on those occasions when the "team" was unable to make a particular decision, team members sought assistance from a higher-ranking management group. Equality was the cultural principle interwoven throughout Saturn's organizational culture. Thus, the key relationships were those within any given "team" (see also Stewart and Bennett 1991). The decision-making process typically involved a group of people representing a range of classification levels and variety of functions.

LEADERSHIP DRIVEN AT OPEL   Opel's decision-making model was leadership driven. In the period prior to the decision, the leader requested input from numerous sources. At this stage, it was possible for employees to provide substantive information as well as an assessment of a given proposal. Employees sensed that they were free to express their opinions. Leaders tried to resolve issues and make decisions that were both consistent with the "data" and tended to reflect widespread support within the organization. In that sense, the Opel decision-making model was consensus based. Hierarchy was the cultural principle shaping relationships at Opel, with the key relationship between a leader and his subordinates. There was a strong recognition of and regard for individuals in positions of authority (see also Hall and Hall 1989). Much of this respect stemmed from their technical areas of expertise and the judgment that they applied in coordinating and managing projects and people. Once the decision was final, organizational members fell in line behind it.

SINGLE VOICE OF AUTHORITY AT ISUZU   Isuzu's decision-making model was driven by the idea of establishing and disseminating one position or single voice internally and then to its partners. The process entailed assigning a task to a subordinate. The subordinate conferred with others—either within or outside the work group or functional area—to complete the assignment. That employee then developed a list of alternatives or proposals to present to the supervisor. While the employee typically made his preferences known, the leader made the decision. The belief was that the leader could apply a broader experience base and a more holistic view of the situation to the particular decision. The employee worked to satisfy his supervisor and through that supervisor the entire organization. Thus, the vertical relationship between the employee and his supervisor was the key relationship. The stability and acceptance of these work roles and the unity of purpose among organizational members contributed to a relatively high degree of internal understanding and harmony—the key cultural principle in Isuzu.

INDIVIDUAL EMPOWERMENT AT GM TRUCK GROUP   The basis of decision making at GMTG was individual empowerment. Employees tended to be highly specialized in their job responsibilities. They typically performed tasks on their own as they developed ideas or proposals to solve technical or business (i.e., finance, purchasing) issues. Employees generally expected their supervisors to uphold their conclusions or decisions. However, individuals often encountered resistance. Multiple positions on any given issue were common and reflected the obstacles in crossing work group and functional boundaries. Consequently, decisions were frequently revisited and changed. Nevertheless, individuals viewed themselves as free and empowered agents who had the potential to make a difference. Individualism was the cultural principle resonating within GMTG's organizational culture (see also de Tocqueville 1840: 98–99). There was no particular key relationship among organizational members that mattered so much as the pivotal role played by individuals operating largely independently in the day-to-day life of the organization.

COLLABORATION AT GM DO BRASIL   Collaboration was the basis for GM do Brasil's (GMBs) decision-making model. Noticeable about the environment at GMB was the apparent ease with which colleagues exchanged information and cooperated with one another. Once assignments were generated, individuals received both solicited and unsolicited input from their peers. This feedback typically occurred in face-to-face situations as colleagues recalled earlier examples—sometimes from other product programs—and offered ideas and commentary on the technical or business issue at hand. This kind of informal information sharing was complemented by the more formal design and engineering reviews. Eventually, a solution or decision became evident to the individual initially assigned the task, and to those participating in any discussions with him/her. The emphasis at GMB was on horizontal relationships, that is, among peers or colleagues. Interdependency was the cultural principle that characterized GMB's organizational culture (see also DaMatta 1991; Oliveira 2001). It was supported by such factors as the extensive social networks, the expectation that colleagues would assist each other, the sharing of work tools and equipment (e.g., telephones, computers), and the small size of the operation in terms of headcount and budget.

The Impact of Decision-Making Differences

The fact that there are distinctive ways of making decisions raises the obvious question: To what extent do these decision-making models aid or hinder the overall effectiveness and efficiency of a partnership? In Briody's partnerships, there were numerous indicators of decision paralysis (2010). Three decision models were in use in each of the two partnerships. One of the participating organizations might have spearheaded a particular initiative, only to find that one or both of the partners were unwilling to go along with it. Delays often resulted in arriving at a final decision. In fact, the delays had their own consequences including cost in labor hours and an inability to meet the partnership lead-time targets. In a number of cases, one (or more) of the partnering organizations would ask its own senior leadership (e.g., President, Managing Director) to intervene and reverse a decision. When decisions did not "stick," rework was typically required, which also led to additional cost and delays. The multiplicity of decision-making models, combined with other partnership issues, resulted in significant levels of frustration, damaged relationships, and irresolvable conflict. The partnership involving Small Car Group, Saturn, and Opel ultimately failed, while the GMTG, GMB, and Isuzu alliance never met expectations.

Lessons Drawn from Decision-Making Models

The first lesson was the *discovery of multiple decision-making models* among the partners. Indeed, each participating organization had its own approach to decision making. Five of these decision-making models were associated with a single corporation (and even within that corporation, there were likely to be many other variants). While decision-making models are associated with both national and organizational cultures, they may also be tied to other subcultural groups related by occupation, job classification, and gender, among others.

A second lesson is that *decision-making models are more closely aligned with organizational-culture attributes* than with national-culture traits. One proof point is that three of the six decision-making models were associated with American national culture, that is, they were associated with organizations based in the United States. Although they were clearly recognizable as sharing some common cultural elements (given their national-culture heritage), they were also easily distinguished from each other on the basis of organizational affiliation. A second proof point was that some Americans worked for organizations located outside the United States and took on the cultural orientation of those organizations. For example, the Americans who worked for Opel expected that decisions would be "leadership driven." A third proof point is that Isuzu's hierarchically oriented decision-making approach was very different than the consensus-based characterization associated with Japanese national culture (see Dore 1973; Hall and Hall 1987; Gannon and Associates 1994; Jun and Muto 1995).

A third lesson relates to *the who and the how dimensions* of any decision-making model. The *who dimension* identifies the individual or group responsible for making decisions. In two of the decision-making models—GM do Brasil and Saturn—an individual's relationships with peers were at least as important as the relationship with his/her immediate supervisor. By contrast, in some of the other models such as GMTG and Opel, peers were not as central to decision making. Instead, the individual tended to work largely alone or with his/her supervisor. This analysis negates simple conventional wisdom that only leaders make decisions, and reveals role diversity in decision making. The *how dimension* of a decision-making model specifies the process by which decisions are made. Sometimes decision making was an overtly collective endeavor such as at Saturn where consensus was essential. In other models such as Small Car Group, the decision-making process was collective, though the decision might not hold if a higher-ranking leader disagreed with it. In still other models such as Isuzu and Opel, decision making was considered a leadership responsibility.

One other important lesson is that *conflict is sure to surface* when multiple decision-making models coexist within the same partnership. Learning how to manage the conflict can lead to significant benefits. Partners on high-performing partnerships have figured out strategies for working together, despite the differences. There is synergy in their relationships and effort behind their joint work. They have created "cultural crossvergence" (Sarala and Vaara 2010), a "hybrid" culture (Adler 1997; Gluesing and Gibson 2004), or a partnership culture that includes a *shared* decision-making model and unites them as a whole.

PARTNERING RELATIONSHIPS AND PROBLEM SOLVING

How individuals, groups, organizations, and other entities conduct themselves in a partnership matters to its success. Partnering is hard work, requiring significant time, energy, and effort. What you are expecting to happen may not occur, while the unexpected may appear without warning. There are always questions, concerns, ambiguity, and second guessing. Cultural differences are a key source of partnership issues. If they are not well understood or if they are ignored, the partners are likely to face ongoing difficulties as long as the partnership is active. In this section we discuss two strategies to foster the work of the partnership and mitigate tension: building and maintaining relationships, and problem solving.

Partnerships are launched when two or more individuals or organizations make a decision to work together. Often they are initiated on the basis of personal, face-to-face introductions, which lead to further discussions about combining resources and expertise toward some set of goals and objectives. Follow-up interactions are essential for understanding perspectives, approaches, and competencies; hammering out roles and responsibilities; creating an initial plan for the joint work; and very importantly, beginning the process of relationship building. Preparing some kind of written agreement (e.g., memo of understanding, contract) to guide the partnership occurs when a formal document is desired.

Robert T. Trotter, II and his colleagues have examined the relationship component of industry–university partnerships. They discovered the importance of reciprocity to collaborative work. Partnership participants emphasized the importance of sharing information and insights, engaging in the joint work, and understanding, trusting, and respecting their counterparts (2008a, 2008b). Indeed, he and his research team concluded that "Without strong relationships, there is neither a commitment to the partner nor the likelihood of achieving partnership goals" (Sengir et al. 2004: 555). This element of reciprocity matters within both "home-grown" partnerships, and those operating in a global context.

Visits help partners build reciprocal relationships.

Partnering with On-Site Work Colleagues

One such home-grown partnership is a multidisciplinary research team at Motorola Mobility. Multidisciplinary work has long been a mainstay of industrial research laboratories. Researchers must figure out ways to collaborate to invent new products, processes, technologies, and software, and then shepherd their inventions into commercialization. The "Experiences Research" group at the Applied Research Center consists of engineers, human-computer interaction specialists, designers, and an anthropologist who also serves as the group's manager. Crysta Metcalf led this team in a discovery process that focused on two key questions related to the group's role within the corporation: "How do we communicate our contributions? How can we persuade others that these contributions are valuable?" (2011: 28). The answers to these questions lay in the group's ability to collaborate to achieve a common goal.

Their approach to collaboration was not additive with each individual performing a specific task. Rather, they opted to engage in the applied research tasks as a group—conducting the field work and analysis together, designing and building prototypes together, and contributing to the final deliverables together. Metcalf comments, "We became successful when we stopped trying to convince each other of our disciplinary value." An increasing number of innovations have resulted from "doing the work together" and being actively engaged in the transfer of their technologies. A key piece of advice from Metcalf is: "You don't throw it over the wall to the product groups for commercialization. You bring in the product groups and get them involved—the earlier the better—and that helps convince them." Interest in the Experiences Research group as a new model of work has risen as the corporation sought to expand its market reach in a tight economy.

Gülcin Sengir and her colleagues discovered that the process of achieving partnership work goals "is both the raison d'être holding the relationships together, and the driving force justifying the establishment of the partnership in the first place" (2004: 547). The joint work promotes ongoing involvement of partnership participants. Working together effectively depends on a number of factors including a strong relational foundation of mutual respect and trust. A field notes excerpt from the larger data set in which she was involved encapsulates this point: "The people who end up working together need to understand and appreciate each other. They need mutual respect and this is the major element of success for us" (Trotter et al. 2008a: 47). In fact, successful work strategies and outcomes can help solidify or reinforce positive team interactions and relationships.

Sometimes the hoped-for, anticipated collaboration within the work group does not materialize immediately. One American RN (Registered Nurse) had to overcome a difficult challenge. She had been hired along with health care professionals from a number of countries to help staff Saudi Arabia's expanding medical sector; English was the mandated language for patient care. The American RN reported, "You got paid by your passport," meaning that the pay rate was contingent upon country of origin. For example, American nurses were paid four times more than their Filipino peers. (From another perspective, American nurses earned a salary that was equivalent to what they would make in the United States while the Filipino salary was more than triple what would be expected in the Philippines.)

The differential pay structure, along with preferential housing accommodations based on nationality, created an undercurrent of discord in the Saudi hospital. This nurse, the only American RN among the largely Filipino nursing staff, reported feeling alienated. There was "resentment about how much I made" independent of her role as assistant manager and charge RN. She learned enough Tagalog, one of the national languages in the Philippines, to understand what the Filipino nurses were saying. Their attitudes became more pronounced when their concept of nursing was inconsistent with hers. For example, patient chart reviews were an essential element for safe patient care and part of the American RN's oversight duties and responsibilities. However, some of the largely Filipino staff did not perceive reading charts as work and "complained that they were doing more work for less money."

What can a global nursing manager do under such circumstances? What are some ways in a partnership to bridge differences in status and power? The American RN used her basic Tagalog to engage with the Filipino nurses. "I had to look for ways to build relationships" she stated. At the hospital, she tried to be as approachable as possible and minimize the differences between her and the nursing staff. She also participated in food shopping, preparation, and meal sharing, as well as weekly mah-jongg games with the Filipino community working at the hospital. The American nurse met with some success, even making a couple of Filipino friends who were able to offer insights and guidance into the social complexities of the Filipino expatriate community.

The American RN actively engaged with her Filipino work colleagues in nonwork contexts with the intent of building relationships. Her approach consisted of repeated interactions and regular communication, built on physical proximity (in that she lived and worked near them), and showed interest in their cultural values (see Shapiro, Sheppard, and Cheraskin 1992). She sought a closeness in her relationship with them as a way to build interpersonal ties (see Bozionelos 2009). Her success was due, at least in part, to her sensitivity to their culture and her ability to encourage openness and sharing (see Phan, Styles, and Patterson 2005).

Sometimes relationships between work colleagues falter and may even fail when the parties perceive the relationship differently. Cultural differences can exacerbate the situation because those involved may not understand each other's assumptions and expectations. A number of Russian scientists and engineers participated in a U.S. government-run partnership with the automotive industry. The Russians came to the United States for a six-month internship as a way to jump-start their international careers. One of the scientists had been asked to talk about his adjustment experiences from the previous year in a cross-cultural training class offered by the program sponsors. He told a story of how difficult it was to work as a team with Americans. He had been assigned to work on a project with one American whom he considered a close friend. As the project was winding down, he told the American that he had made a calculation error, but that he had rectified it. The American reported the error to the local management because error reporting was part of the work process. In the training class, the Russian was still upset. "I remember him saying, 'I thought he (the American) was my friend but he didn't care. He cared only about the task,'" stated Natasha Crundwell, the owner of the firm providing the training and a Russian herself.

This incident represents two particularly difficult lessons in American culture for the Russian scientist. First, he felt that he had been betrayed by his American friend since he had told his friend in confidence about the error. He learned that Americans do not understand friendship as Russians do. For Russians, friendships are "almost like family relationships where there are strong emotional bonds," stated Crundwell. What Americans call friendship seemed superficial to him. The relationship was certainly not fully reciprocal since he cared more for the American than the American for him. Second, the American pointed out to the Russian that "You have to follow the process" and "report every error," stated Crundwell. From the Russian scientist's perspective, the incident did not merit being reported when relationships were on the line. It was only a minor error and not relevant for any important outcome. Moreover, it was not a "cover up" since he had fixed the error. He believed that his American colleague should have discussed this matter with him first before reporting it. Obviously the rigid work process with its rules was more important to the American than their friendship. (The Russian's analysis of the matter was reminiscent of the distinction made between universalistic and particularistic cultures; universalistic cultures favor rules while particularistic cultures favor relationships [Parsons 1951; Parsons and Shils 1951; Trompenaars and Hampden-Turner 1998].)

This promising relationship neither attained its potential nor reached a resolution. The conflict from this single incident continued to overshadow the Russian's recollection of his partnering experience one year later. Managers can play a critical role in transcending the tensions by establishing work practices and processes that are inclusive and empowering, and keep people connected. Unfortunately, there was no managerial strategy in place to help the Russian scientist deal with the culture clash he experienced. Shortly after his internship was over, he returned to Russia.

COWBOYS AND INDIANS

Workplace conflict can be complicated, arising from both individual and organizational factors, and have a direct impact on relationships and productivity. A global investment bank purchased an expensive automated tool for testing software. A leading global IT services company in India was in charge of the testing and assigned one of its experts to test the tool in the United States. Tension soon flared up between the tool expert and the on-site team leader for the global IT services company, as well as between the tool expert and the investment bank's software developers. The team leader was ethnically Indian but raised in the United States, according to anthropologist Patricia Ensworth. He was accustomed to "flat organizational structures, informal communication, and gung-ho attitudes toward taking the initiative," and sent the tool expert off to obtain the specifications from the developers on her own. Ensworth continued, "As one might expect from someone who was used to hierarchical organizations, formal communications, and deference to authority, and who had never visited the United States before, she struggled with the assignment." The already-overworked developers complained to the team leader that they did not have time to write documentation or answer her questions. The tool expert appealed to the team leader for support but was told she must try harder and improve her performance.

The team leader found himself under fire from both the software developers and his own management. One day at a status meeting the tool expert again reported that the problem was a lack of cooperation from the developers. "No," the team leader shouted. "You're the (expletive) problem!" Shocked, she flung her cup of hot coffee in his face and walked away. Within 48 hours, the tool expert and her husband were deported to India. The team leader received a verbal reprimand. According to the bank's Human Resource department, the coffee-throwing constituted "workplace violence" and was grounds for immediate dismissal. Among the employees of both the bank and the IT services company who had grown up in India, the punishment was perceived unanimously as unjust (Patricia Ensworth, personal communication).

Fortunately, the global investment bank viewed this incident as a learning opportunity. Ensworth was given greater authority "to drill down into the teamwork issue" on software projects. She essentially served as "ombudsman," helping raise project team awareness of the cultural elements at play and developing process documents with deliverables that included an effective intercultural team (see Ensworth 2003 for an example of the ombudsman role at a different firm).

Distinctions between Local and Global Partnerships

In the four examples—the Motorola Mobility researchers, the American and Filipino nurses, and the Russian and American scientists, and the relationship between the global investment bank and global IT services company—the parties were physically located together and experienced direct, face-to-face contact with their counterparts. However, many partnerships have members who are geographically separated from each other because they work and reside in various sites around the world. While they may meet regularly to advance their joint work, those meetings do not typically occur in person. Indeed, many partnership participants work "virtually," that is, they use IT and communications technologies to interact. The growth of virtual teams has occurred for many reasons including the possibilities of tapping into a larger talent pool, decreased development time for new products and services, lower travel costs, and reduced time spent in travel (Dekker, Rutte, and Van den Berg 2008; Shachaf 2008).

Julia Gluesing and her colleagues compared global work teams engaged in partnering work, with local work teams that relied primarily on face-to-face interactions. Global teams face complexity challenges that "traditional" teams do not confront. A prominent complexity challenge for global teams involves working across multiple contexts, and doing so virtually. (They define context as "a way of life and work in a specific geographic area with its own set of business conditions, cultural assumptions, and unique history" [Gluesing et al. 2003].) Context affects how work gets done including where the work occurs, the language(s) used, the forms of communication with colleagues, and time of day in which work interactions take place.

In a different study, Julia Gluesing and Cristina Gibson identified a number of characteristics distinguishing global teams from "traditional" teams working in a single context (2004: 202–03). Among the work groups studied were an automotive product development team, a team responsible for tracking and reporting sales, a management team responsible for creating a joint venture, and some software development teams. Typically, global teams

- work in multiple locations, rather than a common location or work environment
- are composed of people from multiple national cultures in multiple geographic locations, rather than in a common national culture in a single geography
- are composed of people from multiple and dissimilar political and economic conditions, compared with teams operating in common political and economic conditions
- include both native and nonnative speakers while traditional teams have native language speakers
- are more likely to be developing or have developed cross-cultural skills, compared with traditional team members
- engage in work tasks that usually involve crossing national and organizational boundaries unlike tasks on traditional teams that generally remain within such boundaries
- rely on various communication technologies much more so than face-to-face interactions
- often work across multiple time zones unlike traditional team members.

Global Virtual Partnerships

Many partnerships are increasingly reliant on virtual interactions—whether as a supplementary or primary strategy. Frequently-used IT and communication technologies include e-mail, telephone, mobile and smartphone devices, instant messaging, application sharing, and virtual private networks. These technologies tend to direct the partners' attention to the specifics of the work, while simultaneously limiting face-to-face encounters.

Global virtual teams interface with their partners differently. Angelika Zimmermann (2011) summarizes some of the communication patterns associated with these teams. They have to learn to communicate so as to build trust and reduce risks and uncertainties related to their work goals. Because communication often contains implicit messages, they have to acquire the skills to communicate in a clear and direct fashion. The fact that much of their communication is nonsynchronous means that they do not benefit from immediate feedback, though regular communication can help. In addition, these teams have to figure out how to evaluate each other's competencies and motivation levels without an ongoing, face-to-face connection.

Tara Eaton has conducted a study on the virtual aspects of offshore outsourcing, a project that has involved globally-distributed work teams (Eaton 2011). Offshore outsourcing refers to situations where client firms contract with one or more providers located in another country. For example, an American automotive company might hire an IT services company in India to create a billing and invoicing system. Eaton found that the structure of virtual work, including the use of technologies, brings "disparate workers together in a committed way." She pointed out that she has observed the gradual development and solidification of a "virtual culture" which she defines as "an adaptive system of learned, shared, and symbolic meanings and behaviors characterizing the virtual group."

The IT and communication technologies "seem to foster a focus on the task at hand, and represent a wider and overlapping range of devices for work in the virtual environment," stated Eaton. Indeed, they contrast markedly with the technologies in use even 10 years ago (i.e., fax, video conferencing) (Riopelle et al. 2003). The current practice of virtual work is associated with a rise in problem solving and learning which, in turn, reinforces the development of the virtual culture. As one of her study participants said, "When I'm trying to explain something technical, I prefer to use e-mail and application sharing software because you can't assume someone else gets all that they need to understand without a visual demonstration."

The importance of written—especially e-mail—communication for global virtual teams cannot be overestimated. Often, nonnative English speakers can express themselves better in writing than verbally, and prefer written communication over verbal because they can spend the necessary time decoding and understanding it, and preparing a well-thought-out response. In addition, written communication eliminates the nonverbal and social cues, and variation in accents associated with these virtual groups, which can help reduce miscommunication and misinterpretation. A field note excerpt of an American virtual team member makes the point this way (Shachaf 2008: 136):

> Communicating with technology [e-mail] with people in other countries…removes some of the problems…you don't have all the cultural, physical aspects of communications. You know, the way you speak to a Japanese is not the way you speak to an Arab is not the way you speak to an American, from the point of view of the distance you have to keep, the way you look at them, the way you express feeling, etc. when you just type a text in an e-mail or a chat system…all that disappears, there is just the plain text there.

One lesson to be drawn from this work is that IT and communication technologies play a dual role in shaping virtual culture: (1) they are the principal mechanisms by which work tasks are completed, and (2) they are the primary ways in which collaborative relationships are formed and maintained. The combination of these elements distinguishes virtual collaborations from those that are grounded largely in face-to-face interactions.

Partnerships are based on cooperative and collaborative activity and not typically on friendship (though friendship might result). Particularly for virtual partnerships, cooperation is essential since it is difficult to create a personal bond which is so highly dependent on face-to-face interaction. An innovative course on Collaborative Innovation Networks (COINs), offered since 2008, is "helping students learn to work in multi-cultural, multi-disciplinary, globally-distributed virtual teams" according to Christine Miller, one of the faculty members teaching

Global business and virtual work have led to the global "virtual conference" connecting multiple sites in real time.

the course. Currently, participating universities include MIT Sloan and Savannah College of Art and Design from the United States, Aalto University Helsinki in Finland, and the University of Cologne in Germany. Students and their faculty advisors work on projects brought to them by client organizations, gathering and analyzing social network data from various sources including the Web, social networking sites, online forums, phone logs, e-mail archives, face-to-face interaction, and blogs (http://sites.google.com/site/coincourse2011/, accessed August 25, 2011). Students rank-order their interest in the projects and then are assigned to a project with peers from at least two of the other three universities.

Once students receive instruction in the current best practices of collaborative networks, they begin to establish the tools they will use for communication (e.g., e-mail, Skype) and how they will use them. After a few weeks, an analysis of the students' own communication behavior is conducted and presented to them. This "virtual mirror" is usually an "eye-opening experience" since it shows the disparities between the COINs' best practices and the students' actual collaborative abilities. In particular, it provides insight on how responsive each student is within his/her project team, as well as the degree of balance in both sending and receiving e-mail messages. Other analyses have revealed some fascinating national-culture differences. The Finns communicate the least, the Germans the most, and the Americans somewhere in between. The tenor and quality of the communication also varies. Finns are "to the point" and appear to be somewhat introverted. Germans tend to communicate with "brutal" honesty. Americans "try to convey unpleasant things in a nicer way," which can be viewed by their partners as evasive (Goor et al. 2011). These patterns of virtual communication are useful in helping students understand the extent to which they are contributing to the team project, and their style of interaction with team members.

Julia Gluesing and Cristina Gibson found that the key way that global teams become effective is by creating a new "hybrid" context or culture for themselves that reflects their emerging work styles, practices, and processes. This effort can be facilitated by team members and leaders who have global experience and/or have previously worked together. Launch time is reduced under such circumstances because there is "likely to be a foundation of trust and shared knowledge of each other's work habits" (2004: 212). Building relationships among team members is particularly important at the outset of a new venture. Their findings dovetail with those of other researchers (Henttonen and Blomqvist 2005: 112) who have found that "Often the first impression...defined the direction and depth of future cooperation...When the other team members did not demonstrate goodwill in her/his actions by answering emails promptly and communicating openly, the interaction faded away."

Gluesing and Gibson also suggest that structuring the team's work (e.g., establishing objectives, assigning roles and responsibilities, making decisions about communication technologies) helps in the organization and coordination of work activities. Creating a sense of community and developing shared models or frameworks of how to work together can help the global team mature and position them to be successful. Similarly, Cristina Gibson and Jennifer Gibbs emphasize the value of a "psychologically-safe communication climate" consisting of features such as openness, mutual respect, and risk taking to facilitate virtual team innovation (2006: 484). Thus, relationship development and maintenance are just as important in global, virtual teams as they are in face-to-face work groups. Moreover, global teams generally need to be more imaginative about the best ways of creating team bonds.

Partnership Life Cycle

A critical part of partnership work involves addressing work-related issues. Partnerships face different issues depending on where they are in the partnership life cycle. Robert T. Trotter, II and his colleagues examined the evolution of industry–university partnership activity through a combination of ethnographic interviews, observation, and social-network data (2004, 2008a, 2008b). They found that partnerships have a life cycle beginning with an early period during which relationships are developed among the key players, progressing through increasingly focused joint work, and ultimately into some transition period.

Initially, potential partners are identified and contacted to gauge mutual interest in forming a partnership. If there is agreement among the parties to proceed, negotiations about the work of the partnership follow. Small work groups consisting of a mix of technical, managerial, and support personnel are formed during the *Initiation Stage.* Over time, these work groups grow in size and density to form a social network structure with a core and periphery. During the *Start-Up Stage,* relationship development continues with the establishment of a strong core membership. The development of trust and mutual respect among the participants occurs, along with good communication and coordination. Some tension occurs as the partners begin to learn about and adjust to their differences. Collaborative work moves into high gear during the *Growth Stage.* Those individuals at the core of the social network focus on such matters as partnership goals and direction, and act as integrators across the partnership network. Those on the periphery are engaged in particular technical tasks, with key players in the core keeping them linked to the overall effort. Distinct subgroups emerge from the core during the *Mature Stage,* each composed of a mix of participants from the partners. Participants are fully engaged in accomplishing the partnership goals through joint work. During *Transition,* the partners examine what they were able to do together as well as what fell short of expectations. They also consider the relationship dynamics and make decisions about the partnership's future. Four outcomes are possible, including continuing the partnership with minimal change, modifying the partnership by adding or deleting certain technical areas, splitting the partnership into two or more fully functioning partnerships, and terminating the partnership. Transition can be

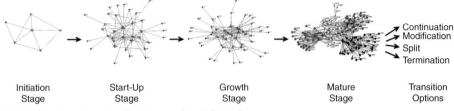

| Initiation Stage | Start-Up Stage | Growth Stage | Mature Stage | Transition Options |

FIGURE 6.1   *Stages in the Partnership Life Cycle.*

associated with conflict since partnership conditions are in flux. Figure 6.1 illustrates this evolution beginning with the Initiation Stage through Transition (Borgatti 2002; Trotter et al. 2008a; Trotter, Sengir, and Briody 2008b).

Partnership Process Outcomes

We use the term *process* to refer to views related to the work process, that is, how the work and problem solving get done and/or should get done. A significant amount of effort goes into keeping partnerships on track so that there is alignment between the work process and the goals and objectives. Cultural rules help to illuminate the process of problem solving and the emergence or existence of a partnering culture. Tracy Meerwarth and her colleagues examined partnership culture as it was in the process of forming. They sought to provide "an understanding of the day-to-day partnership activities, work processes, and participant concerns during the partnership cycle" (2005: 286). They investigated two private-sector partnerships with General Motors—one with Alcan International Ltd. and the other with BP (formerly known as British Petroleum). Through their interviews they identified the concept of *partnership rules*—unwritten prescriptions offered by partnership participants for how partnerships should work. Illustrative examples included:

- *You need to spend time thinking about what you want to solve.*
- *There has to be a benefit for both parties in a partnership.*
- *In the end, if you can't put the product together to satisfy our customers, both lose.*
- *We have to protect our competitive advantage.*

About 40 percent of the 440 rules they discovered were already an active part of partnership problem solving, while others were in the process of crystallizing. Not only was there a higher proportion of rules that were "not yet in place" on the Alcan–GM partnership, but also the rules prescribed numerous ways to improve partnership functioning. By contrast, the BP–GM partnership had a higher proportion of rules already "in place," suggesting a well-functioning partnership. Thus, the number and content of the rules offered insight into perceived differences in partnership performance. The rules indicated distinctive partnership cultures.

When cultural rules are not shared, they can reveal a lack of integration across partnerships, organizations, and groups. Anthropologist Yasunobu Ito has been comparing the work activities of seven different medical departments at a national university hospital in Japan. He has discovered that unofficial "local rules" are specific to departments. For example, in one department where the nurses work three shifts, patient medical notes are taken "using a black pen, a red pen and a blue pen respectively" (2011: 35); this rule does not exist in other departments. Departments also use binder or folder tags in different colors and with different signage to communicate with other medical professionals. A pink tag in one department might mean that a nurse has to check with a doctor on some issue, while in another department, it might mean that the nurse needs to check with another nurse. In some departments, tag color matters, while in others, the writing on the tag is what is relevant. In still other departments, no one uses the tags at all. Indeed, Ito is finding that there is no standardization across hospital departments. Moreover, hospital culture in the division of nursing "makes it difficult to talk about those local rules and the thinking behind them, since according to the official line, they should not exist at all, and if they do, they have to remain secret" (2011: 55).

When a partnership is being initiated, few rules are in place to guide it. Sometimes cultural experts who are familiar with the key people involved, their expectations and assumptions, and their interaction styles are there to assist. One such case involved people in the international programs office at a major U.S. research university. They had been trying for over a year to broker a partnership between their business school and that of a prestigious Chinese university. Now, at long last, discussions were beginning. It was hoped that the resulting agreement would set in motion a series of important research collaborations. The U.S. business school Dean had never been to China before. His Chinese counterpart had been educated in Sweden and spoke some English, though he had little experience with Americans. Also in the room as the conversation started were Riall Nolan, an anthropologist and Dean of International Programs, and his Associate Dean, an American who spoke fluent Mandarin.

Almost immediately the conversation ran into trouble. "The two Deans were talking, but not really hearing one another, and with each exchange, the level of frustration and irritation was growing. Neither one of them understood what was happening or why," stated Riall Nolan. After an hour, Nolan called time out. Nolan took the Business School Dean aside, and the Associate Dean took the Chinese Dean aside, to explain what the cross-cultural communication difficulties were. Each time the Chinese Dean threw out a proposal, the American Dean would say, "That's interesting," or "We can think about that." Although these kinds of statements are often the way Americans will signal genuine interest, such phrases are also used in other cultures to mean the equivalent of "never in a million years." Since this was the way in which the Chinese Dean was interpreting the American Dean's responses, the Chinese Dean became more anxious, then louder, and finally, angry. In contrast, every time the American Dean made a proposal, the Chinese Dean would immediately respond with "Ja, Ja, Ja, Ja, Ja" (Swedish for "Yes"). The American Dean understood this reply as "Yeah, Yeah, Yeah, Yeah, Yeah" which, in an American context, would probably be interpreted as dismissive and sarcastic. However, the time out and personal coaching helped. When the meeting reconvened, each man understood what the other was really trying to say; agreement on the launch of the partnership was reached quickly. In this case, although both sides sincerely wanted to collaborate, and although both could speak English, differences in communication style almost doomed the partnership before it had begun.

Partnership Product Outcomes

Another aspect of problem solving relates directly to the achievement of partnership goals and objectives—that is, the actual or anticipated *products* of the partnership. Anthropologist Sunil Khanna partnered with an NGO (nongovernmental organization) in India on an innovative problem-solving strategy related to the health of mothers and children (Khanna 2010). This organization had been providing health care to slum communities for about 20 years. While it had developed a significant amount of expertise working with such communities, it had simultaneously been challenged by changing funding criteria. For example, funding for HIV-AIDS prevention is typically for specific prevention activities, rather than for a wider range of activities with key community stakeholder groups (e.g., parents, teachers) to ensure high rates of success.

Khanna consulted with the leadership to design and launch a non-profit foundation. This activity was highly unusual among such organizations at the time; the usual reaction would have been to change programs and reporting requirements to meet the changes in funding requirements. However, through Khanna's guidance, the entrepreneurial leadership recognized the important role of community buy-in for any successful HIV-AIDS prevention program. Soon the foundation began approaching private donors in India—including business people and public–private partnerships—to fill its funding gaps. Khanna stated, "Changes are now underway to open a foundation branch in the U.S. so that American donations are tax deductible. Future branches of the foundation are planned for Europe as well."

The products of the partnership included creating a foundation and then expanding fundraising to other settings. The new business model would address changing funding requirements and help to ensure organizational longevity and impact. Indeed, organizational innovation often stems from perceived and actual barriers.

While some anthropologists partner with firms on a wide variety of organizational issues, others work with firms to understand their customer base. A holistic ethnographic approach can help firms make better products, improve their brands, and reduce the likelihood of product failure. In effect, such firms are acting proactively by partnering with the anthropologist, and through him or her, with the customer. For example, Campbell Soup Company wanted to develop a deeper understanding of the "dinner dilemma"—how decisions are made about what to cook for the family dinner—and how Campbell might assist in that process. Anthropologist Timothy de Waal Malefyt led research that consisted of in-depth journaling of thoughts and feelings around meal planning, the creation of a collage of a favorite meal, lengthy in-home interviews, and observations of grocery shopping and meal preparation (2010).

One key finding was that personal connections play a critical role in the meals that women prepare for their families. Women share recipes and meal ideas, often hearing about and trying a new recipe from a friend, family member, or coworker. Thus, their inspiration often comes from other women in their social network. Malefyt and his research team developed a series of recommendations to build on this notion of interconnectedness and make Campbell's products more meaningful. One outcome of this research was targeted advertising in which women are shown "planning weekly meals and talking with other women for meal ideas" (2010). Other outcomes involved website changes including (1) ways for women to expand their meal ideas and share them with their friends through Campbell's website, (2) tips and ideas for both new cooks and experienced ones, and (3) connecting with a larger community of other cooks who also deal with the "dinner dilemma." Campbell's, through Malefyt's work, was able to tap into the cultural dimensions of this everyday practice of meal preparation.

Anthropologists conducted in-home interviews for Campbell's Soup to arrive at insights into the "dinner dilemma."

COLLABORATION FOR COMMUNITY, CAREER, AND TOURISM

Effective partnerships with local communities require time and effort along with paying attention to the internal dynamics of the community. A partnership between the Hopi, a sovereign nation and Native American tribe located in northeastern Arizona, and the Department of Anthropology at Northern Arizona University has resulted in some unexpected outcomes. While the initial focus in 2003 was to integrate aspects of Hopi culture into teacher training and lesson plans, the project has now blossomed to connect Hopi youth and elders, and the scholarly community, through such means as intergenerational-learning and service activities. Archaeologist George (Wolf) Gumerman stated, "The Hopi are facing a challenging task of retaining their distinct cultural identity while preparing youth for successful transition in a fast-paced world of modern lifestyles and different cultures" (*Inside NAU* 2006). Hopi elders and university archaeologists have shared their knowledge and exchanged ideas with Hopi youth on a variety of topics including food, ethnobotany, sustainability, environment, and community.

The Hopi Footprints project has been successful on many fronts. Bonds have been formed between Hopi youth and elders, and between these groups and their university partners. The youth have benefited from what they have learned through the project, including a greater knowledge of Hopi culture as well as career-preparation and business development skills (e.g., filmmaking, website design). According to Gumerman, parents have reported that their "kid was lost and now is on the right path." Public programs held in 2010 in cooperation with

A partnership between the Hopi Nation and Northern Arizona University has led to new career, tourism, and community-building opportunities.

(*continued*)

the Museum of Northern Arizona were heavily attended; they included a cultural exhibit, presentations, and video screenings. The team produced four films as well as a website (http://www4.nau.edu/footprints) that highlights the Hopi youth's perspective on several archaeological sites. The DVDs are available for distribution at the National Parks and other Southwestern tourist locations. The project expands with the transfer of this model of cultural preservation and sharing to other tribes in the United States. The Hopi Footprints Project shows a viable partnering strategy for community change, career preparation, and tourism in the midst of globalization processes.

The NGO, Campbell's Soup, and Hopi Footprints examples are considered successful partnerships from the standpoint of product outcomes. The NGO created a foundation and is bringing in revenue. Campbell's soup improved both its advertising and Web content, and incorporated the findings to benefit the overall direction of its strategic marketing plans. The Hopi Footprints project fostered the cultural transmission of Hopi culture both within and beyond the Hopi Nation through DVDs and public programs, and prepared Hopi youth for a brighter future. In these examples, strong cooperative relationships mattered to the final outcomes.

However, it is important to note that product outcomes may be achieved in partnering arrangements that are "less-than-ideal" (Briody and Trotter 2008: 204). Three of the eight cases in the Briody and Trotter book (2008: 205) were considered successful "despite the lack of institutional support" from one of the partners (Miller et al. 2008), "insufficient cross-agency connections and processes" (Eaton and Brandenburg 2008), and "little concern for the importance of partnering relationships within the hospital" (Jordan 2008). Angelika Zimmermann identified interpersonal variation in virtual teams citing two dominant configurations. One team configuration was characterized by "commitment and tight coupling" where there was "close co-operation and frequent communication ... as well as the integrative leader." In the second configuration, "commitment and loose coupling," "shared understanding and role clarity may be weaker, leading to less effective communication and possibly lower trust" (2011: 73). The relationship aspects of partnerships obviously vary, and vary at different levels from the boardrooms to the conference rooms to the team rooms. More research is needed to explore the relationship between process (both relational and work related) and product outcomes.

Lessons Drawn from Partnering Relationships and Problem Solving

A first lesson is that *partnering is done locally as well as globally*, with global teaming on the rise. The modes of communication vary depending largely on proximity of the partnership participants. Local collaborations continue to rely on face-to-face interactions while global work depends mostly on virtual forms of communication. E-mail, the most prominent means of communication for global teams, has become the key mechanism by which work tasks are coordinated as well as the primary mechanism for relationship development. Lack of communication by e-mail can signal inattention, disinterest, or at worst, a lack of commitment to the partnering relationship. Establishing regular and frequent communication patterns, whether through face-to-face contact, IT and communication technologies, or a mix of the two, will help to keep both local and global partnering efforts on track.

A second lesson is that *conflict, misunderstandings, and miscommunications are unavoidable*. When individuals and groups are from different national, organizational, or institutional cultures, or represent particular cultural subgroups, differences become apparent. Those cultural differences, if not known or accepted by the partners, lead to tensions. Such difficulties can be mitigated by developing open and mutually respectful relationships, making assumptions and expectations as transparent as possible, and identifying and addressing ambiguities and disagreements in a timely fashion.

A third lesson from our review of partnership culture is that *partnerships have a life cycle* during which they grow and change. The evolution of the life cycle parallels the development and accomplishment of partnership goals, and the development and maintenance of partnering relationships. Cooperation and trust are valuable attributes of partnering interactions that tend to emerge over time. Conflict is also present during the partnership cycle—particularly in the early and late stages when participants are adjusting to new circumstances and conditions. Well-functioning partnerships figure out ways to accommodate partner differences.

One additional lesson is that *partnership outcomes matter* to individuals, teams, organizations, and other partnering entities. Partnering is hard work. The majority of partnerships fail due to various types of organizational and cultural differences among the partners. When a failure occurs, the partners incur losses of resources (e.g., time, money), and frequently experience damage to relationships. Perhaps most significantly, they have failed to realize their objectives and produce the desired product and service outcomes they sought. Strategizing continually to uncover and resolve difficulties, compare progress to goals, and cultivate partnering relationships at all levels will contribute substantially to partnership success.

CROSS-CULTURAL SCENARIOS

Read the following cross-cultural scenarios. In each mini-case study, a basic cultural conflict occurs among the actors involved. Try to identify the source of the conflict and suggest how it could have been avoided or minimized. Then see how well your analyses compare to the explanations in Appendix A.

6-1   Bill Higgins had served as the manager of a large U.S. timber company located in a rather remote rain forest in a South American country. Since it began its logging operations in the 1950s, a major problem facing the company has been the recruit-ment of labor. The only nearby source of labor was the sparsely populated local Indian groups. Bill's company has been in direct competition for laborers with a German com-pany operating in the same region. In an attempt to attract the required number of laborers, Bill's company has invested heavily in new housing and offered considerably higher wages than the German company, as well as a guaranteed 40-hour workweek. Yet, the majority of the available workers continued to work for the German company, despite its substandard housing and a minimum hourly wage. Bill finally brought in sev-eral U.S. anthropologists who had worked among the local Indians. The answer to Bill's labor recruitment problem was quite simple, but it required looking at the values of the Indian labor force rather than simply building facilities that would appeal to the typical U.S. laborer.

What did the anthropologists tell Bill?

6-2   Mary Putnam, the president of a Boston publishing company, had been working for several months with a French architectural firm that was designing the company's new printing facility in Fontainbleau, France. However, Mary was becoming increasingly frustrated with the many delays caused by the French architects. When the preliminary plans for the building—which the architects had promised by a certain date—had not arrived, Mary called to inquire when she would be receiving them. The architects, some-what indignant that she had called, felt that Mary doubted their integrity to deliver the plans. Mary was equally annoyed because they had missed the deadline, and what was worse, they didn't seem to be the least bit apologetic about it. By the end of the phone call, Mary was convinced that her company's relationship with the French architectural firm had suffered a major setback.

How might you explain the conflict in this case?

6-3   Sam Lucas, a construction supervisor for an international engineering firm, had been chosen to supervise construction on a new hotel project, in Jeddah, Saudi Arabia, primarily because of his outstanding work record. On this project, Sam supervised the work of about a dozen Americans and nearly 100 Saudi laborers. It was not long before Sam realized that the Saudi laborers, to his way of thinking, were nowhere as reliable as the workers he had supervised in the United States. He was becoming increasingly annoyed at the seeming lack of competence of the local workforce. Following the leader-ship style that held him in such good stead at home, he began reprimanding any worker who was not doing his job properly, and made certain that he did it publicly so that it would serve as an object lesson to all the other workers. He was convinced that he was doing the right thing and was being fair, for after all, he reprimanded both Americans and Saudis alike. He was troubled, however, by the fact that the problems seemed to be growing worse and more numerous.

What advice might you give Sam?

6-4   George McDonald was a chief engineer for a machinery manufacturer based in St. Louis. His company had recently signed a contract with one of its largest customers in Japan to upgrade the equipment and retrain mechanics to maintain the equipment more effectively. As part of the contract, the Japanese company sent all ten of their mechanics to St. Louis for a three-month retraining course under George's supervision. Although George had never lived or worked abroad, he was looking forward to the challenge of working with the group of Japanese mechanics, because he had been told that they were all fluent in English and tireless workers. The first several weeks of the training went along quite smoothly, but soon George became increasingly annoyed with the constant demands they were making on his personal time. They would seek him out after the regularly scheduled sessions were over for additional information. They sought his advice on how to occupy their leisure time. Several even asked him to help settle a disagreement that developed between them. Feeling frustrated by all these demands on his time, George told his Japanese trainees that he preferred not to mix business with pleasure. Within a matter of days, the group requested another instructor.

What was the principle operating here?

6-5   Captivated by the beauty of East Africa during a three-week safari, Jeff Walters and his wife decided to sell their Philadelphia bookstore and start a book-distribution company. Over the first four years, Jeff put together a professional and administrative staff of 18 local Kenyans; his successful enterprise involved supplying books from all over the world to eastern and southern African countries. One day Jeff found that he was behind schedule in preparing a lengthy proposal for a possible government contract due in the USAID (United States Agency for International Development) office in Nairobi the next day. The deadline was so critical that he had to work very closely with some of his staff to make sure that it was met. In the final hours, Jeff found himself helping the secretaries make copies, collate, and assemble the multiple copies of the proposal. But minutes after pitching in to help, he noticed that his staff became very noncommunicative, and he seemed to be getting a lot of cold stares. Jeff couldn't understand why his attempts to be helpful were so unappreciated.

How could you help Jeff understand this cross-cultural problem?

7

■ ■ ■

Coping with Culture Shock

Tom Walters, a 46-year-old fast-track executive from a high-tech company based in Denver, was selected to oversee the construction of a large manufacturing plant in rural China. After discussing the three-year relocation with his wife Laura and two teenage daughters, Tom decided to take the job because it would be a good career move. After several months of attending to the many details involved in any international move, the Walters family arrived at their new home; it was located about 120 miles from Shanghai, China.

Although the company provided the family with a luxurious home, Tom started his job within three days after arrival, leaving most of the details of "settling in" to Laura. With Tom spending long hours at the job site each day, Laura needed to enroll the girls in school, get a driver's license, deal with some immigration issues, find the best places to buy groceries, and generally learn how to navigate in a radically new and different culture. At first Laura was excited about being in such a dynamic, and culturally different, part of the world. It was very much like being on vacation in an interesting and exotic country. But it didn't take long before the "magic" of being in a foreign country began to wear thin. Working with various civil servants proved to be agonizingly slow. Navigating grocery stores, which seemed like a maze to Laura, became increasingly frustrating. Local people seemed unfriendly and unwilling to answer her questions, largely due to the fact that Laura spoke no Chinese other than such basics as "hello" and "thank you." She began to dread having to leave her house because she was having so much difficulty dealing with "those people." In an attempt to preserve her sanity, she joined an organization for expatriate unemployed spouses, where she spent an increasing amount of her time with similarly unhappy foreign dependents. Moreover, their two teenage daughters were not adjusting well to their new school and were suffering from "separation anxiety" from their friends back home in Denver.

Within several months the unhappiness of his wife and daughters began to affect Tom's job performance. He began to feel guilty that his desire for his own career advancement was a major cause of his family's inability to adjust to the new and different cultural environment. Owing to Tom's distractions from his job, the building project he was overseeing fell so far behind schedule that the Chinese partnering company eventually backed out of the project. The upshot was that the building project was cancelled, Tom and his family were sent back to the States, and Tom's company lost tens of millions of dollars in the aborted joint venture.

This unfortunate scenario of Tom Walters and his family is neither hypothetical nor particularly rare. For decades, global businesspeople worldwide have had to overcome numerous challenges of cultural adjustment when living and working abroad on long-term assignments. In Tom's case, the consequences for his company and his own career were indeed serious, and the financial losses were disastrous. Most often, however, foreign assignees do not become "premature returnees," but their job performance is negatively impacted nevertheless. What all of these cases have in common, however, is that the employees and/or their families contract a malady known as "culture shock"—psychological stress resulting from trying to adjust to major differences in lifestyles, living conditions, and business practices in another cultural setting.

THE NATURE OF CULTURE SHOCK

Definition

Culture shock, a term first popularized by anthropologist Kalvero Oberg, refers to the psychological disorientation experienced by people who suddenly find themselves living and working in radically different cultural environments. Oberg describes culture shock as the anxiety that results when all familiar cultural props have been knocked out from under a person who is entering a new culture:

> Culture shock is precipitated by the anxiety that results from losing all our familiar signs and symbols of social intercourse. These signs or cues include the thousand and one ways in which we orient ourselves to the situations of daily life: when to shake hands and what to say when we meet people, when and how to give tips, how to give orders to servants, how to make purchases, when to accept and when to refuse invitations, when to take statements seriously and when not. Now these cues which may be words, gestures, facial expressions, customs, or norms are acquired by all of us in the course of growing up and are as much a part of our culture as the language we speak or the beliefs we accept. All of us depend for our peace of mind and our efficiency on hundreds of these cues, most of which we do not carry on the level of conscious awareness (1960: 177).

Culture shock ranges from mild irritation to a deep-seated psychological panic or crisis. Culture shock occurs when people such as U.S. businesspersons and their family members, all of a sudden, try to play a game abroad in which they have little or no understanding of the basic rules. Here are some examples of statements (from interview data collected by Elizabeth Briody and Judith Beeber

Chrisman) made by American expatriates about the early period of their overseas assignment:

- **Expatriate Spouse:** "I was pregnant. We were not looking forward to moving and had no idea we would be going (on an overseas assignment). It was a surprise...I was sick for two months from the pregnancy. We are at such a high altitude here (in Mexico). We have to boil our water. We eat at home always." (She began to cry and it took her several minutes to regain composure.)
- **Expatriate Spouse:** "We were afraid for him (my husband). He would cry at dinner. We didn't want to tell him about our problems. He was feeling guilty that he got us into this."
- **Expatriate Child:** "Hearing the kids talking to the teachers in Spanish was hard. I thought that they were supposed to be talking in English since it was the American School."

Expatriates must struggle to uncover what is meaningful in this new cultural environment, while acknowledging that many of their own familiar cultural cues may be irrelevant. They are forced to try out new and unfamiliar modes of behavior, all the while never really knowing when they might be unwittingly committing a gross social indiscretion. Culture shock usually carries with it feelings of helplessness and irritability, while producing fears of being cheated, injured, contaminated, or discounted. Even though everyone, to some extent, suffers the anxiety of culture shock when first arriving in an unfamiliar cultural setting, the very success or failure of an overseas living assignment depends largely on how well one can make the psychological adjustment and get beyond the frequently debilitating effects.

Both social scientists and laypeople use the term *culture shock* to define in very broad terms the unpleasant consequences of experiencing a foreign culture. Since the 1960s a number of writers in the field have attempted to elaborate on Oberg's (1960) original formulation by using such terms as *role shock* (Byrnes 1966), *culture fatigue* (Guthrie 1975), and *pervasive ambiguity* (Ball-Rokeach 1973). Yet despite these variations on Oberg's original theme, there is general agreement that culture shock involves the following dimensions:

- A sense of confusion over expected role behavior
- A sense of surprise, even disgust, after encountering some of the features of the new culture
- A sense of loss of the old familiar surroundings (friends, possessions, and routines)
- A sense of loss of self-esteem because the inability to function in the new culture results in an imperfect meeting of professional objectives
- A feeling of impotence at having little or no control over the environment
- A strong sense of doubt when old values (which had always been held as absolute) are brought into question.

Despite the use of the word *shock*, which implies a sudden jolt, culture shock does not occur quickly, nor is it the result of a single event. Rather, it results from a series of cumulative experiences. When you first arrive in a new culture, usually flying into a major city, the cultural contrasts do not seem too obvious. There are usually traffic lights, taxis, tall buildings with elevators, banks, and modern hotels with English-speaking desk clerks. But before long, the very real cultural differences become painfully apparent. People push in front of you in line rather than lining up in an orderly fashion; when people say yes, they don't always mean yes; you try to be thoughtful by asking about the health of your business partner's wife, and he acts offended; you invite local acquaintances to your home for dinner, but they don't reciprocate; you cannot buy things that you are accustomed to having every day at home; people promise to have something done by tomorrow, but it doesn't get done; you tell a humorous story to your colleague at the office and he responds with a blank look on his face; you try to be friendly, but people don't respond. As those first days and weeks pass, the differences become more apparent, and the anxiety and sense of frustration build slowly. Trying to cope with all the newness is beginning to sap you of your energy. Eventually, the cultural differences become the focus of attention. You no longer perceive the foreign ways of thinking and acting as quaint and fascinating alternative ways of living but rather as pathological and clearly inferior to your own. When this occurs, culture shock has set in.

Impact While Abroad

Robert Kohls (1984: 65) and Elisabeth Marx (1999: 32) provide a fairly comprehensive list of the major symptoms that have been observed in relatively severe cases of culture shock:

- Homesickness
- Boredom
- Withdrawal (e.g., spending excessive amounts of time reading; seeing only other Americans; avoiding contact with host nationals)
- Need for excessive amounts of sleep
- Compulsive eating
- Compulsive drinking
- Irritability
- Exaggerated cleanliness
- Marital stress
- Family tension and conflict
- Chauvinistic excesses
- Stereotyping of host nationals
- Hostility toward host nationals
- Loss of ability to work effectively
- Unexplainable fits of weeping
- Physical ailments (psychosomatic illnesses)
- Feelings of isolation
- Weight loss
- Feelings of helplessness
- Tenseness, moodiness, and irritability
- Loss of confidence
- Fear of the worst happening.

Because culture shock is characterized by a large and diverse set of symptoms, the malady is frequently difficult to predict and control. It is important to point out, however, that not everyone will experience all the symptoms, but almost all people will experience some. Moreover, some symptoms, or combination of symptoms, will vary in severity from one case to another. Yet, whenever any of the symptoms manifest themselves while one is living and working abroad, one can be sure that culture shock has set in.

Individual international businesspeople vary greatly in the extent to which they suffer from culture shock. A few people are so ill suited to working in culturally different environments that they repatriate shortly after arriving in the host country. Others manage to get by with a minimum of psychological discomfort. But for most Westerners, operating abroad involves a fairly severe bout with culture shock. According to Oberg (1960), culture shock usually occurs in the following four stages:

1. *The honeymoon stage:* Most people begin their foreign assignment with a positive attitude, so this initial stage is usually characterized by euphoria. At this point, all that is new is exotic and exciting. Attitudes about the host country, and one's capacity to operate in it successfully, are unrealistically positive. During this initial stage, which may last from several days to several weeks, the recent arrival is probably staying temporarily at a Western-style hotel or staff guesthouse where food, conditions of cleanliness, and language are not appreciably different from those at home. The sojourner's time is devoted to getting established—finding a house, a car, and perhaps schools for the children. It is possible that the family's standard of living in this foreign land will be more opulent than they were accustomed to while living in the United States. By and large, it is the similarities between this new country and the United States that stand out—which leads one to the erroneous conclusion that people are really all alike under the skin.

2. *Irritation and hostility:* But as with marriages, honeymoons do not last forever. Within several weeks or perhaps months, problems arise at work, at home, and at the marketplace. Things taken for granted at home simply don't occur. A number of small problems become insurmountable obstacles. Now, all of a sudden, it is the cultural differences, not the similarities, that loom so large. For the first time it becomes clear that, unlike a two-week vacation, one will be in this situation for the next 12–18 months. The second stage of culture shock has set in; this second stage represents the crisis stage of the "disease." Small problems are blown out of proportion. It is during this stage that one or more of the symptoms mentioned are manifested to some degree. A commonly used mode for dealing with this crisis stage is to band together with other expatriates to disparage the local people: "How can they be so lazy?" "So dirty?" "So stupid?" "So slow?" Now is when ethnic jokes proliferate. The speed with which one passes through this crisis stage of culture shock will vary directly with the ultimate success of the international assignment. Unfortunately, some never get past stage 2, and they become premature return statistics or somehow manage to stick it out but at a high cost to themselves, their families, and their companies. Inadequate job performance leads to a "loss of business, low morale among host country national employees, and poor corporate image generally" (Briody and Chrisman 1991: 277).

3. *Gradual adjustment:* Stage 3 marks the passing of the crisis and a gradual recovery. This stage may begin so gradually that the "patient" is unaware that it is even happening. An understanding slowly emerges of how to operate within the new culture. Some cultural cues now begin to make sense; patterns of behavior begin to emerge, which enable a certain level of predictability; some of the language is

becoming comprehensible; and some of the problems of everyday living—which seemed so overwhelming in stage 2—are beginning to be resolved. In short, the culture seems more natural and more manageable. A capacity to laugh at one's situation is a sure sign that adjustment—and ultimate recovery—are well under way.

4. *Biculturalism:* The fourth and final stage, representing full or near full recovery, involves the ability to function effectively in two different cultures. The local customs that were so unsettling months earlier are now both understood and appreciated. Without having to "go native," the international businessperson now accepts many of the new cultural ways for what they are. This is not to imply that all strains in intercultural relationships have disappeared, but the high-level anxiety caused by living and working in a different cultural environment is reduced. Moreover, in a number of situations, those making a full recovery from culture shock find that there are many local customs to which they have become accustomed and which will be missed upon returning home. Again, many people never reach stage 4. It is possible to "get by" with a modicum of success by never going beyond stage 3. But for those who do become bicultural, the international assignment can be a truly positive, growth-producing experience.

A lot has happened in the realm of global business since Oberg's seminal work. More companies are doing business overseas; international assignments continue to rise, as Aahad Osman-Gani and Thomas Rockstuhl point out in their recent review of the expatriate literature (2008). Many firms send employees and their families abroad, particularly as new partnerships are being established (e.g., joint ventures) or as infrastructure is being built (e.g., new plants). Many are on assignment for about three years; they may take subsequent assignments. Others may take short-term assignments of a year or less in duration. Those who are successful will have developed an ability to negotiate and operate not only biculturally, as suggested by Oberg, but also triculturally—within the local host country national culture, within the expatriate community culture, and within their home culture once they have repatriated.

The description of culture shock presented here so far paints a rather bleak picture of the helpless victim suffering from the debilitating psychological effects of a serious illness. Although not glossing over the very serious consequences of culture shock, we can view it more positively as a potentially profound experience leading to cultural learning, self-awareness, and personal growth. For example, Peter Adler (1975) suggested that the conflicts, problems, and frustrations associated with culture shock can result in "transitional experiences" for the international businessperson and accompanying family members, which "can be the source of higher levels of personality and professional development." Cultural learning is most likely to occur under situations of high anxiety, such as is common in moderate to severe cases of culture shock. At lower levels of anxiety, the motivation to learn about the host culture is absent. But when anxiety, frustration, and pain are high, the motivation will be powerful to acquire new knowledge and skills, which can be used to reduce the anxiety. Moreover, culture shock encourages the sufferers to confront their own cultural heritage and to develop a new awareness of the degree to which they are products of it.

Although we are indebted to Adler for reminding us of the more positive consequences of culture shock, the suggestion that it can be growth-producing does have its limitations. As Richard Brislin has suggested, if the anxiety of culture shock is too high, "people may be so upset that they are unable to focus on new learning possibilities" (1981: 158). While a certain amount of anxiety can be positive, there is a point at which it can become dysfunctional. The anxiety of culture shock can interrupt work patterns, increase the number of bad solutions to problems, and impair decision making, planning, and personal relationships on one's overseas assignments.

Ironically, some of the personality characteristics traditionally considered positive for businesspeople at home are the very traits that can most readily contribute to culture shock. To illustrate, many business leaders are type-A personalities, characterized by a high motivation to achieve, competitiveness, and a high level of time consciousness. However desirable these traits are at home, they can become liabilities when attempting to work globally. Wanting to achieve the greatest results in the shortest period of time, type-A personalities tend to be impatient, overly aggressive, domineering, and self-centered. They often do not take the time to listen to others or study and adapt to the local cultural environment.

Impact upon Repatriation

As has been too often the case, many Western businesspeople fail to meet their overseas objectives because they are ill prepared to cope with culture shock. Yet, even for those who are successful at managing culture shock during their foreign assignment (i.e., by reaching stage 3 or 4), the phenomenon has an additional surprise in store—reverse culture shock, or what has come to be known as *reentry shock*. Nan Sussman found that expatriates who were the least prepared for repatriation, experienced greater distress than those who had a better understanding of it (2001). Most Westerners are not prepared for the enormous letdown they feel when returning home after an overseas assignment. In some cases, reentry shock—the disorientation faced when trying to reorient oneself to life and work in your own culture—can be more anxiety producing than the original culture shock. Here are some examples (from research done by Elizabeth Briody and Judith Beeber Chrisma) of reentry shock statements made by expatriates upon their return home:

- **Former Expatriate:** "I experienced a good deal of reverse culture shock in coming back (from Japan)…There is disinterest on the part of the Americans with regard to how the Japanese do things. The attitude is, 'Those (expletive) Japs!' There is resentment about having to hear about the Japanese and how they are taking us to the cleaners. This occurs both in my social life where people essentially do not want to hear about the last four years of your life, and in my work life…When you return to the U.S., you encounter a closed social system. Even with your former friends, it is hard to fit in with them. The disparity of your experience and their lack of experience with a foreign culture make it difficult to fit in."
- **Former Expatriate Spouse:** "I was not happy when I first came back to the U.S. Jack was gone a lot. If we had still been overseas, friends would have known that Jack was away and would have called me to do things. This did not happen when we moved back. In addition, we were living quite close to my parents and they

were always dropping in—a lot. I would have to drop whatever I was doing in order to entertain them. This turned out to be pretty stressful. Also, I was thrown right back in with suburban life—talking about idiotic things in a small town. In general, overseas people were more into foreign affairs, paying more attention to it. No one cared about foreign affairs in Ridgewood since they lived in their own little world there. A lot of the suburbia wives would find out that we had lived overseas and would poo poo it and then say how difficult it must have been for the kids to adjust...."

- **Former Expatriate Child:** "I noticed that American kids were more aggressive. I knew that I couldn't fit in. I didn't like football and baseball because I couldn't understand them. I only knew soccer. It took me a long while to make friends (about 4 years)."

Although most international businesspeople will anticipate a certain number of problems and discomforts when entering a new cultural environment, they are frequently unprepared for the myriad of problems they will face when returning home. First, upon return, home life feels relatively boring and confining. Many foreign assignments of a year or more can be exciting in that they involve travel and learning all sorts of new things. Since coming home to "life as usual" can seem uninteresting by comparison, many returnees experience a generalized malaise or lack of interest in their lives.

Second, many U.S. businesspeople, after returning from a long assignment abroad, soon realize that one problem is finding a new niche in the corporate structure at home. Those who originally decided to send them abroad may no longer be on the scene; consequently, the corporation's plan for how it would use them now may no longer exist.

Third, while trying to overcome the original dose of culture shock, many U.S. businesspeople tend to embellish (in some cases, grossly exaggerate) their fond memories of life in the United States. They remember that things are better made, cheaper, and cleaner and people are more efficient, polite, and competent. But upon reentry to the United States, many of these myths are shattered. One of the by-products of a successful adjustment to the host culture is that our old notions of our culture will never again be the same. After one lives for a while in Switzerland, the United States no longer seems to be the epitome of cleanliness; when compared with the Japanese, the typical American seems loud and boisterous; after returning from an extended stay in Germany you become painfully aware of how unprepared most Americans are to engage in an informed political discussion; after a stint in a developing nation, people in the United States seem rushed and impersonal. Somehow home isn't what one had remembered.

Fourth, one's standard of living may actually decrease when returning to the United States. Such luxuries as servants, large company houses, chauffeurs, live-in babysitters, and other perks used to entice people into an international assignment are likely to disappear. One is now faced with cutting one's own lawn and spending several hours each day commuting to and from work.

Fifth, in those cases in which U.S. businesspeople have made a successful adaptation to a third-world cultural environment, there can be additional problems of adjustment. The returnee and his or her family have seen, on a daily basis, the economic standards of people living in the host country. Per capita income may be no more than several hundred dollars a year; infant mortality may be 15 times as high as it is in the United States; disease and lack of medical facilities keep the average life expectancy to less than 40 years of age; government attention to human rights might be nonexistent; and the prospects of changing these conditions in any meaningful way are highly unlikely. And then, upon return, they encounter friends, colleagues, neighbors, and relatives complaining bitterly that they are unable to find at the grocery store the correct color of toilet tissue for the downstairs bathroom. Such complaints stir up (1) considerable anger at how unaware and unappreciative most Americans are of their own material well-being and (2) guilt for having mouthed many of these same inane complaints at an earlier time.

Sixth, perhaps the most unsettling aspect of reentry shock is the almost total dearth of psychological support for the returnee and his or her household. When encountering the initial stage 2 culture shock during the foreign assignment, there were (it is hoped) some preparations, an understanding (however inadequately developed) that there would be rough times, and other expatriates (who were experiencing many of the same frustrations) who could provide reassurance and support. But when returning home, U.S. businesspeople and their families feel alone and unable to express their feelings with someone who has not been through the same type of experience. Friends and relatives whom they have not seen for months or even years will say, "Oh, I can't wait to hear about your stint in Singapore." But after listening half-heartedly for about two minutes, they will change the subject to a new TV show they have just seen. In short, returnees have a great need to share their overseas experiences (some of which may have been life-altering) with others, but frequently no one seems to be interested. Since the returnees have had the unusual experience of living and working abroad, many of their friends and acquaintances, whose lives may have gone on uninterrupted or changed in other ways, have no way of relating to these experiences. The result is a feeling of alienation from the returnees' own culture because they feel that they are not being understood.

MINIMIZING CULTURE SHOCK

Just about everyone living and working abroad for extended periods of time can expect to experience culture shock to some degree. Tourists and occasional (short-term) business travelers are by and large shielded from some of the more debilitating effects of culture shock because their experiences are limited to hotels and restaurants geared to Westerners. Yet, those who must live and work in a foreign culture for extended periods of time are faced with new ways of behaving, thinking, and communicating. Even U.S. businesspeople who have lived and worked in a number of different countries claim that they have experienced culture shock in each country. For some, each subsequent assignment becomes a little easier, but for many, culture shock must be confronted for each new situation. Although there is no "quick fix" for culture shock, you can take a number of purposeful steps to minimize its negative impact.

Weigh the Alternatives

One very effective way of totally avoiding culture shock is to choose (or have your employer choose) to stay "stateside" or at home in the U.S. rather than enter the global business arena. Some people simply do not have the desire, inclination, or temperament for international assignments. There may be others who are suited for some foreign cultures but not others. Family matters (e.g., medical concerns, education issues, care of elderly parents) need to be considered carefully during the decision-making process because they may be "show stoppers". The old Greek adage "Know thyself" could not be more appropriate than in the process of self-selection for an international assignment. Before deciding to live abroad, it is imperative to have a realistic grasp of your motives and feelings. If individuals possess a high degree of cross-cultural motivation, their adjustment and job performance abroad will be better (Black and Gregersen 1991; Mohr and Klein 2004; Chen et al. 2010). If people decide to move into the global arena solely on the basis of the lure of more money, a possible promotion, or worst of all, to put a little excitement into their less-than-adequate marriage, they will probably do themselves (and their organizations) a favor by staying home. International businesspeople (and any accompanying family members) who are most likely to do well abroad (1) have a realistic understanding of the problems and promises of international business, (2) possess a number of important cross-cultural coping skills, and (3) see the world marketplace as providing vast opportunities for professional and personal growth. Those who cannot meet these criteria may be so ill-suited to living and working abroad that they would be virtually unable to overcome the debilitating effects of culture shock.

Prepare Carefully

For those who do select the international business arena, the best single piece of advice for minimizing culture shock is to be prepared. The more thorough the preparation for an overseas assignment, the fewer surprises there will be, and, consequently, the smaller will be the accumulated negative effect. A major factor in adjusting to a foreign cultural environment is the degree of familiarity with the host culture. It is important to recognize that culture shock will never be totally avoided, but it can be minimized through careful preparation. To prepare for an international business encounter, refer to the major substantive chapters of this book, which really suggest a fourfold approach.

First, as suggested in Chapter 1, a general understanding of the concept of culture can provide a fuller appreciation of other cultures, regardless of where one might be conducting business. For example, that cultures are learned (as opposed to being acquired genetically) should remind the international businessperson and expatriate family members that although culturally different people have learned different things, they are no less capable of learning efficiently. The concept of an integrated culture—where many or most of the parts of the culture are interconnected—should serve to convince us that all cultures, no matter how incomprehensible they may appear at first, do in fact have a consistently logical structure and should not be given such disparaging epithets as "primitive," "savage," "crazy," "stupid," and so on. And we should realize that our culture is so thoroughly internalized that it can have very real effects on our physiological functioning. These and other general concepts—which hold equally true for Indonesians, the French, Bolivians, or Japanese—can be helpful in gaining a greater understanding of the foreign cultural environment.

A second way of preparing for culture shock is to become familiar with local patterns of communication—both nonverbal and verbal (see Chapters 3 and 4). Because any type of business depends on communication to such a significant degree, learning to communicate in a foreign business context is absolutely essential. For the international business person, it enhances rapport with host country national and expatriate colleagues; it enables the international businessperson to understand the full context of the negotiations and transactions; it frequently gives access to otherwise exclusive realms of local business; and it opens a window onto the rest of the culture. For the expatriate family members, learning to communicate in the new cultural environment is also beneficial. It enables adjustment to the local culture—its institutions, economic, political, and social systems, and daily living. Communication facilitates interaction with individuals and groups in the new locale. It also positions the expatriate family to learn, in an in-depth way, about the history and culture of the area.

But proficiency in communications can also play a major role in adjusting to culture shock. Because living in a foreign culture involves doing hundreds of things a day—from taking taxis, to making appointments, to having a watch repaired—knowing how to communicate efficiently can both minimize the frustrations, misunderstandings, and aggravations that always face the linguistic outsider and provide a sense of safety, mastery, and self-assurance. In addition to the mastery of the local language, a vital part of communicating in an international business and living situation involves being able to send and receive nonverbal messages accurately. As mentioned in Chapter 3, any communication event is incomplete without a consideration of the additional layers of meaning conveyed by nonverbal behavior.

The third segment of the fourfold approach, as spelled out in Chapter 2, involves a healthy dose of cultural self-awareness. Before it is possible to understand the internal structure and logic of another culture, it is essential to first understand our own culture and how it influences who we are and what we do. We are as much products of our culture as the Chinese, Indians, and Cubans are products of theirs. All people face a number of universal societal problems, from how to make decisions to how to help young people make the transition to responsible adulthood, from how to gain a livelihood to how to explain the unexplainable.

How any particular culture solves these problems varies widely. Middle-class Americans have worked out one set of cultural patterns, whereas the Indonesians may have developed a radically different set of solutions. In most cases, one solution is probably not more inherently rational than another. They simply represent different responses to similar societal problems. Only after we understand why we do the things we do can we appreciate the internal logic of why other, culturally different people do what they do.

Fourth, before entering the international business scene, it is important to become familiar with as much specific cultural information as possible about the country or countries with which one is conducting business (see Appendix B). There is no shortcut to the acquisition of culture-specific data. It will take time, effort, and no small amount of creativity, but the effort will be worth it. It is important not to be limiting when learning about a new culture. The number of sources of culture-specific information is nearly endless. There are, for example, many scholarly sources (e.g., books, journal articles) from such disciplines as anthropology, religious studies, intercultural communication, cross-cultural psychology, and comparative sociology. Besides the scholarly literature (which is not always easily accessible or comprehensible), there are many other sources of excellent information, including commercially published sources for the business traveler, State Department publications, newspapers, and information published and distributed by the various foreign embassies. And, in recent years a wide variety of information (in terms of both quality and breadth of content) now appears on the Internet. Cross-cultural training classes may be useful for new expatriates, though recent research by John Okpara and Jean Kabongo suggests that cross-cultural training is most effective when focused on the specific host country culture (2011). In addition, people who have spent time in that location, or at least overseas, are also valid sources of information. Work colleagues, expatriate family members, foreign exchange students and faculty, and volunteers and staff of nongovernmental organizations are among the kinds of people who can be particularly helpful. In short, it is advisable to draw on as wide a range of culture-specific sources as possible. The more cultural information at hand, the fewer surprises there are likely to be; consequently, serious culture shock can more likely be avoided.

Additional Suggestions

This approach to understanding the cultural environment constitutes the cornerstone of the *cognitive* approach. By conscientiously pursuing these content areas—general cultural concepts, local communication patterns, cultural self-awareness, and culture-specific information—the global businessperson and expatriate family members will avoid total alienation and some of the more debilitating consequences of culture shock, as well as reentry shock. But one's preparation for coping with, and eventually adjusting to, radically different cultural environments involves more than the mere acquisition of information or new colleagues, friends, and acquaintances. Also required is the development

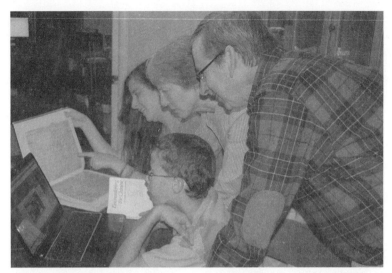

Sources to consult in preparation for an overseas assignment include books, maps, and the Internet.

of life-long skills and competencies that are useful irrespective of the country in which you might be conducting business. These essential competencies, which will be discussed in some detail in the following chapter, include developing a broad perspective, balancing contradictions, appreciating other perspectives, emphasizing global teamwork, and becoming perceptually acute, among others. When developed together, these global skills and competencies establish a global mindset, which is essential for the global business person in the 21st century. What follows are some additional suggestions for reducing culture shock and enhancing the international business experience.

1. *Understand that learning about the host culture is a process that continues throughout your stay in the host culture and beyond.* Far more learning will occur after your arrival in the country than prior to leaving home. Make certain that you use a wide variety of information sources to learn about the host culture. Include local people, newspapers, tourist information, libraries, and your own observations. Find a friend or colleague (either a local resident or an experienced expatriate) to serve as a guide and mentor in helping you learn as quickly as possible.

2. *As soon after arrival as possible, become familiar with your immediate physical surroundings.* Armed with a good map of the vicinity, leave your hotel and walk in a number of different directions, exploring the city or town on foot. Identify local buildings, what they are used for, where they are in relation to one another, the pattern, if any, of how streets are configured, and where people seem to congregate. A familiarity with the "lay of the land," while very tangible and concrete, will provide an excellent base for learning about other aspects of the culture.

3. *Within the first several days of arrival, work on familiarizing yourself with some of the basic, everyday survival skills that your hosts take for granted.* These include such capacities as using the local currency, using the public transportation system, buying

Adjustment to different cultures involves a willingness to get out and explore the cultural landscape.

stamps, interacting with shopkeepers, and ordering from a menu. By mastering these seemingly simple tasks, you will minimize frustrations and embarrassment quickly, as well as gain the self-confidence to master some of the more subtle aspects of the host culture.

4. *As difficult as it may be, try to understand your hosts in terms of their culture rather than your own.* When you encounter a behavior or an attitude that appears strange or even offensive, try to make sense of it in terms of their cultural assumptions rather than your own. This is not to suggest that you should adopt their attitudes or behaviors, or even like them, but you will better understand aspects of the local culture when viewed from within their proper cultural context.

5. *Particularly in the beginning, learn to live with the ambiguity of not having all the answers.* Trying to operate in a new culture is, by definition, a highly ambiguous situation. The person who insists on having immediate and clear-cut answers for everything is likely to be frustrated. Just like the person who is expected to play a game without knowing all the rules, it is important for the cultural neophyte to know that there will be many unanswered questions. By being patient and learning to live with ambiguity, the new arrival is both preserving his or her mental health and "buying time" to learn more answers, reduce the ambiguity, and thus eventually adjust to the new culture.

6. *As a way of enhancing your relationships with your hosts, make a conscious effort to be empathetic; that is, put yourself in the other person's shoes.* People are often attracted to those individuals who can see things from their point of view. Empathy can be practiced by becoming an active listener. First try to understand—then try to be understood.

7. *Understand that flexibility and resourcefulness are key elements to adapting to a new culture.* When living and working in a different culture, the best-laid plans often are not realized. When plans do not work out as expected (as they have a tendency to do

more than at home), you need to make and execute new plans quickly and efficiently without becoming overstressed. Resourceful people are familiar with what is available in the host culture, are comfortable calling on others for help, and know how to take advantage of available opportunities.

8. *Learn to postpone making a judgment or decision until you have sufficient information.* Effective administrators in the United States are defined by their ability to decide quickly and effectively and to bring successful closure to problem-solving tasks. When operating in another culture, however, the capacity of "wrapping things up" or "getting the show on the road" can be a liability rather than an asset. Because people have an imperfect grasp of the rules, norms, and procedures in the host culture, they need to postpone decisions and conclusions until enough facts are at hand.

9. *At least at the beginning of your stay, don't evaluate yourself according to your usual standards of accomplishment.* Any recent arrival to a new culture is bound to be less efficient, productive, or socially competent. The learning curve takes time, so don't be unrealistically hard on yourself.

10. *Work hard at building new social relationships with host country nationals.* Because existing social networks from home have been suspended (at least in a "face-to-face" sense), the sojourner must understand that it is vital to build, nurture, and maintain new social networks in the host country. While it is relatively easy to broaden one's social networks with other expatriates, the cultural adjustment process will be greatly facilitated by focusing on building social relationships with local host country nationals.

11. *Don't lose your sense of humor.* People in any situation, either at home or abroad, tend to get themselves in trouble if they take themselves too seriously. When struggling to learn a new culture, everyone makes mistakes that may be discouraging, embarrassing, or downright laughable. In most situations, your hosts will be disarmingly forgiving of your social faux pas. The ability to laugh at your own mistakes (or at least not lose sight of the humorous side) may be the ultimate defense against despair.

12. *Avoid U.S. ghettos abroad.* Perhaps the best way to ensure an unsuccessful international experience is to limit your social life to an isolated and insulated U.S. enclave where you can get a hamburger and ice in your soft drink but little else. Ghettos are formed when some U.S. travelers attempt to recreate their former lifestyle, while complaining about the lack of amenities, pace of life, and inconveniences of the host culture. Ghetto dwellers might as well have stayed home, for they are neither learning much about the host culture nor about the expatriate culture. By remaining isolated in an American ghetto, expatriates send the local population the message that they feel superior. At the same time, they reinforce their own negative stereotypes.

13. *Avoid going native.* At the opposite extreme of isolating oneself in a U.S. ghetto—and equally as inadvisable—is to "go native." This involves throwing oneself into and idolizing the host culture to such an extent that one loses one's own sense of cultural identity. Expatriates who attempt to imitate the local people are most often met with suspicion, are not taken seriously, and often reject their own cultures so thoroughly that they fail to meet their original personal and professional objectives.

14. *Be adventurous.* All too often, Americans abroad view their overseas assignments as a hardship post that must be endured and will eventually pass, particularly if they become immersed in the job. But living and working abroad should be much more than an experience to be endured. Instead, it can and should be a positively life-altering experience. As long as there is a willingness to experiment and learn about new things, an overseas experience can provide an exciting new world. There are places to explore, people to meet, customs to learn, food to eat, and music and art to experience. These are all available if the traveler is willing to experiment and take risks.

One way of minimizing the negative effects of culture shock is to take care of yourself physically.

15. *Learn how best to manage stress.* Culture shock results from the anxiety brought about by (1) the loss of familiar cultural cues and (2) trying to operate in an unfamiliar cultural setting. How one responds to such anxiety varies considerably, as do the techniques for coping with stress. Some manage stress through regular physical exercise, such as jogging, playing tennis, or taking an aerobics class. Others use such techniques as biofeedback, yoga, or meditation. Still others rely on more spiritual techniques for reducing stress, such as prayer and worship. Whatever technique you choose, it is important to have an effective mechanism for reducing stress, which will in turn enhance the adjustment process.

16. *Take appropriate health precautions.* There is nothing that can ruin an international assignment quicker than serious illness or death. While we cannot eliminate the possibility of illnesses, a number of preventive measures will reduce their occurrence. For example, prior to leaving home, be certain that all required and recommended immunizations are current. If traveling to a malaria-infested area, be certain to take the required malarial suppressant(s) prior to, during, and after your stay abroad. While away from home, follow the same good health habits recommended generally— eat well-balanced meals, allow yourself sufficient rest, exercise regularly, and avoid excesses of alcohol, tobacco, and drugs. Moreover, obtain accurate information about which local foods can be eaten safely and which should be avoided. During home stays, attend to physician and dental visits.

17. *Let go of home (for now).* Before leaving home, it is important to properly say goodbye to friends, relatives, and your familiar way of life that you are temporarily leaving behind. Saying goodbye provides the traveler with a symbolic way of moving from home, a necessary step before you can step into a new culture. This is not to say that you need to cut yourself off from home. In fact, it is advisable to work out ways ahead of time to maintain contact with people at home through letters, telephone calls, or e-mails. Also, before leaving, travelers need to understand

that they (and those remaining at home) will have changed in significant ways upon return to the United States.

18. *Keep in mind that when studying other cultures there are no absolutes.* In a sense, every culture is unique, as is every situation and person within a culture. Moreover, each sojourner brings her or his unique perceptions based on past experiences. In other words, there is no way of predicting with absolute certainty how people will behave in any given situation, irrespective of how well prepared one may be. The generalizations that we read in books written by social scientists should not be viewed as ironclad rules but rather as general statements that are valid for most people, most of the time. The advice we get in training sessions and in our reading should not be viewed as a step-by-step set of prescriptions to be used like a cookbook.

19. *Keep the faith.* After preparing yourself for an international assignment as thoroughly as possible, you need to have confidence in yourself as well as in your hosts. All new arrivals are bound to experience frustrations and make mistakes. Yet, eventually your goodwill and basic humanity will come across to the local people—provided, of course, you make an honest effort to participate in the local culture. At the same time, having faith in the inherent goodwill of the local population is important. By and large, people the world over are tolerant of our indiscretions when they result from an honest attempt to learn about the local culture. If you genuinely communicate that you are the student (interested in learning about their culture) and they are the teachers, very few people in the world would refuse to share their expertise. They are the experts, whereas the visitors are the uneducated, at least in terms of local cultural knowledge. If the sojourner is able to acknowledge openly his or her own subordinate (or at least nondominant) position when dealing with local people, many doors of learning and friendship will be open.

20. *Be conscious about maintaining a healthy balance between work and other aspects of your life such as family, recreation, and social networks.* When working abroad, the demands of working in an unfamiliar setting are likely to make even more demands on your time than would be case at home. The chances of excessive work having a negative effect on one's friends and family are considerably greater than the other way around. Maintaining a healthy work–life balance is particularly important for female expatriates (Fischlmayr and Kollinger 2010).

To be certain, no bottled remedies for culture shock are to be found at the pharmacy. But, by simply knowing that culture shock exists, that it happens to everyone to some extent, and that it is not permanent is likely to reduce the severity of the symptoms and speed the recovery. Don't think you are pathological or inadequate if you experience some culture shock. The anxiety resulting from trying to operate in a different environment is normal. Give yourself permission to feel frustration, homesickness, or irritability. Eventually, you will work through these symptoms and emerge with a much richer appreciation of the host culture. But it is also important to remain realistic. There will be some people, for whatever reason, who will not become close friends. There may be others who, for purely personal reasons, you will not like, and vice versa. And there are some things that may never be understood. But once you understand that these problems, while real and frustrating, are perfectly normal reactions for any sojourner, you can begin to search for solutions.

CROSS-CULTURAL SCENARIOS

Read the following cross-cultural scenarios. In each mini-case study, a basic cultural conflict occurs among the actors involved. Try to identify the source of the conflict and suggest how it could have been avoided or minimized. Then see how well your analyses compare to the explanations in Appendix A.

7-1   Stefan Phillips, a manager for a large U.S. airline, was transferred to Dhahran, Saudi Arabia, to set up a new office. Although Stefan had had several other extended overseas assignments in Paris and Brussels, he was not well prepared for working in the Arab world. At the end of his first week, Stefan came home in a state of near total frustration. As he sat at the dinner table that night, he told his wife how exasperating it had been to work with the local employees, who, he claimed, seemed to take no responsibility for anything. Whenever something went wrong they would simply say "*Inshallah*" ("If God wills it"). Coming from a culture that sees no problem as insolvable, Stefan could not understand how the local employees could be so passive about job-related problems. "If I hear one more *Inshallah*," he told his wife, "I'll go crazy."

What might you tell Stefan to help him understand the cultural realities of Saudi Arabia?

7-2   Randy Hightower, recently appointed to manage his firm's office in Singapore, was anxious to do well in his first overseas assignment. Shortly after his arrival, he called his first staff meeting to outline the objectives for the coming fiscal year. He had already met with his staff individually and was feeling quite confident about the prospects for having a good first year. Toward the end of the staff meeting, Randy, in his characteristic upbeat fashion, told his employees that he looked forward to working with them and that he anticipated that this would be their best year ever. To emphasize his optimism for the coming year, Randy punctuated his verbal remarks by slapping his fist against his palm. The reaction was instantaneous: Most people laughed, giggled, or looked embarrassed. He felt that the point of his dramatic climax was lost amidst the laughter.

How might you explain the cause for the hilarious outburst?

7-3   During the first weeks of an overseas assignment to Buenos Aires, Argentina, Beth Pace was invited to the home of her Argentine business associate for dinner. Beth decided to bring her and her husband a present. Having been told that red meat is a dietary staple in Argentina, Beth decided to take a beautiful set of steak knives as a gift. Upon opening the gift, however, Nick's Argentine hostess and host seemed quite upset.

What did Beth do wrong?

7-4   Sandra Scott was living abroad for the first time in her life as part of a year-long exchange program for a group of post-secondary students. Rotary International had publicized the need for families and mentors for such students. Sandra found her way into the home and life of a French family as a result. She arrived as a smiling, active, and vibrant teenager. Back in the United States, Sandra had been involved in numerous school, volunteer, and athletic activities, including playing on the boys' varsity tennis team. She was enrolled in a local academic program that included language instruction during the day. In the evenings, she interacted with the family as she worked hard to improve her oral communication skills. The weeks wore on and the initial "high" of being in a new place and meeting new people wore off. She found this "total immersion" into a

24-hour per day French-language environment increasingly difficult. There was no relief from it. Everything she did every day required listening to and responding in French. After about two months, her outlook had changed and those around her noticed. She tried to keep up with her studies, said little, and kept to herself. It was clear to Sandra's mentor that culture shock had set in. He wondered what he might do to help her get through this phase. One day he had an idea.

What was he thinking?

7-5   While living and working in Milan, Eric Woodward decided to spend part of a Saturday at a local art museum. Because he was not exactly certain where the museum was located, he asked a man on the street for directions. While the Italian was explaining how to get to the museum, Eric had an uncontrollable itch on his left earlobe. He tried to satisfy the itch by tugging on his earlobe. The Italian man immediately became upset and started yelling at Eric.

What did Eric do to cause such a negative reaction?

8

■ ■ ■

Developing Global Leaders

Most CEOs consider foreign markets to be a key factor in their company's future success. Moreover, a growing number of these same CEOs believe that developing global leaders must be an integral part of their long-term strategic planning. People with global perspectives and work experiences have an ability to work in and across multiple cultural worlds. The following statements are descriptions of a typical day in the lives of a global leader and their views of the skills required for their roles:

- "I want to find out how things can be improved (in my firm's European operations). I have to be very tactful or else everyone will get defensive. It's not helpful if you don't act tactfully. In my job you can lose friends. You can't say that you know it all. The acid test is that we are still friends."
- "As financial assistant to the executive, I investigate management and financial problems. I will get on a plane to Rome (from England) to visit a plant to see what the problems are, for example. I try to find a solution."
- "(In Korea) I had to learn how the people operated—their culture. There was a lot to get used to. We read books and used our heads. We talked to people about it and kept our ears open. If you refuse to pay attention to what you learn, you'll have trouble. You can't do it like you did in the good ol' U.S.A. They'll never understand."

The technical and people-oriented competencies of global leaders are enhanced by their cross-cultural interactions. They confront and deal with "difference" as a routine part of their job. They recognize the value of diverse sources of input. They can apply a broad base of knowledge to the solution of corporate problems. They figure out new ways of targeting opportunities, conceptualizing issues, and implementing initiatives—all of which can help the firm grow and prosper.

Most CEOs today would agree with former head of General Electric Jack Welsh, who observed: "The Jack Welch of the future cannot be like me. I've spent my entire career in the United States. The next head of GE will be somebody who has spent time in Bombay, in Hong Kong, in Buenos Aires" (quoted in Black and Gregersen 1999: 56). Indeed, more and more corporations are seeking a piece of the global pie; their employees are playing a critical role in that investment. One high-profile figure is Carlos Ghosn, Chairman and CEO for the Renault-Nissan Alliance, a partnership that oversees both firms. Born in Brazil in 1954 to a French mother and a Lebanese father, he spent his early years in Brazil, was schooled in Lebanon and France, graduated from the *École Polytechnique* and *École Nationale Supérieure des Mines de Paris* (France's highly selective *grandes écoles* or "great schools"), spent the early part of his career at Michelin Tire in France and Brazil, ultimately becoming the Chairman and CEO of Michelin North America. Renault hired him in the mid-1990s to run its activities in South America. He then went on to become CEO of Nissan while retaining his role at Renault, turning around both companies by the mid-2000s (Hamada 2008).

GLOBALLY ORIENTED FIRMS

More than three decades ago, David Heenan and Howard Perlmutter offered a model for categorizing corporate orientations to the global marketplace. Still valuable today, this model classifies firms on the basis of a national, regional, or global orientation (see Table 8-1). Global leaders, of course, might be found across all three groups. However, it is the globally oriented firms that are most likely to operate using a global strategy and reap the benefits if their strategy is well executed.

The bar is high for firms (as it is for individuals or teams) to achieve a global orientation. Indeed, it is an ongoing pursuit and challenge in all aspects of a firm's operations from customer relations to supplier contracts to work processes to workplace conflicts. Companies and their employees have to step out of their cultural comfort zones into spaces in which they do not recognize the patterns of behavior that they see, or understand the attitudes and assumptions that they hear. Those from corporate headquarters may be surprised to learn that innovative ideas often appear at the "margins"—in the local facilities and neighborhoods rather than in headquarters. They may discover that global policies and procedures developed

TABLE 8-1 Corporate Orientations

Nationally Oriented	Regionally Oriented	Globally Oriented
Operates independently and autonomously within a particular nation	Operates interdependently within a limited area involving more than one nation	Operates interdependently worldwide across nations and world regions
Focuses on local objectives	Focuses on regional objectives	Focuses on worldwide objectives
Exhibits tendency toward national-culture homogeneity	Exhibits limited multicultural heterogeneity	Exhibits extensive multicultural heterogeneity

Source: Adapted from Heenan and Perlmutter (1979: 8–9, 17–21).

with one locale or region in mind may have to be adapted to fit other contexts. Alternately, those situated away from the company's central core may find that they too have something to learn. Baruch Shimoni points out that "local managers mix and hybridize" their own cultural style with that of their company (2006: 231) as in the following example in which a Thai employee talks about his Swedish supervisor:

> He told me I am one of the "slave drivers" [laughing]…so I have changed quite a lot in the past years…now, I have not totally changed, I think, I become more softer…He gave me a lecture…you know, to be sensitive and things like that, and we have to handle them with care, even if they are your subordinates…. (p. 223)

The good news is that *if* those companies learn from their experiences and use those insights to improve their overall effectiveness, they are much more likely to be successful in the global marketplace.

CREATING A GLOBALLY ORIENTED WORKFORCE

Purposeful steps are required not only to create a globally oriented workforce, but also to fold in the knowledge and experiences derived from global and virtual work interactions, issues, and accomplishments into the firm's day-to-day operations. Firms with a global orientation are most likely to maximize their global potential by emphasizing the following organizational processes: (1) seeking job candidates with geographically, culturally, and organizationally diverse experiences, (2) enabling their workforce to gain a stronger global perspective (e.g., through participation on global virtual teams and international travel), (3) preparing and sending selected managers abroad for overseas assignments (whether long term, short term, or commuter), and (4) building a stronger company on the basis of what has been learned from these global interactions.

Many businesses today are becoming increasingly interested in recruiting new employees who have international/cross-cultural experience on their resumes. As a result, a growing number of recent high school graduates are opting to take a "gap year," traveling and interning with organizations abroad before attending college (Mohn 2006: 6). Many middle-class parents are willing to finance these transitional years because their children return home with greater maturity and focus, they often develop fluency in a second language, they are able to "internationalize" their resumes, and they start the process of developing those skills and competencies that multinational corporations often look for. While it is difficult to determine a precise number of students who take a gap year either before or immediately after college, some colleges today are deferring admission for students to take a gap year prior to entering college. In most cases this is not frivolous "bumming around," but rather a way of developing vital global skills for the 21st century. It has been for many a way to leverage their position in the job market when they return home.

Most often, though, businesses hire "good people," meaning that they possess the technical skills, talents, and temperament to be a contributing member of the organization. Once hired, they work on tasks and assignments that reflect that organization's goals and objectives. In today's globalizing environment, a firm is likely to have projects and activities that push the boundaries and traditions of the past. Tracy Meerwarth and her colleagues point out that "The rhythm of work that was once delineated by the ringing of the factory bell or the closing of office doors at the end of the day, now responds to a different rhythm" (2008: 2). Working virtually is now fairly commonplace for corporations and workers alike and an important path into a global work stream. Global teams offer individuals and their organizations an opportunity to engage with different people using different technologies working in different time zones on different projects (see Chapters 4 and 6). That kind of global partnering experience, distinctive in its own right culturally, can be a valuable addition to the organization's work portfolio and to individual growth and learning.

In addition to corporate hiring and global/virtual team processes—which can help propel corporations into global ventures—firms have a long-standing practice of sending employees abroad on overseas assignments. Individual employees are asked to live and work abroad for the company for periods ranging from months to years; the "traditional assignment" lasts three to five years and involves the relocation of the expatriate and his or her family (Collings, Scullion, and Morley 2007: 199). Particularly for extended stays, cross-cultural and language training are often made available to ease adjustment to the new culture.

The new expatriate will engage with host country nationals and others in the course of his or her workday to accomplish the objectives of the overseas assignment. There will be ongoing opportunities for give-and-take including learning the most appropriate ways to implement a new program, sharing current best practices, and figuring out how to reconcile opposing approaches to a particular problem. Whether the assignment involves a position in finance, sales, purchasing, engineering, or public affairs, expatriates typically develop a set of general managerial and negotiating competencies. Anne-Wil Harzing uses three metaphors to describe the kinds of roles expatriates play. The "bear" role is charged with formal and direct decision making and surveillance over operations, the "bumble-bee" with socialization and knowledge transfer across organizational units, and "spiders" with weaving an informal network of communication (2001: 369). While these roles are figurative, they do offer interesting images of some of the skill sets global organizations need.

A word of caution: The organizational process of *preparing and sending selected managers abroad* for overseas assignments does not automatically imply *building a stronger company on the basis of what has been learned* from these global interactions. Companies vary in their ability and willingness to use the skills and knowledge that employees gain when working globally. Moreover, some firms may have internal units that are more globally linked than others. Such was the case in GM where the component and car divisions displayed radically different views of the value of global experience. The component divisions (now Delphi Corporation) were organized as a "coupled system," that is, their domestic and overseas operations were linked structurally and ideologically. Elizabeth Briody and Marietta Baba report one expatriate's experience: "You could end up going to Alabama or France. While overseas you are still getting letters from your general manager. The relationships and communications continue to be present because you haven't left Saginaw Division" (1991: 332–33). The component divisions valued and integrated the work of expatriates into their operations both during and after an overseas assignment; repatriation was straightforward with relatively few hiccups. By contrast, the car divisions were "decoupled systems" in which there were no structural links between domestic and international activities, and where an "anti-international ideology" prevailed (1994: 251–53); repatriation was almost always problematic. GM's component divisions, with their globally integrated facilities, excelled in fostering a global outlook from the executive suite to the plant floor, at home and abroad, unlike their parochial-minded counterparts making Chevys and Buicks.

THE EVOLVING PROFILE OF THE OVERSEAS ASSIGNMENT

Fluctuation in Expatriate Numbers

Since firms have routinely used overseas assignments as a way to break into new markets and build and sell their products, we now turn our attention to the practice of sending employees abroad. The number of expatriates has fluctuated over time based on a number of factors including industry type, size, and maturity; the goals of a particular firm; and host country demand. Periods of infrastructure building involving "greenfield" (new industrial) sites or developing specialized teams are likely to usher in an expansion in the expatriate ranks. Not only will more expatriates be required, but specific expatriates will also be needed—those who have particular technical skills (e.g., plant engineering, "troubleshooting") that may not be available locally. François Vardon, a French expatriate to Mexico for a number of years, explains that an expatriate presence is typically necessary during this infrastructure building phase. His firm, Saint-Gobain (the world's largest building materials company), is active in many developing nations (e.g., Thailand, Poland, Turkey, Russia, China, India). "Once operations are up and running effectively, company policy is to hire locals for the key managerial posts" (François Vardon, personal communication).

Alternately, there may be a "pull" from a host country government or firm for expatriates that have specific skills. Ann Jordan describes the monumental job in the early 20th century of modernizing Saudi Arabia through transnational partnerships in such areas as health care, education, and oil production (Jordan 2011). Individuals signed contracts to engage in various forms of "institution building" from constructing the physical plant to putting in place its work processes and practices to training the locals to work there. Now the country has nationals with these skill sets who have replaced the expatriates.

Large surveys provide insight into current trends. The PricewaterhouseCoopers 2005 survey indicated that an overwhelming majority of firms anticipated growth in the number of overseas assignments. Although figures since the worldwide recession began in 2008 are not available, it is likely that significant expatriate growth continues in China, Central and Eastern Europe, and South East Asia. Many U.S. companies are not only increasing the percentage of workers they are posting abroad, but are also requiring their employees to have more international experience as a precondition for qualifying for leadership positions. KPMG is a global network of firms providing audit, tax, and advisory services. In 2008, KPMG had 2 percent of its workforce on foreign assignment, with the goal of increasing that to 4 percent by 2010, and having 30 percent of its professional staff with international experience in the not-too-distant future (Von Bergen 2008: 4). Mercer's 2008–2009 Benefit Survey for Expatriates and Globally Mobile Employees includes data from 243 global firms for a total of 94,000 expatriates (an increase of 44,000 since 2005–2006). Of these companies, 47 percent reported deploying more expatriates (those working one to five years abroad) and 38 percent reported more "global nomads" (those taking one expatriate assignment after another) (CPA Practice Management Forum 2008: 21).

The Rise in Short-Term Assignments

One relatively recent trend is the growth in short-term assignments, typically defined as less than one year in length (Collings, Scullion, and Morley 2007). An increasing number of managers have been circumventing long-term overseas assignments by relying on more frequent, short-term business trips along with technologies such as e-mail and teleconferencing (Figg 2000). Findings by Cendant Mobility, a global mobility-management company, are consistent with this pattern. They gathered survey data on short-term international assignments and discovered that more than six of every ten companies surveyed reported that they expected to increase the number of short-term assignments over the next two years (Minehan 2004). This trend is driven by three major concerns: cost-cutting, increased concerns for personal safety after September 11, and the increase in dual-income couples. All three concerns can be addressed by cutting back on the number of long-term assignments.

Nevertheless, there are a number of challenges created by short-term assignments. Specifically, some short-term assignments may be too abbreviated for the expatriate to build the long-term relationships needed for success abroad. This problem is further exacerbated by the fact that short-term expatriates are less likely to receive predeparture cultural and language training, even though they are more likely to need it to make the quick adjustment required of a short termer. Short-term assignments can be difficult for the expatriate who may not have a support network abroad. Moreover, if the expatriate has a spouse or children, the separation can cause stress and loneliness; the stay-at-home spouse is often burdened with the extra responsibilities of being a "single parent." Thus, although short-term assignments have certain advantages, it is vital that organizations consider the pros and cons in relation to candidate selection.

SHORT-TERM ASSIGNMENTS MIGHT NOT BE PARTICULARLY COST EFFECTIVE

Since the "great recession" of 2008 many multinational companies have cut back on long-term expatriate assignments to save money. Instead of two to three year assignments abroad, many companies are relying on more short-term assignments that last only several weeks or several months and do not involve relocating the entire family. While this strategy saves money in the short run, companies can get themselves in trouble because they are often violating tax and immigration laws of the host countries. When immigration authorities learn that these short-term "expats" do not have the proper visa and working papers, they are often deported, fined, and in some cases can be jailed. This certainly is not in the best interest of either the global manager or the sponsoring company. According to Tanya Mohn (2006: 6), there are now a growing number of consulting companies that manage these immigration, visa, and tax issues for companies sending managers abroad for short-term assignments.

Companies are also using alternative options to the overseas assignment. We have already discussed global virtual teams, made possible by various IT and communication technologies. Some other options to a long-term assignment abroad include: (1) frequent flyer assignments, which enable face-to-face interaction without the relocation expense, (2) commuter assignments in which the employee commutes back and forth between his or her home to a different country—on a regular basis, (3) rotational assignments, which have much of the same characters as commuter assignments but are characterized by a "time off" period at home (e.g., oil rig work) (Collings, Scullion, and Morley 2007).

Expatriate Strategy Pros and Cons

The expatriate strategy is an important means of connecting the home organization to the overseas environment through a direct exchange of personnel. There are at least three major disadvantages to cutting back too precipitously on the use of one's own expatriates abroad. First, by relying too heavily on host country nationals, the company may become isolated from its overseas operations—whether these operations are wholly owned subsidiaries, joint ventures, strategic alliances, or sales and distribution centers. If the reduction of expatriates proceeds far enough as part of a multinational's strategy, the result could be a corporation that is little more than a loose federation of semiautonomous units located throughout the world (Jeelof 1989). Even in the case of a new start-up venture, having an expatriate "on the ground" can help shape the fledgling organization and keep the goals and objectives front and center; handoffs to a third party tend not to be as effective.

A second and equally important disadvantage of reducing the number of expatriates too severely is that the firm has fewer opportunities for developing valuable managerial skills that can be gained best through long-term international experiences. Without those opportunities, the organizational culture is less likely to be infused with a global character and may exhibit a more provincial outlook. Moreover, those companies will miss an opportunity to develop a cadre of global leaders with (1) the agility to operate in a rapidly changing marketplace, and (2) the experience of working with different legal systems, political structures, languages, tax systems, customs, and ethical systems.

A third factor also comes into play here. It can be tricky to recruit locals who have the desired combination of skills for executive positions for that locale. The pool of available candidates continues to be small compared to the rising demand. The job requirements start with a set of technical skills that includes an understanding of the firm's culture along with some knowledge of the industry. Interpersonal and cross-cultural skills and business ethics are essential given the importance of interacting with suppliers, customers, and the local business and government communities. Language skills matter since candidates should be accomplished in the local language and the language of the global firm—at a minimum business English. Candidates need enough rotational experience, at home and abroad, to ensure that they have the capabilities to take charge in their own regions. Also, global firms are painfully aware that their executive ranks are still short on females (especially for key management positions), with many trying to increase their diversity. Pointing again to Saint-Gobain, François Vardon offered some comments on the ideal candidate to replace him. "Saint-Gobain is looking for a female manager who is Mexican, who has solid international experience, is fully proficient in English, is willing to work long and flexible hours, adapts to jet lag and conference calls with Europe and China, and is well versed in Saint-Gobain's analytic culture where information and numbers are centralized." He concluded his statement (translated from French) with the following tongue-in-cheek remark: *Et je souhaite...« bonne chance ! »* (meaning—"Good luck with that!") (François Vardon, personal communication).

To be certain, there are a number of good reasons for reducing the use of expatriates. First, it tends to be more cost effective to use host country nationals compared to relocating employees and their families. Second, the use of local people is typically required, and well received, by host country governments (e.g., Dowling, Festing, and Engle 2008). Third, an increasing number of local people are both well qualified to manage large operations and well versed in the local culture and language(s).

Expatriate failure rates also may be a contributing factor. However, according to Anne-Wil Harzing, the few documented studies of expatriate failure have shown a relatively low and decreasing rate over time (2002); expatriate failure is defined in terms of early return home, or dismissal from the company. Rosalie Tung reporting on her sample of 80 firms stated, "Seven percent of the respondents indicated that the recall or failure rate was between 20 and 40 percent. 69 percent of the firms had a recall rate between 10 and 20 percent; and the remainder had recall rates below 10 percent" (1981: 77). In a replication of her 1981 study, Tung found that "none of the 163 U.S. multinationals had failure rates in excess of 7 percent, even in assignments to culturally distant countries, such as the Middle East" (1989, 1998). Larger and more detailed data sets are needed to understand the magnitude of and change in this issue over time. Alternately, the definition of expatriate failure and performance could be broadened as a way to assess impact on the firm (Collings, Scullion, and Morley 2007).

Nevertheless, any early repatriation is costly—organizationally and personally. It can affect the quality and output of work at the overseas location, as well as its reputation, especially if there is no replacement in sight. At the home base, there are a number of costs (Briody and Chrisman 1991: 277) including: (1) the cost of repatriating the family early, which may be as high as three times the domestic salary plus relocation (Dowling, Festing, and Engle 2008), (2) finding an appropriate position for the returnee, unless there is a dismissal, (3) selecting and preparing another employee (and family members) for an overseas assignment—a process which can be protracted, and (4) filling the position of the employee who will be sent abroad.

Purnima Bhaskar-Shrinivas and his colleagues discuss some of the ways in which the expatriate (and his or her family members) suffer (2005). Company expectations have not been met, resulting in a failed attempt to perform well on an overseas assignment. The failure may have a long-term negative impact on how the returnee is perceived by him/herself or others (e.g., peers, supervisors). If the returnee remains with the firm, the new domestic position may not be a good fit, particularly if the match is made hastily. The returnee and family members also may experience various sources of stress including (1) having to explain why they returned back to the States early, (2) finding appropriate living arrangements in the event that they sold or rented their home, (3) settling back into a routine and reactivating their social networks, and (4) possibly seeking professional help in the event of a serious health-related, marital, or psychological issue.

Any expatriate failure or, for that matter, any evidence of poor job performance overseas, should be a red flag for both the local overseas management and the home-unit staff managing these international assignments. There are strategies that might be helpful in mitigating some of the difficulties that the expatriate (and/or family members) are encountering during the period of the assignment; these strategies are discussed in the next section of this chapter. Moreover, indications of maladjustment abroad should trigger the personnel staff to reexamine their overseas assignment processes. Were there any indications during the expatriate selection and preparation phases that either the candidate or his or her household would not be able to adapt in the new setting? How could the firm strengthen its existing preparatory assessment so as to choose candidates that are "good bets," thereby increasing the incidence of successful adaption abroad? What elements in the selection and preparation phases need to be more robust? Are the assignments being planned with enough lead time so that adequate attention is given to candidate evaluation, planning, and preparation?

To make the most of global assignments, companies and their expatriates must take a holistic approach to global leadership development. Attention must be paid to all the various phases of the international assignment, including selection, preparation, in-country support, repatriation, and the utilization of the skills and competencies gained while abroad. Moreover, companies should reassess their global strategy over time so as to have the best mix of methods, approaches, and practices to accomplish it. In the remainder of this chapter, we explore the expatriate assignment as part of an overarching global strategy.

SELECTION

Although all companies that send employees abroad go through some sort of selection procedure, some are more effective than others. All too often, personnel are chosen for expatriate assignments on very short notice, according to an insufficient set of criteria, and with little attention to long-term strategic considerations. A number of studies have identified those selection criteria that predict both cultural adjustment and job effectiveness (Black, Gregersen, and Mendenhall 1992; Mendenhall, Dunbar, and Oddou 1992; Teagarden and Gordon 1995; Hechanova, Beehr, and Christiansen 2003; Bhaskar-Shrinivas et al. 2005). These criteria range from job skills to spousal adaptability to a wide range of personal and interpersonal skills.

Technical Skills

Expatriate selection has historically been made on the basis of technical competencies (Katz and Seifer 1996). Most U.S. multinational firms continue to make their selections on the basis of technical skill set primarily, if not exclusively; that is, an engineer expected to be an expatriate in Indonesia will be selected largely on skills and past performance as an engineer at home. Charlene Solomon conducted a study of 50 major U.S. global firms that showed that in nine of every ten cases, expatriates were selected primarily on the basis of their demonstrated technical expertise for a specific job (1994). The assumption is that if one can perform effectively in the job at home, he or she can do so equally well abroad. Selecting expatriates primarily on the basis of technical expertise and past performance may be more prevalent among U.S. corporations than European firms which place greater importance on such criteria as language skills and cross-cultural adaptability (Suutari and Brewster 1999). Although these selection criteria are established by departments of human resources, actual selections are often made by line managers who frequently ignore these criteria (Harris and Brewster 1999). A recent study of Australian expatriates also found that the majority of respondents were selected largely on the basis of technical competence (Chew 2004).

Ability to Adjust

Although technical expertise certainly is an important selection criterion, it should not be the only one. The professional literature is clear that expatriates fail not because of technical incompetence but because they (or their accompanying family members) have not adjusted to the foreign culture. In other words, their professional effectiveness is diminished by the fact that they are suffering from culture shock or are otherwise unable to get along with their local business associates. Thus, technical competency is a necessary but not sufficient selection criterion.

A large number of studies—including some comprehensive reviews of the literature—stress the importance of expatriate adjustment during an overseas assignment (Black, Mendenhall, and Oddou 1991; Hechanova, Beehr, and Christiansen 2003; Bhaskar-Shrinivas et al. 2005; Takeuchi 2010). J. Stewart Black and his colleagues do not formally define *adjustment*, but they do provide examples of the conditions that an expatriate must confront and deal with abroad:

> Moving from the United States to a foreign country often involves changes in the job the individual performs and the corporate culture in which responsibilities are executed; it can also involve dealing with unfamiliar norms related to the general culture, business practices, living conditions, weather, food, health care, daily customs, and political systems—plus facing a foreign language on a daily basis (1991: 292).

The work of Black and his collaborators led to the identification of a model of adjustment consisting of three main dimensions:

- general/cultural adjustment (e.g., to living conditions, local food)
- interaction adjustment with host country nationals whether within or outside of the expatriate work environment
- work adjustment as it pertains to everyday work tasks.

Building on this adjustment model, if adjustment is poor, it will have a negative impact on overseas job satisfaction, job performance, work effort, ability to build relationships, and organizational commitment. It will also contribute to intentions to repatriate and/or early repatriation (Hechanova, Beehr, and Christiansen 2003; Bhaskar-Shrinivas et al. 2005; Harrison and Shaffer 2005). Thus, expatriate selection must be made on a number of criteria that go beyond technical competency and serve as effective predictors of cultural adjustment and consequently expatriate success. These selection criteria can be grouped into four major categories: communication skills, personality traits, motivation, and family circumstances.

Useful Selection Criteria

COMMUNICATION SKILLS   Learning the local language can be a key factor in acclimating to the new environment. Studies have shown a correlation between language skills and general/cultural adjustment (Hechanova, Beehr, and Christiansen 2003; Mohr and Klein 2004; Bhaskar-Shrinivas et al. 2005) and interaction adjustment

(Mohr and Klein 2004; Bhaskar-Shrinivas et al. 2005). The ability to speak to host country nationals in their own language can help ease the period immediately following relocation, as well as open up the possibility of rewarding interactions and relationships over the long term. Interestingly, these same studies do not show the direct link between local language skills and work adjustment. However, in a subsequent analysis, Purnima Bhaskar-Shrinivas and his colleagues found a stronger, positive effect when a "nonnative English-speaking expatriate was relocated to an English-speaking country than when a native English speaker was relocated overseas" (2005: 272). Although they were unable to fully account for this pattern, they suggested that English-speaking countries (e.g., Australia, England, United States) are less accommodating to nonnative speakers than are non-English speaking countries. This finding may also be related to the ongoing use, and in fact, primacy of English as a global business language. For example, Tomoko Hamada pointed out that Carlos Ghosn (discussed earlier in this chapter) insists on the use of English at Nissan even though English was not one of his native languages. In a different way, this statement by one of Alexander Mohr and Simone Klein's interviewees confirms the point: "For my husband it's a lot easier. At the company they are all educated people, all speak English and he doesn't have any disadvantages. This is not always true in my life. You don't know how much of the world is the language (requires language), everything. In the beginning I think this was the hardest part" (2004: 1194).

While these studies may capture the current low level of host country language use by expatriate employees, it is not the case that learning the local language has no or limited value. Just as communication is so vitally important for conducting business at home, it is equally important for successful business abroad. The single best way to become an effective communicator as an expatriate is to learn as much of the local language (verbal, written, and nonverbal) as possible. As discussed in Chapters 3 and 4, an ability to communicate provides an entrée into the culture of both organizations and societies. It demonstrates the expatriate's willingness to understand host country nationals on their own terms in their own modes of communication. It also positions the expatriate to develop relationships with colleagues, customers, and clients more effectively. Therefore, a desire to learn the host country language should be an important selection criterion for expatriates and their spouses. Similarly, ongoing language training or already-acquired language proficiency in the host country language should be considered highly relevant to expatriate selection.

PERSONALITY TRAITS   Research in the area of intercultural communications has identified a number of personality characteristics associated with adjustment and successful overseas experiences (Hechanova, Beehr, and Christiansen 2003; Mohr and Klein 2004). Some of these traits—discussed in greater depth later in this chapter—include self-efficacy (belief in one's competencies), tolerance for ambiguity; ability to bounce back from disappointment; and being nonjudg-mental, willing to experience new things, intellectually flexible, perceptually aware, and culturally empathetic. Unfortunately, many human resources personnel responsible for expatriate placements shy away from such selection criteria because they are not sure how to measure such personality traits. However, a number of effective standardized inventories have been designed to provide information on an individual's potential for cross-cultural effectiveness. For example, the Multicultural Personality Questionnaire can help predict how easily people are likely to adjust to a different cultural milieu (Van der Zee and Van Oudenhoven 2000, 2001). Ekta Sharma used its five dimensions—cultural empathy, open mindedness, social initiative, emotional stability, and flexibility—to assess Indian expatriates to Japan, the United States and the United Kingdom (2011). Another instrument, the Cross-Cultural Adaptability Inventory (CCAI), was originally developed by Colleen Kelley and Judith Meyers in 1987. It examines four basic dimensions that contribute to intercultural effectiveness: emotional resilience, flexibility/openness, perceptual acuity, and personal autonomy (Kelley and Meyers 1995). The CCAI is not intended to predict with absolute certainty the success or failure in overseas assignments. Instead, after exploring candidate strengths and weaknesses along these four dimensions, candidates (and their employers) can assess their readiness for an overseas assignment. The results from such inventories provide useful input for expatriate selection.

MOTIVATION   Another critical variable for expatriate success is the level of motivation to take an assignment in the first place. Some expatriate candidates view overseas transfers as necessary evils that must be endured. They consider overseas assignments as potentially dangerous to their career path and view them as creating a disruption in their home life. Others, by way of contrast, see expatriate assignments as opportunities for professional advancement, learning, and personal growth. These individuals and family members have a general interest in working and living abroad, a specific interest in the host culture, and generally believe that overseas assignments are career enhancing rather than career threatening. It is generally accepted that those with greater motivation for, and more positive attitudes about, overseas assignments are more successful. Gilad Chen and his colleagues found that positive cross-cultural motivation enables expatriates to adjust better to the work, and therefore improves expatriate job performance—even when controlling for other factors such as perceived stressors and previous job performance (2010); David Harrison and Margaret Shaffer (2005) came to a similar conclusion. Other researchers found that level of motivation by expatriate spouses was correlated with level of interaction adjustment (Mohr and Klein 2004). The motivational state of expatriate candidates is an important dimension of the selection process which should not be overlooked.

FAMILY CIRCUMSTANCES   A growing number of studies over the past decade have emphasized the importance of the accompanying spouse for expatriate success. In many respects, the unemployed spouse faces a greater number of challenges in adjusting to the new culture than does the expatriate employee. While the employee has the security and familiarity of the organizational structure, the accompanying spouse is faced with dealing with the butcher, getting the TV repaired, and enrolling the children in school—all with little, if any, institutional support. In addition, whereas the expatriate employee may see the international transfer as a positive career move, the accompanying spouse may see the move as little more than the disruption of his or her own career (Collings, Scullion, and Morley 2007). In addition to spouses, the special circumstances that can influence the cross-cultural adjustment of teenage children must also be considered. It is not hard to imagine how a maladapted spouse or pouting teen can negatively affect the morale and performance of the expatriate employee. Poor spousal adjustment is a major factor in expatriate failure (Tung 1981; Bauer and Taylor 2001) and, spousal adjustment affects all three dimensions of adjustment (Bhaskar-Shrinivas et al. 2005). The implication of these studies is that, in addition to the expatriate employee, spouses and children should be assessed as well on those criteria found to be critical for overseas success.

The number of women expatriates, by and large, in both Europe and the United States, is low relative to the overall labor pool, even though women tend to be better suited for international assignments owing to their stronger intercultural communication skills. The 2005 PricewaterhouseCoopers survey reports that women account for about 10 percent of the expatriate population worldwide, and that this percentage has not changed since the mid-1990s. Although there has been a modest increase in the number of female expatriates, particularly among Scandinavian corporations, the selection procedures presently in place tend to reinforce prejudices against selecting women for overseas assignments (Caligiuri, Joshi, and Lazarova 1999; Linehan and Scullion 2001).

Organizations need to make certain that all members of the family make a smooth adjustment to the new international assignment.

Selection Models

How corporations actually select their expatriates varies widely, and, according to J. Stewart Black and Hal Gregersen, there are a number of effective models (1999). To illustrate, Colgate Palmolive, which has about 70 percent of its markets outside the United States, recruits recent MBAs with considerable study, living, and work experience abroad who are then sent on a series of short-term (6–18 months) training assignments in foreign countries. This is a deliberate approach to selecting those who have already demonstrated a propensity for working in a foreign environment and then providing them with a number of valuable cross-cultural business experiences. Another model, used by the LG Group of Korea, involves a more formal method of selecting candidates for overseas assignments. A 100-item self-assessment instrument of an employee's global knowledge and competencies is used as the basis for discussions between the employee and his or her supervisor to determine what additional training and experiences would be needed to develop strengths and minimize weaknesses. From this series of discussions emerges a long-term plan and timetable for the development of future expatriate candidates. A third, less formal, model of selection is illustrated by Jon Huntsman Jr. (former governor of Utah, Ambassador to China, and a candidate for the 2012 Republican presidential nomination), while serving as an executive of a private chemical company headquartered in Salt Lake City. He frequently invited potential expatriates in his corporation to accompany him on international business trips, during which he personally observed how well they interacted with the local culture. Were they curious about exploring local food and culture, or were they more interested in finding the nearest Burger King before returning to their hotel to watch CNN? Did they seek out foreigners or stick with their own colleagues from home? Such an approach—although often expensive and time consuming—enabled Huntsman to assess potential expatriates before a costly selection mistake was made.

DOING IT ANTHROPOLOGICALLY

During the 1990s, the Samsung Group, the largest company in South Korea, took a very anthropological approach to preparing its employees for overseas assignments. After recruits went through a month-long international "boot camp," they spent the next year in a Western culture engaged, not in any particular functional area of business, but rather in what cultural anthropologists call "participant observation." These junior managers were expected to immerse themselves in the host culture, make systematic observations of how the "natives" live, and develop local tastes and sensibilities. In short, they were expected to become "cultural anthropologists" for the year. Although some corporate leaders might consider the Samsung program to be frivolous, it is based on educating an entire cadre of future corporate leaders in firsthand knowledge of the lifeways of the company's future customers.

A number of general recommendations emerge as "current best practices" for selecting employees for overseas assignments. First, we recommend that companies use as wide a variety of criteria as possible, including technical competence, as well as other predictors of success such as communication skills, personality traits, motivation, and family situation. Once technical competence has been determined, these other dimensions are the best predictors of success in overseas assignments, particularly for those employees who will be expected to interact frequently with host nationals. Second, companies should avoid a "quick and dirty" selection process in an attempt to cut corners and save money. Given the considerable costs of an international posting, companies need to protect their long-term investment by maximizing their chances for selecting successful expatriates. Third, realizing that all candidates will not score high on all selection criteria, firms should be prepared to enhance those weaker areas in either the predeparture preparation phase or during the in-country posting phase.

PREPARATION

Language Training

Once the employee has been selected for an international assignment, the next step is to equip that individual with as much preparation as possible so as to maximize his or her chances for success in meeting professional objectives. To be certain, a vital part of that preparation involves information about the nature of the job description, how it fits into the overall organizational structure, and the relationship between the particular job and the wider objectives of the company. But because the expatriate will be expected to operate within a different cultural context, an essential part of the preparation must involve an understanding of the new cultural realities.

Language training is an important part of the preparation process and is typically supported by organizations sending expatriates on international assignments. Based on our knowledge of the literature and our own research on expatriate households, we believe that expatriates with little or no proficiency in the host country language can be classified into three main groups with respect to language learning. One group, with limited or no proficiency in the host country language, actively seeks language classes or tutoring prior to departure, and then continues instruction while abroad. This group is very disciplined and systematic about language training and makes it a priority. For example, these expatriate candidates may take language classes or hire a tutor (paid for by the firm) prior to relocation overseas and follow up with language instruction once abroad. A second group of expatriate candidates find that they have little time for language instruction because they just recently learned that they were to become expatriates and their departure date is imminent. Of this group, some will access language instruction once abroad.

A third group with little to no host country language skills opts out of taking advantage of language instruction either at home or abroad; instead, this group operates in English and relies on the language skills of those in its social network. We suggest that companies continue to encourage host country language instruction for all of their candidates both prior to departure and while overseas. Companies should also work toward selecting candidates well in advance of the start date to increase the likelihood that language instruction occurs prior to departure. If expatriate candidates have a longer lead time to prepare for their overseas assignments, there would be more time for language instruction and a greater likelihood that language instruction becomes part of their routine.

Cross-Cultural Training

For decades, cross-cultural training (CCT) has been advocated as essential for adjusting to new cultural environments, irrespective of whether we are diplomats, missionaries, Peace Corps volunteers, health professionals, or businesspeople. By facilitating adjustments to the host culture, CCT enhances job performance, reduces the number of incorrect attributions of behavior, increases an understanding of one's own culture, reduces stereotypic thinking, helps in intercultural team building, decreases the social ambiguity that can lead to culture shock, enables the development of cross-cultural competencies, and generally contributes to accomplishing one's professional objectives. Despite what appears to be a compelling case in favor of CCT, Janet Chew reports that many firms still do not provide it for those about to assume an international assignment (2004).

Predeparture cross-cultural training is just the beginning of the learning process for the future expatriate.

The impact of CCT on adjustment has been an area of considerable controversy. Currently, there is no consensus despite numerous studies, including "meta-analytic" studies that merge data from multiple studies to create a larger sample and then analyze it statistically. In one of the most cited review articles, J. Stewart Black and Mark Mendenhall argued over 20 years ago that "cross cultural training is effective in developing important cross-cultural skills, in facilitating cross-cultural adjustment, and in enhancing job performance" (1990: 133). In particular, they identified numerous studies that showed a positive relationship between CCT and self-confidence, relational skills in a cross-cultural context, more accurate cross-cultural perceptions, adjustment to new cultures, and job performance. Two meta-analytic studies drew similar conclusions—one finding reasonably strong correlations for the CCT effects on performance and adjustment (Deshpande and Viswesvaran 1992) and a later study showing a weaker relationship (Morris and Robie 2001). A more recent meta-analytic study shows a negative correlation between CCT and general adjustment (Hechanova, Beehr, and Christiansen 2003). Thus, conclusions drawn from studies involving smaller sample sizes are mixed. However, there are some indications that CCT for Westerners taking assignments in developing nations eases adjustment (Okpara and Kabongo 2011).

CCT is a "hot" topic because it is contested. Research cannot demonstrate consistently that CCT makes a difference in hastening overseas adjustment. At the same time, there is some evidence that when CCT is well done and targeted, expatriate candidates and their family members generally value it, and researchers argue for its inclusion in predeparture programs (Shaffer, Harrison, and Gilley 1999). Moreover, according to a study at Simon Fraser University of 409 expatriate employees from 49 multinational companies, most interviewees felt that their overseas assignments were positive, but two of every three believed that they could have been better prepared through predeparture CCT (Light 1997: 20).

Our view is that CCT is worth doing but that a more rigorous and longitudinal approach to CCT evaluation is necessary. As a rule, firms capture CCT effectiveness data in non-standardized, and often anecdotal ways, which makes comparison across firms (or across expatriates within those firms) difficult. A better approach would be to gather an immediate post-CCT evaluation from the expatriate candidate, followed by subsequent data gathering on expatriate adjustment and performance while overseas from multiple standpoints (e.g., the expatriate, his or her supervisor, colleagues, family members). Mark Morris and Chet Robie have advocated training programs with these kinds of rigorous evaluations (2001). A different approach would entail offering CCT abroad as a way to get expatriates to identify vexing cultural issues and problem solve with their respective work groups. This approach would have team problem solving and performance as primary goals, rather than individual adjustment and performance.

The content of the CCT program is an important consideration during the predeparture phrase. When attempting to answer the question, "What is the syllabus for cross-cultural training?" we should not expect a simple or singular answer.

No generic or packaged program would be appropriate for all situations. Rather, each company must carefully design its own CCT programs (or contract with a reputable CCT firm) to meet its specific requirements and the needs of its trainees. To determine the content, length, intensity, and rigor of a particular CCT program, certain critical issues need to be considered, including previous host-country experience, job type and responsibilities, language capability, the extent of the cultural differences, and previous international experience. However, as a general rule of thumb, the deeper the level of training (in terms of time spent, information learned, and problem-solving scenarios tackled), the more effective the training will be and, consequently, the more likely the expatriate candidate (and family members) will be successful in the overseas assignment.

Even though most Westerners live in an instant society (complete with instant coffee, instant service, and instant gratification), it is shortsighted for Western corporations to expect instant adjustment and immediate benefits. Whatever form CCT might take, preparing people to function effectively in a different cultural environment requires a multifaceted approach and one that might take some time to simmer. The often-heard advice of KISS (keep it simple, stupid) is itself wrongheaded. The world of the 21st century is complex, and any attempt to overly simplify the process of preparing for overseas assignments is bound to fail. Taking our lead from the relatively wide CCT literature and following the basic structure of Chapters 2 through 6, pedagogically sound programs should include the following major components, to one degree or another:

1. *Culture-general component:* A general understanding of the concept of culture provides a fuller appreciation of other cultures, regardless of where one might be conducting business.
2. *Mastering patterns of communication:* Understanding another culture entails familiarization with its patterns of communication, both verbal and nonverbal.
3. *Cultural self-awareness:* It is imperative that we examine cultural values—theirs as well as ours—and recognize how the cultural influences on our own thinking conform to or contrast with those of culturally different peoples.
4. *Culture-specific component:* Host country culture-specific information (including the types of information discussed in Appendix B) along with any cultural details of the particular organizational environments in which the expatriate will be involved can help jump-start the learning process.
5. *Developing cross-cultural skills:* While the preceding four components are all cognitive in nature, the CCT program can begin helping the expatriate (and family members) develop certain skills, acquire new ways of thinking, and modify old ways of doing things.

CCT can be conducted using different methodological approaches, in addition to having a number of content components. These approaches differ in terms of levels of active participation (i.e., experiential learning), which in turn affects the level of training rigor. As one moves from less to more experiential methods, the training becomes more rigorous and consequently more effective. At the least rigorous end of the continuum is the approach that emphasizes the simple imparting of factual information, using such passive techniques as assigned readings, lectures, and videos. At a more intermediate level is the analysis of mini-case studies or scenarios (i.e., attribution training), which involves trying to determine why people in other cultures think and act the way they do. This approach is predicated on the fact that cross-cultural misunderstandings frequently occur because of the tendency to explain (or attribute meaning to) the behavior of others based on our own values and cultural assumptions. At the highest level of interactivity are such experiential training strategies as role playing, simulations, field trips, and interactive multimedia CDs, which involve the individual trainees to as great an extent as possible.

As the reader should now be aware, this book draws heavily upon the use of cross-cultural scenarios (found at the end of each chapter) as a pedagogical device. These cross-cultural scenarios enable the reader to explore the principle(s) behind breakdowns in communication and understanding in an international setting. Because they are short, scenarios work well in even crowded CCT programs. Like the longer, more complex case studies used routinely in business school curricula, cross-cultural scenarios provide the opportunities for honing analytical, decision

---

INTERACTING CROSS-CULTURALLY WITHIN INTEL

Semiconductor giant Intel provides an example of a company committed to a high level of experiential learning for cross-cultural competency. The company's 91,000 employees work in 48 different countries and 70 percent of its revenues come from sales outside the United States. Wisely, Intel has made exposure to different cultures a cornerstone of its leadership program for middle managers. Company officials reason that with so much at stake, it is imperative that all employees learn to understand their international coworkers and customers as thoroughly as possible. This, of course, involves, learning to work on foreign assignments, with culturally diverse colleagues at home, and as part of global cross-cultural teams.

The goal of the Intel leadership program (which was designed by employees from Russia, China, Israel, and the United States) was to expose its employees to three different levels of culture: (1) the overall corporate culture, (2) the subcultures of various business units within the company, and (3) the cultures in their facilities around the world. The training sessions, which are held at various locations throughout the world, do not draw upon reading materials, lectures, or "class discussions." Rather, training sessions are organized around culturally diverse teams that have a week to develop a business plan for a new product. Even though cross-cultural concepts are not the main "subject matter" of the training sessions, participants, who come from different cultural backgrounds, are forced (by their interactions) to consider cultural differences in their week-long planning process. This Intel approach to training for cross-cultural competency is highly experiential because trainees are learning to cope with cultural differences in a real, live work setting (Frauenheim 2005).

making, and communication skills. Moreover, these scenarios encourage the search of multiple explanations, even if there is only one correct explanation for some scenarios. Thus, the value of the scenarios as an educational device is that it trains people to seek a number of possible explanations for potential cross-cultural misunderstandings.

The Specifics of Overseas Life and the Job

Companies usually send expatriate candidates on a short trip to their expected overseas location on what is sometimes referred to as a "look-see" visit. In the best case, candidates explore housing options, gain some familiarity with the surroundings (e.g., grocery stores, school, neighborhoods), and often have a chance to meet work colleagues or other expatriate families. Such trips are vital to candidates both as an introduction to life and work abroad, but also as a kind of "test" (for themselves and their firms) of how they respond to the overseas assignment opportunity.

A different form of preparation involves engagement between the expatriate candidate and his potential work colleagues and partners overseas. Given the importance of collaboration in today's world (both virtual and face-to-face), it is likely that many candidates will have been working with overseas peers, suppliers, and customers for some time. What is valuable about these prior relationships is that they help to make the transition to an expatriate assignment much smoother. Expatriate candidates can build on those relationships. Rather than walking into the office or plant that first day not knowing a soul, expatriate candidates have a relational foundation already in place. In such instances, there is also the potential that the work tasks have some continuity with work back home. For those expatriate candidates without such connections, organizations should make efforts to link the departing employee with contacts at the overseas site. Establishing even initial e-mail or phone contact can provide an important entrée into work activities abroad. This approach can help facilitate collegial interaction and reduce the expatriate's learning curve so that the expatriate can get up to speed more quickly and effectively.

IN-COUNTRY SUPPORT

One way to conceptualize adjustment and performance on an overseas assignment is in terms of those who have a "stake" in the expatriate's (and accompanying family members') success. Riki Takeuchi has proposed a framework that highlights four stakeholder groups that can influence, or are influenced by, the arriving expatriate (2010). The four stakeholder groups include spouse–family, parent company, host country nationals, and the foreign subsidiary (or overseas operations). What is helpful about this framework is that it serves as a starting point for understanding potential sources of in-country support. While some of this support is through "formal" channels—such as the personnel departments in the home and overseas units—much of the support is "informal" through the establishment of new relationships. Our discussion below encompasses these and other stakeholders.

Despite careful preparation at home, as soon as the expat and his family arrive in the new host country, they are confronted with a host of challenges, many of which were discussed in Chapter 7. The challenge of adjusting to a new national culture (and for the expatriate a new organizational culture) is all of a sudden no longer hypothetical, but very real. Because this initial phase is a vulnerable period, the expatriate and family need all of the support they can get in order to avoid, or at least minimize, some of the more debilitating effects of culture shock.

A Role for the Corporation

To be sure, corporations provide an array of financial inducements as well as support services to their expatriates (Guzzo, Noonan, and Elron 1994; PricewaterhouseCoopers 2005). Though each firm is different, some of the types of financial incentives include a housing differential, relocation payments, educational allowance for the children, tax equalization, reimbursement for tax return preparation, and occasionally other kinds of allowances (e.g., hardship, goods and services, spouse). Often the firm pays for or subsidizes a health or athletic club membership. Firms typically provide general support in the form of home leave (sometimes as much as once per year), emergency leave, company car allowance, driver (depending on location), access to Western medical care, and language training, to name some of the key services. Companies have found it necessary to "sweeten" expatriate packages as a way to attract high quality candidates. Consequently, these forms of support tend to be generous.

However, one issue has been that many corporations are not particularly attentive to the next (absolutely vital) step of providing expatriates with the in-country support services and resources to enable them to make a successful adjustment to their new foreign assignments. While companies may have followed a rigorous search and selection procedure, and provided the employee and his or her family with an excellent predeparture training program, it is generally the case that the home unit's connection to the expatriate weakens over time. Expatriates have a phrase for this situation: "Out of sight, out of mind." Historically, this "syndrome" has been most visible in the months prior to repatriation, when the home office has been scrambling to find the expatriate a return position. One strategy that could make a significant difference is enabling the expatriate to stay connected with the home unit. An ongoing connection with peers (say, on project work) or senior leaders (say, on overseas initiatives that would be valuable at home) might even pave the way for the next career move.

For the U.S. businessperson, work is the primary mechanism that shapes the day and that offers a handy opportunity for building and maintaining relationships. Much of the businessperson's schedule involves engaging with people to plan projects, problem solve, and implement decisions. Thus, the job offers a ready-made structure and a set of social interactions for the day's activities—largely with host country nationals. Indeed, Soo Min Toh and Angelo Denisi point out that the locals are the "often overlooked partners" in the expatriate's adjustment experience (2007: 281). "Socializing behaviors" such as providing the expatriate with information and offering social support are not typically required of the local staff (with the possible exception of the role of administrative assistant); instead, it is an "extra" role that one or more of the local staff may take on as a goodwill gesture (2007: 282). However, Toh and Denisi suggest that host country nationals might be more likely to help expatriates if there were work-related beliefs and expectations about doing so. The local overseas operation might consider implementing this suggestion if its own organizational culture is not already attuned to the importance of integrating the expatriate as quickly as possible.

Making available, or at least raising awareness about, local learning opportunities could also contribute to expatriate adjustment. Both organizational-sponsored programs and organizational-encouraged activities may be helpful (Andreason 2003). For example, local staff might suggest travel to different parts of the country (whether for business or pleasure), concerts and performances, museums and places of national interest, or an entrée into local professional, civic, and social organizations. Such counsel enables expatriates to *continue* to learn about both the new national culture and the new organizational culture—a process initiated during their predeparture training. In the event that local colleagues accompany the expatriate (and possibly family members depending on the particular collegial relationship) on such ventures, the expatriate can learn directly from a "native." Such gestures demonstrate a willingness to help the expatriate acclimate and emphasize the value in throwing oneself into the local scene. When the home and local overseas offices encourage and support their employees in these ways, they are sending several unmistakable messages:

- the best way to adjust to one's new cultural surroundings is to experience first-hand what the new culture has to offer
- the quicker and more thoroughly one adjusts to the new cultural environment, the more successful one will be in the new work assignment
- cultural learning is no longer hypothetical; everyday life in the new assignment becomes the best possible classroom for learning another culture and language
- the firm as a whole is interested in supporting its expatriates in the best ways possible because it is a "win-win" for both the company and the expatriates.

While companies should provide such support to their expats, it is equally imperative that the expatriates avail themselves of these in-country learning experiences.

Accessing Local Networks

For the children in an expatriate household, school and after-school activities provide an institutional (routine) structure similar to what the office/workplace provides for their employed parent(s). Indeed, their schooling and leisure interests not only fill children's time, but also present opportunities for developing friendships that can facilitate adjustment both overseas and upon return home. The diversity of children's networks (e.g., expatriate, host country national) largely depends on whether they attend an American, international, or local school. It has been well established that if household members are unhappy—particularly teenagers—everyone in the family suffers. Schools and the social networks connected with schools (or for that matter, places of worship, clubs, and other community-based groups) can be a valuable resource for expatriate families and can play a critical role in the adjustment of both the children and their parents.

Unlike the U.S. businessperson or school-age children, the spouse on an overseas assignment is not automatically integrated into life in the new setting. He or she does not usually have the option of working outside the home due largely to host country work permit restrictions or because the job in the States was not transferable; some spouses also choose not to work while abroad. Instead, the spouse is the one responsible for managing the household and caring for the children. If the spouse is unable to adapt, it can have detrimental effects on family life (e.g., increasing conflict, divorce), the effectiveness of the employed businessperson at work, and the likelihood of the household's premature repatriation (Tung 1982; Black and Stephens 1989; Black and Gregersen 1991; Shaffer et al. 2001).

Spouses have to "create their own structure and then fill it with selected activities" according to Elizabeth Briody and Judith Beeber Chrisman. With time, the spouses they interviewed usually identified members of the expatriate community

Expatriate children often make smoother adjustments to new cultures because of both school friends and cross-cultural flexibility.

in their locale with whom they were able to interact and develop relationships. "That community, by virtue of its clubs, church, and sponsored activities, furnished a potential structure around which the spouses could organize their lives" (1991: 276). Many spouses, of course, also developed long-lasting relationships with host country nationals through some common activity, hobby, or routine (e.g., their children attended the same school). The longer it took the spouses to create a structured environment for themselves, the longer it took them to adjust during the overseas assignment. The need for spouses to develop and maintain social relationships is no less pressing today than it was in the early 1990s when Briody and Chrisman conducted their study. The task of initiating social contacts is made easier today owing to the blogs and networking opportunities found in cyberspace.

Strangely, neither educational institutions nor the expatriate community were part of Riki Takeuchi's (2010) four-stakeholder framework of expatriate adjustment (spouse/family, parent company, host country nationals, and the foreign subsidiary/overseas operations). But it is clear that new networks at work and school and in leisure activities are critical for all members of the expatriate household. Ideally, these networks should include both host country nationals and other expatriates—whether they are from the United States or from other countries. The most efficient way of learning to adjust to a foreign work assignment is by *expanding one's social and professional networks as widely and as intensively as possible.* Of course, the expatriate is often tempted to confine his or her networks (particularly social networks) to other Americans and/or expatriates, rather than making the effort to cultivate social relationships with host country nationals. But getting out of one's comfort zone is absolutely essential for adjusting to the new assignment. The best way to learn about another culture is experientially—that is, by interacting with the practitioners of the new culture.

REPATRIATION

Although many expatriates anticipate dealing with a host of adjustment problems when entering a new culture, few are prepared for the adjustments they face when coming home. Most returning expatriates—particularly those who have successfully acclimated to their overseas assignments—expect (or at least hope for) a ticker-tape parade upon returning home. In many cases, they have made enormous sacrifices by uprooting themselves and their families, managed to adjust to many new situations, and generally succeeded in meeting their personal and professional objectives. Having accomplished some major achievements, they view themselves as extremely valuable resources for their firms. Yet, if they expect to be seen as "conquering heroes or heroines" by their employers, colleagues, friends, and loved ones, they are in for a rude awakening.

Returning home is oftentimes as challenging as the original adjustment to the foreign assignment. Ideally, preparation for repatriation should be taken as seriously as predeparture preparation. Coming home should be treated as yet another foreign assignment. Because successful expatriates have experienced some life-altering changes while abroad, they are different people than they were when they left home. Moreover, home is not the same. During one's time away, many changes will have occurred at the home office, in the neighborhood, at the children's schools, in the economy, and even in the physical surroundings. Expatriates who left the United States in 2006 would come home to a very different political and economic climate in 2009 when the country, and indeed the world, was in a deep economic recession. Leaving the country at a time of rapid stock market growth and returning during a Dow Jones downturn can be jolting. Even the amount of commercial development (and the resulting traffic congestion) in one's old neighborhood can seem startling upon returning after a four-year assignment abroad. Whereas the expatriate may have been a "big fish in a little pond," he or she may be just the opposite after returning home. One's status, authority, and even physical amenities are likely to be diminished after returning home from an overseas assignment. There are also bound to be a number of changes at the home office in terms of personnel, strategy, leadership, technology, and even corporate culture. Little wonder that returning expatriates may feel that they are coming back to a foreign environment.

Repatriation Track Record

Unfortunately, the track record of U.S. firms dealing with repatriation leaves a good deal to be desired. General inattention to the reentry process has negative consequences for both the returnee and the organization. Research conducted on U.S. expatriate executives provides some insight into the dimensions of the problem (Briody and Baba 1991; Black, Gregersen, and Mendenhall 1992; Stroh, Gregersen, and Black 1998). For example, they found that:

1. A majority of all repatriating employees and more than 90 percent of their spouses received no repatriation preparation.
2. Most were given very little lead time before ending their overseas assignments. Only 4 percent were given more than six months' notice, with most receiving less than three months.
3. About two-thirds of all repatriates did not have a specific job to return to when they repatriated.
4. In nearly half the cases, returning Americans wound up in jobs with less authority and autonomy than they had in their overseas assignments.
5. Only 11 percent of returnees received a promotion upon return, whereas 77 percent were actually demoted to lower-level positions.
6. More often than not, the returnees had no opportunity to use their internationally acquired skills in their next position. (*Message*: Most employers do not recognize or appreciate the skills that are developed overseas or how they can be applied to helping the company in the future.)
7. Owing to their dissatisfaction with the "coming home" process, approximately 20 percent of all U.S. expatriates left the company within the first year of returning to the States.

If these data are even remotely accurate, the message that U.S.-based multinational corporations send is both clear and unfortunate: Overseas assignments are detrimental to one's long-term career development. Because most expatriates make considerable sacrifices for the company by disrupting their personal and professional lives (and those of their families), they expect to be rewarded upon their return. Not only are most not rewarded, but many are actually penalized. In the end, both the company and the returning household suffer. After making an enormous investment in the international transfer, the company sees many of its returning expatriates, feeling unappreciated and under-valued, take their valuable assets somewhere else—perhaps to a competitor! What an inexcusable waste of talent.

Global Strategy Reimagined

How firms accomplish their global strategy changes over time. What strategies might be appropriate for a start-up operation such as an export jewelry busi-ness could create havoc for a well-established venture producing HD 3D TVs. Corporations can and do rethink their approach to the market. At one time, the overseas assignment was the primary mechanism for establishing and managing overseas "outposts." However, the world has changed with the ability to travel to centers of business and commerce worldwide with expediency, and the develop-ment of IT and communication technologies. Global-virtual teams, short-term and commuter assignments, and interesting combinations thereof can often serve as alternatives to the 3–5-year hitch. While they too have their own challenges, both on the work and home fronts, they appear to be less career-disruptive and reason-ably effective from an organizational standpoint.

Yet, even with a reduction in the number of a firm's expatriate pool, there is still the nagging issue of repatriation and reintegration for those on overseas assignments. What needs to be done to ensure that the returning expatriate (a corpo-rate asset far more valuable upon return than before the international assignment) is integrated smoothly back into the corporate mainstream and retained over the long haul? The answer to this question goes beyond merely looking at the issue of repatriation. Instead, it requires that the company understand and attend to the larger issue of why it is making the international transfer in the first place. What is the *strategic* purpose of the foreign assignment? What will it accomplish?

- If it is no more than filling a position, it may well make more sense to hire a host-country national to accomplish a specific task.
- If the company (in addition to filling a job position) wants to achieve greater control over a foreign subsidiary, then it will need to know how the expatriate executive will accomplish that.
- If the company is interested in global leadership development, it will need to be very explicit up front about what skills and capacities should be nurtured during the over-seas assignment.
- If the company is hoping to use the overseas transfer as a mechanism for increasing its flow of global information, products, or services, then it must be purposeful in identifying what information will be transferred and how best to use the expatriate in that capacity.

Corporations all over the world face the issue of expatriate return, although some do it better than others. According to a Conference Board survey in 1996, 74 percent of European corporations gave written guarantees of a position upon reentry as compared to only 38 percent of U.S. corporations. Repatriation is often treated as if it were an anomaly in organizational functioning. At a minimum, firms need to devote much more time and energy to strategic problem solving around repatriation using the following types of questions as a foundation: How can expatriates repatriate smoothly? What organizational changes need to occur to guarantee expatriates return employment in a position that maximizes the use of their combined skill set and knowledge (pre and post-assignment)? What policies, processes, and practices must be put in place to raise the status, value, and input of expatriates once they have returned from an overseas assignment? What measures should be used to evaluate returnee impact on the firm once the overseas assignment has concluded? What can be done to enhance returnee retention over the long term? How should the organizational structure of the corporation change to ensure an integrated system of people and assignments linking the home office with its overseas facilities? The "coupled system" model described earlier in this chapter offers some clues.

Moreover, companies need to examine repatriation and expatriate retention in light of employee career planning generally (Caligiuri and Lazarova 2001). The successful repatriate brings back to the corporation a wealth of information about the culture, potential markets, and the local workforce, as well as a number of valuable competencies useful for future work assignments. The purposeful tracking of this information can be invaluable not only for developing the future leaders of a corporation, but also for dealing more effectively with foreign markets, negotiations, and labor relations (O'Connor 2002). The generalist skills developed by expatriates while overseas have broad applicability within a firm but have not typically been designated as valuable; as companies become more global in their orientation, attitudes about generalist skills may change. Companies also need to be upfront with expatriate candidates about the repatriation issue. Expatriates assume that if the firm is spending all this money on them to help them be as successful as possible abroad, then they must be highly valued employees worth that investment. One way to relieve the anxiety and ensure a more effective return adjustment is to provide expatriates (and their families) with as much information as possible at every step of the overseas assignment process. It is a difficult path that companies must navigate—on the one hand finding the appropriate candidates to take international assignments, and on the other raising awareness of the potential challenges that returnees often face upon return. However, without that degree of honesty about the return risk, companies will continue to face enormous credibility problems and the unhappy prospect of continuing to jeopardize their chances of attracting high-quality expatriate candidates in the future.

GLOBAL LEADERS FOR THE 21ST CENTURY

The management literature is becoming increasingly inundated with descriptions of behavioral traits for successful management in the 21st century. Although each commentator puts a slightly different spin on his or her list of characteristics, there remains a basic core set of competencies upon which most would agree. These competencies, discussed in some detail here, involve developing a broad perspective; appreciating points of view other than one's own; understanding issues holistically; being able to balance contradictions and operate comfortably in ambiguous situations; working effectively in cross-cultural teams; being able to bridge the local and the global; becoming emotionally resilient, open-minded, autonomous, and perceptually aware; and being willing to make decisions in the absence of all of the facts. These are the traits that leaders will need in a world that is becoming increasingly more global and multicultural. Moreover, they can be put to immediate use in any job where an individual or team confronts global issues, deals with global perspectives, or proposes global applications. While this list represents a good inventory of competencies that could be used as selection criteria (or predictors of success) for overseas assignments, it is also useful with respect to global virtual teams and short-term and commuter assignments.

Serving in overseas assignments is the best single training ground for developing executive leadership skills needed for the 21st century.

GLOBAL LEADERS AND CONFLICT RESOLUTION

In her analysis of a retirement party of an American executive who worked for a Japanese subsidiary in the United States, Tomoko Hamada Connolly illustrated the skill set of a global manager. The retiree, Mr. O'Casey, was the Human Resources Director. At the party, the Japanese plant manager spoke warmly of him, praising his abilities to guide the firm through difficult times over a 17-year period; a number of the supervisors drank the local micro-brew "Legends" as a way to honor and recognize him.

But, rituals can be "full of hidden dangers and pot holes" (Hamada Connolly 2010: 43). Barb, the female with the highest seniority and one that remembered a sexual discrimination lawsuit, baited Mr. O'Casey about the "secrets" he held in working with the Japanese and "whether working with the Japanese gentlemen was the most challenging thing in his long career or not" (2010: 39). The Japanese management present responded by sucking in their breath through their teeth—an indication of significant discomfort. However, Mr. O'Casey tackled the notion of "secrets" as one might expect of a superb cultural broker. He joked in response by inviting Barb to "come to my office tomorrow," a phrase interpreted by attendees that a serious work-related issue had occurred. Indeed, Mr. O'Casey's statement signaled to Barb that she had moved beyond the acceptable norms of the occasion—which she seemed to understand. In this instance, Mr. O'Casey was successful in dealing with this very public threat of organizational conflict.

Later during the party, Mr. O'Casey offered his perspective on the trajectory of the multinational by proposing three general guidelines. The first was aimed at the American work force: recognize that the firm is Japanese-owned, implying that American input would be limited. The second targeted both the Japanese and the Americans: profitability is a shared goal. The third guideline was directed at the Japanese management: run the business humanely and ethically. By highlighting general guidelines rather than specific incidents, and by side-stepping controversial questions from employees like Barb, Mr. O'Casey was able to present a potential model and a hopeful outlook for the future.

What follows is a discussion of the major competencies needed for global leadership in the 21st century. The first four competencies, which establish a *global mind-set*, provide the base of the learning pyramid. The next three competencies provide *personal stability* needed to function effectively in any cross-cultural business environment. The last three competencies provide the *professional confidence* needed for the challenges of global work. These three levels of competencies provide a firm foundation for *successful leadership*, which is the capstone competency needed for effectiveness in today's global economy.

1. *Broad perspective:* Unlike the more traditional domestic leader, the global leader needs to develop the broadest possible perspective. The emphasis should be on seeing the big picture. This involves a type of systems thinking whereby one can see how the various parts are interconnected to make a whole. A fundamental generalization

Successful managers for the 21st century need to know how to manage cross-cultural teams.

from the discipline of anthropology is the functional interrelatedness of the parts of culture; that is, any culture is composed of a number of parts, many of which are interconnected to form a systemic, well-integrated whole.

2. *Appreciation of alternative perspectives:* A key aspect of learning for global leaders is being able to make the bridge from their own point of view to many different points of view. Perhaps the best way to understand other points of view is to learn how to listen effectively, discuss appropriately, and try to put yourself into someone else's shoes. Learning the applicable modes of communication (e.g., that group's language) and the cultural rules surrounding communication (e.g., relationships first and business later) allows you to send and receive messages with relative efficiency. Both provide entry into a way of thinking and acting, as well as a frame of reference for understanding alternative viewpoints.

3. *Cognitive complexity:* Global leaders need what Stefan Wills and Kevin Barham (1994: 50) refer to as "cognitive complexity," composed of the twin abilities to differentiate and integrate. *Differentiation* involves being able to see how a single entity is composed of a number of different parts; *integration* involves the capacity to identify multiple relationships between the different parts. The truly complex thinker—needed for success as a global leader—is the person who can engage in both types of thinking and can move comfortably between the two. He or she has the ability to focus on the unique needs of the local situation while maintaining a good grasp of how it fits into the overall operations.

4. *Cognitive flexibility:* On most lists of competencies for international leaders is the need to be curious, nonjudgmental, and open to new ways of thinking and explaining phenomena. This essentially means that the individual is willing to learn and

postpone making evaluations until more facts are known. Such a capacity involves the suppression of your ego, the letting go of old paradigms and cultural certainty, learning how other cultures view you, and being willing to see the internal logic of another culture. This type of cultural literacy actually enables you to understand your own culture and those of others, mobilize diverse people, serve diverse clients and customers, and operate across cultures with maximum success.

5. *Personal autonomy:* Another important competency of the successful global leader is personal autonomy. To be open, flexible, and nonjudgmental does not entail adopting the thoughts and behaviors of others as your own—that is, "going native." But while remaining open minded (to learn more about another culture), you must not abandon your own identity in favor of theirs. Personally autonomous global leaders are not threatened by culturally different people. They have high self-esteem, value their cultural roots, and come to the global arena as mature adults.

6. *Perceptual acuity:* Successful leaders need to be perceptually acute in a number of ways. They need to derive meaning as accurately as possible from interactions with people from a wide variety of cultures and subcultures. This competency involves being attentive to both verbal and nonverbal communication and being sensitive to the feelings of others and to your effect on others. Those with perceptual acuity focus on alternative explanations rather than relying on explanations that might seem logical or obvious from their own cultural perspective. They get good at considering not only the words exchanged but also the nonverbal communication, the social context, and the assumptions embedded in the other culture.

7. *Emotional resilience:* Things rarely go as planned when working globally. Frustrations are frequent and stress is high. Although unanticipated problems occur in any leadership situation, they occur with greater regularity when operating in an environment in which the cultural rules differ and each party has an imperfect understanding of each other's rules. Global work becomes a training ground for learning how to deal with unanticipated problems, annoyances, and stress. To succeed, the global leader must learn to get back in the game immediately after disappointment and maintain a positive, upbeat attitude in the face of adversity.

8. *Balancing contradictions:* A major requirement for being an effective global leader is being able to balance contradictory needs and demands rather than prioritizing or attempting to eliminate them. Contradictions and conflicts should be seen as opportunities rather than liabilities. Conflicting values, behaviors, and ideas are a fact of life in the world today, and are not diminishing in number. The world is not becoming culturally homogenized into a monolith. If anything, the cultures of the world are becoming increasingly more diverse and insistent upon maintaining their unique identities. When exposed to logical alternatives to one's own way of thinking and behaving, global leaders can learn to cope with the contradictions and actually use these differences for the sake of achieving synergy. In other words, grasping multiple perspectives can lead to a wider range of options and approaches to problems and challenges.

9. *Willingness to make risky decisions:* Making decisions, as all leaders must, always involves a certain amount of risk. Being a new global leader entails being an adventurer. It often requires a willingness to act on "gut feelings," and, if unsuccessful, bounce back. Because leaders in cross-cultural situations often need to act with less than a perfect grasp of all the facts, the range of risks is frequently greater than in a more culturally familiar environment. In other words, working with members of another culture familiarizes the individual with the risks inherent in decision making; perhaps more importantly, it provides the opportunity for taking risks, experiencing failure on some occasions, but learning from those failures.

While global work has its risks, it also presents opportunities to learn from both failure and success.

10. *Global teamwork:* Global leaders need to emphasize cultural awareness and cross-cultural teamwork, not just personal awareness and individual mastery. With the ubiquity of foreign subsidiaries, joint ventures, and offshore facilities, global leaders need to be able to value and facilitate multicultural teamwork. Yet, before one can build fully effective multicultural teams within an organization or with business partners, people must first understand the cultural assumptions and the behavior of others in the group in comparison with their own. So, in a sense, the personal and cross-cultural awareness needed for multicultural team building is mutually reinforcing.

In many ways, the development of global leaders is greatly enhanced when a global perspective has been built into the fabric of the corporate culture, when global work infuses the domestic environment, and when people have ongoing opportunities to interact with others from different cultural settings both at home and abroad. Assessing or reassessing the long-term goals for training, leadership development, and human resources management will help—particularly if global leadership competencies are encouraged, rewarded, and routinely part of the culture. Exposing more employees to work projects and activities with global content and global colleagues will help make the meaning of "global" tangible to them. Hiring a culturally and linguistically diverse workforce at home to lead key work efforts can also be an effective globalizing strategy.

Of course there are many other small steps, none of which is particularly expensive, but when taken together can have a positive cumulative effect. For example, companies can (1) bring in speakers from corporate divisions in other countries or from other global organizations; (2) offer internationals visiting the company, the opportunity to interact socially with host families during their stay; (3) sponsor "brown bag" lunches (open to all) where employees can present interesting insights from recently completed international travel; (4) use in-house non-American employees as part of CCT as advisors for Americans going abroad on extended business trips or international assignments; (5) encourage globally oriented behavior among all employees, such as taking foreign-language classes, serving on local boards of international non-profit organizations, and attending international/cross-cultural seminars. The list is endless. However, what makes any item on such a list meaningful to employees is its connection to their current and/or future work activities. Knowing that you are scheduled for a short-term assignment in Germany can be a highly motivating reason for dusting off your old high school German books. Or, realizing that the composition of your global work team is mostly Chinese nationals can be enough of an incentive to get you to finally sign up for that CCT class you have been meaning to take. Thus, creating global leaders is at least partly contingent on finding ways to link their job responsibilities to global colleagues, issues, and interests. When that happens it sends an unequivocal message that the organization is committed to its global mission over the long haul.

CROSS-CULTURAL SCENARIOS

Read the following cross-cultural scenarios. In each mini-case study, a basic cultural conflict occurs among the actors involved. Try to identify the source of the conflict and suggest how it could have been avoided or minimized. Then see how well your analyses compare to the explanations in Appendix A.

8-1 Harold Mariani, an internal consultant with one of the large accounting firms, was transferred to work in his firm's Mexico City office for nine months. His immediate supervisor, who was Mexican, assigned him a week-long project. After the boss described the project, Harold told him that he didn't think it was a good idea and that it would be a waste of his, and the company's, time. Angered by Harold's reaction, his supervisor tells him to implement the project anyway and storms out of the office.

Why was the supervisor so angry?

8-2 Jon Starrett, a senior executive working in his company's office in Brussels, wanted to make a good impression on his Belgium staff. In order to facilitate good relations with his staff, Jon decided to do several things. First, he arrived at the office early in the morning so he could interact with his subordinates over coffee. Second, he initiated an "open-door" policy so that everyone would feel free to stop by and chat. However, in spite of his best efforts, Jon ended up alienating his subordinates.

What did he do wrong?

8-3 Linda Harmon, a vice president of a U.S.-based courier service, was sent to open an office in Madrid. The company had recently expanded its overnight delivery services to several other countries in Europe (including the Netherlands), and these operations were doing very well. The company's "bread-and-butter" service was overnight delivery anywhere in Europe, provided that the package was in the pickup box by 5:00 P.M. Even though Linda and her husband, John, were getting along well in Spain, she could not understand why the Spanish people were not responding more favorably to the company's services.

Why was the overnight delivery system not catching on in Spain?

8-4 While working on a six-month assignment in her company's Taipei office, Kathryn Skye made arrangements to meet for dinner a former classmate from the Harvard Business School. While enjoying the food and getting caught up on each other's lives, the Taiwanese classmate, who currently worked for a large software company, told Kathryn about his plans for starting his own software consulting business. Unfortunately, he said that he needed to wait before he launches the business because he was unable to get the proper telephone number for the business from the telephone company. Given all of the work he has done to write his business plan, it strikes Kathryn that a telephone number should not delay the opening of the business. But Kathryn's former classmate insists that he cannot start his new enterprise until he has the right telephone number.

How can you explain to Kathryn what is going on?

8-5 Right after completing a master's degree in international business, Dick Sutton decided to accept a job with a firm in Tokyo. He had studied Japanese for a year and was most interested in immersing himself in Japanese culture. Within the first month of his arrival, he was invited to an office party. As was the custom, most of the employees were expected to entertain the group with a song, poem, or joke. Knowing the keen interest the Japanese have in baseball, Dick recited the poem "Casey at the Bat," which seemed to be well received. Dick was having a good time at the party and was secretly congratulating himself on his decision to come to Japan. In fact, he couldn't help thinking how informal and playful all his colleagues were, including the upper-level executives—a far cry from all the descriptions he had read of the Japanese as austere and humorless businesspeople. Later in the evening, Dick found himself talking with two of his immediate superiors. Wanting to draw on the informality and good humor of the moment, Dick casually brought up some plans he had for a new marketing strategy, only to be met with near total indifference. For the remainder of the evening, Dick felt as though he was not being included in the party.

What advice could you give Dick?

Appendix A

■ ■ ■

Cross-Cultural Scenario Discussions

CHAPTER 1

1–1   In most of Europe when people write the date as 6/5/01, they are placing the day first, the month second, and the year last. So Bernice's request for information by 6/5 was not for June 5 but for May 6. Therefore, Bernice was not three and one-half weeks early but five days late!

1–2   The Chinese, and particularly those in Shanghai, are resentful of the Japanese, who bombed and brutally occupied Shanghai during World War II. Moreover, these Chinese businessmen believe that Japanese culture is a derivative of Chinese culture.

1–3   Although cameras can be valuable for documenting a foreign culture, they must be used with care. There is the simple matter of violating one's privacy, a notion to which most Americans can relate. How would a typical middle-class American, for example, feel if someone dressed in foreign clothing started taking his picture while he was cutting his front lawn? At the very least, such behavior would be met with suspicion. For a number of other cultural reasons, many East Africans would be reluctant to have their picture taken. First, a sizable number of people living along the Kenya coast are Muslims and as such resist being photographed because of the Koranic prohibition of depicting the human form. Second, whereas the Westerner looks for "picturesque" scenes of people doing traditional things, the local people themselves may feel that the foreign photographer is documenting their "backwardness" or lack of modernization. Third, some East Africans who do not understand the technology of the camera believe that having their pictures taken is tantamount to having their soul entrapped in the camera. In a society where witchcraft is widely believed, the thought of anyone, particularly a witch, capturing one's soul can be terrifying.

1–4   France, along with other European countries, still suffers the memories of Hitler's reign of terror. Uniformity in logos, slogans, or signs are reminiscent of the German swastika and the humiliation of the period of occupation. The "gifts," coupled with the hostile takeover, started the Fortune 500 corporation off on shaky ground, considering French history.

1–5   Although this fertilizer company did a good deal of research in developing its product, it was woefully lacking in cultural information that would have enabled the company to market it. First, the company tried to convince the village men to accept an agricultural innovation, when in fact it was the women who were the farmers. That they failed to understand this basic ethnographic fact did little for their general credibility. Second, many East Africans have two important beliefs that can help explain their reaction: (1) the theory of *limited good*, which assumes that there is a finite amount of good in the world (such as fertility), and (2) witchcraft, the notion that evil forces embodied in people can harm members of the community. Given these two beliefs, any individual East African farmer would never participate in any scheme that promises to produce considerably more per acre than her neighbor, for to do so would open her up to charges of having bewitched the fertility from the neighbor's soil. In short, to continue to grow the same amount as one had in the past is a far preferable alternative to being killed for witchcraft.

CHAPTER 2

2–1 Saudis do not budget their time in the same way as Americans do. Time is considered to be a much more flexible commodity. The best piece of advice we might give Bill is to be patient and allow more time when conducting business affairs in Saudi Arabia than would be normal in the United States. Moreover, what Bill considered to be "small talk" is a very important part of the process of doing business in Saudi Arabia. Trust is an important ingredient in business affairs. Before engaging in meaningful business relations, most Saudis need time to get to know those with whom they are about to do business. They feel that there is no better way to do this than to discuss a wide variety of nonbusiness topics while drinking coffee. Finally, Saudis define private and public space somewhat differently than is done in Dallas. Although Saudis are extremely private in their personal lives, they are quite open in those things they consider to be public, and business is thought to fall into the public domain. Thus, even though the Western businessperson may want to discuss confidential business matters, it is not at all uncommon for a "personal" appointment to be conducted with other people in the room.

2–2 The demise of these joint-venture negotiations cannot be explained by the fact that contemporary Japanese firms are inextricably wedded to traditional practices. Present-day Japanese firms have shown an enormous willingness to adopt innovative policies and strategies, which has contributed to their rapid rise in the world economy. Yet, equally high on the Japanese list of cultural priorities is the value placed on respect for elders and saving face. Even though Hayakawa may have disagreed with his grandfather's position, it would have been totally inappropriate for him to have disagreed with his grandfather in a *public* meeting. The Japanese way would have involved private discussions between Hayakawa and his grandfather to try gently to convince the former president of the need for these innovative policies. Tom's impassioned attempt to change the retired president's mind in the public meeting was seen as a serious breach of etiquette, which caused the old man to lose face.

2–3 Mexicans place a high value on fiestas because they represent an opportunity to get together with friends and family. Work, for the sake of work, is not as highly valued as it is north of the Rio Grande. Mexicans, unlike their counterparts from the United States and Canada, have no difficulty putting off a task until tomorrow, particularly if it helps to maintain important social relationships between friends and family.

2–4 Asians in general, and Koreans in particular, place a high value on harmonious personal relationships. Conflicts are avoided at all costs, and every effort is made to be polite and nonconfrontational. Also, Koreans have great difficulty in admitting failure, for to do so is to be humiliated or shamed—that is, to lose face. It is therefore important to maintain a high degree of *kibun*, translated as "morale" or "self-esteem." The reporting or acknowledging of a problem is far more serious than the problem itself, for it causes a loss of face for the teller and a loss of morale for the hearer. Thus, when the Korean employees withheld knowledge about plant problems from Jennifer, they did so to (1) preserve her *kibun*, and (2) not lose face themselves. If anything negative has to be reported it should be done, according to the Korean way, at the end of the day so that the parties involved will at least have the evening to restore their damaged *kibun*.

2–5   This scenario illustrates the high value Americans place on science, logic, and rational thought. Because there were no logical links between any of these unfortunate happenings at the plant, Ned and his fellow Americans concluded that they were just an unfortunate, yet unrelated, series of accidents. The local workforce, on the other hand, believed that sinister forces were at work that required the services of a religious specialist. This belief was the direct cause of Ned's two managerial problems—morale and absenteeism. Unfortunately, Ned and his colleagues got caught up in their own value system and missed the major point: It makes little difference whether the belief in evil spirits is true or false. Ned was no more capable of proving that evil spirits did not in fact cause this series of events than the local workers could prove that they did. What Ned and his American staff failed to understand was that (1) the workers believed that evil spirits were at work, and (2) this belief, whether true or false, was causing a major problem for the company. The only reasonable way to solve that problem was to take an action that would enable the workers to perceive that the power of evil spirits had been neutralized and that their safe work environment had been restored.

CHAPTER 3

3–1   An open kitchen design reflects the typical American lifestyle of using the kitchen for both food preparation as well as socializing. It is, in other words, not at all unusual for dinner guests in the United States to socialize in the kitchen (with or without drinks) while the host may be putting the final touches on the dinner. However, for many Nairobi residents (most of whom retain strong ties to their traditional rural cultures), the place where food is cleaned, prepared, and cooked is considered an unclean place totally unsuitable for entertaining one's guests, or, for that matter, even letting them see. To serve their guests dinner in the dining room, while being able to look into the "unclean" place where food is prepared, is as unthinkable as having a doorless bathroom adjoining the dining room. After people complained to the public housing officials, the units were modified by building a door between the dining room and kitchen. Lily failed to remove her cultural blinders by assuming that people the world over deal with their personal domestic space in similar ways. Perhaps the Municipal government of Nairobi could have been spared the needless expense of altering the kitchens had Lily done her cultural homework.

3–2   In any society, gifts are given as a way of symbolizing certain thoughts. Yet, like other aspects of culture, certain gifts symbolize different thoughts in different cultures. In the United States, chrysanthemums are given for a number of general purposes. But in Italy and in some other European countries, chrysanthemums are used traditionally as funeral flowers. Also, George's flowers sent another unintended message. Although it is appropriate to take flowers as a gift when invited to someone's home for dinner, to present flowers to the mother of an unmarried woman is seen as an expression of a man's serious intentions toward the daughter.

3–3   Life in rural Turkey is quite different from life in Istanbul. Located in two different continents (Europe and Asia), Istanbul reflects a good deal of its past European influence. The farther one gets from Istanbul, the more traditional, non-Western, and Islamic the people become. The arrival of a foreigner in a small Turkish town is not a common event. Andy and Nancy received stares not out of hostility but rather out of curiosity. In addition to the general interest in foreigners, there was another source of confusion, which many of the local people no doubt felt. The presence of a woman in the generally all-male domain of the coffeehouse was an unusual sight. Rural Turkish women (who frequently wear dark clothing, cover their faces, and have little contact with the general public) do not enjoy the same liberties as their urban counterparts.

3–4   In a sincere but misguided attempt to convey to their Japanese counterparts their interest in the project, the Americans made two serious cultural blunders. First, by taking off their jackets and rolling up their sleeves, they were trying to communicate sincerely, in a nonverbal way, that they were interested in working hard to arrive at a satisfactory agreement between the two corporations. The Japanese, however, who tend to be much more formal in dress, interpreted this symbolic gesture as most unbusinesslike and inappropriate—a breach in professional protocol. The second faux pas resulted from Harry's invitation to start their discussions off on a first-name basis. Although by making such a suggestion Harry was genuinely interested in facilitating their work relationship, he failed to realize that Japanese business relationships tend to be based on quite rigid status differences. In the eyes of the Japanese, being on a first-name basis involved an unacceptable level of informality and egalitarianism.

3–5   This is just one more example of how the same hand gesture can have very different meanings in two different cultures. Although beckoning someone with a "crooked" index finger is perfectly normal in the United States, in Korea it is an obscene gesture.

CHAPTER 4

4–1   In Uruguay it is considered impolite to use a blanket greeting ("¡Hola!") for an entire group. Stan should have personally greeted everyone at the party, and, when leaving, he should personally say farewell to everyone individually as well. Also, the greeting "Hola!" is a more informal greeting and should only be used in casual situations.

4–2   In fact, Claire had inadvertently committed two cross-cultural gaffes. First, in this part of the world, the head is considered to be the most sacred part of the body, where one's spiritual power resides. Although patting a child on the head in North America is a gesture of endearment, in Malaysia it is viewed as a violation of the most sacred part of the body. Second, complimenting a child on her beauty or health is regarded in Malaysia as inviting bad fortune for the child. If evil people or evil spirits believe that a child is particularly healthy or beautiful, they might become jealous and want to harm the child. So, unlike parents in North America who often boast about their children's beauty, health, and intelligence, parents in Malaysia will downplay those traits to protect their children from harm.

4–3   The candidate is demonstrating a presentation style that the French are accustomed to and respect. The French prize eloquence and knowledge of history and literature as a means of conveying that one is a cultured, well-educated person. The inclusion of these types of references would be a normal part of a well-executed presentation in France. This knowledge of French culture, however, should never be a substitute for product knowledge and technical expertise.

4–4   Mark failed to realize that his upbeat way of communicating (by speaking at a high decibel level, and using animated facial expressions and strong hand gestures) was intimidating to the Thai women, who tend to be soft-spoken and demure. The women interpreted his loudness and animated expression as being either angry or out of control. Mark was intimidating the female candidates with his overly assertive communication style, which, while perfectly appropriate in Minneapolis, doesn't play well in Bangkok.

4–5   The key to understanding this apparently innocent exchange, which left Pettersson offended and Lars confused, revolves around the use of personal questions. People in the United States think it perfectly natural to ask a number of personal questions early on in one's initial conversation; this is considered a normal way of finding a common ground on which to build a relationship quickly. In other societies like Sweden, people move to establish social relationships at a slower pace. The personal lives of the Swedes and their families are considered private. They will be quite reluctant to make any moves toward intimacy until there has been sufficient time to assess the newcomer. Thus, Lars' questions appeared overly personal to Pettersson, whose culture handles such introductory amenities much more slowly.

CHAPTER 5

5–1 Despite Ray's Hispanic heritage, his dramatic rise in his company's organization required him to adopt the mainstream U.S. cultural interpretation of time; that is, Ray was operating under the assumption that because time is money, there is no reason to waste it. Such a definition of time assumes that the end product of negotiations between two companies is more important than the process that brings it about. But in Chile and many South American cultures, the *process* is also very important. It is not enough just to make a decision on the merits of the product; to many South Americans, it is equally important that those entering into a business relationship enjoy one another's company and build a strong foundation of mutual trust. To the Chileans, Ray's insistence on getting down to business as quickly as possible was bypassing some very important components of the negotiation process.

5–2 In Brazil, ideas are often reinforced with touch. Larry should not have been insulted by the taps on his shoulder and arm. Indeed, it would have been appropriate for him to have emphasized his views in a similar fashion.

5–3 The unwillingness of these four Korean accountants to leave their current employers stems from a sense of loyalty felt by many Korean workers that is not shared by their U.S. counterparts. The vast literature on Japanese business practices suggests that Japanese workers have a strong loyalty to their employers because their lives revolve around the company, and they in fact gain a sense of their own importance primarily through the prestige of the company. However, Koreans, unlike the Japanese, have relatively little loyalty to their companies, per se. There is a good deal of job mobility in Korea, for employees are always on the lookout for better job opportunities. Koreans, however, have a strong sense of loyalty to their *bosses* within the company. When Korean employees do change companies, they frequently follow bosses who take them along when they move. Even though it may be every bit as difficult for foreign firms to recruit Koreans away from their current jobs as it would be to recruit Japanese, the nature of employee loyalty is different in these two countries.

5–4 Americans place such importance on words that the absence of words becomes very disorienting. Because most Americans feel that silence is inherently unnatural, they frequently say things that get them into trouble in their haste to fill the silence. Roger would have been better off to have waited out the silence and then come back with another proposal or a question that would have kept the discussions on track.

5–5 Among middle-class men in the United States, it is customary to shake hands as a gesture of friendship, as it is also among men in Kuwait. When communicating extreme friendliness, an American man may grasp his friend's right hand with both of his hands. If, however, an American man gives such an emphatic handshake to a Kuwaiti man, he will be sending an extremely offensive message. In Kuwait and generally throughout the Muslim world where the right hand is sacred and the left hand is profane, touching someone with the left hand is highly offensive.

CHAPTER 6

6–1 For the local Indian labor pool, flexibility of time was of greater significance than housing or high wages. Under the German system, which paid an hourly wage (rather than a 40-hour-per-week salary, as with Bill's company), local laborers could take time off for their festivals and ceremonies without fear of losing their jobs. The solution to Bill's labor recruitment problem required the relatively simple task of changing to a more flexible hourly wage system rather than a weekly salary system.

6–2 Although both U.S. and French culture are what Edward Hall would call monochronic (emphasizing promptness and schedules), they differ in terms of the degree to which each emphasizes the primacy of meeting deadlines. For Americans, keeping to an agreed-upon schedule takes priority, even when confronted with unanticipated contingencies. If need be, personal pleasure or even quality will take second place to meeting the deadline. The French, too, are interested in efficiency and meeting schedules, but they don't give deadlines the same top priority as in the United States. For the French, the emphasis is on quality. In the event that time runs short, the French will choose to take additional time to ensure high quality, whereas Americans are more willing to sacrifice a number of things—including quality—to meet the deadline.

6–3 In the United States, public humiliation is one of a number of techniques that can be used quite effectively to change people's behavior. In the world of Islam, however, where the preservation of dignity and self-respect is absolutely essential, public reprimand will be totally counterproductive. If Arabs feel that they have suffered a loss of personal dignity because they have been criticized in public, they take it as a dishonor to both themselves and their families. And when Sam insisted on using this "motivational" technique, he alienated not only the individual to whom the reprimand was directed, but also all his fellow workers who felt hurt on his behalf. When this happens, the person giving the reprimand loses the respect of those witnessing the situation.

6–4 The employee–employer relationship in Japan is very different than in the United States. When a Japanese firm hires an employee, he or she becomes part of the corporate family. Whereas labor and management in the United States operate largely from an adversarial perspective, the relationship between the Japanese worker and the company is based on loyalty and a long-term commitment to one another. Though there is some evidence of change, many employees hope to stay with their firm for the duration of their careers and have the firm take an active role in their personal lives in areas such as housing, recreation, and schooling for their children. Moreover, far less separation of business and personal matters occurs between Japanese employees and their supervisors. Thus, it is little wonder that the Japanese mechanics thought that George was not acting like a responsible supervisor because he was unwilling to become involved in their personal lives.

6–5 In Nairobi, as in many other parts of the world, status and rank are important elements of social and business relationships. In the United States, where people have a tendency to play down status differences, the boss may often roll up his or her sleeves and start working alongside those of lower rank and position. In fact, the boss in the United States is likely to become more popular by engaging in manual labor alongside the workers, for it shows a true spirit of empathy and democracy. In Kenya, however, a boss doing manual labor is seen as a deliberate rejection of self-respect. If those in high positions are not willing to maintain their high status and self-respect, they will unlikely continue to receive the respect of their employees. To the African employees, it would have been far preferable to have missed the deadline than to have their boss lose his self-respect by engaging in manual labor.

CHAPTER 7

7–1 The scenario can best be understood by first appreciating the very different views in U.S. culture and Saudi culture concerning *locus of control*. In the United States, it is believed that people are ultimately responsible for their own destiny. If something goes wrong, it is believed that it is frequently possible for the individual to *do* something (that is, to change certain behavior) to bring about the desired outcome. In Saudi Arabia and throughout the Arab world, people are taught from an early age that all things are subject to the direct will of Allah. All plans for the future (including, of course, business plans) are viewed with a sense of inevitability and will be realized only if Allah wills it. This is not to say that people in the Arab world would not work hard to help bring about the desired results. Rather, they believe that despite the effort the desired ends will not happen unless Allah is willing. Perhaps Stefan would have been less frustrated if he had translated *Inshallah* to mean "if possible" or "Allah willing" rather than as a knee-jerk response used to absolve oneself of all responsibility for one's actions.

7–2 Here is another example of how certain nonverbal actions—in this case, the pounding of one's fist into one's palm—have a very different meaning in a foreign country than in the United States. In Singapore, as well as in several other Southeast Asian countries, such a gesture is a sexual insult, comparable in the United States to extending the middle finger.

7–3 Giving knives in Argentina has a negative connotation because it symbolizes severing, not starting, a friendship. Beth's business associate was, therefore, insulted by the choice of gift. A better choice of gift might have been a bottle of French champagne or imported chocolates.

7–4 Sandra's host family belonged to a tennis club not far from the house. The father of the family decided to drive her there one day. He introduced her to the club manager and explained that Sandra had played competitive tennis in the United States. The manager welcomed Sandra to the club and immediately arranged for her to play with some of the club's members. When Sandra got out on that court and began her first set, she realized that tennis freed her from having to engage in any kind of verbal communication. She could keep score in her head and just enjoy the round of play. Tennis gave Sandra the confidence that she could succeed. Within just a few weeks, her spirits were lifted. She was back in the French game of life.

7–5 To tug on one's own earlobe is the Italian way of questioning a person's manhood by suggesting that he is so effeminate that he should be wearing an earring. No wonder the man on the street became incensed.

CHAPTER 8

8–1 In Mexico, subordinates are not expected to question their assignments. In other cultures, however, subordinates are urged to more independent, which, in some cases, involves questioning the wisdom of the decisions made by one's supervisor. But in Mexico, as a general rule, supervisors do not appreciate having their authority challenged.

8–2 Despite his good intentions, Jon made two serious mistakes. First, senior executives in Belgium usually get to the office later in the morning than do their subordinates. By going in early, Jon created an awkward situation for his staff members, who were not sure how to react when their superior came in early. Second, Belgians tend to be relatively quiet and reserved. Office doors are usually kept closed and people knock before entering someone else's office. Forcing his subordinates into an open-door policy made them feel uncomfortable.

8–3   Unlike the Netherlands, where offices generally close promptly at 5:00 P.M. and the workers go home, it is common for Spaniards to work until 8:00 P.M. or later. Therefore, a 5:00 P.M. deadline would not be advantageous to a Spanish operation. Failure to seek out cultural differences when trying to establish new territory can result in a less than successful operation.

8–4   Taiwanese, despite their great economic leap into the global economy, still retain a good deal of superstition. This is particularly true about certain numbers. Some primary numbers, associated with very negative things such as death or excrement, are to be avoided at all costs. Other numbers, associated with positive things such as money, growth, and wealth, should be used in house addresses, license plates, and telephone numbers. In Taiwan, the telephone company receives many requests for numbers that include the lucky numbers, leaving those with unlucky numbers unused. Thus, Kathryn's classmate believed strongly that unless he had a telephone number with lucky numbers in it, his business would be doomed from the start.

8–5   Dick's problem stemmed from making the unwarranted assumption that informality at the party could carry over into a business context. In fact, Japanese make a very real distinction between these two social situations. Japanese senior executives can be informal and playful at parties, but this is not the environment in which to discuss business matters. The two realms are kept quite distinct in Japan.

Appendix B

■ ■ ■

Locating Relevant Cultural Information

In recent years an increased awareness has risen in the international business literature regarding the need for a fuller understanding of the cultural environment of global business. Whether one is managing a firm's overseas operations, directing an international sales force, or helping expatriate employees and their families adjust to living and working in a foreign culture, the need for understanding the cultural environment has never been greater than it is today.

The difficulty lies not with identifying the problem but rather with knowing how to solve it. Much of the literature from international business tends to be anecdotal, illustrating by endless examples how well-meaning but shortsighted businesspeople can run amok because of their cross-cultural insensitivity. Or the literature deals with general pleas for cross-cultural understanding. This approach is of little assistance to the global businesspeople (and their accompanying family members) who must deal with culture-specific problems. Clearly, global businesspeople need to be able to acquire culture-specific data that are accessible, relevant, and applicable to their immediate business situations.

THE TRADITIONAL ANTHROPOLOGICAL APPROACH

Although the discipline of anthropology, with its central focus on the concept of culture, is the logical place to turn for culture-specific information, most international businesspeople contend that the conventional anthropological approach to research is not particularly well suited to meeting their informational needs. Cultural anthropologists collect data in a particular culture by means of the time-consuming technique known as *participant observation*. The field anthropologist must master the language, gain acceptance into the foreign culture, and develop networks of relationships before the formal data gathering can even begin. Thus, most international businesspeople view the traditional data-gathering process used by anthropologists as so snail-like in pace that it is virtually useless for their more immediate needs.

As time consuming as traditional cultural anthropological research is, there may well be international business situations that would require such an approach. For example, a U.S. multinational corporation about to invest millions of dollars in a manufacturing facility in Colombo, Sri Lanka, will not be acting extravagantly by hiring one or more anthropologists to conduct a cultural study of the local people, who would eventually make up its workforce. Such a study might include traditional techniques such as participant observation and interviewing, as well as drawing on the already existing ethnographic and social science literature on the region. Although conducting such firsthand research would cost thousands of dollars, it nevertheless provides the best assurances that the corporate values and assumptions will be integrated into those of the local workforce. Also, many MNCs are using cultural anthropologists for the purpose of developing new products. Anthropologist John W. Sherry, who years ago studied communications technology among the Navajo, is now a member of an interdisciplinary team of design ethnographers with Intel Corporation. Their purpose is to learn as much as possible (by using anthropological methods) about how people work and use high-tech tools so that Intel can design better ones for the future. Sherry and his teammates venture out to homes, businesses, public spaces, and any other places where they can observe people interacting with technology. Anthropologists are trained to patiently observe human behavior for hours on end while recording those behaviors in minute detail. Intel (along with other high-tech companies such as IBM, Hewlett-Packard, Motorola, and Xerox) is betting that useful insights will emerge from those minute details. Because technology design always carries with it a number of assumptions about the people who eventually use it, Sherry and his band of high-tech ethnographers frequently must determine the degree to which those design assumptions actually jibe with those of real end users.

As one example of this application of anthropology, Sherry and his fellow design ethnographers spent large amounts of time hanging out in teenagers' bedrooms. They talked to more than 100 teenagers, analyzed still photos, and studied hours of videotapes that catalogued how teenagers' bedrooms were used. The team concluded that teenagers would like to be able to send photos to one another by transmitting images over telephone lines that would enter a friend's computer, and then be displayed in a bedside electronic picture frame. Such a product is now available for mass consumption.

DOCUMENTARY SOURCES USEFUL IN DEVELOPING A CULTURAL PROFILE

Culture-Specific Associations

A particularly effective way to access culture-specific information is by contacting the many associations, both at home and abroad, that focus on a particular country or culture. A primary reference book that can be found in the reference department of any good research library is the four-volume *Encyclopedia of Associations* (Thompson, 2009, vol. 47). Suppose you are interested in obtaining culture-specific information on Japan. By consulting the Keyword Index (Part 3) of this encyclopedia under "Japan," you will find entries having to do with Japan for approximately 150 associations based in the United States, including the Japan-American Society, the Japan Foundation, the Japan National Tourist Organization, the Japanese American Citizens' League, and the Japanese–American Curriculum Project. Parts 1 and 2 of the encyclopedia provide pertinent descriptive data on these culture-specific associations, including address, telephone number, contact person, membership, and publications.

Some Country-Specific Sources

Proquest and Brigham Young University produce a series entitled *Culturegrams*, brief cultural orientations covering 25 cultural categories of customs, courtesies, and lifestyles in more than 200 different countries. Each *Culturegram*, now in electronic, downloadable form, represents a condensation of a wide variety of data sources. Although these minicultural briefings are by design not in-depth cultural profiles, they do provide some valuable information on a wide variety of contemporary cultures.

In their cross-cultural compendium entitled *Kiss, Bow, or Shake Hands*, Terri Morrison and W. A. Conaway (2006) examine cultural features, behavioral styles, negotiating techniques, protocol, and business practices in 60 countries throughout the world. Each country description, written succinctly in nine to eleven pages, deals with a standardized set of issues such as cognitive style, negotiating strategies, locus of decision making, power distance, punctuality, business entertaining, nonverbal communication, forms of address, and gift giving. Although hardly definitive, this entry into the cross-cultural business literature is a convenient and reasonable place to start.

Intercultural Press, a boutique publishing house in Yarmouth, Maine, specializes in books and videos dealing with intercultural communication and the cultural aspects of global business. Get on their mailing list to receive a 25- to 30-page catalogue (issued several times a year) describing both general books on culture and business and a wide variety of well known titles on specific countries. Or contact them online at: www.nicholasbrealey.com/boston/subjects/interculturalpress.html

For a convenient way of locating the latest books on specific cultures, there is no better source than the electronic bookseller Amazon.com (www.amazaon.com). You can find the newest books on Amazon (and, in some cases, reviews) even before they are available at the best research libraries. The best part is that, with several clicks of the mouse, the books can be at your doorstep in a few days.

U.S. Government Sources

The U.S. Department of State periodically publishes a series entitled *Background Notes* (www.state.gov/r/pa/ei/bgn), short pamphlets (four to eight pages in length) on approximately 160 countries. Each pamphlet in the series includes information on the demography, geography, government, economy, history, and foreign relations of the country. Included also are a statistical profile, brief travel notes, a map, a listing of government officials, and a brief reading list. Single issues or annual subscriptions of *Background Notes* can be obtained from the Government Printing Office.

The Central Intelligence Agency (CIA) makes available basic factual information on most countries in a source called the *CIA Factbook* (www.cia.gov/library/publications/the-world factbook/index.html). Each entry contains three to five pages of background information on such topics as geography, climate, land use, population, birth and death rates, ethnic divisions, religions, languages spoken, government divisions, membership in world organizations, and considerably more.

Sources of Country-Specific News and Current Events

It would be difficult to find any successful U.S. businesspeople in Chicago, New York, or Atlanta who were not in the habit of keeping abreast of local, national, and international news through newspapers, periodicals, and the electronic media. Hardly a day passes without something being reported that affects one's business or personal life. The same holds true for those conducting business abroad. In addition to knowing the language, history, and culture of the host country, international businesspeople must also be well aware of current happenings. When living and working in any of the major cities of the world, procuring local English-language newspapers or news magazines would not be difficult. However, if the U.S. international businessperson is in the United States or wants to supplement the in-country news coverage, a number of very adequate alternatives are available.

The most complete and convenient news-reporting system available is the World News Connection (WNC), an online search service for world current events, sponsored by the National Technical Information Service of the federal government. WNC offers timely news information gathered from thousands of media services, including newspapers, periodicals, radio and TV broadcasts, and books. Subscribers get the most extensive collection of up-to-date information (military, political, social, scientific, environment, and technical) from around the world, all of which has been translated into English. The data are organized into eight regions of the world: Central Asia, East Asia, Near East and South Asia, China, East Europe, West Europe, Latin America, and sub-Saharan Africa. Under certain subscription plans, WNC will provide custom-designed profiles, whereby the subscriber defines the type of information required (subject and geographic location) and WNC will e-mail only those media reports that fit the profile.

The Electronic Library

Many of the preceding documentary sources can be located in any good research-oriented library through the card catalog or the indexing system for U.S. government documents. Within the last several years, however, the nature of libraries has changed dramatically. Today, the search for relevant literature on different cultures and business cultures has been made infinitely easier than in the past owing to online electronic searching, which is both fast and comprehensive. For example, the *College InfoTrac* databases include vast quantities of periodic literature, including academic/scholarly publications, business literature, and newspaper articles (all easily referenced) going back to the early l980s. *CARL UnCover* provides access to articles from more than 17,000 journals from the Colorado Alliance of Research Libraries. *FirstSearch* is a menu-driven electronic service providing access to journal databases, newspaper articles, and government reports from 16,000 libraries. *EUREKA* is an electronic bibliographic catalog containing more than 56 million items held by the Research Libraries Group, Inc.

Although websites on the Internet are always changing, there are a number of sites at any given time that can provide valuable sources of country specific information. Below are listed some of the better known sites:

Bureau of Consular Affairs: U.S. Department of State (http://travel.state.gov). This site, sponsored by the U.S. State Department, is absolutely essential for expatriates or frequent business travelers. It provides valuable information on visa requirements, travel advisories, help for Americans abroad, document authentication, medical services around the world, and international legal issues and services, among other things.

Business Culture: (http://www.businessculture.com/index.php). This site, which charges for its information, provides predeparture reports and executive reports on a wide range of countries throughout the world.

Executive Planet: (http://www.executiveplanet.com/community). This is an extremely comprehensive site that provides a guide to the business cultures found in 42 major countries of the world. In addition to providing some basic facts about the countries, it provides well-written and insightful information on business expectations (e.g., appointments, dress, entertainment), negotiating strategies, tips on intercultural communication, and proper public behavior.

Federation of International Trade Associations: (http://www.fita.org). This site is a gateway to hundreds of sites dealing with various aspects of international trade. It aims to provide the most content rich materials on international trade as well as a comprehensive outlet for goods and services needed by those interested in engaging in international trade.

Intercultural Relations: (http://www.interculturalrelations.com). This is a major site for free, interdisciplinary information having to do with all aspects of intercultural communications. The interdisciplinary journal entitled *The Edge: The E-Journal of Intercultural Relations* can be accessed from this site.

International Business Etiquette Internet Sourcebook: (http://atn-riae.agr.ca/export/4027-e.htm). Sponsored by the Agriculture and Agri-Food Canada division of the Canadian Government, this site provides a wide range of helpful information on etiquette and business culture in many regions and countries in the world.

International Business Etiquette and Manners: (http://www.cyborlink.com) This site provides valuable information on the cultural practices of 30 different countries. Each country's page has the same format, including introductory country facts, fun facts, explanation of Hofstede's cultural dimensions, appearance, behavior, communication, and resources.

In addition to these online bibliographic services, vast quantities of cultural data can be found by surfing the Internet. By using such search engines as Netscape, Google, or Yahoo!, it is possible to find a great deal of helpful information about the country/culture in which one wants to do business. It is important to say from the outset that all information found on the Internet is *not* created equal. With the advent of the mass use of television in the 1950s, anyone could become a viewer. Today, with the widespread use of the Internet, anyone can become a broadcaster: Anyone with a little bit of technical know-how can construct his or her own Web page and put any type of information on it. This necessitates that we learn to look at the sources of information on the Internet with a critical eye. There are no methods for assessing the accuracy or validity of Internet information with absolute certainty. Nevertheless, you should look for the reason(s) that a particular site exists in the first place. Do the people constructing the site have a "hidden agenda"? Are they putting this information on the Internet for the purpose of educating you in an objective way? Are they trying to sell you something? Are they trying to convert you to their particular cause? In most cases, websites that are the property of universities, libraries, museums, and governments are likely to be the most reliable. Those sites that are put on the Internet by individuals or small, noninstitutional groups and organizations require considerably more scrutiny.

HUMAN RESOURCES FOR CULTURE-SPECIFIC INFORMATION

Given the generally inaccessible nature of much culture-specific information, the successful international businessperson must be creative in his or her search for relevant information. This search, of course, requires the use of human resources as well as published ones. Every businessperson bound for a foreign assignment has a vast variety of experts to draw on, but it requires knowing where to look. Unfortunately, most businesspeople do not take advantage of the resources at hand, many of which are free. Here are some major sources of expertise that should be utilized.

One's Own Company

Frequently, expertise on the cultural environment of a particular country can be found in one's own corporation. Depending on the size of the corporation, people working right down the hall may have experience in living and working in a specific part of the world. Western multinational corporations are so large and decentralized, with divisions operating independently of one another, that most divisions usually do not know what types of international expertise exist in other divisions. If this is the case, the wise international businessperson will do well to contact the one division within the corporation that might have that type of information—the Human Resources department. Once the appropriate persons have been identified, they will likely be willing to share all sorts of culturally relevant information, if for no other reason than they have become instant experts on a subject of mutual concern.

Academia

Local colleges and universities are excellent sources of culture-specific information. Interestingly, U.S. businesses have turned to universities for technical assistance but have not by and large utilized the cultural, social, or political expertise that is also part of the academic world. Many mid- to large-sized universities have well-established area studies programs composed of faculty, and often graduate students, who have had considerable experience conducting research in various parts of the world.

For many of these faculty members, the prime purpose for living abroad was to study firsthand the sociocultural realities of the area. Perhaps the most relevant are the small but growing number of academic programs in the United States that are designed to integrate international business studies with area studies (i.e., language and culture). Although it would be impossible to list them all, this type of program is exemplified by the Masters of International Management offered at the American Graduate School of International Business in Glendale, Arizona; the Masters in International Business Studies (MIBS) offered at the University of South Carolina at

Columbia; and the M.B.A./M.A. in International Management and International Studies at the Wharton School, University of Pennsylvania. Yet, even those institutions that do not offer programs in international business employ faculty from a wide variety of disciplines with extensive knowledge of different parts of the world. For example, a sociology or foreign language professor who lived and conducted research at the Cairo University for several years will no doubt be a valuable resource on the general cultural, social, political, and economic environments of Egypt. Such academic experts can be identified with a few well-placed phone calls to the office of the director of the International Studies Program, the dean of the Business School, or the dean of Arts and Sciences.

Foreign Trade Offices

In the United States, many foreign governments maintain foreign trade offices (FTOs), whose very existence is to assist U.S. importers and exporters. Although most FTOs are located in Washington or New York, some of the larger foreign governments may have branches in other major cities throughout the country. These offices publish excellent (and usually free) brochures, booklets, and so forth, on both the technical and the cultural aspects of doing business in their countries. The extent of the services provided by any FTO will vary according to the country's relative affluence and its commitment to stimulating trade with the United States. The Japan External Trade Organization (JETRO) maintains the most elaborate services (https://www.jetro.go.jp). To illustrate, JETRO makes available more than 100 complimentary publications and films on doing business in Japan and employs Japanese trade experts in New York, Houston, Los Angeles, and San Francisco to answer individual questions. Not all foreign governments provide such extensive services, but frequently helpful culture-specific information can be obtained from the appropriate embassy in Washington, DC or consulate in other U.S. cities.

Private-Sector Consultants and Trainers

Before the 1950s there were virtually no cross-cultural consultants specializing in business. Then with the appearance of William Lederer and Eugene Burdick's *The Ugly American* (1958) and the "discovery" of culture shock by Kalvero Oberg (1960), there was an increasing awareness of the hazards involved in conducting business in an unfamiliar cultural environment. In the past several decades, an entire specialized consulting and training industry has developed. The problem today is not a shortage of qualified cross-cultural consultants and trainers but rather sorting through all their credentials to find someone with the particular knowledge and skills needed to address a firm's particular and frequently unique situation. By simply searching any search engine on the Internet by using the term *cross-cultural training*, you will be directed to the home pages of many of the leading cross-cultural trainers and consultants.

Consultants and trainers must be able to address the firm's special needs and problems. Does the consultant have the proper culture-specific experience and training? Are the proposed training and/or services designed to meet the specific needs and objectives of the corporation? Are the learning objectives clearly stated? Are the methods of training realistic and compatible with company policies and procedures? How will the program be evaluated to determine if it has accomplished what it promised? Once these questions have been answered to the firm's satisfaction, a program can be designed and executed. These may include predeparture briefings for international businesspeople and their families on such topics as customs, history, political structure, and practical matters necessary for living and working in the assigned country.

In recent years a relatively dramatic increase has occurred in the number of people claiming to be cross-cultural trainers or consultants. Many are well trained and effective, but others may be considerably less effective or just plain charlatans. Before hiring such cross-cultural trainers, insist that they demonstrate six important qualifications. First, they should possess considerable knowledge of the target area, gained through both formal academic study and first-hand living experience. Second, they should understand a number of important anthropological principles and concepts that they can apply to their country-specific area of expertise. Third, they should have personal experience with culture shock and should have made a successful adjustment to living in another culture. Fourth, they should have a sound understanding of their own culture and how their own values and attitudes influence them. Fifth, they should be experienced trainers who feel comfortable using a wide variety of educational strategies, including experiential learning techniques. Finally, they should have a "presentation of self" that corporate personnel do not find offensive.

THE SEARCH FOR CULTURAL INFORMATION UPON ARRIVAL

So far we have considered a number of possible sources of cultural information that should be consulted before one's departure for a foreign business assignment. This constitutes the predeparture aspect of one's preparation, which should provide a solid background for the most important learning that is yet to come. Regardless of how much predeparture preparation has taken place, the new arrival will be a stranger in a very different, and perhaps frightening, cultural environment. Despite occasional claims to the contrary, this is no different from the position most cultural anthropologists find themselves in when first arriving at the site of a field research project. It is now time for the newly arrived Western businessperson to become his or her own "ethnographer" by becoming an active learner while immersed in the culture. If the businessperson is serious and purposeful about mastering the new cultural environment, there should be no shortage of sources of cultural information, both documentary and human. Moreover, the quality of one's cultural learning during this on-site phase should be significant because it will be acquired *experientially*. In short, if the newly arrived businessperson realizes that the culture *is* the classroom, the amount of cultural learning that can occur is virtually limitless.

In-Country Documentary Resources

Because tourism represents a welcome source of foreign exchange, most countries make considerable efforts to attract tourists and make certain that they see the sights, spend their money, and leave with a desire to return. Consequently, most foreign countries, even small third-world countries, maintain tourist information centers (at least in the major cities), where the new arrivals can obtain printed information (brochures, booklets, maps, and so on) on things to do and see while in the country. Thus, one of the first stopping places in your continuing search for cultural information should be the local tourist center. However, having in your possession information on national monuments, historic sites, scenic areas, and museums is just the beginning of the learning process. Your understanding of the culture will be greatly enhanced by actually exploring these places and learning about them firsthand.

It is hard to imagine any country without a public or university library with books on national history, culture, and contemporary issues. Shortly after arrival, seek permission to use the local library and get to know the most valuable person there, the reference librarian.

Private-sector bookstores can also be valuable sources of local cultural data. Not only are you likely to find a number of valuable written sources, but it is also possible to learn a good deal about a culture by noticing how the bookstores are organized. Are some topics or categories of books not sold? Are some topics or categories unusually large? Frequently, it is possible to get a feel for what a particular culture emphasizes by looking at how much space is devoted to certain topics in local bookstores.

One of the best entries into a culture, and by far the most accessible type of documentary source, is local or national newspapers, some of which will be printed in English. Not only are local newspapers the best source of contemporary happenings, but they also reflect a wide range of cultural values. To illustrate, what does it say about a society if there are no letters to the editor? If there is an editorial page, are certain topics restricted or limited? What clues might one get about a culture if male suitors advertise for "brides wanted" in the classified section? Can information be gleaned from the jobs' section of the classifieds about the degree of labor specialization within the society? What can you learn about the family structure by reading the obituary pages? What insights into the culture can one pick up by reading the comics? These are only some of the questions that the culturally sensitive businessperson should raise when reading local newspapers in a foreign country.

In addition to reading in-country newspapers daily, many have found it helpful to clip and file some of the more interesting articles. Clipping articles is more convenient than taking notes and can provide a sizable amount of data that can be referred to and studied for years to come.

In-Country Human Resources

Clearly, it would be unwise to spend all or most of your time in a new country reading various printed materials. There is no substitute for people, for most of the important insights into a culture will come from interacting with local people. After all, they are the real experts in the local culture. Although cultural anthropologists do, in fact, draw on whatever reliable documentary materials are available, most of their data come from a combination of being a participant observer and asking questions of knowledgeable local people. These are the two best sources of cultural data for the international businessperson as well.

Of course, most international businesspeople operate under certain work and time constraints not usually facing the field anthropologist, thereby making a total immersion into the local culture impractical if not impossible. Yet there are a number of opportunities for expatriate businesspeople to become involved in the local culture. The critical question is whether you choose to take advantage of these opportunities. If you do, you will increase your cultural learning geometrically, and you will most likely enjoy yourself in the process.

Being a participant observer in the local culture involves making a conscious decision and taking some personal risks. As a newly arrived participant observer, you will feel very much out of control of the situation, particularly at first. Much of what will be observed will not be understood, and there will be opportunities at every turn to contract "foot-in-mouth" disease. Yet, to succeed as a field anthropologist or curious international businessperson, you must be patient and able to live with ambiguity. Gradually, more and more of what is observed begins to make sense until eventually an increasingly logical and coherent picture of the culture emerges.

Once you decide to become a participant observer in the new culture, the question of how best to record the cultural data arises. The best advice is to always carry a pocket notebook. As new bits of cultural information are experienced, it is important to jot down as soon as possible some key words that can be transformed into more elaborate notes at the end of the day. Periodically, perhaps every month or two, your daily notes should be reviewed to discover both recurring themes and possible inconsistencies, which may require additional focused research to resolve.

When acting as your own ethnographer, participant observation alone is not enough. Bound by your own cultural perspective, you can possibly misinterpret what is observed. Thus, as a check, you should ask questions of local people. Key informants'—those willing and able to provide insights into the culture—can be invaluable sources of local knowledge. The sampling of conversations and interviews should be chosen carefully, and the sample of interviews should be as large and representative of the total society as possible.

CONCLUSION

We have explored a number of sources of information available to the international businessperson when attempting to construct a cultural profile of another country. These sources of cultural data include both written materials and human resources. They also include resources that should be consulted in the United States before entering the international business arena, as well as those likely to be found abroad. This discussion of sources certainly does not pretend to be definitive but is rather meant to be suggestive. Many valuable data sources have not been mentioned specifically.

The international businessperson should keep three major points in mind when constructing foreign cultural profiles. First, there is a direct correlation between the amount of culture-specific information a person has and the success of his or her personal and professional overseas experience. Second, it is important to be constantly on the lookout for new sources of cultural information *and* to be sufficiently creative and open minded to see how they can be integrated with other sources. Finally, the cultural learning process does not end with an orientation program or the completion of a reading list; rather, it is an ongoing process that starts before leaving home and continues throughout one's assignment abroad and beyond.

The aim of this appendix has been to explore some sources of information that can help the international businessperson acquire a measure of "cultural literacy" when entering a foreign business setting. According to E. D. Hirsch (1987), literacy requires more than knowing how to read; it also requires a certain level of comprehension of background information about the culture. Just as a U.S. high school graduate cannot be considered culturally literate if he or she identifies Karl Marx as one of the Marx Brothers or the Great Gatsby as a magician, the international businessperson attempting to conduct business in Germany cannot be considered culturally literate without knowing something about Nietzsche, Wagner, and the Schwarzwald. The sources discussed in this appendix are intended to provide the Western international businessperson with a starting point in the quest for "literacy" in another culture.

References

Adams, Michael with Amy Langstaff and David Jamieson. 2003. *Fire and ice: The United States, Canada, and the myth of converging values.* Toronto, ON: Penguin Canada.

Adler, Nancy J. 1997. *International dimensions of organizational behavior*, 3rd ed. Cincinnati, OH: Southwestern.

———. 2002. *From Boston to Beijing: Managing with a world view.* Cincinnati, OH: Southwestern.

Adler, Peter. 1975. The transitional experience: An alternative view of culture shock. *Journal of Humanistic Psychology* 15(4): 13–23.

Allport, Floyd H. 1924. *Social psychology.* Boston, MA: Houghton-Mifflin.

Andreason, A.W. 2003. Direct and indirect forms of in-country support for expatriates and their families as a means of reducing premature returns and improving job performance. *International Journal of Management* 20(4): 548–555.

Applebaum, Herbert A. 1981. *The culture of construction workers.* New York, NY: Holt, Rinehart and Winston.

Archer, Dane. 1997. Unspoken diversity: Cultural differences in gestures. *Qualitative Sociology* 20(1): 79–105.

Argyle, Michael and Mark Cook. 1976. *Gaze and mutual gaze.* Cambridge, UK: Cambridge University Press.

Arnould, Eric J. and Craig J. Thompson. 2005. Consumer culture theory. *Journal of Consumer Research* 31(4): 868–882, March.

Arunthanes, Wiboon, Patriya Tansuhai, and David J. Lemak. 1994. Cross-cultural business gift giving: A new conceptualization and theoretical framework. *International Marketing Review* 11(4): 44–55.

Atterberry, Tara E. (Program Director). 2011. *Encyclopedia of associations.* Detroit, MI: Gale Publishing.

Axtell, Roger. 2007. *Essential do's and taboos: The complete guide to international business and leisure travel.* Hoboken, NJ: John Wiley and Sons.

Baba, Marietta L. 1986. *Business and industrial anthropology: An overview.* NAPA Bulletin No. 2. Washington, DC: American Anthropological Association.

———. 2006. Anthropology and business. In *Encyclopedia of anthropology*, edited by H. James Birx, 83–117. Thousand Oaks, CA: Sage Publications.

———. 2009. W. Lloyd Warner and the anthropology of institutions: An approach to the study of work in late capitalism. *Anthropology of Work Review* 30(2): 29–48.

Ball-Rokeach, Sandra J. 1973. From pervasive ambiguity to a definition of the situation. *Sociometry* 36(3): 378–389.

Barney, Jay B. 1986. Organizational culture: Can it be a source of sustained competitive advantage? *Academy of Management Review* 11(3): 656–665.

Barrett, Richard A. 1991. *Culture and conduct: An excursion in anthropology.* Belmont, CA: Wadsworth Publishing Co.

Bauer, Talya N. and Sully Taylor. 2001. When managing expatriate adjustment, don't forget the spouse. *Academy of Management Executive* 15(4): 135–137, November.

Beals, Ralph L., Harry Hoijer, and Alan R. Beals. 1977. *An introduction to anthropology*, 5th ed. New York, NY: Macmillan.

Beauregard, Mary. 2008. Cultural training partnerships: Who has the power? In *Partnering for organizational performance: Collaboration and culture in the global workplace*, edited by Elizabeth K. Briody and Robert T. Trotter, II, 75–89. Lanham, MD: Rowman and Littlefield.

Befu, H. 1979. Konnichiwa, essay read at the meeting of the Japan Society, April 1975, San Francisco, CA; quoted in Sheila J. Ramsey, Nonverbal behavior: An intercultural perspective. In *Handbook of intercultural communication*, edited by M.K. Asante, E. Newmark, and C. Blake, 105–143. Beverly Hills, CA: Sage Publications.

Bhaskar-Shrinivas, Purnima, David A. Harrison, Margaret A. Shaffer, and Dora M. Luk. 2005. Input-based and time-based models of international adjustment: Meta-analytic evidence and theoretical extensions. *Academy of Management Journal* 48(2): 257–281.

Birdwhistell, R.L. 1963. The kinesis level in the investigation of the emotions. In *Expression of the emotions in man*, edited by Peter H. Knapp. New York, NY: International University Press.

Black, J. Stewart and Hal B. Gregersen. 1991. The other half of the picture: Antecedents of spouse cross-cultural adjustment. *Journal of International Business Studies* 22(3): 461–478.

———. 1999. The right way to manage expats. *Harvard Business Review* 77(2): 52–62, March–April.

Black, J. Stewart, Hal B. Gregersen, and Mark E. Mendenhall. 1992. *Global assignments: Successful expatriating and repatriating international managers.* San Francisco, CA: Jossey-Bass.

Black, J. Stewart and Mark Mendenhall. 1990. Cross-cultural training effectiveness: A review and a theoretical framework for future research. *Academy of Management Review* 15(1): 113–136.

Black, J. Stewart, Mark Mendenhall, and Gary Oddou. 1991. Toward a comprehensive model of international adjustment: An integration of multiple theoretical perspectives. *Academy of Management Review* 16(2): 291–317.

Black, J. Stewart and Gregory K. Stephens. 1989. The influence of the spouse on American expatriate adjustment and intent to stay in Pacific Rim overseas assignments. *Journal of Management* 15(4): 529–544.

Blomberg, Jeanette, Mark Burrell, and Greg Guest. 2003. An ethnographic approach to design. In *Human-computer interaction handbook: Fundamentals, evolving technologies, and emerging applications*, edited by Julie A. Jacko and Andrew Sears, 964–989. Mahwah, NJ: Lawrence Erlbaum Associates.

Bolton, Ralph. 2010. Chijnaya: The birth and evolution of an Andean community: Memories and reflections of an applied anthropologist. In *Vicos and beyond: A half century of applying anthropology in Peru*, edited by Tom Greaves, Ralph Bolton, and Florencia Zapata, 215–263. Lanham, MD: Altamira Press.

Borgatti, Stephen P. 2002. *NETDRAW*. Boston, MA: Analytic Technologies.

Boroditsky, Lera. 2009. How does our language shape the way we think? In *What's next: Dispatches on the futures of science*, edited by Max Brockman, 116–129. New York, NY: Vintage Books.

Bozionelos, Nikos. 2009. Expatriation outside the boundaries of the multinational corporation: A study with expatriate nurses in Saudi Arabia. *Human Resource Management* 48(1): 111–134, January–February.

Brake, Terence, Danielle Medina Walker, and Thomas Walker. 1995. *Doing business internationally: The guide to cross-cultural success.* Burr Ridge, IL: Irwin.

Brannen, Mary Yoko and Jane E. Salk. 2000. Partnering across borders: Negotiating organizational culture in a German–Japanese joint venture. *Human Relations* 53: 451–487.

Brett, Jeanne and Tetsushi Okumura. 1998. Inter- and intracultural negotiations: U.S. and Japanese negotiators. *Academy of Management Journal* 41: 495–510.

Briody, Elizabeth K. 2010. *Handling decision paralysis on organizational partnerships*, Course Reader (Internet Access), Detroit, MI: Gale.

Briody, Elizabeth K. and Marietta L. Baba. 1991. Explaining differences in repatriation experiences: The discovery of coupled and decoupled systems. *American Anthropologist* 93(2): 322–344, June.

———. 1994. Reconstructing a culture clash at General Motors: An historical view from the overseas assignment. In *Anthropological perspectives on organizational culture*, edited by Tomoko Hamada and Willis E. Sibley, 219–260. Lanham, MD: University Press of America, Inc.

Briody, Elizabeth K., S. Tamer Cavusgil, and Stewart R. Miller. 2004. Turning three sides into a delta at General Motors: Enhancing partnership integration on corporate ventures. *Long Range Planning* 37: 421–434.

Briody, Elizabeth K. and Judith Beeber Chrisman. 1991. Cultural adaptation on overseas assignments. *Human Organization* 50(3): 264–282, Fall.

Briody, Elizabeth K. and Robert T. Trotter, II, eds. 2008. *Partnering for organizational performance: Collaboration and culture in the global workplace.* Lanham, MD: Rowman and Littlefield.

Briody, Elizabeth K., Robert T. Trotter, II, and Tracy L. Meerwarth. 2010. *Transforming culture: Creating and sustaining a better manufacturing organization.* New York, NY: Palgrave Macmillan.

Brislin, Richard W. 1981. *Cross-cultural encounters: Face-to-face interaction.* New York, NY: Pergamon Press.

Burgoon, Judee K., David B. Buller, and W. Gill Woodall. 1989. *Nonverbal communication: The unspoken dialogue.* New York, NY: Harper and Row.

Byrnes, Francis C. 1966. Role shock: An occupational hazard of American technical assistants abroad. *Annals of the American Academy of Political and Social Science* 368: 95–108, November.

Caligiuri, Paula M., Aparna Joshi, and Mila Lazarova. 1999. Factors influencing the adjustment of women on global assignments. *International Journal of Human Resource Management* 10(2): 163–179, April.

Caligiuri, Paula M. and Mila Lazarova. 2001. Strategic repatriation policies to enhance global leadership development. In *Developing global business leaders: Policies, processes, and innovations*, edited by Mark E. Mendenhall, Torsten M. Kuhlmann, and Gunter K. Stahl, 243–256. Westport, CT: Quorum Books.

Caulkins, D. Douglas and Ann T. Jordan, eds. 2012. *A companion to organizational anthropology.* Malden, MA: Wiley-Blackwell.

Cefkin, Melissa, ed. 2009. *Ethnography and the corporate encounter: Reflections on research in and of corporations.* New York, NY: Berghahn Books.

Champness, B.G. 1970. Mutual glance and the significance of the look. *Advancement of Science* 26: 309–312.

Chen, Gilad, Bradley L. Kirkman, Kwanghyun Kim, Crystal I.C. Farh, and Subrahmaniam Tangirala. 2010. When does cross-cultural motivation enhance expatriate effectiveness? A multilevel investigation of the moderating roles of subsidiary support and cultural distance. *Academy of Management Journal* 53(5): 1110–1130, October.

Chew, Janet. 2004. Managing MNC expatriates through crises: A challenge for international human resource management. *Research and Practice in Human Resource Management* 12(2): 1–30.

Chhokar, Jagdeep S., Felix C. Brodbeck, and Robert J. House. 2007. *Culture and leadership across the world: The GLOBE book of in-depth studies of 25 societies.* LEA's Series in Organization and Management. New York, NY: Lawrence Erlbaum Associates.

Chijnaya Foundation, "The Chijnaya Foundation: Purpose and promise," http://www.chijnayafoundation.org/chijnaya-foundation-purpose-and-promise

Coincourse2011, "Home," http://sites.google.com/site/coincourse2011/

Collings, David G., Hugh Scullion, and Michael J. Morley. 2007. Changing patterns of global staffing in the multinational enterprise: Challenges to the conventional expatriate assignment and emerging alternatives. *Journal of World Business* 42(2): 198–213, June.

Condon, John. 1984. *With respect to the Japanese: A guide for Americans.* Yarmouth, ME: Intercultural Press.

Condon, John and Fathi Yousef. 1975. *Introduction to intercultural communication.* Indianapolis, IN: Bobbs-Merrill.

The Conference Board. 1996. Managing expatriates' return: A research report, Conference Board Report No.1148-96-Rr, New York, NY.

Coy, Michael W., ed. 1989. *Apprenticeship: From theory to method and back again.* Albany, NY: State University of New York Press.

CPA Practice Management Forum. 2008. Expatriate employee numbers double as companies see increased value in expatriate assignments, November, 21–22.

Crouse, Karen. 2011. British women face hurdles and indifference, *New York Times*, Special Report: Women's British Open, July 27.

DaMatta, Roberto. 1991. *Carnivals, rogues, and heroes: An interpretation of the Brazilian dilemma.* Translated by John Drury. Notre Dame, IN: University of Notre Dame Press.

Darrah, Charles, James Freeman, and J.A. English-Lueck. 2007. *Busier than ever! Why American families can't slow down.* Stanford, CA: Stanford University Press.

Darwin, Charles R. 1872. *The expression of emotions in man and animals.* London, England: John Murray.

Dekker, Daphne M., Christel G. Rutte, and Peter T. Van den Berg. 2008. Cultural differences in the perception of critical interaction behaviors in global virtual teams. *International Journal of Intercultural Relations* 32: 441–452.

Deshpande, Satish P. and Chockalingam Viswesvaran. 1992. Is cross-cultural training of expatriate managers effective: A meta-analysis. *International Journal of Intercultural Relations* 16(3): 295–310, Summer.

Diamond, Nina, John F. Sherry Jr., Albert M. Muniz Jr., Mary Ann McGrath, Robert V. Kozinets, and Stefania Borghini. 2009. American girl and the brand gestalt: Closing the loop on sociocultural branding research. *Journal of Marketing* 73: 118–134, May.

D'Iribarne, Philippe. 2002. Motivating workers in emerging countries: Universal tools and local adaptations. *Journal of Organizational Behavior* 23(3): 243–256, May.

Dore, Ronald. 1973. *British factory, Japanese factory: The origins of national diversity in industrial relations.* Berkeley, CA: University of California Press.

Dowling, Peter J., Marion Festing, and Allen D. Engle Sr. 2008. *International human resource management: Managing people in a multinational context*, 5th ed. London, UK: Thomson Learning.

Dubinskas, Frank A., ed. 1988. *Making time: Ethnographies of high-technology organizations.* Philadelphia, PA: Temple University Press.

Eaton, Tara. 2011. A cultural analysis of information technology offshore outsourcing: An exercise in multi-sited ethnography of virtual work. Paper 370. Wayne State University Dissertations, Detroit, MI.

Eaton, Tara A. and Dale C. Brandenburg. 2008. Coordinated autonomy? Culture in emergency response partnering. In *Partnering for organizational performance: Collaboration and culture in the global workplace,* edited by Elizabeth K. Briody and Robert T. Trotter, II, 91–106. Lanham, MD: Rowman and Littlefield.

Efron, David. 1941. *Gesture and environment.* New York, NY: King's Crown.

Eibl-Eibesfeldt, I. 1971. Transcultural patterns of ritualized contact behavior. In *Behavior and environment: The use of space by animals and men,* edited by Aristide H. Esser, 297–312. New York, NY: Plenum Press.

———. 1972. Similarities and differences between cultures in expressive movement. In *Non-verbal communication,* edited by Robert A. Hinde. London: Cambridge University Press.

Eisenberg, A.M. and R.R. Smith. 1971. *Nonverbal communication.* Indianapolis, IN: Bobbs-Merrill Co.

Ekman, Paul, Wallace V. Friesen, and Phoebe Ellsworth. 1972. *Emotion in the human face: Guidelines for research and an integration of findings.* New York, NY: Pergamon Press.

Elahee, Mohammad and Charles M. Brooks. 2004. Trust and negotiation tactics: Perceptions about business-to-business negotiations in Mexico. *The Journal of Business & Industrial Marketing* 19(6): 397–404.

Ellsworth, Phoebe C. 1975. Direct gaze as a social stimulus: The example of aggression. In *Nonverbal communication of aggression,* edited by P. Pliner, L. Kramer, and R. Alloway. New York, NY: Plenum Press.

Engholm, Christopher. 1991. *When business East meets business West: The guide to practice and protocol in the Pacific rim.* New York, NY: John Wiley and Sons.

Engholm, Christopher and Diana Rowland. 1996. *International excellence: Seven breakthrough strategies for personal and professional success.* New York, NY: Kodansha International.

Ensworth, Patricia. 2003. "Patricia Ensworth on managing multicultural project teams at Moody's." *CIO,* October 1, http://www.cio.com/article/29821/ (accessed April 8, 2011).

Fang, Tony. 2005–06. From "onion" to "ocean": Paradox and change in national cultures. *International Studies of Management and Organization* 35(4): 71–90, Winter.

Fang, Tony, Verner Worm, and Rosalie L. Tung. 2008. Changing success and failure factors in business negotiations with the PRC. *International Business Review* 17: 159–169.

Farb, Peter. 1968. How do I know you mean what you mean? *Horizon* 10(4): 52–57.

———. 1974. *Word play: What happens when people talk.* New York, NY: Knopf.

Figg, J. 2000. Executives shun expatriate opportunities. *Internal Auditor* 57(1): 13–14, February.

Fischlmayr, Iris C. and Iris Kollinger. 2010. Work-life balance—a neglected issue among Austrian female expatriates. *The International Journal of Human Resource Management* 21(4): 455–487, March.

Fisher, Roger, William Ury, and Bruce Patton. 1991. *Getting to yes: Negotiating agreement without giving in,* 2nd ed. New York, NY: Penguin Books.

Foster, Dean Allen. 1992. *Bargaining across borders: How to negotiate business anywhere in the world.* New York, NY: McGraw-Hill.

Frauenheim, Ed. 2005. Crossing cultures: As the world gets smaller understanding country-specific differences becomes a business imperative: Culture of understanding. *Workforce Management* 84(13): 1, 26–32, November.

Friedman, Thomas L. 1999. *The Lexus and the olive tree.* New York, NY: Farrar, Straus and Giroux.

———. 2002. India, Pakistan, and G.E. *The New York Times,* August 8, p. 13.

Furman, Nelly, David Goldberg, and Natalia Lusin. 2010. *Enrollments in languages other than English in United States institutions of higher education, Fall 2009.* New York, NY: Modern Language Association, December.

Gamst, Frederick C. 1980. *The hoghead: An industrial ethnology of the locomotive engineer.* New York, NY: Holt, Rinehart and Winston.

Gannon, Martin J. 2001. *Cultural metaphors: Readings, research translations, and commentary.* Thousand Oaks, CA: Sage Publications.

———. 2009. The cultural metaphoric method: Description, analysis, and critique. *International Journal of Cross Cultural Management* 9(3): 275–287.

Gannon, Martin and Associates. 1994. *Understanding global cultures: Metaphorical journeys through 17 countries.* Thousand Oaks, CA: Sage Publications.

Gannon, Martin J., Edwin A. Locke, Amit Gupta, Pino Audia, and Amy L. Kristof-Brown. 2005–06. Cultural metaphors as frames of reference for nations: A six-country study. *International Studies of Management and Organization* 35(4): 37–47, Winter.

Gannon, Martin J. and Rajnandini Pillai. 2010. *Understanding global cultures: Metaphorical journeys through 29 nations, clusters of nations, continents, and diversity*, 4th ed. Thousand Oaks, CA: Sage Publications.

Gardner, Burleigh B. 1945. *Human relations in industry*. Homewood, IL: Irwin.

Gardner, Burleigh B. and Sidney J. Levy. 1955. The product and the brand. *Harvard Business Review* 33(2): 33–39, March–April.

Geertz, Clifford. 1973. *The interpretation of culture*. New York, NY: Basic Books.

Gibson, Cristina B. and Jennifer L. Gibbs. 2006. Unpacking the concept of virtuality: The effects of geographic dispersion, electronic dependence, dynamic structure, and national diversity on team innovation. *Administrative Science Quarterly* 51(3): 451–495.

Gluesing, Julia with Tara Alcordo, Marietta Baba, David Britt, Willie McKether, Leslie Monplaisir, Hilary Ratner, Kenneth Riopelle, and Kimberly Harris Wagner. 2003. The development of global virtual teams. In *Virtual teams that work: Creating conditions for virtual team effectiveness*, edited by Cristina B. Gibson and Susan G. Cohen, 353–380. San Francisco, CA: Jossey-Bass.

Gluesing, Julia C. and Cristina Gibson. 2004. Designing and forming global teams. In *Handbook of global management: A guide to managing complexity*, edited by Henry W. Lane, Martha L. Maznevski, Mark E. Mendenhall, and Jeanne McNett, 199–226. Oxford, UK: Blackwell.

Gluesing, Julia C., Kenneth R. Riopelle, Kenneth R. Chelst, Alan R. Woodliff, and Linda M. Miller. 2008. An educational partnership for immediate impact. In *Partnering for organizational performance: Collaboration and culture in the global workplace*, edited by Elizabeth K. Briody and Robert T. Trotter, II, 125–141. Lanham, MD: Rowman and Littlefield.

Goffman, Erving. 1963. *Behavior in public places*. Glencoe, IL: Free Press.

Goldin-Meadow, Susan. 2003. *Hearing gesture: How our hands help us think*. Cambridge, MA: Belknap Press.

Goldman, Alan. 1988. *For Japanese only: Intercultural communication with Americans*. Tokyo: The Japan Times.

Goor, Peter, Maria Paasivaara, Casper Lassenius, Detlef Schoder, Kai Fischbach, and Christine Miller. 2011. Teaching a global project course: Experiences and lessons learned. *Conference proceedings—Collaborative teaching of globally distributed software development—Community building workshop*. International Conference on Software Engineering (ICSE), supported by the National Science Foundation.

Gordon, Sarah. 2011. "Royal Wedding to provide £50m tourism boost on Friday, and that's just the beginning…" *Daily Mail On-Line*, April 28, http://www.dailymail.co.uk/travel/article-1381459/Royal-Wedding-2011-tourism-boost-London-visitors-spend-50m-Friday.html?ito=feeds-newsxml

Gorer, Geoffrey. 1935. *Africa dances: A book about West African Negroes*. New York, NY: Knopf.

Gravel, Alain. Le Point, Radio-Canada. 29 juin 1994. "Gentleman only ladies forbidden," Running time 21:20, http://archives.radio-canada.ca/sports/golf/clips/11730/

Gregory, Kathleen L. 1983. Native-view paradigms: Multiple cultures and culture conflicts in organizations. *Administrative Science Quarterly* 28: 359–376.

Gregory-Huddleston, Kathleen. 1994. Culture conflict with growth: Cases from Silicon Valley. In *Anthropological perspectives on organizational culture*, edited by Tomoko Hamada and Willis E. Sibley, 121–131. Lanham, MD: University Press of America.

Gudykunst, William B. and Young Yun Kim. 2003. *Communicating with strangers: An approach to intercultural communication*. Boston, MA: McGraw Hill.

Guthrie, G.M. 1975. A behavioral analysis of culture learning. In *Cross-cultural perspectives on learning*, edited by Richard W. Brislin, Stephen Bochner, and Walter J. Lonner. New York, NY: John Wiley and Sons.

Guzzo, Richard A., Katherine A. Noonan, and Efrat Elron. 1994. Expatriate managers and the psychological contract. *Journal of Applied Psychology* 79(4): 617–626.

Hall, Edward T. 1959. *The silent language*. New York, NY: Doubleday.

———. 1966. *The hidden dimension*. New York, NY: Doubleday.

———. 1976. *Beyond culture*. New York, NY: Doubleday.

———. 1983. *The dance of life: The other dimension of time*. New York, NY: Doubleday.

Hall, Edward T. and Mildred R. Hall. 1987. *Hidden differences: Doing business with the Japanese*. New York, NY: Doubleday.

———. 1989. *Understanding cultural differences: Germans, French and Americans*. Yarmouth, ME: Intercultural Press.

Hall, Judith A. 1978. Gender effects in decoding nonverbal cues. *Psychological Bulletin* 85(4): 845–857.

Hamada, Tomoko. 1991. *American enterprise in Japan*. Albany, NY: State University of New York Press.

———. 2008. Globalization and the new meanings of the foreign executive in Japan. In *Multiculturalism in the new Japan: Crossing the boundaries within*, edited by Nelson H.H. Graburn, John Ertl, and R. Kenji Tierney, Asian Anthropologies, Vol. 6, 43–62. Oxford, UK: Berghahn Books.

Hamada, Tomoko and Willis E. Sibley, eds. 1994. *Anthropological perspectives on organizational culture.* Lanham, MD: University Press of America.

Hamada Connolly, Tomoko. 2010. Business ritual studies: Corporate ceremony and sacred space. *International Journal of Business Anthropology* 1(2): 32–47.

Harris, Hilary and Chris Brewster. 1999. An integrative framework for pre-departure preparation. In *International HRM: Contemporary issues in Europe*, edited by Chris Brewster and Hilary Harris, 223–240. London, UK: Routledge.

Harrison, David A. and Margaret A. Shaffer. 2005. Mapping the criterion space for expatriate success: Task- and relationship-based performance, effort and adaptation. *International Journal of Human Resource Management* 16(8): 1454–1474.

Harrison, Randall P. 1974. *Beyond words: An introduction to nonverbal communication.* Englewood Cliffs, NJ: Prentice Hall.

Harzing, Anne-Wil. 2001. Of bears, bumble-bees, and spiders: The role of expatriates in controlling foreign subsidiaries. *Journal of World Business* 36(4): 366–379.

———. 2002. Are our referencing errors undermining our scholarship and credibility? The case of expatriate failure rates. *Journal of Organizational Behavior* 23: 127–148.

Harzing, Anne-Wil, Kathrin Köster, and Ulrike Magner. 2011. Babel in business: The language barrier and its solutions in the HQ-subsidiary relationship. *Journal of World Business* 46(3): 279–287.

Hechanova, Regina, Terry A. Beehr, and Neil D. Christiansen. 2003. Antecedents and consequences of employees' adjustment to overseas assignment: A meta-analytic review. *Applied Psychology: An International Review* 52(2): 213–236.

Heenan, David A. and Howard V. Perlmutter. 1979. *Multinational organizational development.* Reading, MA: Addison-Wesley Publishing Co.

Helms, Brigit. 2006. *Access for all—Building inclusive financial systems* («La finance pour tous – Construire des systèmes financiers inclusifs»), Washington, DC: The World Bank.

Henttonen, Kaisa and Kirsimarja Blomqvist. 2005. Managing distance in a global virtual team: The evolution of trust through technology-mediated relational communication. *Strategic Change* 14: 107–119, March–April.

Herbig, Paul A. and Hugh E. Kramer. 1991. Cross-cultural negotiations: Success through understanding. *Management Decision* 29(8): 19–31.

Heron, John. 1970. The phenomenology of social encounter: The gaze. *Philosophy and Phenomenological Research* 31(2): 243–264, December.

Hickerson, Nancy P. 2000. *Linguistic anthropology*, 2nd ed. Belmont, CA: Wadsworth.

Hirsch, E.D., Jr. 1987. *Cultural literacy: What every American needs to know.* Boston, MA: Houghton Mifflin.

Hofstede, Geert. 1980. *Culture's consequences: International differences in work-related values.* Beverly Hills: Sage Publications.

———. 1991. *Cultures and organizations: Software of the mind.* London, UK: McGraw-Hill.

———. 2001. *Culture's consequences: Comparing values, behaviors, institutions, and organizations across nations*, 2nd ed. Thousand Oaks, CA: Sage Publications.

House, Robert J., Paul J. Hanges, Mansour Javidan, Peter W. Dorfman, and Vipin Gupta, eds. 2004. *Culture, leadership, and organizations: The GLOBE study of 62 societies.* Thousand Oaks, CA: Sage Publications.

Huang, Elaine M., Gunnar Harboe, Joe Tullio, Ashley Novak, Noel Massey, Crysta J. Metcalf, and Guy Romano. 2009. Of social television comes home: A field study of communication choices and practices in TV-based text and voice chat, *Proceedings of CHI*, ACM Press, Boston, MA, April 7, 585–594.

Inside NAU. 2006. Following Hopi footprints, 3(38), September 20 (Campus Publication, Northern Arizona University, Flagstaff, Arizona).

Ito, Yasunobu. 2011. "Prohibited ingenuity at the workplace: An ethnographic study of medical information and nurses' practice in Japan," *Presentation at Lancaster University*, Lancaster, UK, March 10.

Jamali, Dima. 2004. Success and failure mechanisms of public private partnerships (PPPs) in developing countries: Insights from the Lebanese context. *International Journal of Public Sector Management* 17(5): 414–430.

Jeelof, Gerrit. 1989. Global strategies of Philips. *European Management Journal* 7(1): 84–91, March.

Jensen, J.V. 1982. Perspective on nonverbal intercultural communication. In *Intercultural communication: A reader*, edited by Larry A. Samovar and Richard E. Porter, 260–276. Belmont, CA: Wadsworth.

Jessup, Jay M. and Maggie L. Jessup. 1993. *Doing business in Mexico*. Rocklin, CA: Prima.

Jordan, Ann T. 1994. *Practicing anthropology in corporate America: Consulting on organizational culture*. NAPA Bulletin No. 14. Arlington, VA: American Anthropological Association.

———. 2003. *Business anthropology*. Prospect Heights, IL: Waveland Press.

———. 2008. The making of a modern kingdom: Transnational partnerships in Saudi Arabia. In *Partnering for organizational performance: Collaboration and culture in the global workplace*, edited by Elizabeth K. Briody and Robert T. Trotter, II, 177–192. Lanham, MD: Rowman and Littlefield.

———. 2010. The importance of business anthropology: Its unique contributions. *International Journal of Business Anthropology* 1(1): 15–25.

———. 2011. *The making of a modern kingdom: Globalization and change in Saudi Arabia*. Long Grove, IL: Waveland Press.

Jun, Jong S. and Hiromi Muto. 1995. The hidden dimensions of Japanese administration: Culture and its impact. *Public Administration Review* 55(2): 125–134, March–April.

Kalmbach, C. Jr. and C. Roussel. 1999. Dispelling the myths of alliances. *Outlook*, Special Edition, Andersen Consulting, October.

Katz, Jeffrey P. and David M. Seifer. 1996. It's a different world out there: Planning for expatriate success through selection, pre-departure training and on-site socialization. *Human Resource Planning* 19(2): 32–47.

Katzner, Kenneth. 1975. *The languages of the world*. New York, NY: Funk & Wagnalls.

Keegan, Warren J. and Mark C. Green. 1997. *Principles of global marketing*. Upper Saddle River, NJ: Prentice Hall.

Kelley, Colleen and Judith Meyers. 1995. *CCAI: Cross-cultural adaptability inventory: Manual*. Minneapolis, MN: National Computer Systems, Inc.

Kennedy, Gavin. 1985. *Doing business abroad*. New York, NY: Simon and Schuster.

Khanna, Sunil K. 2010. *Fetal/fatal knowledge: New reproductive technologies and family-building strategies in India*. Belmont, CA: Wadsworth/Cengage.

Kluckhohn, Clyde. 1968. *Mirror for man*. New York, NY: Fawcett.

Kluckhohn, Florence and Fred L. Strodtbeck. 1961. *Variations in value orientations*. New York, NY: Harper and Row.

Knapp, M.L. 1972. The field of nonverbal communication: An overview. In *On speech communication: An anthology of contemporary writings and messages*, edited by C.J. Stewart and B. Kendall. New York, NY: Holt, Rinehart and Winston.

Kohls, L. Robert. 1984. *Survival kit for overseas living*. Chicago, IL: Intercultural Press.

———. 2001. *Survival kit for overseas living: For Americans planning to live and work abroad*, 4th ed. Boston, MA: Intercultural Press Inc., Nicholas Brealey Publishing.

Kottak, Conrad P. 2004. *Cultural anthropology*, 10th ed. New York, NY: McGraw-Hill.

Kramer, Cheris. 1974. Folk-linguistics: Wishy-washy mommy talk. *Psychology Today* 8(1): 82–85.

Kuethe, J.L. 1962. Social schemas. *Journal of Abnormal and Social Psychology* 64(1): 31–38, January.

Kumar, Rajesh and Verner Worm. 2003. Social capital and the dynamics of business negotiations between the northern Europeans and the Chinese. *International Marketing Review* 20(3): 262–285.

———. 2004. Institutional dynamics and the negotiation process: Comparing India and China. *International Journal of Conflict Management* 15(3): 304–334.

LaBarre, Weston. 1947. The cultural basis of emotions and gestures. *Journal of Personality* 16(1): 49–68.

Lakoff, Robin Tolmach. 1975. *Language and women's place*. New York, NY: Harper and Row.

———. 2004. *Language and women's place: Text and commentaries*. Revised and expanded edition, edited by Mary Bucholtz. Studies in Language and Gender. New York, NY: Oxford University Press.

Lederer, William J. and Eugene Burdick. 1958. *The ugly American*. New York, NY: W.W. Norton & Company, Inc.

Lee, Kam-hon, Guang Yang, and John L. Graham. 2006. Tension and trust in international business negotiations: American executives negotiating with Chinese executives. *Journal of International Business Studies* 37: 623–641.

Lewellen, Ted C. 2002. *The anthropology of globalization: Cultural anthropology enters the 21st century*. Westport, CT: Bergin and Garvey.

Lewicki, Roy J., Stephen E. Weiss, and David Lewin. 1992. Models of conflict, negotiation and third party intervention: A review and synthesis. *Journal of Organizational Behavior* 13: 209–252.

Lewin, Kurt. 1947. Frontiers in group dynamics: II. Channels of group life; social planning and action research. *Human Relations* 1: 143–153.

Light, David A. 1997. Expatriate employees: Getting the most out of their experience. *Harvard Business Review* 75(6): 20, November/December.

Linehan, Margaret and Hugh Scullion. 2001. Factors influencing participation of female executives in international assignments. *Comportamento Organizacional E Gestao* 6(2): 213–226.

Lipset, Seymour Martin. 1986. Historical traditions and national characteristics: A comparative analysis of Canada and the United States. *The Canadian Journal of Sociology* [Cahiers canadiens de sociologie] 11(2): 113–155.

———. 1990. The values of Canadians and Americans: A reply. *Social Forces* 69(1): 267–272.

Little, Kenneth B. 1965. Personal space. *Journal of Experimental Social Psychology* 1(3): 237–247.

Malefyt, Timothy de Waal. 2010. Using anthropology to understand the American 'dinner dilemma'. CourseReader (Internet Access), Detroit, MI: Gale.

Malefyt, Timothy deWaal and Brian Moeran, eds. 2003. *Advertising cultures.* Oxford, UK: Berg.

Malinowski, Bronislaw. 1922. *Argonauts of the western Pacific: An account of native enterprise and adventure in the archipelagoes of Melanesian New Guinea.* New York, NY: E.P. Dutton and Co., Inc.

Marx, Elisabeth. 1999. *Breaking through culture shock: What you need to succeed in international business.* London, UK: Nicholas Brealey Publishing.

Maurer, Steven D. and Shaomin Li. 2006. Understanding expatriate manager performance: Effects of governance environments on work relationships in relation-based economies. *Human Resource Management Review* 16(1): 29–46.

Mauss, Marcel. 1923. *Essai sur le don* [The gift: The form and reason for exchange in archaic societies]. London, UK: Routledge.

Mayo, Elton. 1933. *The human problems of an industrial civilization.* New York, NY: Macmillan Company.

Mbiti, John S. 1969. *African religions and philosophy.* New York, NY: Praeger.

McCracken, Grant C. 2009. *Chief culture officer: How to create a living, breathing corporation.* New York, NY: Basic Books.

McCune, Jenny C. 1999. Exporting corporate culture: A cohesive culture helps hold far-flung operations together. *Management Review* 88(11): 52–56, December.

McKean, Erin. 2009. Redefining definition. *New York Times Magazine*, December 20, p. 16.

Meerwarth, Tracy L., Elizabeth K. Briody, and Devadatta M. Kulkarni. 2005. Discovering the rules: Folk knowledge for improving GM partnerships. *Human Organization* 64(3): 286–302.

Meerwarth, Tracy L., Julia C. Gluesing, and Brigitte Jordan, eds. 2008. *Mobile work, mobile lives: Cultural accounts of lived experiences.* NAPA Bulletin No. 30. Malden, MA: Blackwell.

Meerwarth, Tracy L., Robert T. Trotter, II, and Elizabeth K. Briody. 2008. The knowledge organization: Cultural priorities and workspace design. *Space and Culture* 11(4): 437–454.

Meissner, Martin and Stuart B. Philpott. 1975. The sign language of sawmill workers in British Columbia. *Sign Language Studies* 9: 291–308.

Mendenhall, Mark E., Edward Dunbar, and Gary R. Oddou. 1987. Expatriate selection, training and career-pathing: A review and critique. *Human Resource Management* 26(3): 331–345.

Meschi, Pierre-Xavier. 1997. Longevity and cultural differences in international joint ventures: Towards time-based cultural management. *Human Relations* 50(2): 211–228.

Metcalf, Crysta J. 2011. Circulation of transdisciplinary knowledge and culture in a high-tech organization. *Anthropology News*, February, p. 28.

Metcalf, Crysta J. and Gunnar Harboe. 2006. Sunday is family day. *Ethnographic Praxis in Industry Conference Proceedings*, September 1, pp. 49–59.

Miller, Christine Z., Jörg Siebert, Julia C. Gluesing, and Amy Goldmacher. 2008. The challenge of partnerships in complex cultural environments. In *Partnering for organizational performance: Collaboration and culture in the global workplace*, edited by Elizabeth K. Briody and Robert T. Trotter, II, 159–176. Lanham, MD: Rowman and Littlefield.

Miller, Daniel. 1994. *Modernity, an ethnographic approach: Dualism and mass consumption in Trinidad.* Oxford, UK: Berg.

Millington, Andrew, Markus Eberhardt, and Barry Wilkinson. 2005. Gift giving, *guanxi* and illicit payments in buyer–supplier relations in China: Analysing the experience of UK companies. *Journal of Business Ethics* 57: 255–268.

Minehan, Maureen. 2004. Don't ignore short-term assignment challenges. *Society for Human Resource Management Online*, http://www.shrm.org/Pages/default.aspx.

Mitchell, Charles. 2000. *A short course in international business culture*. Novato, CA: World Trade Press.

Mizutani, Osamu. 1979. *Nihongo no seitai* [The facts about Japan]. Tokyo: Sotakusha.

MobiThinking. http://mobithinking.com/

Moeran, Brian. 1996. *A Japanese advertising agency: An anthropology of media and markets*. Honolulu, HI: University of Hawai'i Press.

Mohn, Tanya. 2006. How to become a world citizen, before going to college, *New York Times*, September 3, p. 6.

Mohr, Alexander T. and Simone Klein. 2004. Exploring the adjustment of American expatriate spouses in Germany. *International Journal of Human Resource Management* 15(7): 1189–1206, November.

Molinsky, Andrew L., Mary Anne Krabbenhoft, Nalini Ambady, and Y. Susan Choi. 2005. Cracking the non-verbal code: Intercultural competence and gesture recognition across cultures. *Journal of Cross-Cultural Psychology* 36(3): 380–395, May.

Montague, Susan P. and Robert J. Morais. 1976. Football games and rock concerts: The ritual enactment of American success models. In *The American dimension: Cultural myths and social realities*, edited by William Arens, and Susan P. Montague, 33–52. Port Washington, NY: Alfred Publishing Company.

Moran, Robert T. and William G. Stripp. 1991. *Dynamics of successful international business negotiations*. Houston, TX: Gulf Publishing.

Morgan, Gareth. 1980. Paradigms, metaphors, and puzzle solving in organization theory. *Administrative Science Quarterly* 25(4): 605–622, December.

Morris, Desmond, Peter Collett, Peter Marsh, and Marie O'Shaughnessy. 1979. *Gestures: Their origins and distribution*. New York, NY: Stein and Day.

Morris, Mark A. and Chet Robie. 2001. A meta-analysis of the effects of cross-cultural training on expatriate performance and adjustment. *International Journal of Training and Development* 5(2): 112–125.

Morrison, Terri and Wayne A. Conway. 2006. *Kiss, bow, or shake hands: The bestselling guide to doing business in more than 60 countries*, 2nd ed. Avon, MA: Adams Media.

Morsbach, Helmut. 1982. Aspects of nonverbal communication in Japan. In *Intercultural communication: A reader*, 3rd ed., edited by Larry A. Samovar and Richard E. Porter, 300–316. Belmont, CA: Wadsworth.

National Association for the Practice of Anthropology, "American breakfast & the mother-in-law: How an anthropologist created go-gurt," April 30, 2002, http://practicinganthropology.org/stories/2002/american-breakfast-the-mother-in-law-how-an-anthropologist-created-go-gurt/

Netlingo. http://www.netlingo.com/acronyms.php

Northern Arizona University, "Footprints of the ancestors," http://www4.nau.edu/footprints

Oberg, Kalvero. 1960. Culture shock: Adjustments to new cultural environments. *Practical Anthropology* 4: 177–182, July–August.

O'Connor, Robert. 2002. Plug the expat knowledge drain. *HR Magazine* 47(10): 101–104, October.

Okpara, John O. and Jean D. Kabongo. 2011. Cross-cultural training and expatriate adjustment: A study of Western expatriates in Nigeria. *Journal of World Business* 46: 22–30.

Olie, René. 1990. Cultural issues in transnational business ventures: The case of German–Dutch cooperation. In *Cross-cultural management and organizational culture*, edited by Tomoko Hamada and Ann Jordan, 145–172. Studies in third world societies, February, Publication No. 42, Williamsburg, VA: College of William and Mary.

Oliveira, Jacqueline. 2001. *Brazil: A guide for businesspeople*. Yarmouth, ME: Intercultural Press.

Orr, Julian E. 1996. *Talking about machines: An ethnography of a modern job*. Ithaca, NY: Cornell University Press.

Ortlieb, Martin. 2009. Emergent culture, slippery culture: Conflicting conceptualizations of culture in commercial ethnography. In *Ethnography and the corporate encounter: Reflections on research in and of corporations*, edited by Melissa Cefkin, 185–210. Studies in Public and Applied Anthropology, Vol. 5. New York, NY: Berghahn Books.

Ortony, Andrew. 1975. Why metaphors are necessary and not just nice. *Educational Theory* 25(1): 45–53.

Osman-Gani, Aahad M. and Thomas Rockstuhl. 2008. Expatriate adjustment and performance in overseas assignments: Implications for HRD. *Human Resource Development Review* 7(1): 32–57, March.

Parsons, Talcott. 1951. *The social system*. New York, NY: The Free Press.

Parsons, Talcott and Edward Shils, eds. 1951. *Toward a general theory of action*. Cambridge, MA: Harvard University Press.

Phan, Michel C.T., Chris W. Styles, and Paul G. Patterson. 2005. Relational competency's role in Southeast Asia business partnerships. *Journal of Business Research* 58: 173–184.

Plog, Fred and Daniel Bates. 1980. *Cultural anthropology*. New York, NY: Knopf.

PricewaterhouseCoopers. 2005. International assignments—Global policy and practice: Key trends 2005.

Ramsay, John. 2004. Trope control: The costs and benefits of metaphor unreliability in the description of empirical phenomena. *British Journal of Management* 15: 143–155.

Reeves-Ellington, Richard. 2009. Enviroscapes: A multi-level contextual approach to organizational leadership. In *Multi-level issues in organizational behavior*, Vol. 8, edited by Francis J. Yammarino and Fred Dansereau, 337–420. Bingley, UK: JAI Press.

Richardson, Friedrich and Charles R. Walker. 1948. *Human relations in an expanding company*. New Haven, CT: Yale University Labor Management Center.

Ricks, David A. 1999. *Blunders in international business*, 3rd ed. Oxford, UK: Blackwell

Ridgwell, Henry. 2011. "Britain hopes for billion-dollar economic boost from royal wedding." *Voice of America News*, April 30, http://www.voanews.com/english/news/europe/Britain-hopes-for-billion-dollar-boost-from-royal-wedding-120852234.html

Riopelle, Kenneth, Julia Gluesing, Tara Alcordo, Marietta Baba, David Britt, Willie McKether, Leslie Monplaisir, Hilary Ratner, and Kimberly Harris Wagner. 2003. Context, task and the evolution of technology use in global virtual teams. In *Virtual teams that work: Creating conditions for virtual team effectiveness*, edited by Cristina B. Gibson and Susan G. Cohen, 239–264. San Francisco, CA: Jossey-Bass.

Roethlisberger, F.J. and W. J. Dickson. 1939. *Management and the worker: An account of a research program conducted by the Western Electric Company, Hawthorne Works. Chicago*. Cambridge, MA: Harvard University Press.

Rosenthal, Robert, Judith A. Hall, Dane Archer, M. Robin DiMatteo, and Peter L. Rogers. 1979. Measuring sensitivity to nonverbal communication: The PONS test. In *Nonverbal behavior: Applications and cultural implications*, edited by Aaron Wolfgang, 67–98. New York, NY: Academic Press.

Sachs, Patricia, ed. 1989. Special issue: Anthropological approaches to organizational culture. *Anthropology of Work Review*, Editorial 10(3): 1, Fall.

Safadi, Michaela and Carol Ann Valentine. 1990. Contrastive analyses of American and Arab nonverbal and paralinguistic communication. *Semiotica* 82(3–4): 269–292.

Salacuse, Jeswald W. 1991. *Making global deals: Negotiating in the international marketplace*. Boston, MA: Houghton Mifflin.

———. 1998. So, what is the deal anyway? Contracts and relationships as negotiating goals. *Negotiation Journal* 5–12, January.

———. 2003. *The global negotiator: Making, managing, and mending deals around the world in the 21st century*. New York, NY: Palgrave Macmillan.

Sapir, Edward. 1929. The status of linguistics as a science. *Language* 5(4): 207–214, December.

Sarala, Riikka M. and Eero Vaara. 2010. Cultural differences, convergence, and crossvergence as explanations of knowledge transfer in international acquisitions. *Journal of International Business Studies* 41: 1365–1390.

Schwartzman, Helen B. 1993. *Ethnography in organizations*. Qualitative Research Methods, Vol. 27. Newbury Park, CA: Sage Publications.

Segil, L. 1996. *Intelligent business alliances: How to profit using today's most important strategic tool*. New York, NY: Times Books.

Sengir, Gülcin H., Robert T. Trotter II, Elizabeth K. Briody, Devadatta M. Kulkarni, Linda B. Catlin, and Tracy L. Meerwarth. 2004. Modeling relationship dynamics in GM's research-institution partnerships. *Journal of Manufacturing Technology Management* 15(7): 541–559.

Serrie, Hendrick, ed. 1986. *Anthropology and International Business*. Studies in Third World Societies, No. 28. Williamsburg, VA: College of William and Mary.

Sethi, S. Prakash and Oliver F. Williams. 2000. Creating and implementing global codes of conduct: An assessment of the Sullivan Principles as a role model for developing international codes of conduct—Lessons learned and unlearned. *Business and Society Review* 105(2): 169–200.

Shachaf, Pnina. 2008. Cultural diversity and information and communication technology impacts on global virtual teams: An exploratory study. *Information and Management* 45: 131–142.

Shaffer, Margaret A., David A. Harrison, and K. Matthew Gilley. 1999. Dimensions, determinants, and differences in the expatriate adjustment process. *Journal of International Business Studies* 30(3): 557–581.

Shaffer, Margaret A., David A. Harrison, K. Matthew Gilley, and Dora M. Luk. 2001. Struggling for balance amid turbulence on international assignments: Work-family conflict, support and commitment. *Journal of Management* 27(1): 99–121.

Shapiro, Debra L., Blair H. Sheppard, and Lisa Cheraskin. 1992. Business on a handshake. *Negotiation Journal* 8(4): 365–377, October.

Sharma, Ekta. 2011. Global adjustment perspectives of Indian professionals. *Global Business Review* 12(1): 87–97.

Sheer, Vivian C. and Ling Chen. 2003. Successful Sino-Western business negotiation: Participants' accounts of national and professional cultures. *The Journal of Business Communication* 40(1): 50–85, January.

Sheppard, Pamela and Bénédicte Lapeyre. 1993. *Meetings in French and English [Tenir une réunion en Anglais comme en Français]*. London, UK: Nicholas Brealey Publishing.

Sherry, John F., Jr., ed. 1995. *Contemporary marketing and consumer behavior: An anthropological sourcebook.* Thousand Oaks, CA: Sage Publications.

Sherzer, Joel. 1991. The Brazilian thumbs-up gesture. *Journal of Linguistic Anthropology* 1(2): 189–197.

Shimoda, K., M. Argyle, and R. Ricci-Bitti. 1978. The intercultural recognition of emotional expressions by three national groups—English, Italian, and Japanese. *European Journal of Social Psychology* 8: 169–179.

Shimoni, Baruch. 2006. Cultural borders, hybridization, and a sense of boundaries in Thailand, Mexico, and Israel. *Journal of Anthropological Research* 62(2): 217–234, Summer.

Slater, Jonathan R. 1984. The hazards of cross-cultural advertising. *Business America* 7(7): 2, 20–23, April.

Solomon, Charlene M. 1994. Success abroad depends on more than job skills. *Personnel Journal* 73(4): 51–60, April.

Sommer, R. 1959. Studies in personal space. *Sociometry* 22: 247–260.

Spekman, R.E. and L.A. Isabella. 2000. *Alliance competence: Maximizing the value of your partnerships.* New York, NY: John Wiley and Sons.

Spindler, George and Janice E. Stockard, eds. 2007. *Globalization and change in fifteen cultures: Born in one world living in another.* Case Studies in Cultural Anthropology. Belmont, CA: Wadsworth, Cengage Learning.

Squires, Susan. 2002. Doing the work: Customer research in the product development and design industry. In *Creating breakthrough ideas: The collaboration of anthropologists and designers in the product development industry*, edited by Susan Squires and Bryan Bryne, 103–124. Westport, CT: Bergin and Garvey.

———. 2005. Telecommunication-product meaning and use: Two examples of needs assessment. In *Creating evaluation anthropology: Introducing an emerging subfield*, edited by Mary Odell Butler and Jacqueline Copeland-Carson, 79–88. NAPA Bulletin 24 Arlington, VA: American Anthropological Association.

Squires, Susan and Bryan Byrne, eds. 2002. *Creating breakthrough ideas: The collaboration of anthropologists and designers in the product development industry.* Westport, CT: Bergin and Garvey.

Stewart, Edward C. and Milton J. Bennett. 1991. *American cultural patterns: A cross-cultural perspective*, Revised ed. Yarmouth, ME: Intercultural Press.

Stroh, Linda K., Hal B. Gregersen, and J. Stewart Black. 1998. Closing the gap: Expectations versus reality among repatriates. *Journal of World Business* 33(2): 111–124.

Suchman, Lucy A. 1987. *Plans and situated actions: The problem of human-machine communication.* Cambridge, UK: Cambridge University Press.

Sunderland, Patricia L. and Rita M. Denny. 2007. *Doing anthropology in consumer research.* Walnut Creek, CA: Left Coast Press.

Sussman, Nan M. 2001. Repatriation transitions: Psychological preparedness, cultural identity and attributions among American managers. *International Journal of Intercultural Relations* 25: 109–123.

Suutari, Vesa and Chris Brewster. 1999. International assignments across European borders: No problems? In *International HRM: Contemporary issues in Europe*, edited by Chris Brewster and Hilary Harris, 183–202. London, UK: Routledge.

Tages Anzieger, April 27, 2010, "Schlechte Noten fürs Grossraumbüro," http://www.tagesanzeiger.ch/wirtschaft/konjunktur/Schlechte-Noten-fuers-Grossraumbuero/story/11770162

Takeuchi, Riki. 2010. A critical review of expatriate adjustment research through a multiple stakeholder view: Progress, emerging trends, and prospects. *Journal of Management* 36(4): 1040–1064, July.

Tannen, Deborah. 1990. *You just don't understand: Women and men in conversation.* New York, NY: William Morrow.

————. 1998. *The argument culture: Moving from debate to dialogue.* New York, NY: Random House.

Teagarden, Mary B. and Gary Gordon. 1995. Corporate selection strategies and expatriate manager success. In *Expatriate management: New ideas for international business,* edited by Jan Selmer. Westport, CT: Quorum Books.

Teegen, Hildy J. and Jonathan P. Doh. 2002. U.S.–Mexican alliance negotiations: Impact of culture on authority, trust, and performance. *Thunderbird International Business Review* 44(6): 749–775, November–December.

Thomas, David C. 2002. *Essentials of international management: A cross-cultural perspective.* Thousand Oaks, CA: Sage Publications.

Thompson, Verne, ed. 2009. *Encyclopedia of associations: International organizations.* Three-volume set, 48th ed. Detroit, MI: Gale Publishing.

Thompson, Ann Marie and James L. Perry. 2006. Collaboration processes: Inside the black box. *Public Administration Review,* Special Issue 20–32, December.

Tinsley, Catherine H. and Madan M. Pillutla. 1998. Negotiating in the United States and Hong Kong. *Journal of International Business Studies* 29(4): 711–728.

de Tocqueville, Alexis. 1990 [1835]. *Democracy in America,* Vol. 1. New York, NY: Vintage Classics.

————. 1990 [1840]. *Democracy in America,* Vol. 2. New York, NY: Vintage Classics.

Toh, Soo Min and Angelo S. Denisi. 2007. Host country nationals as socializing agents: A social identity approach. *Journal of Organizational Behavior* 28: 281–301.

Trompenaars, Alfons and Charles Hampden-Turner. 1993. *The seven cultures of capitalism.* New York, NY: Currency/Doubleday.

————. 1998. *Riding the waves of culture: Understanding cultural diversity in global business,* 2nd ed. New York, NY: McGraw Hill.

Trotter, Robert T., II, Elizabeth K. Briody, Linda B. Catlin, Tracy L. Meerwarth, and Gülcin H. Sengir. 2004. The evolving nature of GM R&D's collaborative research labs: Learning from stages and roles, GM Research and Development Center Publication No. 9907, October 15.

Trotter, Robert T., II, Elizabeth K. Briody, Gülcin H. Sengir, and Tracy L. Meerwarth. 2008a. The life cycle of collaborative partnerships: Evolutionary structure in industry-university research networks. *Connections* (International network for social network analysis) 28(1): 40–58, June.

Trotter, Robert T., II, Gülcin H. Sengir, and Elizabeth K. Briody. 2008b. The cultural processes of partnerships. In *Partnering for organizational performance: Collaboration and culture in the global workplace,* edited by Elizabeth K. Briody and Robert T. Trotter, II, 15–54. Lanham, MD: Rowman and Littlefield.

Tung, Rosalie L. 1981. Selection and training of personnel for overseas assignments. *Columbia Journal of World Business* 16(1): 68–78, Spring.

————. 1982. Selection and training procedures for U.S., European, and Japanese multinationals. *California Management Review* 25(1): 57–71, Fall.

————. 1989. "International assignments: Strategic challenges in the twenty-first century." *Paper presented at the 49th Annual Meetings of the Academy of Management,* August 14–16, Washington, DC.

————. 1998. American expatriates abroad: From neophytes to cosmopolitans. *Journal of World Business* 33(2): 125–144.

————. 2008. The cross-cultural research imperative: The need to balance cross-national and intra-national diversity. *Journal of International Business Studies* 39(1): 41–46.

Tung, Rosalie L. and Alain Verbeke. 2010. Beyond Hofstede and GLOBE: Improving the quality of cross-cultural research. *Journal of International Business Studies* 41: 1259–1274.

Van der Zee, Karen I. and Jan P. Van Oudenhoven. 2000. The multicultural personality questionnaire: A multidimensional instrument of multicultural effectiveness. *European Journal of Personality* 14(4): 291–309.

————. 2001. The multicultural personality questionnaire: Reliability and validity of self- and other ratings of multicultural effectiveness. *Journal of Research in Personality* 35(3): 278–288.

Van Maanen, John. 1978. *Policing: A view from the street.* New York, NY: Random House.

Van Marrewijk, Alfons. 2010. European developments in business anthropology. *International Journal of Business Anthropology* 1(1): 26–44.

Von Bergen, Jane M. 2008. More U.S. workers being sent to international posts. *The Charlotte Observer,* August 17, p. 4D.

Warner, W. Lloyd and J.O. Low. 1947. *The social system of the modern factory: The strike: A social analysis.* New Haven, CT: Yale University Press.

Warner, W. Lloyd and Paul S. Lunt. 1941. *The social life of a modern community.* New Haven, CT: Yale University Press.

Wasson, Christina and Susan Squires. 2011. Localizing the global in the field of technology design. In *Applying anthropology in the global village*, edited by Christina Wasson, Mary Odell Butler, and Jacqueline Copeland-Carson, 251–284. Walnut Creek, CA: Left Coast Press.

Watson, O. Michael. 1970. *Proxemic behavior: A cross-cultural study.* The Hague, The Netherlands: Mouton.

Watson, Warren E., Kamalesh Kumar, and Larry K. Michaelsen. 1993. Cultural diversity's impact on interaction process and performance: Comparing homogeneous and diverse task groups. *Academy of Management Journal* 36(3): 590–602.

Weiss, Stephen E. 1993. Analysis of complex negotiations in international business: The RBC perspective. *Organization Science* 4(2): 269–301, May.

Weiss, Stephen E. 2006. International business negotiation in a globalizing world: Reflections on the contributions and future of a (sub) field. *International Negotiation* 11(2): 287–316, February.

Whorf, Benjamin Lee. 1956. *Language, thought, and reality.* Cambridge, MA: MIT Press.

Williams, Oliver F. 2004. The UN Global Compact: The challenge and the promise. *Business Ethics Quarterly* 14(4): 755–774.

Wills, Stefan and Kevin Barham. 1994. Being an international manager. *European Management Journal* 12(1): 49–58, March.

Wilson, Meena and Maxine Dalton. 1996. Selecting and developing global managers: Possibilities and pitfalls. Unpublished paper, May.

Wood, Julia T. 1994. Gender, communication, and culture. In *Intercultural communication: A reader*, 7th ed., edited by Larry A. Samovar and Richard E. Porter, 155–165. Belmont, CA: Wadsworth.

Wordnik. http://www.wordnik.com/

World Almanac and Book of Facts. 2010. New York, NY: World Almanac Education Group.

Würtz, Elizabeth. 2005. Intercultural communication on Web sites: A cross-cultural analysis of web sites from high-context cultures and low-context cultures. *Journal of Computer-Mediated Communication* 11: 274–299.

Ya'ari, Ehud and Ina Friedman. 1991. Curses in verses. *Atlantic* 267(2): 22–26, February.

Zimmermann, Angelika. 2011. Interpersonal relationships in transnational, virtual teams: Towards a configurational perspective. *International Journal of Management Reviews* 13: 59–78.

Photo Credits

■ ■ ■

Chapter 1:

Page 5: Ed Tronick/Anthro-Photo; **page 7:** Timothy de Waal Malefyt; **page 12:** Michael McCoy/Photo Researchers, Inc.; **page 13** (top and bottom): Michael McCoy/ Photo Researchers, Inc.; **page 16:** Curt Wiler/Alamy; **page 16:** Elizabeth K. Briody; **page 20:** Andrea Booher/Stone/Getty Images

Chapter 2:

Page 30: Elizabeth K. Briody; **page 35:** Gary P. Ferraro; **page 44:** Elizabeth K. Briody; **page 46:** Polka Dot/Jupiterimages/Alamy; **page 53:** Phil MacKenzie; **page 56:** Elizabeth K. Briody

Chapter 3:

Page 72: Ken Kim; **page 74:** Ken Kim; **page 77:** Greg Pease/Stone/Getty Images; **page 84:** Elizabeth K. Briody; **page 86:** U. Ejiro O. Onomake-Anthropologist; **page 92:** Tracy L. Meerwarth; **page 95:** Image by Bruno Moynie for Pacific Ethnography

Chapter 4:

Page 106: Elizabeth K. Briody; **page 108:** Dr. Adam Koons; **page 115:** iofoto/Shutterstock; **page 118:** Chung Sung-Jun/Getty Images; **page 123:** Elizabeth K. Briody; **page 128:** George Brandon/WENN Photos/Newscom; **page 131:** Elizabeth K. Briody

Chapter 5:

Page 141: Douglas E. Walker/Masterfile; **page 144:** Elizabeth K. Briody; **page 150:** wavebreakmedia ltd/Shutterstock; **page 153:** Elizabeth K. Briody; **page 155:** Elizabeth K. Briody; **page 157:** Elizabeth K. Briody; **page 159:** Elizabeth K. Briody

Chapter 6:

Page 167: Elizabeth K. Briody; **page 171:** Elizabeth K. Briody; **page 179:** Tracy L. Meerwarth; **page 185:** Elizabeth K. Briody; **page 191:** Timothy de Waal Malefyt; **page 192:** George Gumerman

Chapter 7:

Page 209: Richard J. Rybak; **page 210:** Steve Vidler/SuperStock; **page 212:** Galina Barskaya/Shutterstock

Chapter 8:

Page 229: DreamPictures/Photodisc/Getty Images; **page 232:** Duncan Crundwell; **page 239:** Carole Vardon; **page 244:** SuperStock/SuperStock; **page 246:** Bruce Ayres/Stone/Getty Images

Index

■ ■ ■